[illegible]

Mahdist Faith and Sudanic Tradition

Monographs from the African Studies Centre, Leiden

Mahdist Faith and Sudanic Tradition The History of the Masālīt Sultanate 1870–1930

Lidwien Kapteijns

KPI

London, Boston, Melbourne and Henley

First published in 1985
by KPI Limited

Routledge and Kegan Paul PLC
14 Leicester Square, London WC2H 7PH

Routledge and Kegan Paul
9 Park Street, Boston, Mass. 02108, USA

Routledge and Kegan Paul
464 St Kilda Road, Melbourne,
Victoria 3004, Australia

Set in Times Roman by
Hope Services, Abingdon, Oxon
and printed in Great Britain by
St Edmundsbury Press Ltd
Bury St Edmunds, Suffolk

Library of Congress Cataloging in Publication Data
Kapteijns, Lidwien,
Mahdist faith and Sudanic tradition.
Bibliography: p.
Includes index.
1. Darfur (Sudan) – History. I. Title.
DT159.6.D27K36 1984 962.4 84–3891

British Library CIP data available

ISBN 0–7103–0090–5

To my parents, Harrie and Bertje

Contents

Preface ix

Note on transliteration xiii

Abbreviations xv

Ethnic map of Dār Fūr and Wadai xvi

Map of the Masālīt Sultanate c. 1900 xvii

Sultans of Dār Masālīt xviii

Sultans and 'shadow-sultans' of Dār Fūr xviii

Sultans of Wadai xviii

Introduction 1

1 The western Sudan before 1874: the political and geographical context 13

2 Masālīt society during the Ancien Regime (before 1874) 18

3 Prelude to the rise of the Masālīt Sultanate: Hajjām Ḥasab Allāh and the unification of the Masālīt 62

4 The rise of the Masālīt Sultanate from a regional perspective (1883–1898) 73

5 The rise of the Masālīt Sultanate from within: Sudanic tradition re-enacted 123

6 'The sultan is like a buffalo in the fight': struggle for independence and prelude to colonial rule 171

7 Some direct results of indirect rule: Dār Masālīt in the 1920s and 1930s 208

Glossary 244

Notes 251

Appendix 319

Sources and bibliography 331

Index 357

Preface

This book is the product of research begun in January 1978, when I was teaching history at the University of Khartoum, Sudan. Since the secondary literature on western Dār Fūr is nearly non-existent and relevant travel accounts few, it is almost completely based on primary sources. The (Arabic) Mahdist Archives and (English) Condominium Archives kept at the Central Records Office, Khartoum, have been consulted intensively over a period of four years. I spent three academic vacations (in total seven months) doing oral history in Dār Masālīt, Dār Qimr and al-Fāshir, and interviewed Masālīt residing in Khartoum during the academic year of 1980–1. One summer I spent in French and British Archives, while the Sudan Collection of the History Department in Bergen, Norway, was consulted during two visits of altogether three months.

In the face of uneven and relatively inaccessible sources, the reconstruction of a chronological framework and a general political history of western Dār Fūr was a major undertaking. The oral sources have made it possible to go beyond this and to write the history of Dār Masālīt 'from within', i.e. to write local history in both its political and socio-economic aspects. This is, I hope, this study's contribution to the history of Dār Fūr, and this is what may make it a worthy companion to R. S. O'Fahey's *State and Society in Dār Fūr*.

Many persons and institutions have directly or indirectly contributed to this research. I owe an old debt of gratitude to my history and language teachers at the University of Amsterdam and the School of Oriental and African Studies, London, particularly to Dr R. Peters, and to Prof. Dr M. C. Brands who has been a stimulus and a challenge from 1970 onwards. In Khartoum my colleagues and friends of the History Department, in particular Prof. ʿUthmān S. A. Ismāʿīl, Prof. Muḥammad al-Ḥājj, Dr H. A. Ibrāhīm, Dr ʿAbd al-Wahhāb 'Bob', and Dr al-Ḥājj Ḥāmid Muḥammad Khayr, have encouraged and supported me throughout. Dr M. I. Abū Salīm, Director of the Central Records Office, Khartoum, has helped me in word, deed and example, while his staff has gone out of its way to help me obtain the files I needed. I am especially indebted to my students Ibrāhīm Yaḥyā ʿAbd al-Raḥmān, who initiated me into Masālīt language and history, and took me on a long walking tour through Dār Masālīt in 1978, to ʿAlī Yūsuf Adam, who gave me a hand with some of the Arabic manuscripts, and to ʿAlī Baḥr al-Dīn ʿAlī Dīnār and ʿAbd Allāh Bulād Idrīs, who assisted me during fieldtrips in al-Fāshir and Kulbus.

Thanks are due to the authorities in Khartoum and Dār Fūr Province, especially to Sultan ʿAbd al-Raḥmān of Dār Masālīt, for facilitating my research where they could. Those Darfurians who have answered questions and provided hospitality are far too numerous to list here. I hereby thank them all, in particular my 'foster parents' in El Geneina (the household of al-*ḥājj* Dafaʿ Allāh ʿAjab and ʿAzza ʿAlī Ab Shanab), my hosts in al-Fāshir (the household of *amīr* Baḥr al-Dīn ʿAlī Dīnār), and in Khartoum, the household of al-*ḥājj* Muḥammad Aḥmad Abū Lafta.

I would like to acknowledge the late Dr Mūsā al-Mubārak, who has laid the trail for historians of Dār Fūr. Dr Paul Doornbos, with whom I shared some of the pleasures and rigours of field work, has been a support and source of inspiration throughout. The same is true for Dr Sean O'Fahey and particularly for my favourite Sudan scholar, Dr Jay Spaulding. I am grateful to these three colleagues and to Dr R. Buijtenhuijs for reading earlier drafts of this study. The African Studies Centre, Leiden, has functioned as my academic home base from 1979 onwards. For moral support and indispensable help in pratical matters I am grateful to Dr G. Grootenhuis, Dr W. van Binsbergen and Dr R. Buijtenhuijs. For typing a complicated manuscript I would like to thank Sunniva Björkelo, Bergen, Norway.

I am grateful to the Arts Faculty Research Board, University of Khartoum, and, in particular, the Netherlands Foundation for the

Advancement of Tropical Research (WOTRO) for providing the financial support which made this study possible.

To my parents, whose minds are infinitely wider than their radius of action, I have dedicated this book.

Sint-Michielsgestel, January 1982 Lidwien Kapteijns

Note on transliteration

The problems of transliteration posed by a book containing classical Arabic, Sudanese colloquial Arabic and Masālīt texts cannot be satisfactorily solved by a non-linguist. Quotations from Arabic documents have been transliterated according to the system used by the *Encyclopedia of Islam*, but with the omission of the subscript ligatures and the substition of 'j' for 'dj' and 'q' for 'ḳ'. Quotations from oral, Sudanese colloquial Arabic texts, which cannot be 'retranslated' into classical Arabic, have been represented phonetically, in a way which is perforce unsophisticated as long as linguistic data and research are not available. In the transliteration of place-names no consistency has been aimed at. In general the spelling used here is that of the maps of the Sudan Survey Department, but some place-names (such as al-Fāshir and Kabkābiyya) have been transliterated as Arabic words. Apart from a manuscript grammar by R. Davies and the BA Honours Thesis of Ibrāhīm Yaḥyā (1980), the Masālīt language has not been studied or described systematically. The system followed here is a modified form of that used by R. Davies.

Abbreviations

ANSOM	Archives Nationales, Section Outre Mer (Paris).
B.I.F.	Bibliothèque de l'Institut de France (Paris).
B.S.G.	Bulletin de la Société de Géographie (Paris).
B.S.K.G.	Bulletin de la Société Khédiviale de Géographie (Cairo).
CRO	Central Records Office (Khartoum).
IJAHS	International Journal of African Historical Studies (Boston).
JAH	Journal of African History (London).
PRO	Public Records Office (London).
SHAT	Service Historique de L'Armée de Terre (Paris).
SNR	Sudan Notes and Records (Khartoum).
SOAS	School of Oriental and African Studies (London).

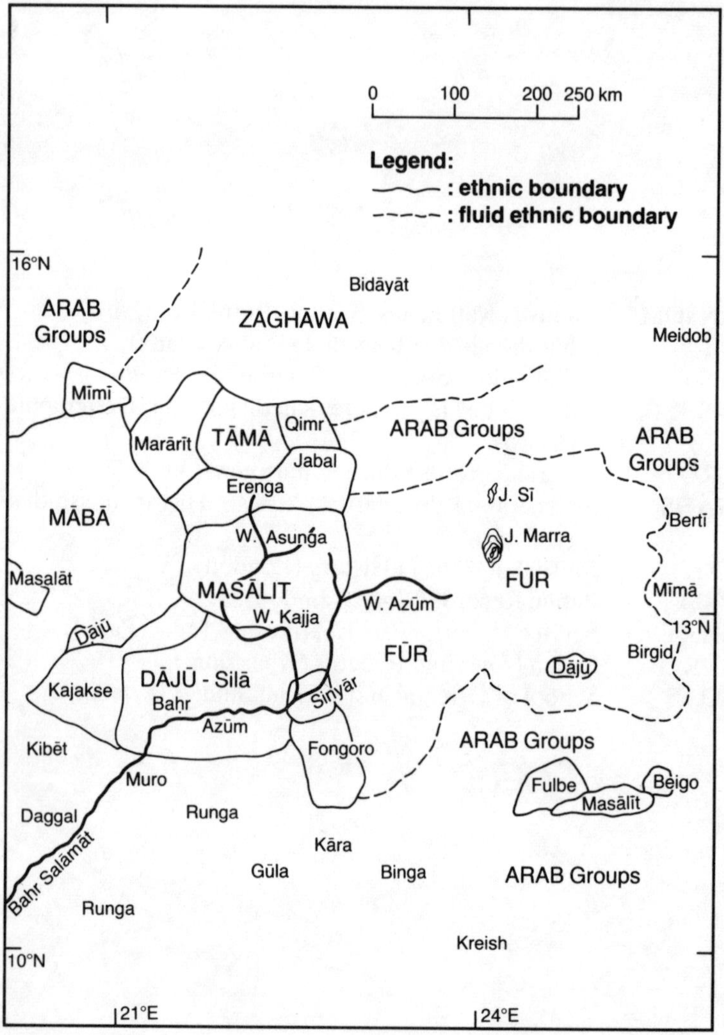

Ethnic map of Dār Fūr and Wadai

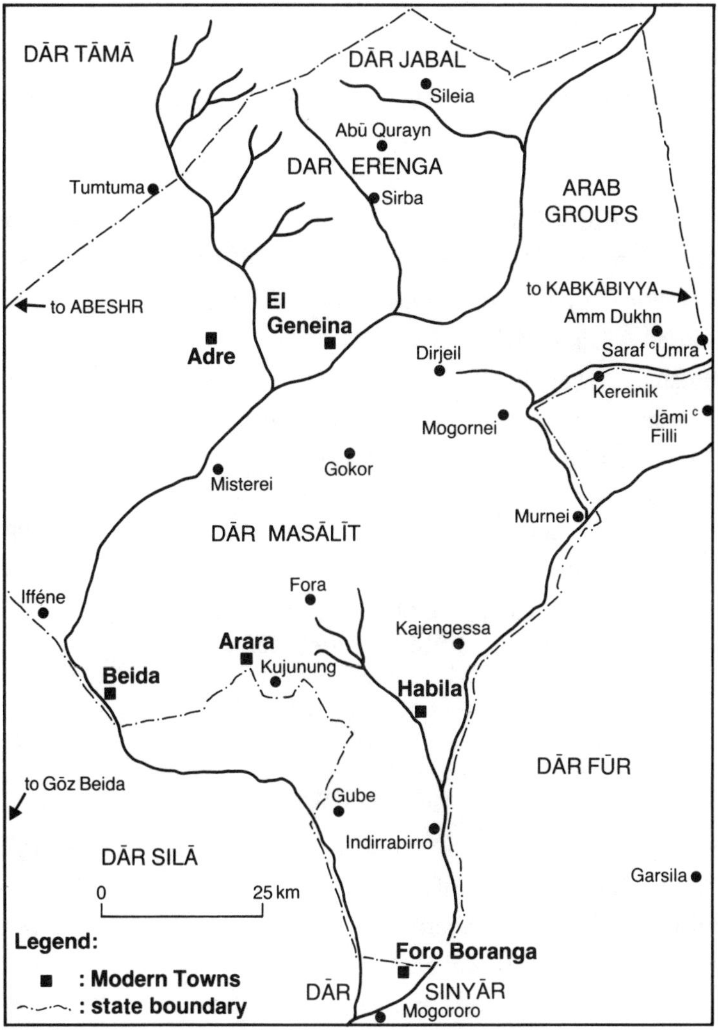

Map of the Masālīt Sultanate c. 1900

Sultans of Dār Masālīt

Ismāʿīl b. ʿAbd al-Nabī	1884–1888
Abbakr b. Ismāʿīl	1888–1905
Tāj al-Dīn b. Ismāʿīl	1905–1910
Baḥr al-Dīn (Andōka) b. Abbakr b. Ismāʿīl	1910–1951

Sultans and 'shadow-sultans' of Dār Fūr

Muḥammad al-Faḍl	1803–1838
Muḥammad al-Ḥusayn b. Muḥammad al-Faḍl	1838–1873
Ibrāhīm Qaraḍ b. Muḥammad al-Ḥusayn	1873–1874
*Ḥasab Allāh b. Muḥammad al-Faḍl	1874
*Bōsh b. Muḥammad al-Faḍl	1874
*Hārūn b. Sayf al-Dīn b. Muḥammad al-Faḍl	1874–1879
*ʿAbd Allāh Dūd Banja b. Abū Bakr b. Muḥammad al-Faḍl	1879–1884
*Yūsuf b. Ibrāhīm Qaraḍ	1884–1888
*Abū'l-Khayrāt b. Ibrāhīm Qaraḍ	1888–1891
*ʿAlī Dīnār b. Zakāriyya b. Muḥammad al-Faḍl acceded in March/April 1891, surrendered to the *anṣār* in October 1891, reigned	1898–1916

* = 'shadow-sultan'

Sultans of Wadai

Muḥammad Sharīf	1834–1858
ʿAlī b. Muḥammad Sharīf	1858–1874
Yūsuf b. Muḥammad Sharīf	1874–1898
Ibrāhīm b. Yūsuf b. Muḥammad Sharīf	1898–1901
Aḥmad al-Ghazālī b. ʿAlī b. Muḥammad Sharīf	1901–1902
Muḥammad Ṣāliḥ Dūd Murra b. Yūsuf b. Muḥammad Sharīf	1902–1909
Adam Asīl b. ʿAbd al-Maḥmūd b. Muḥammad Sharīf, deposed by the French	1909–1912

Source: Tubiana, 1960

Introduction

This is a study of the emergence and development of one of the most recent Sudanic kingdoms, the sultanate of Dār Masālīt, in the period 1870–1930. The study is organized chronologically, i.e. it traces the history of Dār Masālīt from 1870 (before the foundation of the sultanate) to 1930 (after the establishment of Anglo-Egyptian rule). It describes the Masālīt state from the basis upwards: an analysis of the different social groups making up Masālīt society in relation to each other and to their main source of livelihood, the land, precedes a description of the new central government and ruling class which came into being in the decade 1888–1898. Although this book is primarily a history of the Masālīt Sultanate, it is regional in its approach and pays attention to developments in the other sultanates of the eastern Sudanic belt, those of Wadai, Dār Fūr, Dār Silā, Dār Tāmā and Dār Qimr, all adjoining Dār Masālīt.[1]

The background to the emergence of the sultanate is given in the first three chapters. A description of the political and geographical setting of Dār Masālīt in Chapter One is followed by a reconstruction of Masālīt society during the period before 1874, when most of Dār Masālīt was part of the Keira Sultanate of Dār Fūr. This early period is only vaguely remembered in Dār Masālīt as the time in which 'the old ways' were still in force. The reconstruction of these 'old ways', presented in Chapter Two under the name of Ancien Regime, is based on relatively few, mainly oral, and partly anachronistically used sources and is perforce static. The virtue of this necessity is that this basic description of the means of subsistence of the lower echelons of Masālīt society, which is the first of its kind in the field of Sudanese studies, is valid for almost the whole period under study.

The fall of the Ancien Regime, the developments triggered off by the Turco-Egyptian occupation of Dār Fūr (1874–1883) and the unification of the Masālīt clans by Hajjām Ḥasab Allāh of the Masālīt Mistereng are discussed in the third chapter.

The fourth chapter gives an analysis of the emergence of the Masālīt Sultanate from a regional perspective. It disentangles the complex political history of western Dār Fūr during the Mahdiyya (1883–1898), and analyzes the political, ideological and economic dimensions of the new sultanate's relations with its neighbours. The political developments offered the Masālīt the opportunity to establish their state. The ideological element is the 'Mahdist faith' of the title. Mahdist faith, or Islam in a Mahdist guise, came to represent the corporate identity of the state *vis-à-vis* the outside, that is to say, became the ideology of state in its formal external relations. Politically and economically the young Masālīt Sultanate was dominated by its western neighbour, the sultanate of Wadai. Yet, in this period, its capital became a station and (minor) southern terminus of the trans-Saharan trade with North-Africa.

The foundation of the sultanate from within is the subject of the fifth chapter. While the sultanate was presented to its neighbours as a miniature Mahdist state, internally it was organized as a Sudanic state, patterned on the Keira Sultanate of Dār Fūr of which the Masālīt had been a part until 1874. Sultan and subjects of the Masālīt Sultanate as it were reenacted a play, which they knew both from direct experience and from hearsay, and in which they themselves now became the major actors. This is the 'Sudanic tradition' of the title. Sudanic tradition is here not used as a clearly defined or definable theoretical concept, for this would be premature. It is used to indicate those organizational features of the Masālīt Sultanate – discussed in Chapter Five – which were derived from the Keira Sultanate (in whose shadow the new state emerged), and which resembled features of the other, less well documented, sultanates of the area.[2]

The sixth chapter discusses, from a regional perspective, the political crises through which the Masālīt Sultanate passed in the first decade of the twentieth century. In 1909 the sultanate of Wadai came under French colonial rule. Dār Masālīt was conquered militarily, but did not come under French administration, since it was, by international agreement, assigned to the British. In Dār Masālīt, the period 1909–1922 was therefore not one of revolutionary economic change as in some of the neighbouring sultanates, but of dramatic political change. This intensified certain structural features of this Sudanic state (e.g. the factionalism of the nobility), and reactivated the Mahdist faith of its subjects, since popular revolt against the sultan's French connection placed itself in the Mahdist tradition and took a religious form.

Dār Masālīt's occupation by Condominium (Anglo-Egyptian) troops and its incorporation into the British Empire marked the beginning of a new era. The detailed and full study of Dār Masālīt under Condominium Rule is beyond the scope of this study. Yet three major themes are discussed in the final chapter. Firstly, how the British 'indirect rule' policy gave the Masālīt Sultan more power and wealth than he had ever had. Secondly, how British policy, particularly the new taxation system, revolutionized the local economy. Thirdly, how British development of the central Sudan (the Nile valley) – not studied here – 'underdeveloped' the Sudan's periphery, of which Dār Masālīt was a part. While 'Sudanic tradition' fell by the wayside. Mahdist faith reemerged as the ideology of resistance against these hated changes.

Studies of the history of Dār Fūr (Sudan's westernmost province of which Dār Masālīt is a part) are few. The most important modern works are Mūsā al-Mubārak's *Tārīkh Dār Fūr al-siyāsī, 1882–1898* ('The Political History of Dār Fūr, 1882–1898') and R. S. O'Fahey's *State and Society in Dār Fūr*. The former is a detailed account of political events in Dār Fūr (including the western frontier area) during the Mahdiyya. The latter is an administrative history of the Dār Fūr Sultanate in the periods 1750–1874 and 1898–1916, with an emphasis on the central institutions of the state. By focusing upon a smaller area at the periphery of Dār Fūr, and by basing itself to a large extent on oral sources, the present study has attempted to complement these studies by reconstructing the wider society as well as the state, and by throwing light upon the periphery rather than the centre.

This book deals with themes and subjects on which there is an ongoing theoretical debate between Africanists of different disciplines and specializations. These are, for example, the issues of slavery and long-distance trade – both involving the vexed question of what mode(s) of production existed in the states of the eastern Sudanic belt – and the question of the use of oral sources.

The debate on African slavery has been dominated by two approaches or interpretations, the functionalist or 'absorptionist' interpretation of the American historians Miers and Kopytoff, and the neo-Marxist approach of Meillassoux and other French anthropologists.[3] The former regarded the concept of African 'slavery' as essentially different from Euro-American conceptions of slavery. They argued that in Africa transactions in 'rights-in-people' were an integral part of systems of kinship and marriage, and that slavery was part of a continuum of social relationships involving such rights. While in the west the antithesis of slavery was freedom, in Africa it was not freedom as autonomy, but 'belonging', that is to say membership in a local community, e.g. a kin group. A slave (or 'acquired person') was by definition 'not belonging' when he first arrived. Yet, normally he was gradually absorbed into the kin system of the host society.[4] It is this process, the gradual reduction of the slave's marginality, the lifetime and inter-generational mobility of the slaves, and the relative absence of slave revolts, that are central to Miers and Kopytoff's editorial foreword, and that have earned their approach the label of 'absorptionist'[5] and the criticism of presenting a too benign image of African slavery.

In contrast, neo-Marxist anthropologists like Meillassoux looked upon African slavery as an exploitative relation of production, and upon the slave as a means of production in the hands of his master. They advocated a class analysis – the slaves being an 'objective' class without historical or political vocation in most African societies – and criticized Miers and Kopytoff for being too much concerned with the jural status of slaves, and for neglecting the costs of obtaining slaves and the effect of slaveholding upon the distribution of wealth and power.[6] Similar criticism came from the American historians Cooper, Klein and Lovejoy. Cooper criticized Miers and Kopytoff for failing to analyze the causes and consequences of the different ways in which the slaves' marginality was used by the different social groups of a society.[7] Klein and Lovejoy believed that the functionalist interpretation divorced the discussion from historical reality. 'For functionalists like Miers and Kopytoff', they wrote, 'there has been an unwillingness to appreciate the economic basis of social relationships and the importance of slavery as a source of labor.'[8] Following Terray (1975), they argued for the existence of a slave mode of production in many parts of West Africa in the nineteenth century, and for the existence of plantation slavery in those areas of the savanna or (western) Sudanic belt which had a relatively dense population. Although they distinguished two types of savanna slavery (differing in the pattern of slave residence, the density of slave population, and the degree of economic rationality or exploitation), they analyzed only the harsher, more exploitative, system of slavery of societies in which the products of slave labour were largely marketed, and not used for subsistence.[9] If Miers and Kopytoff depicted African slavery as too benign because of a distortion in the scope of the collection of essays they edited,[10] Klein and Lovejoy can be accused of distorting the reality by neglecting the milder form of slavery which existed in societies which were less oriented to the market.

The critics of Miers and Kopytoff have correctly argued that slavery cannot be studied in isolation from the political economy of the society in which it exists. This argument should be a warning against sweeping generalizations of the type made by Lovejoy and Klein, when they propose the (poorly defined) label of slave mode of production for parts, if not most of West Africa.[11] What is striking, when one compares the studies of slavery in various societies of the western Sudanic belt (Klein and Lovejoy, 1979; Boutillier, 1975; Klein, 1977) and even the section on slavery in Dār Masālīt presented below, is the number of formal similarities in the institution of Sudanic slavery. It is these formal or functional similarities in the institution of African slavery which are the subject of the editorial foreword of Miers and Kopytoff. Although one may query the relevance of generalizations on this level and of this ahistorical, functionalist type, for the time they might be the only generalizations about African slavery possible.

As a result of the nature of the available sources, it was mentioned above, the reconstruction of Masālīt society during the Ancien Regime is perforce static. Since there are no data on the ways in which slaves were used by individuals and social groups to control access to wealth and power, this also applies to the section on slavery in Dār Masālīt during the Ancien Regime. For the later period, after the emergence of the Masālīt Sultanate, there is much more information about the uses of slaves. Chapter Five contains an analysis of how slaves became one of the means by which the new ruling elite, particularly the sultan, came to dominate the commoners and local nobility both politically and economically. This usage of slaves was institutionalized in the *jihādiyya*, a body of professional slave soldiers who were skilled in the use of firearms and were in the personal service of the rulers.[12]

The new use(s) to which slaves were put by the ruling class of the new Masālīt Sultanate in the decade 1888–98, coincided with a numerical increase of Dār Masālīt's slave population as a result of the Mahdist wars.[13] The same decade witnessed the beginning of the long-distance trade between Dār Masālīt and the Mediterranean coast. The abundance of slaves, their low price, and the ease with which they could be sold may have negatively affected their position, but neither slaves nor the product of slave labour formed the main source of income or political power of the new ruling class (see Chapter Five). If the label of 'slave mode of production' is at all useful in a Sudanic context, it certainly is not in characterizing Masālīt society.

Another theme of the present study which is the subject of debate between Africanists, is that of the links between long-distance exchange and state formation. The debate focuses on two questions. Firstly, whether there was a causal relationship between the development of long-distance trade and the historical formation of states in the Sudanic belt. Secondly, whether long-distance trade was the major factor which allowed the ruling classes of African states to maintain their wealth and power or, in Marxist terminology, to reproduce the existing relations of production. To the first question this study is not really relevant. The Masālīt state emerged in the shadow of an earlier and larger state during the political upheaval of the Mahdiyya. Neither states nor long-distance trade were new to the eastern Sudanic belt, and the connection between the two has been lost in time. In Dār Masālīt, it is argued in Chapter Five, long-distance trade followed in the wake of, and did not cause the rise of the sultanate.

To the debate on the second question this study may have something to contribute. Several Africanists such as Godelier, Coquery-Vidrovitch, and Person have argued that the power and wealth of the aristocracies of African states derived mainly from their control of the long-distance trade.[14] Underlying this theory was the belief that the 'tribute' or taxes which these aristocracies levied from their subjects was mainly of symbolic value and not large. The French anthropologist Terray criticized this theory in his study of the Gyaman kingdom of Abron, a province of Asante. Terray denied that the state controlled the long-distance trade in the way in which other scholars had thought it did. The rulers did not control the trade routes or tax the traders at will, he argued, for they were too keen on attracting trade and there were too many competing trade routes to make this kind of control attractive or effective. The rulers dominated the export trade only because the major exports (gold in the Gyaman kingdom of Abron and kola nuts in Asante) could only be produced by those who controlled a sufficient labour force of slaves, i.e. by the rulers. Not long-distance trade but slavery was the origin of the wealth of the rulers, Terray argued, and it was slavery (i.e. the need to keep the slaves subordinated) that determined the military character of the ruling class and the light 'tribute' it levied from the commoners.

> Abron and Ashanti aristocracies were anxious to take part in long-distance trade because apart from hoarding it was the only means at their disposal for 'realising' the surplus product they extorted from their captives, and so to obtain for themselves on the one hand the luxury goods which served as material basis for their social superiority, and on the other hand goods – captives, weapons – which enabled regular reproduction of the social formation.[15]

The present study (of a different kind of state) points in a different direction. In the Masālīt Sultanate long-distance trade was not the main source of revenue of the sultan and other members of the ruling class. Their main source of revenue was formed by the taxes and other customary dues levied by the rulers from their (free) subjects. It is true that much of this tax revenue was redistributed to the commoners and to members of the ruling class, but there is no reason to call these payments of basic necessities such as grain, cotton, butter and livestock, symbolic and to belittle their real value. Long-distance trade was certainly important to the ruling class. It indeed provided the prestige goods which served as the material basis for the rulers' social superiority, as Terray noted; it also provided the rulers with guns and ammunition. However, it would go too far to say that guns 'enabled the regular reproduction of the social formation', as

Terray does for the Gyaman kingdom. In Dār Masālīt firearms were not the only or most important means by which the rulers monopolized the (legal) use of force, for swords, horses and trained horsemen were at least as important to the military superiority of the ruling class. In Dār Masālīt the major export goods (ostrich feathers, ivory, rhinoceros-horn, skins and slaves) were not the product of slave labour, as in the state studied by Terray, but were obtained by the rulers as part of the customary dues and taxes demanded from their subjects, through the regional exchange of goods obtained as taxes, and through raiding into neighbouring territory.

While this case study of the Masālīt Sultanate does not support theories that long-distance trade, and not taxation, was the main source of revenue of the ruling class of Sudanic states, it gives evidence of the fact that long-distance trade was to a large extent controlled and regulated by the state. Within Sudanese studies it thus disproves the analyses of foreign trade by O'Fahey (1980) and Walz (1978), who have denied or ignored state regulation of the trade between the Mediterranean coast (particularly Egypt) and the sultanates of the eastern Sudanic belt. The argument presented below (see Chapters Four and Five) tends to support the analysis of foreign trade in the Funj Sultanate, proposed by Spaulding, but generalizations about the Sudanic belt as a whole seem premature.[16]

The Masālīt Sultanate and the other eastern Sudanic states can be briefly characterized as follows. They were predominantly agrarian states, based on extensive rainfed agriculture and nomadic animal husbandry. Apart from local exchange of goods and services which embodied a principle of reciprocity and was not bound to the marketplace, there was regional exchange across ecological boundaries (the sedentary–nomad boundary, the 'desert-side economy',[17] and finally long-distance trade, to a large extent controlled by the sultans. Eastern Sudanic states were multi-ethnic states, and the two major strata were those of the rulers (the local and state nobility) and the ruled (the commoners). About the role and position of slaves in the eastern Sudanic states other than the Masālīt Sultanate (particularly the large and important sultanates of Wadai and Dār Fūr) little is as yet known. The rulers did not monopolize the means of production, but controlled the agricultural surplus, which was extracted from the commoners (in kind) through regular taxation and *ad hoc* demands, and which was consumed conspicuously, redistributed, or exported abroad. The label of 'tributary' mode of production, a concept formulated by S. Amin and popular among neo-Marxists,[18] may suggest itself. However, the present author would rather refrain from distinctively defining the dominant mode of production of eastern Sudanic states, particularly because of the lack of knowledge about slavery in Wadai and Dār Fūr, and partly because at this stage labels would conceal more than they reveal.

The present study of the Masālīt Sultanate is a case study. The theories and models discussed above have guided the author in deciding what questions to ask from the sources, and what aspects of the Masālīt past to single out for discussion. However, this case study is too narrow a base, and present knowledge of the eastern Sudanic belt too limited to formulate general answers to the issues raised. It is hoped that this book, apart from pointing the way to future research on Dār Fūr, can provide some new insights to the present debate on slavery, state formation and long-distance trade.

Another important issue in African historical studies which this study cannot ignore is that of oral history, 'the collection of oral testimony as an ancillary technique of historical study'.[19] In this field much work has been done since the publication of Vansina's *De la Tradition Orale* in 1961. Behind the screen of respectability provided by this work, many historians ignored those who were sceptical of both the existence of African history and the feasibility of writing it on the basis of oral sources, and turned to concrete research projects involving the use of oral interviews for historical purposes. The work they produced in the two decades following 1961 has certainly contributed to the recognition of the importance of African history and of oral history as one of its techniques among professional historians. In the meantime techniques of interviewing and recording were improved. Standards of transcribing, annotating, translating and referring to oral texts became more rigid. Oral historians usually evaluated oral texts like any other text, that is to say, applied the rules of internal and external textual criticism. They examined the internal consistency of oral texts, compared them with other written and oral sources, and tried to take subjective and social biases into account. Although they worried about the vagaries of memory, problems of chronology, appropriate sampling techniques etc., to the outside they presented oral history as a possible solution to the problem of how to democratize history and how to give a voice to the inarticulate.

Although the debate on oral history continued, partly because Vansina himself vainly struggled against the canonization of his *De la Tradition Orale*, it was not until the second half of the 1970s that the dominant tendency among oral historians 'to be overly enthusiastic in public print, and deeply suspicious in private conversation' was reversed.[20] Oral history was again openly admitted to be problematic, but this time by the practitioners of oral history themselves, and with the object of improving its standards rather than of discrediting it as a useful technique. One group of historians openly stated that for them Vansina's *De la Tradition Orale* was irrelevant, since they were studying societies where there were no fixed oral traditions (with a set wording), which had been handed down from generation to generation. Their oral sources were eyewitness accounts and personal reminiscences, sometimes told second or third hand. Instead of trying to reconstruct a 'prototestimony' by collecting as many variants of an oral tradition as possible – as Vansina's book proposed – they tried to reconstruct 'converging lines of evidence' by recording as many different perspectives on particular historical events and phenomena as could be found.[21] Another group of historians, studying the same kind of societies and traditions as Vansina, did not reject *De la Tradition Orale*, but tried to rescue it from the criticism of anthropologists by improving upon it. These historians still tried to reconstruct the different lines of transmission of an oral tradition, but they no longer did so 'to eliminate variation, on the assumption that points on which all narrators could be shown to have agreed must have passed down unchanged from an original prototestimony and would thus be historical.' Rather than trying to detect 'a kind of historical lowest common denominator',[22] these historians looked at the variations of oral traditions as clues to historical change in the past. Van Binsbergen's interpretation of the myth of the Tunisian 'Sidi Mhâmmad' is an excellent example of this approach by an anthropologist.[23] Miller's *The African Past Speaks* contains similar exercises from the hand of historians. The tone of the latter was outright defensive, for structuralist anthropologists had seriously criticized the methods by which Vansina and his students had set about discovering historical realities in what anthropologists regarded as timeless statements about the world and moral values (i.e. myths or traditions of origin). While incorporating and disproving elements of this criticism, these historians greatly improved the methods of analyzing myths and increased our understanding of their structure.[24]

Compared to mythlike oral traditions of this type, eyewitness accounts and personal reminiscences are very simple. However, even here oral historians aimed at exposing rather than concealing problematic aspects. It was realized that the oral interview in its final form, the transcript, was not identical to any other primary written source. Grele coined the term 'conversational narrative' for the oral interview, 'conversational because of the relationship of interviewer and interviewee, and narrative because of the form of exposition – the telling of a tale'.[25] Unlike the traditional written sources, Grele wrote,

> oral history interviews are constructed, for better or worse, by active intervention of the historian. They are a collective creation and inevitably carry within themselves a pre-existent historical ordering, selection and interpretation. Unlike letters, records, archival materials or other manuscript sources, they are created after the fact, by historians.[26]

Moreover, not only the interviewer's historical perspective shapes the oral interview, but also the view of history of the informant.

> The informant's view of history (its use, its structure, a system of cause etc.) are [*sic*] developed only in relation to the historian's view of that process, while the historian's organization of his questions (the structure of the interview) is in turn developed in response to the answers of the interviewee. Each view is thus a standard of reference for the other.[27]

Grele was rather pessimistic about the state of the art in 1975 and called his essay 'Movement Without Aim'. It is true that recognizing the problematic character of oral sources does not mean that the solutions are readily available. Boasting that oral historians, in contrast to their colleagues in the field, the anthropologists, at least attempt to account for their use of oral sources (see below under Sources and Bibliography), can only be dutch comfort and no real excuse for the imperfections. However, there is no reason for undue pessimism. Complicated, even untrustworthy sources and unperceptive historians are as old as history writing itself. Careful analysis and comparison with other, independent sources (both written and oral) can explain and expose the former, while the precept of making historical statements verifiable makes it possible to unmask the latter. The present study is not an explicit contribution to the theory of oral history. It is a concrete example of how oral and written sources complement each other, and shows to those who still need to be convinced – including some of the colleagues and students of the University of Khartoum – what is to be gained when Sudanese history is written from both written and oral sources alike.

Chapter 1

The western Sudan before 1874: the political and geographical context

State formation and Islamization: the sultanates of Wadai and Dār Fūr

The tradition of state formation in the eastern part of the Sudanic belt before the eighteenth century is of long standing, but poorly documented. The early Arab geographers have very little to say about this area in comparison with areas to the west (e.g. Kanem-Bornu) and east (the Nile Valley, Nubia). Pending archaeological investigation of the many sites associated with prehistoric states in Dār Fūr, the historian must rely on the few references in contemporary documents and on oral tradition, recorded from the nineteenth century onward.[1]

Summarizing the present state of scholarship, one can say that of the three empires remembered to have existed in this area in early times the first was the Dājū state, which centred upon the area south and southeast of Jabal Marra. The Dājū state may have temporarily co-existed with, but was finally peacefully superseded by the Tunjur state, which had its centre of gravity to the north of Jabal Marra and comprised both Dār Fūr (now the Sudan's westernmost province) and Wadai (now eastern Chad). Very little is known about the Tunjur state, but it flourished some time between 1500 and 1650 A.D., a period of which the beginning, at least, is in this area regarded as pre-Islamic.

In the period 1600–50, two states arose as successor states to the Tunjur Empire. The Tunjur were first superseded in the east by the Fūr-based state of the Keira dynasty, here referred to as the Dār Fūr Sultanate. Shortly afterwards the Tunjur were overthrown in the west, where the Mābā became the ethnic core of the sultanate of Wadai.

Wadai and Dār Fūr were Islamic states. Tradition associates the beginnings of the process of Islamization with the founding fathers of the sultanates, who introduced their families and courts to Islam and gradually made Islam the state religion. O'Fahey has argued that as a result of the important role which the sultans and the central political institutions played in spreading Islam, the heartlands of the sultanate of Dār Fūr were Islamized (and Arabized) earlier and more thoroughly than the outlying areas.[2] It is true that the frontier area between Dār Fūr and Wadai, and the Masālīt in particular, had a reputation of not being proper, let alone exemplary, Muslims as late as the twentieth century.[3] Nonetheless local tradition in Dār Masālīt places the initial spread of Islam in the seventeenth century; in view of the country's proximity to both the capital of Wadai and the heartlands of the Dār Fūr state (constituted until the end of the eighteenth century by the Fūr lands on the western slopes of Jabal Marra), this may well be correct. Until the 1880s, however, Islam in the area remained 'corporate Islam' or Islam in its 'mixing stage', that is to say that people were Muslims in the sense that they were subjects of Muslim rulers (*cuius regio*, *eius religio*), but continued to observe many traditional, non-Islamic, religious practices.[4] The new stage, that of 'reforming Islam', will be discussed below.

In the eighteenth century both Wadai and Dār Fūr were expanding, the former to the east and the latter to the west. This resulted in the period 1680–1750 in many wars between the two states, during which Wadaian troops invaded Dār Fūr and Fūr troops Wadai. In the early nineteenth century the Dār Fūr Sultan succeeded in replacing the reigning sultan of Wadai with his own candidate and thus, for a short time, in becoming Wadai's political overlord. After this episode, however, there were no major clashes until 1874, when the fall of the Dār Fūr Sultanate ushered in a new period of Wadaian expansion to the east.

It is not known to what extent and how the frontier zone between the two warring states was affected by these wars. Both al-Tūnisī, who crossed the border from east to west in 1811, and Nachtigal, who crossed it in the opposite direction in 1873, described the frontier between the two sultanates as a strip of uninhabited and unadministered land about one day's march wide.

From their descriptions it is evident that this frontier of 'negative land' was not the result of the physical features of the area, but the result of the conflicting ambitions of the sultans of Wadai and Dār Fūr, who both aspired to rule it but were unable to balance their ambition to tax it with their power to protect it.[5] As al-Tūnisī put it:

> L'intervalle qui sert de démarcation entre le Dârfour et le Ouaday, est le seul espace ou les Arabes ne stationnent pas. Cet espace est trop resserré pour leur permettre d'y vivre en sécurité et à l'abri des exigences spoliatrices des sultans fôriens et ouadayyens, car le trajet, d'une frontière à l'autre, n'est guère plus que d'une journée à marche ordinaire.[6]

Local tradition in western Dār Fūr has preserved hardly any memories of the relations between Dār Fūr and Wadai and their impact upon the frontier area in this period, but the uninhabited or unadministered zone may well have originated in the wars mentioned above.

In peacetime there were three routes linking Wadai with Dār Fūr, of which the direct one, passing through the northern part of modern Dār Masālīt, was in 1874 the main route.[7] Not only the east–west or trans-Sudanic trade passed along this route, but also a large part of Wadai's trade with Egypt came this way, even after the discovery of the northern desert route. What it meant to the Masālīt and other peoples of the frontier area to be situated on a major trade route is again hard to establish. However, the travel accounts and local traditions suggest that the impact of the trade route was extremely limited. The Masālīt participated in this trade only by raiding the caravans – often with considerable success.[8]

The frontier area between Dār Fūr and Wadai

Although the frontier between Wadai and Dār Fūr in the period before 1874 was not clear-cut or static, it was politically defined on the one hand by the unadministered zone with frontier posts on either side, and on the other by the traditional boundaries of the tributary or dependent sultanates and chiefdoms straddling the frontier. A short survey of these kingdoms and peoples, whose history is entangled with that of the Masālīt, is indispensable to this study.

The northern part of the frontier was formed by the Bidāyāt, a nomadic people. The Bidāyāt seem to have paid taxes to Dār Fūr.[9] They now live on both sides of the international boundary. South of them lived the Zaghāwa, who were also nomads and whose political allegiance was divided and alternated between Wadai and Dār Fūr. The sultanate of Dār Qimr, now in the Sudan, lay south of the Zaghāwa. It was incorporated into Dār Fūr at an early stage, at the beginning of the eighteenth century, but remained a sultanate and retained its customary ways; this is evident in the survival of a number of ancient titles.[10] West of Dār Qimr lay the mountainous kingdom of Dār Tāmā, now in Chad. Dār Tāmā was tributary to Dār Fūr until it was conquered by Wadai in the beginning of the nineteenth century.[11] However, to whatever side it paid tribute, Dār Tāmā retained a high degree of independence, if only because its physical configuration made it a natural fortress.[12] By 1874 – and possibly long before – the sultanates of the Zaghāwa, Qimr and Tāmā lay astride a trade route which linked Wadai with Dār Fūr and with Egypt.[13]

Although the frontier sultanates were called after their dominant ethnic group, it would be wrong to regard them as ethnically homogeneous; nor is it correct to assume that all the ethnic groups of the area formed the core of, or belonged to, one such sultanate. With regard to the Jabal (also called Mileri, Mūl or Mūn), who lived south of Dār Qimr, their ruler was probably not a sultan but a *firsha*, who governed Dār Jabal as a district of Dār Fūr's western province. Dār Jabal was conquered by the Fūr sultans at the same time as Dār Qimr, of which it may have once been a part.[14]

The two major ethnic groups living south of Dār Jabal did not form sultanates during the period before 1874. These were the people who are today called the Erenga and the Masālīt, who – being the main subject of this study – will be discussed in a separate section below. The area south of Dār Jabal and north of the Masālīt homeland is today called Dār Erenga. This area was inhabited by a collection of ethnic groups – the Awra, Asungor, Marārīt, Girga, Dula, Erenga, etc. – which spoke related languages, and in most cases represented immigrant groups from Wadai and Dār Tāmā, where peoples of the same name still exist today. Each small group had its own ruler (*malik* or sultan), who was part of the administrative hierarchy of western Dār Fūr. The Erenga proper constituted only one of these groups, but since the area came to form an administrative unit in the late 1880s, it came to be called Dār Erenga, while the different ethnic groups increasingly came to be referred to as subsections or clans of the Erenga, the leading political group.[15]

Two sultanates – the one a full-fledged frontier state and the other a small dependent kingdom – straddled the frontier south and southwest of the Masālīt. Dār Sinyār, now divided by the international boundary, was an integral part of Dār Fūr until – and here the traditions differ – some time between 1860 and 1880, when it was annexed by its western neighbour, Dār Silā.[16] Dār Sinyār was a tiny kingdom, but it was crossed by an important trade route, which linked Dār Fūr with its slaving grounds in Dār Fongoro and Dār Runga, and by a pilgrim route, along which West African pilgrims travelled east to Mecca.[17] Southwest of Dār Sinyār and Dār Masālīt, now in Chad, lay the sultanate of Dār Silā, also called Dār Dājū after its most important ethnic group. Nachtigal called Dār Silā a comparatively old Muslim kingdom, whose inhabitants were nevertheless 'very nearly pagan'.[18] The Dājū of Dār Silā came originally from Dār Fūr, where memories of a Dājū empire preceding that of the Tunjur are still alive. The dates and stages of this westward migration are remembered by Dājū tradition, which places the arrival in Dār Silā in approximately 1700 A.D.[19] Nachtigal noted that the historical memories, customs and beliefs of the Dājū linked them more closely to Dār Fūr than to Wadai. Yet at the time of his visit (1873), as well as that of al Tūnisī in 1811, Dār Silā paid tribute to both Dār Fūr and Wadai, maintaining a position of semi-independence from both.[20] The introduction of the states and major ethnic groups of the area surrounding the Masālīt has set the stage for the latter, who are the main actors in the historical process analyzed below.

Chapter 2

Masālīt society during the Ancien Regime (before 1874)

The Masālīt during the Ancien Regime

The survey of Wadai/Dār Fūr relations and of the states and chiefdoms of the frontier area between the two sultanates has set the scene for the main actors in the historical process analysed below, the Masālīt.

Definition of Dār Masālīt

The literal meaning of Dār Masālīt, or more correctly, *dār al-Masālīt*, is the home of the ethnic group of the Masālīt. However, the Masālīt homeland never formed a single separate administrative unit except for the period 1874–84. For long periods of time it was part of more than one such unit, and/or was grouped together for administrative purposes with the *dār*s of other ethnic groups. The term Dār Masālīt therefore came to mean different things in different times. Before 1874 there was no administrative unit called Dār Masālīt. The Masālīt homeland, here also referred to as Dār Masālīt, was divided up between Dār Fūr and Wadai, while some Masālīt lived from hand to mouth in the so-called uninhabited strip of land separating the two sultanates. After 1874 most Masālīt were united by one of their *firsha*s, Hajjām Ḥasab Allāh who, with the support of the new Turco-Egyptian regime, obtained a kettledrum, the title of bey, and the right to administer *dār al-Masālīt* in the literal sense. However, when in 1884, after the downfall of the Turco-Egyptian regime (and Hajjām Bey), *faqīh* Ismāʿīl ʿAbd al Nabī founded the Masālīt Sultanate, Dār Masālīt came to include the *dār*s of the Erenga, Jabal, and several

'Arab' groups, apart from that of the Masālīt. Part of the latter ceased to belong to the sultanate after 1912, when the fourth Masālīt Sultan ceded the western part of his country (now in Chad) to the French conquerors of Wadai. Finally, in 1924, as a result of the delimitation of the Chado-Sudanese boundary, Dār Masālīt came to include part of Dār Sinyār in the south.[1] It then had an estimated population of 65,000.[2] The meaning of Dār Masālīt in this study will therefore in each case depend on the time period to which it refers. Since the analysis of the emergence and consolidation of the sultanate in the period 1884–1905 is central to the present study, Dār Masālīt is often equivalent to the area governed by 'the old Sultanate', *i.e.* including most of the homeland of the Masālīt, and the *dār*s of the Erenga, Jabal and several groups of nomads or sedentarized nomads. The following section deals with the Masālīt during the Ancien Regime, *i.e.* before 1874.

The Masālīt in Wadai

> Peu de temps après, lorsque Sâboun était dans sa demeure, tout à coup un grand bruit arrive jusqu'à lui; des cris d'alarmes retentissent; il regarde sur la place du fâcher, et la voit remplie d'une foule de blessés, de gens dépouillés, qui lui criaient: 'Le pillage, la guerre nous ont ruinés.' Qui sont ces gens? dit Sâboun. Que leur est arrivé? Ce sont, lui dit-on, des Maçâlyt qui se plaignent des incursions du roi de Tâmah.[3]

The earliest evidence for the fact that some Masālīt of the frontier area were subjects of Wadai is given by al-Tūnisī, who recorded the incident quoted above in approximately 1811. Yet in contrast to what has been contended elsewhere,[4] the Masālīt were in 1811 not newly conquered subjects of Wadai. According to Nachtigal they had been brought into Wadai from Dār Fūr before 1655, i.e. during the reign of the first sultan of Wadai (1635–55), whose successors had compelled them to stay in the homes imposed upon them by bloody violence.[5] Their name, *Masālīt al-Ḥōsh*, ('Those Who Guard the House'), suggests that they were brought in to guard the frontier. One of the Masālīt sections making up these *Masālīt al-Ḥōsh* were the Surbang ('Zirban'), who were the maternal relatives of the first Keira Sultan of Dār Fūr, Sulaymān Solong (1655–80), and hid the young prince Sulaymān from his father's political rivals.[6] Oral tradition confirms that the subjects of Wadai included Masālīt from the time of the foundation of the sultanate. Sultan ʿAbd al-Karīm, remembered as the founder of Wadai and as *jadd al-Islām*,[7] introduced his people to Islam. He taught them how to read the *Qurʾān*, established mosques and *faqīh*s in each village, and demanded – for the first time – the Islamic dues of *fiṭra* and *zakāh*. When these taxes in the course of time increased, the Masālīt refused to pay. They lodged a complaint with the *shartay* of Kerne who informed the Dār Fūr Sultan. The latter took immediate action. He had a stone wall built to demarcate the Fūr/Wadai border, which was further fortified by the settlement of Fūr Kunjāra[8] (who live there until this day) as boundary guards. From that day on there were Masālīt on both sides of the Wadai/Dār Fūr border. Those of Wadai, the informant added, all became *faqīh*s, while those of Dār Fūr remained ignorant of Arabic and of the *Qurʿan* until recently.[9]

The mention of a stone wall as a boundary mark brings up the question of the *trija*; for with the exception of al-Tūnisī, who described a boundary marked by large spikes fixed in the bark of trees, all accounts of the Wadai/Dār Fūr border – both oral and written – use the term *tirja*. No two descriptions of the *tirja*, however, are the same. Nachtigal called the two ranges of hills which each marked one edge of the uninhabited zone *tirja*s or border mountains; Masālīt opinion today refers to the *tirja* as a range of hills which is situated east of Abesher and which used to demarcate the western border of the Old Dār Fūr Sultanate, the western border of the Masālīt Sultanate until 1912, and (roughly) the ethnic border between Masālīt and Borqū.[10] It is evident that *tirja* covered or came to cover many meanings, from 'the place where Sultan Hussein lost his ring' to any hill with buildings on its top.[11] However, most reliable references to the *tirja* have three points in common: they associate the *tirja* with Dār Fūr's western and northwestern border with Wadai; they locate the *tirja* west of the modern international boundary; and they define the *tirja* as ranges of hills, fortified with stones and thornbushes to make crossing difficult, if not impossible.[12] In reality probably only parts of the border were demarcated by fortified hills; other parts may have had iron spikes as boundary marks, or no boundary marks at all. In any case Dār Fūr's claims to all territory east of the *tirja* – as those of Wadai to all territory to its west – were probably more permanent than any actual administration of the border zone. What really counted were the frontier posts on both sides of the line. From there the governors of the border districts, with the aid of a few hundred armed horsemen, administered the surrounding area and guarded the frontier, directing what was the equivalent of a passport-office, customs-station and 'quarantaine', and if need be, meeting force with force.[13]

'Where traders fear to tread'; the Masālīt in the no-man's land between Dār Fūr and Wadai

The existence of buffer zones of uninhabited or unadministered bush country between different states was a common phenomenon in the Sudanic belt. Wadai's frontiers with Bagirmi, Dār Tāmā and Dār Fūr were all of this type, as was – in 1918 – the frontier between Dār Fūr and the sultanate of Dār Masālīt.[14] It is therefore possible that this type of frontier was not only the result of the discrepancy between the ability and ambition to administer the border area, but also of a conscious frontier policy which minimized contact with the outside in order to maximize the chance of keeping the peace. The fate of several early visitors to Wadai and Dār Fūr, and the formalities which attended the frontier crossing of the caravans of al Tūnisī and Nachtigal, are evidence for such a policy of 'splendid isolation', particularly with regard to foreigners and (foreign) traders.[15] For indigenous people, particularly those who had relatives and clansmen on the other side, it was much easier to move across political borders. Yet oral data suggest[16] that they were discouraged or actually prohibited from doing so for different reasons than those applying to foreigners and traders; for even if the neighbouring sultan was glad to see them come, their own sultan was loath to see them go. In this part of the Sudanic belt subjects, not land, were the scarce commodity.

With regard to the buffer zone between Dār Fūr and Wadai, in 1873–4, when the Wādī Asunga and Wādī Kajja formed its western edge and its eastern edge followed a north–south (-west) line along the Wādī Bīr Daqīq through Umm Sibayḥa and Murle, it covered approximately one-third of the area known as the Masālīt homeland.[17] However, although it was an unadministered zone, it was not uninhabited. Masālīt tradition does not remember the existence of this stretch of no-man's land, the bonanzas of successful caravan raids, or former homes further to the west or east. Several Masālīt sections have their centres and homelands in the area described as a no-man's land in the travel accounts.[18] Moreover, even the latter agree it was infested with Masālīt – who either as permanent inhabitants or as irregular visitors terrorized the buffer zone and ambushed the caravans which crossed it. Nachtigal called the Masālīt of the borderland 'Masalit et-Tirge' (the Masālīt of the border mountain) and 'Masalit Ambus' (or Amm Būs, those who live along the *wādī*s with the tall grass called *būs*).[19] They were notorious for two habits, that of cannibalism, and that of raiding the caravans, the latter of which is much better documented than the former.[20] Although the name Amm Būs is no longer in use, it is still remembered in Dār Masālīt, and is said to refer to the wild and unruly Masālīt of the area southwest of the confluence of the Wādīs Kajja and Asunga, that is to say, the Dudonga, Urta, Adukong, Kunjāra, Aryeng, Jerkereng and Amburthung clans of the Masālīt. The Amm Būs never effectively belonged to either Wadai or Dār Fūr, nor to the Masālīt Sultanate, and escaped the armed horsemen of either side by temporarily crossing the border.[21]

The Masālīt in Dār Fūr

Between latitudes 13.30° and 12.15°, east of Dār Fūr's frontier with Wadai and west of the Wādī Azūm, lay the homeland of other Masālīt. It bordered on the Erenga groups in the north and on the Tarjam, Ta'ālba (or the Tha'āliba), Maḥāmīd etc., in the northeast. The Sinyār and Dājū were its southern neighbours, while in the east the Wādī Azūm marked roughly the porous ethnic border between Masālīt and Fūr. Yet although the Masālīt homeland was a geographical unit, administratively it was divided up between different districts and provinces of the Dār Fūr Sultanate. To which administrative division it belonged is not easy to establish, partly because of our limited knowledge, and partly because of some inherent characteristics of the administrative structure of the state. One of these was the lack of homogeneity, probably resulting from the fact that the many regions and peoples had been incorporated into the Keira state at different times. The survival of a mish-mash of titles of pre-Keira origin is another feature which suggests that some parts of the state (particularly the north and west) had been part of an earlier state or earlier states.[22] The continuous attempts by the central government to check the ever-increasing autonomy of the local hereditary nobility led to the appointment of new agents and the creation of new lines of command, which partly account for a third characteristic of the administrative structure, the fact that it was not static. Offices were created and abolished, districts and ethnic groups shifted from one province to another,[23] blurring the picture of what the administrative structure of Dār Fūr may have looked like at any particular time. From the reign of Sultan Muḥammad al-Faḍl (1803–1838) onwards, however, there is more clarity, while for the reigns of his successors, when the Old Regime drew to a close in 1874, oral testimonies add to the written sources to provide colourful detail.

From the point of view of the central administration the Masālīt homeland did not exist. Its northern part (at least as far south as the present Murne) belonged to the Fia and Kerne districts (or *shartaya*s) of the western province (magdumate), while its southern part was probably included in the Tebella and Zami Baya districts (or *shartaya*s) of Dār Dīma, the old southwestern province of the sultanate, which had become part of a larger southern province (the magdumate of the South) in about 1800. In about 1870 the western province consisted of four districts, those of Madi, Fia, Konyir and Kerne.[24] The most northern one, Madi, with its capital at Bīr Juways, included the Qimr, part of the Zaghāwa, the Banī Ḥusayn nomads around Jabal ʿUtāsh, and other ethnic groups, but no Masālīt. South of it lay the district of Fia, with its capital at Muʿallaqa (not far from Kabkābiyya), which was the residence of *shartay* Ḥanafī.[25] Fia was a Fūr district, but included also the Erenga groups, the Jabal, a number of nomadic groups, and the northern sections of the Masālīt . The small district of Konyir lay northwest of Kabkābiyya and east of the hill at which the boundaries of Fia, Madi and Konyir came together. South of the Wādī Barei, which formed part of the northern boundary with Fia, lay the district of Kerne. Kerne, which stretched from the western slopes of Jabal Marra to the border with Wadai, was the largest *dār* of the area. It was ruled by *shartay* Muzammil Nūr from Gilli (Gulli) or Korāre, respectively to the northwest and north of the modern Zalingei.[26] Like Fia, Kerne was primarily a Fūr district, but it also included other ethnic groups, among whom were many sections of the Masālīt . Kerne was the southernmost district of the western province. To its south lay the old Fūr chiefdom of the Abū Dīma.[27] Dār Dīma consisted of many *shartaya*s, of which those on its western fringes – Tebella, Zami Baya, Kulli and Zami Toya – are important to this study. The mountainous canton of Tebella (see map Dereisa) lay south of Kerne and south and west of the Wādī Azūm, which here bends to the south. That part of Tebella which lay west of the Azūm – roughly the country south of Murne and north of Habīla – was populated by Masālīt. The district of Zami Baya, straddling the Wādī Azūm south of Tebella, may have included what is today the Masālīt area of Indirrabirro. Zami Toya (see map Bindisi) and/or Kulli (see map Garsila) probably extended to the (south-) west as far as the border with Dār Silā, including part of the Masālīt's southern neighbours, the Sinyār.[28]

Although the administrative divisions of the Dār Fūr Sultanate outlined above were not ethnic divisions and cut across ethnic boundaries rather arbitrarily, the contradiction with the principles of administration at a lower level, where the ethnic group, or rather subgroup, was the basic administrative unit, is only apparent. Dār Dīma, Fia and Kerne were old chiefdoms with a strong ethnic core of Fūr, and may well have pre-dated the Keira state. The *shartay*s of Kerne and Fia, which belonged to closely related Fūr families, were answerable directly to the sultan, as the *abū dīma* or *dimanqāwī*, head of all the *shartay*s of his district, used to be.[29] Before analysing the relations between the Masālīt and their Fūr overlords more must be said about the Masālīt themselves, both in relation to the land, which was their main sustenance, and in relation to each other.

The commoners and their means of subsistence

> Green and gold the landscape steams under a milk-blue sky. Against a background of huge acacias by the Wadi Barei, where there are still pools shrinking in the whitish sand, a village of conical thatched huts cowers roof-deep in the giant millet, little of most of them visible but the apex of the cone, strangled in pumpkin creeper.[30]

This impressionist picture of Dār Masālīt during the rains was sketched by a Condominium official after decades of desiccation and desertification. It evokes a picture of an abundance of water, lush vegetation and fertility. During the Ancien Regime – even more than in the 1950s – the western plains of which *dār al-Masālīt*, the Masālīt homeland, was a part, were indeed a well-watered and fertile area, and a granary for the nomads of the desert in the north and for the Fūr of Jabal Marra in the east. *Dār al-Māsalīt*, bounded by the 13.30° parallel of latitude in the north and that of 12.15° in the south, enclosed the land between three major *wādīs*, the Wādī Kajja (running from northeast to southwest), the Barei and the Azūm together forming its eastern border. It was crossed by innumerable smaller streambeds (*khūr*s and *rijl*s), where water was at all times close to the surface and easy to obtain. All streambeds were lined with large and shady trees such as the sycamore and *acacia albida*, which could offer shade to scores of people and animals. These trees, together with the hills and rocky outcrops which one encounters everywhere in the *dār*, were the major landmarks, important enough to serve as boundary marks, to give local villages and people their names, and even to serve as shrines for rainmaking and fertility rituals. Game was abundant. The same country where one today encounters but an occasional tree and no animal more dangerous than the white ant, was then the wooded abode of lions, buffaloes, elephants, rhinocerosses, leopards, waterbucks, gazelles, kudus, giraffes, ostriches, partridges, guinea-fowl, hyaenas and monkeys. The rainfall, increasing from north to south with corresponding variations in vegetation and fauna, added to the difference in soil types – clays in the south and sandy soils in the north, with streaks of alluvial clay along the streambeds – to distinguish the northern from the southern part of the country.

The Masālīt commoners were primarily farmers, the main crop being millet (*dukhn*) on the sandy soils of the north, and sorghum (*dhura*) on the clays of the south. Fields were selected, cleared and burnt in the dry season. Crops were sown after the first rains in June or July, and after several weedings – the most labour-intensive agricultural activity – harvested in October at the end of the rainy season. Then the grain was threshed, winnowed and stored, either in straw hut-shaped silos on a raised platform (Masālīt, *tukuli*; Arabic, *surrāya*), or less commonly in underground pits (*maṭmura*s). Every nuclear family had several farms. A few vegetables might be grown inside the compound. A number of fast-ripening crops were grown on the land immediately surrounding the compound, which was called *jubrāka*, and was cultivated by all the members of the family. The main grain crop was grown by the man, who might well have two or three farms with an average size of one and a half hectares. The loose sandy soil called *qōz* (*qūz*) was favoured for millet farms, while the cotton – another predominantly male crop – required the more humid soil of streambeds. Watermelons, grown towards the end of the rainy season, were again grown mainly by men. The field of the woman was usually smaller and had a larger variety of crops. She also grew millet, but was assisted by her children to whose labour she, and not her husband, had the sole right.[31] Possibly as a consequence of this it was her crop that the family would eat first. She also grew groundnuts, sesame, okra, beans etc., and often had a small patch of irrigated farmland near the streambed, where she grew onions. At the end of the rains, in the *darrat*, the grain was threshed and the farmers paid their taxes. Below a minimum of (normally) approximately 2400 *raṭl* (10 *rayka* of 30 *midd* or *mudd*, each of 8 *raṭl*) no grain crop was in theory taxable. Those who reached this minimum paid one tenth of their crop (one *rayka* out of ten) in taxes. In practice even smaller crops were taxed, but at a lower rate of one *midd* out of every thirty *midd* harvested, i.e. one thirtieth of the harvest.[32] The *zakāh*, as the tax was called, was measured out and paid in public, namely on the village threshing floors, and was immediately stored in the public granary.

If agriculture was the main economic activity of the Masālīt, there were other means of subsistence, one of which was animal husbandry. The Masālīt never had very large herds, but most commoners had a few cows, goats, sheep, donkeys, a horse, plenty of hens – but few camels. Herding the village cows was a communal responsibility and families took turns in providing cowherds to tend the cows which were kept by night in thorny enclosures (*zarība*s) just outside (or if one feared for their safety, inside) the village. It is uncertain whether livestock was taxed on a local level; but when it was taxed by higher authorities, it was the herd of the whole village or clan section that was assessed, and the details of compensating the owners of the animals which were physically removed were left to the villagers.[33] The *nafīr* or communal labour party by which the villagers combined their forces, e.g. to cultivate the fields of one of their members, was another activity of the whole community. However, among the Masālīt, in contrast possibly to other areas of Dār Fūr, it was held on special occasions only and was by no means the most common way in which agricultural activities were performed.[34] Although every individual selected his own fields, the farms of one village and of kinsmen were usually close together; the decision to let the land lie fallow – once in every ten years or so – was again a communal one, people say. When the *būde* weed came up in one man's field, all the surrounding fields were abandoned as well, and new fields were opened up in a different direction.[35] Farming and animal husbandry together provided the basic necessities of life. Grain, served as porridge (*'asīda*) or beer (*marissa*), was the staple food, while livestock provided milk, clarified butter and meat. The hides were worn as clothes, used as *farwa*s to sit on, made into *qirba*s to carry water, or into *jurāb*s or general purpose bags, into horse furniture, shields to fight with, and sandals to wear. The locally grown cotton also provided clothing. It was spun by men, women and children alike and woven into strips of coarse cotton cloth called *tukkiyya* (plural, *takākī*), two of which formed a *tōb* or *thawb*.[36]

Raiding, hunting and gathering were other important means of subsistence. Raiding seems to have been an economic institution with its own well-established rules and distinct (Masālīt) name, *martu*. The Masālīt made raids into Dār Silā, the land of the nomads in the south, into Wadai and into Fūr territory. They raided for cows, e.g. to replenish their shrunken herds after a period of drought, or to enlarge their herds for less pressing reasons. For the young men *martu* offered the opportunity to obtain the capital required to get married, while there was also a non-economic factor involved – for it was said that no marriageable young woman would allow herself to be wooed by a suitor who had not 'blooded his spear'.[37] The hunting parties, often made up of the able-bodied men of one or more villages and led by *'aqīd*s, provided a more or less regular supply of meat.[38]

Gathering – regarded as women's work – supplied a welcome change of diet and a store of reserve food which could well be a matter of life and death;[39] for however fertile the land, and however varied the means of subsistence, against the failure of the rains nothing could avail. In case of droughts, which were not an uncommon phenomenon in this area even in the past, gathering was the only means of subsistence left. The Masālīt claim to have always had a knowledge of survival techniques superior to that of their neighbours (who allegedly did not know what was eatable or how it should be prepared), and which included gathering grains from the inside of termite hills, plundering nests of insects for honey, luring foxes and snakes from their holes, and preparing bitter or even poisonous roots and seeds in complicated and laborious ways. In ordinary circumstances, however, the edible fruits of the bush were no more important than its other products: the woods and grasses which were popular as building materials and fuel, or were strong and supple enough to be woven into ropes, baskets, foodcovers, containers, etc.

This is how the bulk of the Masālīt, and all those who are here called commoners, made a living; they farmed, kept livestock, hunted and gathered. But some of the commoners had special skills and functions (and hence often revenues) on the side. The weavers are a good example, for in each village only one or two people – always men – had a pit-loom and for a small fee would weave *tukkiyyas* from cotton brought to them by the individual villagers. There were specialized tanners, and people who were good at making the *amm chang* sandals or horse furniture. Many people made straw mats of various kinds and qualities, and rope, while weaving baskets and food covers of plain straw or stronger fibres dyed in many colours was a feminine speciality. The wooden bowls called *qadaḥ*, from which people ate, also required some skill and experience, as did a host of other items used in the house. There were the 'swimmers' (singular, *ʿawwām*) who would help people cross the streams in the rainy season and the bone doctors who specialized in setting the broken bones of animals and human beings; there was the root doctor, who with his concoctions of medicinal roots cured the ill and provided charms for the anxious; the *dumbāri* or locust charmer who, from his lonely abode on the top of a hill, was to divert the swarms of locusts from the village farms; the rain priests or owners of local shrines who led the rainmaking ceremonies when the rains were late, or prayed for wind when people were winnowing;[40] and finally, there was in every village a *faqīh*.

In western Dār Fūr as elsewhere the concept of *faqīh* is a very wide and comprehensive one, including all gradations between the small village *faqīh* who might not even have memorized the *Qur'ān* and the great *'ālim* or expert in the Islamic sciences who attracted scores of students from faraway places. It is the small village *faqīh* who concerns us here. He read the *Qur'ān* regularly and had memorized at least part of it. He led the village people in prayer at the *masīk*, the open place in the middle of each village where all adult men spent their evenings and had their meals, where guests were accommodated, where people performed their prayers, and where – by the light of a large wood-fire – the *faqīh* taught his pupils the *Qur'ān* and the basic principles of Arabic. The *faqīh* also made amulets, wrote *maḥāya* for the ill, named the newly-born, read the *fātiḥa* at marriage ceremonies, and said the funeral prayers. However even the *faqīh*s, with the exception of those who travelled around and sustained themselves by the services they provided to the local people, farmed for a living with or without the assistance of their pupils. This is true for all the specialists or craftsmen of the type mentioned above with one important exception, that of the *ḥadāḥīd*. The *ḥadāḥīd* (sing. *ḥaddādī*) were professional blacksmiths and potters, and although they seem to have had farms and livestock, they were a despised caste and were not regarded as full members of the village community.[41]

Within the village or group of villages all community members were involved in the exchange of goods and services generated within the community. The exchange relationships were face-to-face and based on mutual trust, and did not necessarily involve the use of currencies. The local exchange activities were not bound to specific times or localities but, although they were to a large extent regulated by custom, could occur anywhere at any time. Many local exchange activities embodied an element of reciprocity. This is best illustrated by the *nafīr*, the communal labour or beer party, whereby the adult members of the community combined their forces to weed the fields or build the house of one of its members. What was exchanged in the *nafīr* was not so much labour for beer (or meat and beer) as labour for future labour; for the circumstances of tomorrow might force any member of the community to appeal to his neighbours and kinsmen for similar help. The same is true for other – more exclusively female – occasions for joint labour, the celebrations attending the *rites de passage*. Then all the young women had to go and assist in the preparation of food at the house where feast or funeral was held, while the matrons and their men had to go there to present their congratulations or condolences, to partake of the food, and to pay a contribution toward the expenses. Again the exchange was not one of labour and goods for food, but services and goods for similar services and goods at future weddings, funerals, etc. The comparison with a modern insurance or savings plan does not seem too far-fetched. Obligatory gift-giving also occurred when a member of the community had to travel, e.g. to attend the funeral of a distant relative, or to act as a midwife for a faraway daughter. In that case the contributions which the community members made towards the travel expenses created the right to the same help on similar occasions, but also the right to a small present of whatever was cheaper or of better quality at the traveller's destination when he returned.

The same element of reciprocity can be seen in the *ngōre* and the *morota*. *Ngōre* was an institution which allowed those members of the community who had a shortage of millet to go and work on anybody's farm for a fixed reward of six *midd* of millet per day.[42] The *morota* resembled the *nafīr* but was limited to the young men and women of the community who, on someone's request or at the initiative of their leaders, gathered to weed someone's fields or build his house. It is true that they were rewarded in goats, which constituted the capital for their parties and dances,[43] but their assistance was given on the silent understanding that everybody's children could expect and be expected to exchange labour services for party funds in this way. A major occasion for exchange was marriage. Masālīt tradition claims that the Masālīt commoners (in contrast to their rulers) always married women of their own clan, who usually lived in nearby villages.[44] The bridewealth was paid in two stages. Before the marriage could be consummated the groom had to pay ten cows, eight to twelve goats and a number of *tukkiyyas*, which were all distributed by the girl to her close relatives. After the wedding the groom and bride lived with the latter's parents for a period of two or three years during which the groom owed his inlaws all kinds of labour services called *kumal*. Only after this period could he move his wife, his two or three children and the most indispensable household items to a compound of his own.[45] The frequency of the above-mentioned exchange activities was limited by custom. In the case of marriage and other *rites du passage* this is obvious, but the occasions on which one organized *nafīr*s were limited as well. Normally every adult man or woman worked his own fields. Only if someone was newly married and was making a farm for the first time, or if someone was ill, old and disabled, or if the local chief felt the need for a *nafīr*, would the community get together to work, drink, dance and be merry.[46] In contrast to other local exchange activities, the exchange of goods for the services of the craftsmen and specialists mentioned above did not have an element of reciprocity, nor was the frequency with which they were offered or called upon limited by custom. Yet they belonged to the sphere of local exchange and were paid for in locally produced goods – some beer or a hen for the weaver, some grain for the *faqīh* and the *dumbāri*, etc. – without interference by the local authorities.[47]

The exchange activities described above were part of a local sphere of exchange. However, the community was also involved in other exchange activities which were regional in scope, involved the use of currencies, were subject to some control by the local or central government, and were bound to a specific time and place – namely, to the marketplace. The sphere to which these activities belonged will be called the regional sphere of exchange.

The marketplace was the place where producers met to exchange or barter their products, where the farmers of the *qōz* mingled with the nomads of the semi-desert and where the mountain products of Jabal Marra were displayed side by side with those of the lowlands. Most of the products exchanged in the marketplace were produced in the *dār*s of the Masālīt and their neighbours, only a small percentage being imported from further afield. The majority of people who participated in exchange were therefore known in the area, at least as a group, and were not professional middle-men but sold goods in the production of which they had been involved. The few full-time traders were mainly strangers of the type called *jallāba*.[48] who were named after their characteristic occupation: travelling from place to place to peddle goods. Markets were held wherever there was a concentration of people, and were usually under the auspices of the local authorities who collected small market fees in kind from all those who offered goods for sale.[49] Samples of the products of the farming, animal husbandry, hunting, gathering, weaving, tanning and smithing activities mentioned above were offered for sale in most marketplaces in Dār Masālīt. They were marketed mainly by the inhabitants of the villages in the immediate surroundings of the market, and rarely by people who lived more than one day's travel away. Many markets were also visited by the nomads of the north, northeast and northwest, who came to buy grain in exchange for sour milk, clarified butter, hides, leather strings and bags, ropes, whips, etc. The Zaghāwa of the north were often too poor to barter their own produce, it was said, and came to Dār Masālīt to work for grain.[50] Most nomads, however, did come to barter; for example the Maḥāmīd sections and the Banī Ḥusayn from the northeast, and from the northwest the Maghārba, who came all the way from Arāda (in Chad) to graze their camels on the wooded banks of the *wādī*s and to exchange the red salt called *deime* and natron for grain.[51]

The latter visited markets to the west and southwest of the present Geneina, while the former exchanged their goods in the markets of Dār Erenga and probably further south in Dār Masālīt.[52] Relations with the cattle nomads to the south were strained, and cattle raiding is said to have been more common than cattle trading. Another kind of salt, together with red pepper and possibly tobacco came from the mountains east of Dār Masālīt. The salt was called *falgo* and came in little cones which Fūr and Masālīt traders carried on their heads in big baskets called *raykas* to the markets of the lowlands. There were two types of *falgo*. The type which came from Dango near Kabkābiyya came in units of three small cones tied together, while that of Keibe and Dabanga in Jabal Marra was sold in bigger and single cones. Whether the Masālīt bought *falgo* salt at the source or at the lowland markets on either side of their eastern border (Garsila, Dereisa, Keira, Amm Dukhn, Murne), it was bartered for grain and *tukkiyya*s.[53] Inside Dār Masālīt *falgo*s were a currency and had a fixed value in relation to the *midd* of grain and the *rubṭa*, a unit of cotton thread. Since the Fūr and Masālīt lived constantly at loggerheads with each other the *falgo* trade was a hazardous one. That it continued to be so is evident from a topical song from the 1890s, which was composed when Fūr highway robbers attacked one of the most powerful traders of the day called Kuttūk:

Yā ṣibyān,
ukurbu ḥizām,
darb Keibe mā lahu amān,
Kuttūk bigūl: anā walā māshī bittān
law kut folgōy bi tamanya riyāl.

You young men,
gird your loins [to fight];
the road to Keibe is unsafe;
Kuttūk says: I will not go again
even if one cone of salt would cost
eight *riyāl*.[54]

Slaves were imported from two directions, namely from Dār Silā in the southwest and from Kūbe, in the country of the Masālīt of southern Dār Fūr, in the southeast. The trade with Kūbe had been brisk since olden times; the fact that its inhabitants were relatives of the Masālīt of the west made the enterprise less hazardous, while Kūbe's location near the land of the blacks, where slaves were cheap and easy to obtain, guaranteed good prices.[55] It seems that the Masālīt in this period imported slaves for use rather than for resale, and most slaves imported from the southeast therefore never entered the marketplace.[56] When the roads were open, slaves were also imported from Dār Silā by Masālīt, Dājū and some *jallāba* traders. Some of the slaves, particularly those peddled by the Dājū, did enter the marketplace in Dār Masālīt. Local tradition remembers how slaves were groomed and greased for the purpose, and how prospective buyers would appraise them as chattels and make bids, arguing not so much about the price of the slave – which was more or less fixed for each category based on age and sex – but about the qualities and defects of the slave, and the category in which he was.[57]

A last category of products offered for sale in the marketplace was that of imported goods: paper, needles, incense, possibly some cloth, and particularly beads of many kinds and qualities. Originally imported into the Sudan from Egypt, beads reached Dār Masālīt through the small *jallāba* peddlers who laid in their stores in Kobbei (northwest of al-Fāshir), Kabkābiyya (another old *jallāba* settlement), and after 1850 possibly Abesher. Like the Maghārba from the northwest the *jallāba* travelled from chief to chief. Through the chiefs they obtained the right to enter the marketplace to buy the goods peculiar to the area, and through the chief they obtained goods which did not enter the marketplace such as ivory, ostrich feathers and rhinoceros-horn.[58] The latter products were sometimes taken to the towns and administrative centres further east by the Masālīt, it was said, but this was certainly not common practice since the nobility or local rulers who had the right to dispose of them were bound to their districts.

Neither in Wadai nor in Dār Fūr was there a standardized coin currency. As al-Tūnisī noted in about 1800: 'Le sultan n'a jamais ordonné de suivre pour les échanges, un mode uniforme, dans tous les marchés; il en résulte que chaque localité demeure attaché à ses habitudes.'[59] In the *dār*s of the Masālīt and the other frontier peoples there was no coin currency at all. Yet while all the goods circulating in the marketplace were commodities with an intrinsic value, some of them were also currencies, i.e. media of exchange with fixed price relationships towards each other. There were fixed equivalences for the *midd* of grain (the basic measure of value in these grain-producing lands), the *rubṭa* (or *rabṭa*) and the *falgo*, and for the *tukkiyya*, goat and cow; the first set serving as small change, while the latter was used in major purchases. All these 'moneys' were media of exchange, measures of value, and stores of wealth.[60] Dār Fūr womanhood considered beads a right of every married woman, as is evident from a song which travelled from al-Fāshir to Dirjeil and elsewhere:

> Manṣūṣ Kobbei
> sallū galbī
> nimshī nishkī
> li-iya Amm Būsa.
>
> The amber beads of Kobbei
> have stolen my heart;
> I will go and complain
> to *iya* Amm Būsa. [for not having received any][61]

However, beads were also money. In the early nineteenth century strings of beads were used as money in Kobbei, Kabkābiyya and Saraf al-Dajāj, and when Nachtigal travelled through in 1873–4 they were a currency in the whole area between Abesher and Kabkābiyya.[62] But in contrast to *tukkiyya*s and cows, beads were liable to changes in fashion,[63] and moreover were only sold by the local women if they were forced by circumstances and had no other way out of a precarious financial situation. This is evident from Nachtigal's comment upon the women of Abesher:

> Even the poorest woman will always sooner try to increase her bead decorations than to get a new shawl, though that forms the whole of her clothing. The men never resist their wives' propensity to adorn themselves, or seek to limit their expenditure in either their own interests or those of the household. The head of the household, however, provides only limited means for running the household; on the other hand, he makes no claim to any share in the proceeds from the milk, hens and other things which are left to the care of his wife. If the supply of provisions runs out, the wife will not tell her husband about it, and try to get fresh supplies from him, but goes to her relations, and if this attempt is fruitless, she then tries to procure provisions by selling her ornaments. Money to spend she never receives.[64]

One may conclude from this that for the Masālīt and other sedentary inhabitants of the frontier area beads were primarily a store of value, and only secondarily a medium of exchange. Nachtigal's commiseration with the skin-clad and beadless women of the Maḥāmīd nomads whom he saw in the marketplace of Umm Zuwayfa, and whom be believed to be so much poorer than their fully-beaded Tarjam neighbours,[65] may well have been misplaced; for while the Tarjam women wore their whole capital around their necks and in their ears, noses and hair, the stored wealth of the Maḥāmīd was grazing and ruminating among the trees nearby. The beaded Tarjam women were more fortunate than their camel-owning sisters in only one respect – camels were subject to taxation, while beads were not.

All these exchange activities were taking place both during the Ancien Regime and after it. They followed the rhythm of the seasons, slackening during the rains when the sedentaries were farming, the nomads far away in the bush and the roads impassable, and picking up again after the harvest. The picture would be almost idyllic if one were to leave out politics. However, insecurity was one of the various serious impediments to trade in the area. Part of the Masālīt homeland was unadministered and regarded as a no-man's land 'where traders feared to tread'. In the eyes of the central government in al-Fāshir, the frontier Masālīt were highway robbers and cannibals; their reputation among their neighbours was scarcely any better. Particularly the myth of cannibalism was (and is) widespread and persistent.[66] Whatever the truth may be, in a culture area where traditions of the origin of ordered (and Islamic) rule often metaphorically refer to food and the introduction of proper eating habits,[67] the sin of cannibalism may well be identified with that of anarchy. Before 1874 the Masālīt were not politically or administratively unified. In Dār Masālīt itself this period is remembered at best as a period of isolation, in which people lived clan-by-clan without much contact either with each other or with strangers; and at worst as a period of internal strife between the clans. This period did not come to an end until 1874, when Hajjām Ḥasab Allāh, one of the Masālīt *firshas*, forced the Masālīt to forget 'the blood that was between them' and to sit down and eat together.[68] The enmity was not only directed inwards. Local tradition looks upon foreign relations in the past as always precarious and often openly hostile; the fragile *modus vivendi* with the Fūr, Wadaians and the cattle nomads to the south often broke down as a result of mutual raiding. Masālīt xenophobia lives on in old folk beliefs that the Fūr can change themselves into hyaenas and other despicable animals, and that the Erenga change into bloodsucking spirits by night, and leave their graves after having been dead and buried.[69] 'In the past the Masālīt used to beat up any stranger who came to their *dār* and take their clothes', an informant in Beida remarked, and another asked rhetorically: 'In whose *dār*, by which road could one have traded? There were no roads, no secure roads. Particularly in the west there were continuous wars . . . Except for *falgo* there was no trade.'[70] This was the tone of most oral testimonies from the southern and western parts of Dār Masālīt, although even there informants admitted that there used to be some paper even before 1874, and that their women had always worn the necklace called *tagāga*.[71] However, oral data from the north of the country evoked a very different picture of trading conditions in Dār Masālīt during the Ancien Regime. Talking about the trade between the Masālīt of the west and those of southern Dār Fūr in the days of his great-grandfather, an informant said:

In those days the world was secure, you see. People were not

> altogether bad. They united under 'Abdulla Runga, and had respect for law and order. One had nothing to fear from human beings, only maybe from hyaenas. Everybody was going and coming. There was no one [from here] who did not go there, and no one [from there] who did not come here. If you had cows, or even one horse, you would just go.[72]

This apparent contradiction in the oral sources may be interpreted as an indication of the different conditions prevailing in the unadministered southwestern part and the administered north-eastern part of Dār Masālīt; and moreover of the importance of positive action by the government to create conditions which allowed and favoured trade.

In the case of the third sphere of exchange, that of the long-distance trade (involving foreign import goods, foreign traders and strict regulations as to where, when and to whom goods could be sold), the role of the central government and its agents along the trade routes is obvious.[73] Regional exchange also was only possible if the central government officials and indigenous authorities of the region maintained law and order and offered protection to traders, particularly foreign traders. In Dār Masālīt the biggest markets were those held near the residence and under the supervision of the highest local authority, and in every market-place the local lord collected a small percentage of everything offered for sale.[74] Apparently the regional tradition of government protection and control of trade was widespread and long-lived. 'The [Masālīt] sultan is in the habit of taking a small tax from all people bringing salt from Darfur into Masalit',[75] a Condominium official wrote in June 1918; and another wrote much later with regard to the Zalingei area, just to the east of Dār Masālīt: 'Each shartai regards the markets in his boundaries as his own property, and invariably levies a small due on all sales.'[76] Typically enough the opposite of protection, that is to say the disturbance of regional trade, was often a government affair as well; for from the late 1920s to the late 1940s the second source of income (after taxation) of the sultan of Dār Qimr was said to be highway robbery and intercepting the camel routes – a common alternative to levying a tax or toll on trade.[77]

If the lack of government action and protection was an impediment to trade, so was too much interference by the government, e.g. through taxation. It goes without saying that the volume and frequency of exchange activities depended on the exchange potential or surplus of the individuals and groups involved. The size of this surplus depended on many factors, only two of which will be discussed here: the threat of natural disaster and taxation. As for the first, the failure of the rains or epidemics striking man or beast would eliminate any surplus. Exchange might temporarily be more brisk than ever, because the hungry would sell goods and chattels, and even their own persons, for food.[78] However, in the long run the volume and frequency of exchange decreased. Not only famine itself, but also the fear of famine formed a check on exchange, for experience had taught people the importance of storing surplus food for the hard times to come.

The second check on the exchange potential of the Masālīt and their neighbours was taxation by the local and central government. During the Ancien Regime the central government's standard way of tax collection in the un- or half-administered borderland was tax raiding; but in the districts of Fia and Kerne at least, more regular means were employed. In both cases what was carried off was livestock, which was also a favourite item of regional exchange, since cows took care of their own transport. The central governments of Wadai and Dār Fūr had another habit which had the effect of limiting the exchange potential fo their subjects; this was the tax which Nachtigal called *dīwān*. The *dīwān* was an annual tax which differed from region to region and was to be paid in those products for which the region was famous, and which would have been the most likely goods to be exchanged.[79] On the local level people paid taxes mainly on grain and livestock, but their stores of honey, ghee and *tukkiyya*s were regularly broken into by the collection of 'customary dues'.[80] Nachtigal analyzed the effect of taxation upon market prices and conditions of exchange in Abesher:

> In calculating the taxes to be paid to the king and the administrative officials, the man, too, is never taken into account; on the contrary, the women's huts are counted, and the *salam*, the *difa*, the *kodmula*, etc., are collected from them. Needless to say, these conditions help to raise prices and to make market transactions difficult.[81]

The most important goods circulating in the marketplace functioned therefore at the same time as commodities, currencies and the means of paying taxes. This was true for grain, cotton cloth, goats and cows, but not for *falgo* salt and beads, which were not taxed. Prices were to a large extent fixed by custom, as were the price relationships between the goods used as currencies. Yet there was room for fluctuations corresponding to the vagaries of supply and demand and for bargaining – although in bargaining it was the quality of the product, and only indirectly the price, that was argued about. Finally, there was room for the adjustment of prices to specific circumstances. In the case of a drought, for example, the real nature of custom was exposed, and the accumulated individual decisions taken in the past were superseded by a new decision made by the local authorities. For example, one informant related how a drought in the 1890s brought a large number of Zaghāwa into Dār Masālīt to barter livestock for grain. In order to deal with (and profit from) these special circumstances the village head, his *warnang*,[82] and the representatives of the age groups of the young and elder men gathered to set the price of grain, and to change the equivalencies between the *midd*, the goat and *tukkiyya*, and the cow. Since grain was scarce the amount of grain which was determined to be worth a cow was much smaller than usual. A separate and smaller *midd* or measure of grain was set for the goat, while a few of these *midd*s equalled the value of a sheep. The value of the *tukkiyya* was also expressed in terms of the *midd* set for the goat. It should be noted that the new prices were valid not only for the strangers, but also for the Masālīt amongst themselves.[83] How often local authorities in Dār Masālīt set prices and the value of the currencies is not known. They certainly did so in extreme conditions, and probably every year for the purpose of taxation. The evidence from the Zalingei area, which borders upon Dār Masālīt, suggests an even more frequent and close price-control. There a Condominium Government official discovered the existence of a

> pre-government Fur price control, which helped to create a scheme of values for commercial transactions. It was one of the functions of the Warnang in each village or village group to settle by consultation with the villagers the size of the 'midd' of grain. This was the standard value, and although it varied in size

> according to the plenty of the harvest or season of the year, its variations were regulated by consult and were subject to causes obvious to all. Anyone who altered the size of the 'midd' without the consent of the warnang was subjected to the odium of his fellows as a 'blackleg' and according to some informants might also be mulcted by popular consent.[84]

Regulating the grain price and supervising regional trade was only one of the responsibilities of the local authorities. The identity of the latter, their rights and duties *vis-à-vis* the commoners and the Fūr overlords will be considered below.

The local nobility and their Fūr overlords

While the commoners were referred to in Dār Masālīt as *masākīn* (Ar., sing. *miskīn*), the nobility or local rulers were called *ḥukkām* (Ar., sing. *ḥākim*), i.e. those who have *ḥukm* (judicial and administrative authority). The lowest indigenous *ḥākim* was the village *shaykh*, originally called *khalīfa*. His direct superior in the administrative pyramid was the head of the Masālīt *khashm al-bayt* (clan or section), of which there are at present more than a hundred.[85] Each section had its own territory or rather, territories (called *dār*, *ḥākūra* or *balad*) in different parts of the Masālīt homeland with known boundaries demarcated by trees, hills, streambeds, piles of stones of iron spikes hammered into trees and termite hills. Each section also had at least one *dinggar* or wooden drum, which symbolised the ownership of the land and was the badge of authority of the head of the land-owning clan, the drumchief, who was called *dala* (plural, *dalajei*) in Masālīt, and *malik* or *dimlij* in Arabic.[86] Although the drumchiefs, here called *maliks*, were not the highest indigenous rulers, and although their importance varied according to the number of their people and the fertility and location of the clan's territory, during the Ancien Regime they were the most common and basic type of local ruler. They formed the pillars of the clan's internal administration and conducted its 'foreign affairs'. The *malik* was the titleholder to the land owned by the clan, representing the clan in all matters relating to the land. He gave out land to newcomers, allowing them to bring new land into cultivation and become *fās* owners, or to settle on land already opened up by others.[87] Together with the *ajāwīd* or board of elders, he also solved land and cultivation disputes – usually disputes about boundaries, which were decided on the basis of oral testimonies of knowledgeable old men of both parties, who rode the boundary accompanied by the Book and the Sword, representing heavenly and worldly sanctions against distortions of the truth.[88] As 'owner of the land', the *malik* had the right to a part of all the game killed in the clan's territory (and of all the animals slaughtered and sold in its markets), namely, to that part of the animal that 'had rested on the earth'. He also received in his house the ivory of the elephants, the horn of the rhinocerosses, the feathers of the ostriches killed or found dead in his *dār*, and the runaway slaves and stray animals (the *hāmil*) captured in it. At least in theory he had to pass on a part, if not all of these, to a higher authority, but in practice ivory, ostriches, rhinoceros-horn and possibly some slaves were sold to the itinerant traders, the *jallāba*.[89]

The *malik*'s jurisdiction was not restricted to land questions. In the old days no type of criminal offence was outside his jurisdiction, although the power over life and death seems to have been a right reserved to the sultan or *maqdūm*.[90] The *malik* combined judicial and executive powers. He was the upholder of law and order inside the clan territory. If a girl was made pregnant, if during beer-drinking sessions feelings ran high and fights broke out, it was the *malik* who had to find and punish the culprit, if need be by making use of the services of the *warnang* and his men, who thus functioned as local police.[91] When there was a case of murder within the clan the *malik* tried to solve it by arranging for the payment of *ṣadaqa* to the victim's closest relatives and by the ceremony of 'biting the liver' (of the animals slaughtered for the meal of reconciliation). Murder cases involving two clans were settled on the basis of precedent, that is to say, sometimes by the payment of *ṣadaqa* or a ceremony of reconciliation and sometimes by *diya* or blood-money. If the clan heads could come to an agreement they set the rate of the *diya* payment themselves, sending at best a present (or rather a fine) to the higher authorities.[92] However, even if the *diya* was fixed by the *maqdūm* or the sultan, it was the *malik* who was responsible for its collection and for spreading its burden among the members of his clan. The *malik* received a certain percentage of the taxes levied on the grain crop, the *zakāh* and *fiṭra*, collected and forwarded to him by his village *shaykhs*, and managed the public granary which was opened in case of droughts or less general disasters to lend grain to those who had exhausted their grain stores before the new crop was ripe and to provide millet for 'the ill, the blind, and those who had so many children that they could not feed them'.[93] There is no evidence that the *malik* had a right to people's labour without compensation or for other purposes than those of the public weal, and those sanctioned by tradition. Yet he (and his *ajāwīd*) decided which poor or needy community members came into account for a *nafīr*, and when he organized a *nafīr* himself, this *nafīr* was better attended, achieved more, and was more of a festive occasion than that of the average commoner.[94]

The *malik* also represented the clan in its external relations (both peaceful and violent) with other Masālīt clans, with other ethnic groups such as the nomads visiting his *dār*, and with the higher authorities. He received messengers, important travellers and pilgrims, and foreign traders. He negotiated with the nomads to have certain fields fertilized with animal dung and fixed a price for pasturing livestock in the millet fields after the harvest. He was consulted when the *'aqīd* and *warnang*s planned to raid into neighbouring territories, and was held responsible for this by his superiors. With his *ajāwīd* he decided upon war or peace.[95] From all these functions and rights the *malik* derived extra revenue. He received a share of the game killed in his *dār*, and presents (demanded or expected) from new settlers. He disposed of valuable trade items such as ivory and rhinoceros-horn and received a share of the animals captured during a raid, and probably a part of the runaway slaves and stray animals caught in his *dār*. A more steady source of revenue were the fines paid for criminal offences and the 'fees for victory' (Ar. *ḥaqq al-naṣr*) payable by the winners of lawsuits, while he also received customary dues such as the 'greeting gifts' (*salāmāt*) of his village heads, traders and travellers.[96] Oral sources suggest that the village heads brought the *malik* whatever was demanded from them, but what was an acceptable or legitimate demand, and what was *ẓulm* or oppression is not known. Taxation was another source of revenue for the *malik*, but oral sources are not in agreement about what percentage was for the village *shaykh*, what was for the *malik*, and how much was passed on to the central government.[97]

The office of *malik* was hereditary. A new *malik* was chosen from the nearest male relatives of the previous one, normally his son or brother. If, however, the *malik* was oppressive and unjust, or if he was disqualified for another reason (e.g. by committing a crime), he could be deposed and replaced by a new man from either his own or another subsection of the clan. The central government did not seek an active role in the appointment of the *malik*s. Yet it customarily confirmed the candidate chosen by the clan, decided succession disputes in favour of the candidate who could rally most supporters and paid best, and opposed an occasional *malik* whom it considered unacceptable. Nevertheless, being often the popular choice, the *malik* was politically a 'man of the people'.[98]

The extent to which the *malik* distinguished himself from the commoners in life-style and standard of living depended on the numerical, economic and political strength of his clan. A *malik* of a small clan occupying an isolated and wild part of the Masālīt homeland was a 'man of the people' in an economic and political sense. A more powerful *malik* who had many followers and a fertile *dār*, and was in close contact with his Fūr overlords, had in compensation for more numerous obligations towards the Fūr, more opportunity to distinguish himself from the commoners. He would have a robe of office, a clean *jallābiyya*, a turban, a shawl and a pair of shoes, which were all privileges of the *ḥukkām* upon which the commoners could not encroach with impunity. A powerful *malik* had a rifle, drank tea and coffee, and had more horses, wives, slaves and hangers-on than the average commoner.[99] In an anecdote dating from the 1890s the son of the clan head of the Minjiri, called Sulaymān Nīdim, so impressed a newly-married local woman with his fancy clothes, perfume, rifle, fine horses and escort of slaves that she refused to take her own husband back after Sulaymān had playfully taken over bride and bridal hut for the period of his visit.[100] Yet although the more important *malik*s did distinguish themselves from the commoners, like the commoners they farmed, kept livestock, hunted and gathered for a living. Much of their revenue from jurisdiction and taxation was spent in conspicuous consumption and in redistribution, that is to say, on allowances to the poor, lavish hospitality, and the maintenance of a number of (free and slave) hangers-on, to which their status obliged them.[101] Among the sedentaries outside the Masālīt homeland the drumchiefs and clans were sometimes called by different names, but their significance and functions were similar to those among the Masālīt.

The highest indigenous *ḥākim* was the *firsha*. The *firsha* was primarily a powerful *malik* of the type described above, but apart from being the *malik* of his own clan he represented several smaller *maliks* of other clans in their relations with the central government (and to some extent, with each other).[102] At the end of the Ancien Regime the Masālīt had four *firsha*s. The *firsha* of the Fukkunyang represented all Masālīt living in Dār Fia before the central government, while that of the Nyerneng originally represented all those living in Dār Kerne. In the nineteenth century two *maliks* broke away from the Nyerneng and established independent *furūshiyya*s. The *firsha* of the Mistereng came to share the headship of the Masālīt clans of Dār Kerne, while the *firsha* of the Minjiri, probably subject to the Tebella *shartāya* in Dār Dīma, headed a number of southern *malik*s, some of whom, however, were not subject to any Masālīt *firsha* and maintained direct (but minimal) relations with their Fūr overlords.[103]

There are indications that the northern part of the Masālīt homeland was more closely administered than its southern part. Masālīt tradition has preserved the memory of Masālīt contacts and dealings with the *shartay*s of Fia and Kerne, and with the *maqdūm* of the west, ʿAbd Allāh Runga, who ruled during the reign of Sultan Muḥammad al Ḥusayn (1838–73). Of the contemporary *shartay*s and governors of Dār Dīma, however, not even the names are remembered, while Aḥmad Shaṭṭa, *maqdūm* of the southern province of which Dār Dīma was a part, figures only in stories which have no relation to the Masālīt. *Maqdūm* ʿAbd Allāh Runga was a slave official, possibly a Dinka, who was the direct representative of the Fūr Sultan. Although he formed in theory the top of the administrative pyramid made up by the *shartays*, *firsha*s, *malik*s and village *shaykh*s, in practice this pyramid functioned independently, while the *maqdūm* travelled around in the western province, inspecting the local administrations and dealing with the people over the heads of their local rulers.[104] Although (or possibly because) he was a eunuch, Masālīt tradition associates a number of piquant stories with his name, one of which relates his ill-starred and short-lived marriage to a *jallāba* girl of Kabkābiyya who was circumcized – a phenomenon with which the *maqdūm* was not familiar, and of which he did not approve![105] In a more serious vein, he is remembered as an oppressive ruler, and the Masālīt claim to have attacked and killed him at his residence in Jāmiʿ Filli, where there was a stone mosque.[106] Of the *shartay*s of Fia and Kerne only those who were in power just before the fall of the Dār Fūr Sultanate are remembered by name: Ḥanafī of Dār Fia and Ibrāhīm Bōsha and his successor Muzammil of Dār Kerne. They were the direct overlords of (at least three of) the Masālīt *firsha*s. Although the main residence and 'place of customs' (or shrine) of the Fia *shartay*s was at Muʿallaqa near Kabkābiyya, *shartay* Ḥanafī lived much closer to the Masālīt homeland at Tineat. He had an advance post, a frontier guard under the command of an *urrundulung*, near Amm Sibayḥa, just north of the Masālīt, while his son ʿAbd al-Qaffā, nicknamed Sultan of Rōro, also lived as a neighbour to the Masālīt at Dirjeil Siminyang. From there he ruled the *shaykh*s of the Tarjam, Taʿālba and Maḥāmīd, the *malik*s of the Erenga and the small sultans of the Awra, Marārīt and Jabal.[107] There were probably many more central government officials who were not indigenous to the area and people they ruled, but only the memory of those who were sufficiently accommodating and whose local power-bases were strong enough to survive the Turco-Egyptian period and the foundation of the Masālīt Sultanate has been preserved. The command of *maqdūm* Ndelngongo of the Awlād Māna, who was the ruler of Mokū and Ḥajar Laban in the 1890s, was said to date from Fūr times and to have been associated with ʿAbd al-Qaffā. *Maqdūm* Andokoi owed his command in the area of Keira and Tineat to the fact that his mother was a Fūr princess.[108] In contrast, the Masālīt clans of the south – with the exception of those living on the Wādī Azūm – had no Fūr or other non-indigenous central government officials as their neighbours. Moreover there were no southern equivalents to the *ḥākūra*s which the Fūr Sultans had carved out for Borno *faqih*s (at Tamr Ab Jiddo, Shinggilba and Konge) on the Masālīt's eastern border in Dār Fia.[109]

Another indication that the northern part of the Masālīt homeland was more closely administered than the south is possibly the fact that the two clans whose *malik*s became the first *firsha*s were northern clans (the Fukkunyang and Nyerneng), while the two offshoots of the Nyerneng *furūshiyya* were southern clans (the Mistereng and Minjiri). The *firsha* of the Fukkunyang, moreover, had at least two indigenous rulers under him whose titles were Fūr creations and who were confirmed, if not actually appointed in their functions by the Fūr. These were the *sambei* of the Gernyeng (who was allegedly superior to the Gernyeng *malik* of the Dirjeil area) and the *maqdūm* of the Lere section of the Masālīt (who seems to have ranked above the village *shaykh*s as a *malik* would). The inauguration of the last *sambei* – which took place in the early 1870s in al-Fāshir, where he went under the escort of *shartay* Ḥanafī of Dār Fia – was still remembered by an old informant, as were the songs which were sung at the *sambei*'s return to Dirjeil and his visit to the 'place of customs' there.[110] In the south there is no memory of indigenous rulers with such close relations to the Fūr, with the exception of the two *firsha*s of the Minjiri and the Mistereng. Although all informants confirmed that they had been nominally subject to the Fūr, and wẹre visited at intervals by Fūr agents, all stressed the autonomy, autarchy and isolation of the southern clans in the olden days.[111] Whether it was the area's situation on the Wadai/Dār Fūr border that was responsible for this isolation; or the nature of the land, which had enough rocky outcrops and areas of dense bush to offer an easy refuge from central government officials; or possibly the small numbers of the area's Masālīt population, which expanded most after the foundation of the Masālīt Sultanate, is a question which only future research may solve. It is possible that this southern and south-western part of the Masālīt homeland was looked upon by outsiders as an uninhabited frontier zone.

R. S. O'Fahey has characterized the relationships between the central government and the local communities in Dār Fūr as follows:

> Local communities . . . were self-governing, and their ideal of good government was probably as little government as possible, a view no doubt reciprocated by the ruling institution once its demands had been met. The communities' main contact with their rulers was confined to war, justice in matters such as homicide that could not be settled within the community, and taxation.[112]

This also applies to the relations between the Masālīt and their Fūr overlords. One may add one more point of contact between local communities and the central government, namely active government involvement in the appointment or confirmation of indigenous *ḥukkām*. This is illustrated by the accounts of how, in the nineteenth century, the Mistereng and Minjiri broke away from the Nyerneng and established their own *furūshiyya*s. The Mistereng *malik* declared war upon the Nyerneng after a conflict which began when he was deeply insulted by a Nyerneng visitor to his house, who called him a Nyerneng slave. When the *malik* declared that he would no longer obey the Nyerneng *firsha*, the latter appointed a new *malik*. The old *malik* thereupon declared war upon the Nyerneng and was killed. His sons went to the Fūr Sultan in al-Fāshir to demand their independence from the Nyerneng. 'They told him: in our *dār* we used to have one ancestor, and we followed him. Now they have killed our father and drove us out.' Their demand was granted, and the indignant sultan sent out Fūr officials to accompany them and to demarcate the boundaries of the *furūshiyya* of the Mistereng.[113] As for the Minjiri, their *malik* refused to obey the Nyerneng *firsha* after Minjiri blood had been shed in a conflict involving calves which had been stolen in a time of drought and famine. When the Minjiri *malik* was imprisoned in al-Fāshir by the central government, he staged a hunger strike; the Fūr Sultan, concluding that Minjiri/Nyerneng hostility was irreconcilable, gave him a separate *furūshiyya* in return for a present in cows.[114] Whether all the details of these accounts are correct or not, like the anecdote about the *sambei* described above, they illustrate the way in which central government appointed indigenous rulers and interfered in their relations with each other, particularly when there was a question of homicide.

The collection of taxes was another occasion on which the Masālīt *ḥukkām* came into contact with the central government. Usually the taxes were collected by Fūr officials sent out for that purpose by the *shartay* and the *maqdūm* of the west. However, it is not unlikely that the Masālīt *firsha*s, like their southern neighbours the Sinyār, took part of the taxes demanded from them to their Fūr overlords in person as 'greeting presents'. The name associated with the tax obligations to the Fūr is *dīwān*.[115] Tax payments consisted mainly of livestock, but probably the government collected *tukkiyya*s as well (although some Masālīt informants contended that in the olden days, when the Masālīt wore mainly skins, *tukkiyya*s were very scarce). Some ivory, ostrich feathers and slaves probably served as greeting-presents, as did certain delicacies of the bush.[116] That Fūr rule is not remembered as oppressive does not necessarily mean that it was not; for so much dust has been raised and so much history has been made and retold during the turbulent years of the Turkiyya and Mahdiyya that the memories of the pre-1874 period are vague and sometimes confused. Apart from raids by Fūr clans, which were not sponsored by the central government, and the punitive expedition against Masālīt villages which were allegedly inhabited by cannibals, which was, there are few memories of armed conflict between the Masālīt and their Fūr overlords.[117] As for the defence policy of the Dār Fūr state, the Masālīt proudly maintain that they never contributed soldiers to the Fūr armies. This might indicate that the Masālīt enjoyed a high degree of autonomy, but it was more probably inherent in their frontier position; while the sultanate waged war in the east and south, those Masālīt who were under Fūr administration were to guard the western frontier.[118]

Slaves and masters

While the commoners (*masākīn*) were one notch below the rulers and their close relatives (*ḥukkām*), the slaves (Ar. singular *ʿabd*, plural *ʿabīd*; Mas. singular *maji*, plural *majir* for a male slave; Ar. singular *khādim*, plural *khadīm*; Mas. singular *khadimmo*, plural *khadimmar* for a female slave) ranked below the commoners.[119] The definition of a slave in Masālīt society in the second half of the nineteenth century is a definition of what a slave was not, rather than what he was. The main onus of being a slave was that of not belonging, of not being a Maslātī but a stranger; in particular of being a stranger who had not come voluntarily, of his own accord, but who had come by force of necessity or had been brought by force. One informant used the term slaves even for strangers who had come to Dār Masālīt on their own initiative:

> Formerly we lived here clan by clan, but now we have mixed with slaves, and spend the day together [as if nothing distinguishes us]. Those slaves, those Borgū and Dājū, came here and mixed with the Masālīt and filled the *dār*. It is true that the people made the *dār* prosperous and that was to the advantage of the *ḥukkām*, but we don't want them.[120]

Being a stranger meant first of all that the acquired person had no (near or known) kinsmen, and no ties with the new society except for those with his master and – in a limited number of cases – with his master's *ḥukkām*. Not only did the slave have no father (or was regarded as having none), he could also not become a father, since the children whom he begot belonged to the owner of his wife, who was often also his own master; these children could be, and often were, given away or sold.[121] Moreover, although the aspect of 'not belonging' may have been more important than that of being unfree or bound, the latter is also emphasized by oral sources; the slave was bound to work for his master without compensation; he was neither free to leave his master if he wanted to, nor stay if his master decided to sell him. Fleeing, refusing to work (or to work hard enough) and other forms of disobedience eventually led to his being sold.

The ethnic origin of the slaves of the Masālīt was varied, as were the ways in which the slaves were acquired. Many slaves, particularly those acquired through trade, were Fartīt and Kirdī from the southern marches of the sultanates of Dār Fūr and Wadai, that is to say, people who belonged to ethnic groups which were (or were conveniently regarded as) pagans. Many slaves, however – particularly those acquired through raids or warfare or as refugees – were subjects of neighbouring Islamic states; for them slave status could be a temporary status since returning home would set them free. Slaves were acquired in many ways. Many were brought back from raids or wars, while many others, forced to flee their countries because of war, were captured during their flight. Refugees from drought and famine were often enslaved as well, while kidnapping was common throughout Dār Fūr. A very important and more regular source of slaves was the slave trade, which goes further back in time than any oral or written source for the history of Dār Fūr, and which at least in western Dār Fūr did not end until the beginning of the Condominium rule in the 1920s.[122] Most of the concrete examples of how slaves were acquired which were remembered by informants refer to the period after 1874. They are nevertheless used in this study of slavery during the Ancien Regime since the ruling elite of the new sultanate of Dār Masālīt, which emerged in the 1880s, acquired slaves in basically the same ways as the traditional *ḥukkām* and commoners before them. Below it will be argued that the Masālīt acquired more slaves, and acquired more slaves by force after the foundation of their sultanate than during the Ancien Regime.[123] The section which follows should be read with this qualification in mind.

The fate of refugees from war is illustrated by the large numbers of Fūr who were enslaved by the ruling elite of the new Masālīt Sultanate. Many of these 'slaves of the sultanate' came to Dār Masālīt as a result of Dār Fūr's 'Time of Troubles' which began in 1874, when Dār Fūr was conquered by al-Zubayr. Although Fūr resistance against the Turco-Egyptians and their successors, the *anṣār*, did not collapse until 1891, the flight, defeat and death of a number of Fūr 'shadow sultans' forced many members of the Fūr royal family and their followers to take refuge in Dār Masālīt, where they were enslaved. Some of the wives of Sultan Ibrāhīm (1873–4), the daughter of Saʿīd Burūs, and many less glamorous ladies who have not been remembered, became the captive wives of the Masālīt, while sultan Ibrāhīm's gatekeeper, a slave called Ab Maṭar, ended up performing his old function in the capital of Dār Masālīt. When in the early 1880s the Turco-Egyptian regime was toppled by the *anṣār*, many of those who had been part of the former's administrative and military establishment in Kulkul and Kabkābiyya fled westward to Dār Masālīt. Most of them were enslaved, only the Masālīt and very important personalities like *faqīh* Abāy (who became *qāḍī*) being incorporated into the administration of the new sultanate as free men.[124] The fate of war captives is illustrated by the large numbers of people who were enslaved during the many wars which the Masālīt fought, first with the *anṣār* in the decade 1889–98, and then with the Fūr armies of ʿAlī Dīnār. As a result of the defeats of the Mahdist armies sent out against Abū Jummayza, the withdrawal of the cholera-stricken army of the Mahdist general ʿUthmān Jānū, who occupied Dār Masālīt in 1890, and the defeat of the Mahdist lieutenant 'Dardama' in 1895, the Masālīt captured and enslaved many people of many different ethnic backgrounds.[125] They enslaved both free men and slaves, although captives who were slaves already were apparently preferred to free men. When the Masālīt Sultan in 1888 decided to rid himself of the Mahdist garrison which was residing in his capital, he retained only the horses, firearms and the black slave troops called *jihādiyya*, 'who had no cause to fight for'; the free soldiers were provided with sandals and a waterskin and were escorted out of the *dār*. Women were captured as well, for each *jihādī* was accompanied by his wife, who – with her *rayka* on her head – joined her husband everywhere, even into slavery with the Masālīt.[126] In 1890 the Masālīt acquired many slaves by nursing the victims of the cholera epidemic which was decimating the Mahdist army of occupation back to health. The Masālīt Sultan ordered every Maslātī to capture, confine and cure as many diseased Mahdist soldiers as he could but to take care not to bring them to Dirjeil, his residence. When the epidemic died down, the dead had been buried and the survivors had regained their health, most captives were taken to Dirjeil and settled there. The *jallāba* village of Wiḥayda, close to Dirjeil, traced its origin back to this epidemic.[127] Yet in contrast to many others, the *jallāba* soldiers settled in Wiḥayda, with their Nile Valley origins, their claims to be descendants of the Prophet, their superior knowledge of Arabic and Islam, and their business acumen, apparently commanded enough respect to be given their freedom and to be allowed to develop Wiḥayda into a bustling trading community.

If the Masālīt acquired many slaves in wars in which they were victorious, in case of defeat the tables were turned. When the Mahdist army invaded the country in 1890, nearly the whole free and slave population of Dār Masālīt fled to the west. Many Masālīt lost goods and chattels, including slaves, and even their lives. When *bāsī* Aḥmad Abū Lafta was killed during the Dājū invasion of 1896, many of his slaves scattered and were never heard of again, while one of his free wives and her two daughters were captured and taken to Goz Beida, where they became wives and concubines to the Dājū royal family.[128] In 1905, after the battle of Shawai in which the Fūr defeated the Masālīt and captured their sultan, many Masālīt again fled to the west. Those who took refuge in Wadai received a fair treatment, but of those who fled to Dār Silā many were robbed of all their possessions, particularly horses, rifles and slaves, while some were enslaved; the wives of the Masālīt Sultan were paraded in front of the Dājū Sultan, I was told, who selected all those who had no children and retained them in Goz Beida as love mates, wives and servants for his relatives.[129] In 1905 also my informant al-*ḥajj* Muḥammad Aḥmad Abū Lafta lost his first concubine, Anjumma bint Ḥalīma, who was the daughter of one of his father's concubines, herself an ex-wife of the Fūr Sultan Ibrāhīm. During the fighting, mother and daughter fled to Zalingei, and from there to al-Fāshir, where Anjumma entered the *ḥarim* of Sultan ʿAlī Dīnār.[130] During this war, local tradition says, thousands of Masālīt were captured and carried off by the Fūr. It is said that the bottom dropped out of the Fāshir slave market as a result of this influx of Masālīt captives. A wife and daughter of the captured Masālīt Sultan became the concubines of Adam Rijāl and of Sultan ʿAlī Dīnār himself.[131] That slave status could be temporary is evident from the fact that the Fūr set many of the Masālīt captives free in return for the firearms which the Masālīt captured from the French in 1910.[132]

People brought to Dār Masālīt by drought or famine were often enslaved as well. During a drought in the late 1870s a Masālīt family left their home in Zeina, northeast of Dirjeil, and migrated to Wadai. When their situation became really desperate the man ordered his wife to sell him as a slave. Thus it came about that the man maintained himself by drawing water for his master's livestock, while his wife and children survived the famine thanks to the grain, the cows and the donkey which his new master had paid for him. However, when news got around that Dār Masālīt had recovered and that the crops of Dirjeil were standing in the fields, the man sent his family ahead and soon caught up with them in Zeina.[133] Most victims of drought were less lucky. During the drought called 'Khaffaltīnī' in the 1890s a Zaghāwa woman nursing a child came south to Dār Masālīt in search of food, but died on the way. When the Masālīt Sultan Abbakr was informed of this he provided a *tukkiyya* to have the woman buried, and gave the baby girl to his wife, *iya* Ḥumāra, who brought her up. Eventually the girl became the (slave) wive of Abbakr's son and gave birth to *abbo* Muḥammad Nimr, the elder brother of the present sultan.[134] Drought victims enslaved by commoners were often sold as soon as they had regained their health, for at the beginnings of the rains they might either escape and flee back home, or be reclaimed by relatives who had come to search for them. During the drought of 1913, which affected the whole eastern Sudanic belt, many Masālīt took in stray children from Wadai.[135] In Dār Silā the sultan encouraged his people – possibly at the instigation of the French – to give the Wadaian refugees from drought lands to cultivate and not to retain (that is to say, enslave) them when improved circumstances allowed them to return to their country.[136] Kidnapping was so common throughout Dār Fūr that parents are extremely conscious of this danger even today. It is not at all rare to meet someone who had a close relative kidnapped or who had been kidnapped himself; and more general oral references to the institution of kidnapping are plentiful.[137]

A more important source of slaves was the slave trade. Although slaves were in general traded from south to north they were bought and sold in all directions, gaining in value as the distance from their homes increased. Like *tukkiyya*s and cows, slaves were generally accepted and used in financial transactions in the whole area between al-Fāshir and Abesher and beyond. They crossed political frontiers as part of bridewealth payments for royal brides, as part of tribute paid to political superiors, as diplomatic presents exchanged between sultans, and as objects of purely commercial transactions.[138] Outside the termini of the long-distance trade such as Kobbei and Abesher slaves were bought for cows, transport animals (bulls and donkeys) and grain.

In Dār Masālīt the standard price for a good quality slave was said to be three cows, the age, sex and quality of the cows corresponding with those of the slave.[139] Most slaves were imported into Dār Masālīt from Dār Silā, where slaves were cheap and plentiful, it was said, because the Dājū neighboured on Fartīt groups such as the Binga, Banda, Kara, Gula and others, and had hence easy access to slaves. The traders on the Silā-Masālīt route were Dājū, Masālīt and *jallāba*, who crossed Dār Masālīt in all directions on their way to and from the centres of the long-distance trade. Other slaves entered Dār Masālīt from Wadai and Dār Fūr.[140] They were not always 'raw' slaves, that is to say, newly imported from the pagan south. ʿĀyisha, for example, who became the concubine of *faqīh* Makkī of Murle, had been born in the slave community of Birinjil near al-Fāshir. *Bāsī* Aḥmad, mentioned above, bought his concubine Bakhīta Bandiyya for ostrich feathers from the *anṣār* of Kabkābiyya. From the fugitive Fūr Sultan Abū'l-Khayrāt he bought a male slave called Abd Allāh Abū Ḥaraka for the small price of three *rayka*s of grain and a donkey, because ʿAbd Allāh had been wounded by a horse and could no longer accompany Abū'l-Khayrāt's war band which was moving on from Dār Masālīt to fight the *anṣār* in al-Fāshir.[141]

Slaves were also imported from southern Dār Fūr, particularly from Kūbe in the area of modern Gereida, which was the base of many small-scale slave traders who went south to trade their grain and livestock for slaves. The Gereida area was populated by Masālīt and had close relations with the Masālīt of the west, who came to southern Dār Fūr to sell their horses for cows and slaves, or to join in small trading expeditions into Dār Fartīt. Although some such expeditions – possibly with an emphasis upon raiding rather than trading – were organized from Dār Masālīt itself, and led by *ʿaqīd*s such as *ʿaqīd* Zokko and his son *ʿaqīd* ʿUmar, contemporaries of the Fūr Sultan Ḥusayn, most probably started from southern Dār Fūr.[142] An account of an expedition which started out from Kūbe was given by an informant who did some slave trading himself around the turn of the century. At the beginning of the rains he and a small group of other people set out for the south. He himself took one bull loaded with grain and one donkey south to Jaʿalī, where he was given one slave girl for the bull, one for the grain, and one for the donkey. The Fartīt actually sold the children of their own close relatives, he related, although they did so reluctantly and mainly because they were hungry! Therefore they always tried to overtake the buyers after the slaves had been handed over and the party had set out for the north. To escape from their pursuers, and to prevent the slaves from fleeing back home by bringing them quickly into a new and unfamiliar environment, the return trip was made in forced marches. Back in southern Dār Fūr the slaves were sold either in the marketplace or in private houses.[143] *Abbo* ʿAlī Ab Shanab, a Maslātī who had been born in southern Dār Fūr but who came to Dār Masālīt in c. 1900, was said to be more fluent in 'Fartīt' than in Masālīt; and although he undertook no more trading expeditions into Dār Fartīt after he had been incorporated into the sultanate's *corps diplomatique*, he still sent his slaves to the south to collect ivory, giraffe meat and possibly some slaves.[144]

Dār Silā figures in the oral sources as the major source of trade slaves. That this was still so after the emergence of the Masālīt Sultanate is confirmed by a song popular in 1896, just before the Dājū invasion:

Abbakr sīdī
jawādak shiddī
li-sayf al-naṣr qaddimī
[. . . .]
aḍribū Goz Beida
wa-arsinī rajul ʿabīd.

Abbakr, my lord
saddle your horse
take the sword of
victory [to Dār Silā]
attack Goz Beida
and [bring back] a
slave in chains.[145]

This song of course expressed the hope of acquiring slaves (or possibly one particular 'slave', the Dājū Sultan himself) through victory in war. A more specific reference to the trade in slaves from Dār Silā in the same period is the anecdote about the Masālīt youngsters who returned to Dirjeil from a slave-trading expedition to Dār Silā. When the slave girls who had to prepare them a late supper composed a praise song for them, the young traders gallantly rewarded them with the present of a slave girl.[146] That this slave girl could be taken to the Fezzān traders residing in Dirjeil and exchanged for perfume which the girls divided amongst themselves was an innovation, which resulted from the foundation of the sultanate and the emergence of Dirjeil as a centre of the long-distance trade. How many slaves were imported into Dār Masālīt and what percentage was resold inside or outside the *dār* is unknown. Reselling slaves was common practice. It occurred when people were forced to draw upon their reserves in times of drought, or wanted to rid themselves of slaves who – recurrently and for no good reason – attempted to run away. The latter were sold either on the local market, or through the good offices of the *malik* to the perambulatory *jallāba* (and later, Fezzān) traders. Sometimes, e.g. when the traders did not come, slaves were sold further afield in Kobbei or Kabkābiyya.[147]

Although slaves were property, the ownership of which could be shared and transferred according to the wishes of the owner, they were a special kind of property for the obvious reason that they were human beings with whose feelings one had to reckon. For example,when a master bought a slave husband for one of his female slaves (or *vice versa*) he consulted both parties to make sure that the planned union was acceptable.[148] Yet in general the extent to which slave feelings were taken into account was very limited. It is true that the sale of second-generation slaves was frowned upon, as was the separate sale of mothers and small children, but both were common.[149] Only few slave complaints were regarded as legitimate. One of these was enforced celibacy, that is to say, not to be provided with a spouse. The institutionalized solution for this was the 'ear-cutting ceremony'. Although this institution was said to be very old, the concrete example given below dates from the 1890s. One of the male slaves of *bāsī* Aḥmad was in charge of a vegetable garden near one of the wells in Dirjeil. In protest against the fact that he had not been provided with a wife, and out of love for a slave woman who daily came to fetch water from his well, he decided to make a small cut in the ear of the son of his beloved's mistress, Khadam Allāh Ismāʿīl, half-sister of Sultan Abbakr. Dissuaded from this by his friends, he only (temporarily) kidnapped the boy, and was brought before the sultan to explain himself. The outcome of the incident was that he was indeed handed over to Khadam Allāh and married to the lady of his heart, while *bāsī* Aḥmad was offered a cow with a calf in compensation.[150] Unmarried slave girls and concubines lived inside the master's compound and were supervised by his free wife (or wives). The male slaves and their families lived just outside their master's compound and if they were numerous, formed a village (or quarter of a village) of their own. Residence was both a function of the number of slaves and an indication of the use to which they were put.

The Masālīt acquired slaves for two (closely related) reasons: to acquire extra labour for their households and to expand the kin-group. Slaves were primarily a source of permanent domestic and agricultural labour, in contrast to sons, who became heads of their own households, and daughters, who were married off and joined their husband's kin-group. Slaves did basically the same – but more, and more of the heaviest and most dangerous – work as the commoners. This is particularly true for the female slaves and less so for the male slaves, much of whose labour was typically women's work which no free man would ever do.[151] The heavy domestic chores such as fetching wood and water, grinding and pounding millet, preparing great quantities of food for guests, were performed by slaves. Male slaves watered and pastured cows, donkeys and horses, built and repaired huts and fences, and sank wells – a very laborious and dangerous operation which cost many a slave his life. Slaves of both sexes performed all kinds of agricultural labour, such as clearing the land of trees and underbrush and burning it, sowing, weeding, harvesting, threshing, winnowing and finally, storing the grain. In contrast to the slaves of the nomads of the area, who cultivated while their masters were away pasturing their livestock, the slaves of the Masālīt worked in the fields side by side with their masters and other free men and women.[152] During the growing season they worked three days of the week on the farm of their master, it was said, one day on those of his master's wives, and one day on their own plot allotted to them by their master. On Fridays they would rest or attend to their own crops of ground nuts, sesame, or okra, which were grown on a smaller scale and might require irrigation.[153]

If a master had many slaves, the slaves had an overseer. That of the slaves of *bāsī* Aḥmad in the village of Amm Sidayre, not far from Dirjeil, was a third-generation freed slave called Somīt Abarranjāl, who took disciplinary measures when slaves were lazy and did not come to work, but also provided grain and clothes from the master's stores when slaves were hungry or went in rags. Beating slaves was common practice but risky, since it often motivated slaves to run away. During the rains slaves worked in the fields from sunrise to the middle of the afternoon. Then they would go off to fetch wood, water and fodder for the horses, bring in the cows and calves for the night, and perform their own domestic chores.[154] Once a year, on the occasion of the Feast of Fastbreaking, the slaves received a set of clothes from their master. Theirs were also the remnants or inferior parts of the animals they slaughtered for their master and of the grain which they threshed for him.[155] Nevertheless they supported themselves and their families by their own labour. They grew their own millet, grew and spun their own cotton, built their own houses, entertained their own guests, and went to the market for their own purposes. Some slaves, particularly slaves who belonged to the nobility, were quite well off. Owning a horse, a rifle, a number of cows and slaves, and several wives, they were better off than many commoners and shared in their master's prestige and wealth. In general it seems that the standard of life of slaves was just a notch below that of their masters, whether the latter were commoners or *ḥukkām*.[156]

Like livestock slaves performed useful services; they reproduced themselves and formed a store of wealth which could be drawn upon when the need occurred. Moreover, in contrast to cattle, they could maintain and care for themselves. The labour of the slaves relieved their owners of at least part of their agricultural and domestic labour, and allowed for some specialization. It gave the *faqīh* more time to teach religion, the *malik* to govern, the commoners to spin more cotton, to go to more distant markets, or to grow more vegetables in the *wādī*. However, apart from in the weeding season the Masālīt were never short of time; and neither commoner nor *ḥakim* depended on slave labour for his living. Slave labour also contributed to the surplus of grain and cotton the slave owner could accumulate. Part of this surplus was stored for times of hardship; part of it was conspicuously consumed on weddings and other festivities, while part of it was sold. Small quantities of grain and *rubṭa*s were exchanged in the marketplace to obtain the necessities of daily life not provided for by the household's own production. Bigger quanitities might be exchanged for livestock with nomads visiting the *dār*, exchanged with the Maghārba and Maḥamīd for salt, or once in a blue moon sold to the *jallāba* of the town of Kobbei, 'which was always hungry.'[157] Although slaves normally had a smaller surplus than their masters, they used it in the same ways. If they found the opportunity to sell grain to nomads, they could take it or leave it just like their masters.[158] Slave labour was not used to maximize production for the market, oral sources suggest, but to make life easier and more comfortable for the slave owners. This is what Ḥabbo Janna meant when she said:

> Those to whom Allah gave slaves have slaves; those who do not have slaves just do the hard work themselves.[159]

Slaves were also acquired as 'artificial' kinsmen for the purpose of expanding the kin-group. Marrying a slave girl rather than a girl of free birth was cheaper and easier, since it required only three cows and did not involve the groom in tiresome negotiations with in-laws or cumbersome labour services to which they had a right. When female slaves became mothers of their master's children, these children were legally and automatically free, although they might be discriminated against socially and when competing for political office.[160] When female slaves were married to the male slaves of their master, the children of this union belonged to the master and – as oral sources put it – 'became brothers and sisters to his own children.' Yet how unreliable kinship terms are when describing the status of slaves is obvious if one realises that such children were often given away or sold, and that at their master's death they did not inherit together with the latter's children, but were inherited by them; and what was more logical, if one inherited a single slave together with someone else, than to sell the slave for cotton cloth which could be more easily divided?[161]

It also happened that a male slave was married to his master's daughter, and was even acquired (and freed) for that purpose. The advantages of such a marriage are obvious, for instead of being married off 'to give birth to other people's children' the daughter would stay with her father and bear children who became free and full-fledged members of her father's kin-group. Since the father was thought to gain most from marrying his daughter to a slave, and since the slave could not pay bridewealth, it was the father who paid bridewealth for the girl to her mother, i.e. his own wife.[162] Although several examples of this type of marriage have been recorded, it is obvious that there was an emergency situation of some kind in every case. *Bāsī* Karam Allāh was one such father who married his daughter to his slave; when one is told that *bāsī* Karam Allāh had no son, the reason for this choice of husband is not hard to guess. In another case the father had reason to believe that his daughter might become a spinster, and when no free husband presented himself he gave her as wife to his slave.[163] Slaves had the right to marry. As the 'ear-cutting ceremony' demonstrated, the Masālīt were very conscious of the fact that the sexual activities of a slave needed to be controlled, lest he be killed or confiscated as a penalty for illicit love affairs. However, a slave not only had the right to marry, he was expected and obliged to marry, lest the owner lose the profit of his reproductive faculties. In a third example of a marriage between a slave and his master's daughter the reason was that the master had failed to find, or could not afford, to buy a slave wife for his slave.[164] In general the Masālīt looked upon such a marriage with contempt, and their derision often caused the whole family to move from the village and establish a hamlet of their own.[165]

Female slaves were usually integrated into the kingroup smoothly and automatically. If they bore their master a child, 'they were given the *fātiḥa*' (during the marriage ceremony before the *faqīh*) and were freed.[166] The slave descent of their children and their children's children would be known mainly to insiders, and would not be brought up except in situations of conflict. This silent and gradual integration probably explains in part why informants – the oldest of whom were born in the late 1870s – could not estimate the numbers of slaves owned by the Masālīt during the Ancien Regime, with the exception of those of their own close relatives and neighbours.[167] The manumission and integration of male slaves was a much slower process which usually required two or three generations. First-generation male slaves could be manumitted and adopted as artificial kinsmen only through a *tour de force* like the one described above; but even the slave who was acquired in order to become his master's son-in-law could not be manumitted before one year had passed, and before his behaviour, particularly at night, had been carefully watched; for 'who could be sure that he would not change into a hyaena, or [a blood-sucking spirit called] *massās*, or what not?'[168] Manumission was a simple ceremony at which the *faqīh* read the *fātiḥa*, the slave received a proper Muslim name, and at which a bull or goat was slaughtered for those who came to offer their congratulations. Manumission meant first of all that the slave gained freedom from labour obligations without compensation. From the moment of his manumission, it was said, he owed his master 'nothing but what the master's own sons owed him'. The terminology used in the oral sources is again that of kinship; freed slaves became their master's sons, their children his children, etc.[169] From the point of view of the kin-group or clan this was probably true, for the ex-slave became a member of his master's *diya* group. His position in his master's household, however, is not known in any detail. Manumission was often the prelude to the freedman's marriage with a free woman, whom he was expected to choose from amongst the close relatives of his ex-master.[170] If he did so, he had not only severed the old ties of bondage – which was one aspect of manumission – but also created a new bond which tied him to the master's kin-group as a kinsman by marriage. Although in the eyes of an outsider the position of suitor, or brand-new son-in-law, was hardly an improvement upon slave status, it solved the problem of not belonging, and had moreover the advantage of being temporary; eventually the freedman could move his bride and their children to his own compound. In theory manumission meant that the slave could pack up and leave, but since the freedman was usually a second or third generation slave, this rarely happened.

In conclusion, one can say that slaves were not indispensable to the Masālīt. They made life easier for their owners, and since they contributed to most stages of the productive process, they increased the wealth of those who controlled their labour. As artificial kinsmen, moreover, they strengthened the household and kin-group of their masters. The continuity in the institution of slavery in Dār Masālīt between the Ancien Regime and the period after 1874 will be discussed in Chapter Five.

Chapter 3

Prelude to the rise of the Masālīt Sultanate: Hajjām Ḥasab Allāh and the unification of the Masālīt

The fall of the Ancien Regime and the beginning of the Turkiyya

In 1874 the Ancien Regime came to an end. Although it expired on the battle field, it had suffered from a cancer which had been developing since the 1850s. From that date onwards traders from the Nile valley, bypassing the sultanate to the east and south, had begun to penetrate into Dār Fūr's economic hinterland and to compete for the resources of slaves, ivory and rhinoceros-horn, which were Dār Fūr's major exports to the mediterranean world and beyond. The new trading companies operated as slave armies equipped with modern firearms and were led by able trader-generals from a series of fortified camps. When al-Zubayr Raḥma, the most powerful of these *baḥḥāra* trader-kings, picked a quarrel with the Dār Fūr Sultan and invaded the country, the old-style Fūr armies were defeated in a number of battles and the sultan was killed. While the *baḥḥāra* were fighting their way into Dār Fūr from the south, the Turco-Egyptians, who had occupied the Nile valley and Kordofan since 1821, stole in from the east without meeting any resistance and declared Dār Fūr a province of Egypt.[1]

At the fall of the Ancien Regime the Keira Sultanate fell into its constituent parts; tribal units in most cases, and in some cases miniature multi-ethnic states dominated by one ethnic group. Although the new regime immediately divided Dār Fūr into four districts with garrison towns at al-Fāshir, Dāra, Umm Shanga and Kulkul,[2] for the local rulers the fall of the Old Regime meant that each ethnic group was thrown back upon its own resources, and recovered its independence and the freedom to negotiate its own terms with the invaders. While for the Banī Ḥusayn and other peoples of western Dār Fūr 'being a tribe again' was apparently a spontaneous reaction,[3] in the case of the Masālīt this was not at all obvious. They had never – within living memory – formed a political unit, and when Hajjām Ḥasab Allāh of the Masālīt Mistereng united them after the fall of the Ancien Regime, he united them by force.

The defeat of the Fūr armies and the death of Sultan Ibrāhīm had not eliminated all Fūr resistance; concentrating around the Fūr princes-in-exile in Jabal Marra, this resistance outlasted the Turco-Egyptian regime. The guerilla activities of the 'shadow sultan' Hārūn Sayf al-Dīn (1874–1879), and the many government attempts to eliminate him kept western Dār Fūr in turmoil; physically, because soldiers of either side kept plundering villages and disrupting trade;[4] politically, because the local rulers who had submitted to the new regime still had to reckon with a possible restoration of the sultanate, and kept considering and reconsidering their attitudes. The sultan of Dār Tāmā, for example, was waiting to see what way the cat would jump. In 1879 he sent his son to Kulkul to pay his respects to the Turco-Egyptian governor of Dār Fūr. He also allowed the tax collectors in his country, but he declared frankly that he was neutral in the struggle between Hārūn and the government, and would side with the winner.[5] On the other hand, the Qimr Sultan openly chose the side of the 'Turks'. He had fought against al-Zubayr on the Fūr side, but by 1878 he had already made himself so useful to the new regime that he was decorated. He committed himself to the new regime irrevocably in 1880, when he betrayed Hārūn and thus became acessory to the latter's death at Aptar in Dār Qimr.[6] The same is true for Hajjām Ḥasab Allāh of the Masālīt. Hajjām dutifully paid taxes, showed up to salute the governor of al-Fāṣhir whenever he came out west, and obtained both the title of bey and his kettledrum as a reward for joining the regicides of the new regime.[7]

The Turco–Egyptian occupation of Dār Fūr lasted for nine years, most of which were spent fighting the Fūr 'shadow sultans' in the west and the *baḥḥāra* in the south. The new administration was preoccupied with three things, eliminating the rebels, collecting taxes and abolishing the slave trade. To root out the slave trade it ordered all *jallāba* and *baḥḥāra* out of southern Dār Fūr, and closed the desert route from Kobbei to Asyūt, which had been Dār

Fūr's main artery of trade with Egypt.[8] However, the government was not hostile towards *jallāba* and *baḥḥāra* on principle, and large numbers of them entered its service as military commanders and civil administrators, or became associated with it as traders. A number of Kobbei traders, for example, came to hold high offices, and al-Nūr Bey ʿAnqara, ex-lieutenant of al-Zubayr, was appointed as governor of the Kulkul and Kabkābiyya district.[9]

The collection of taxes, one of the *raisons d'être* of the state, was all the more urgent in view of the administration's eternal budgetary deficit.[10] Taxes were paid in kind. In October 1879 Messedaglia, the new governor, explained the tax rate to a number of western rulers gathered in Kulkul; three *midd* of grain and one sixth of a bull were payable by each person of over ten years old – the total number of the population being estimated by the local rulers themselves.[11] He added the stipulation that those who lived very far away would be allowed to pay in cash, for which purpose the government fixed the price of grain and cows. This stipulation might be an indication of official ignorance of economic conditions in western Dār Fūr, but it was more probably made to pay lip-service to official regulations. Von Slatin, who succeeded Messedaglia, was certainly aware that:

> there is very little money in Darfur. The northern Arab tribes who act as camel-men, and who supply transport for the great caravan road between Asyut and Darfur, have a small amount of gold and silver coin; but in all other parts of the province payments are made principally in 'takia', a sort of native-made cotton cloth, cut in various lengths.[12]

Slatin was quite explicit about the fact that although 'taxes were paid in kind, such as corn, honey, camels, cows, sheep and native-made cloth', the government was able to assess them in Egyptian piasters by arranging a fixed tariff for these local products. The latter were sold to traders who generally paid the government in grain, which the government again used to pay its soldiers and officials. 'As the price of corn varied, it happens as often as not that the cash value of the salaries was in excess', Slatin noted. However, since the grain which was not consumed was undoubtedly again exchanged for other goods with the traders, the profits resulting from price fluctuations more likely went to the latter.[13]

The Turkiyya in Dār Fūr was a period of commercialization and monetization. In the minds of Masālīt informants it is associated with heavy taxation, with the first introduction of money, and with a small-scale labour migration to Kulkul and Kabkābiyya, where Masālīt youngsters, attracted by the promise of salaries in coins and imported cloth, went to join the new regime's military establishment.[14] Although the process of monetization was cut short by the overthrow of the Turco-Egyptian administration in 1883, as long as it lasted it had a revolutionary effect. F. S. Ensor, who travelled from Umm Badr to al-Fāshir in 1875, only a few months after the occupation, noted that:

> the 'tobe' is the money standard and had always served as a dollar; now however, it fluctuated materially and he [the Fūr *shaykh* of Broosh] complained bitterly of his loss. The introduction of real silver dollars, and the rejection of the 'tobe' in exchange by the newcomers, had caused its value to diminish. In Broosh it had already reached a third, and was falling still lower every day.[15]

Although this devaluation may have been more dramatic in the case of cloth than other local products such as grain and livestock, the trend of the new development is clear. Since taxes were assessed in Egyptian piasters the deflation of the local currencies must have been felt by the local people as an increase in taxation. In reality, however, it is doubtful whether there was any other system than that worked out on the spot between the armed bands of tax collectors and the local rulers. An Egyptian clerk who had collected taxes from the Masālīt in 1876 noted that 'no particular system was adhered to in this, although the manner in which it was carried out resembled that of the Darfur Sultans.'[16]

Paying taxes was the touchstone of loyalty to the new regime. The Sinyār, who refused to pay, were raided by Turco-Egyptian troops until the sultan of Dār Silā drove the latter out.[17] As long as the Tāmā Sultan was still sitting on the fence he paid only a limited amount of corn and cows. The Jabal and Erenga, however, who had to feed the garrison at Abū Qurayn, claim that the 'Turks' collected piles of grain as high as mountains, and took grain, *tukkiyyas* and livestock to their treasury in Kulkul.[18] The chiefs of the 'Arabs', the Taʿālba, Tarjam and Maḥāmīd, all paid taxes to Kulkul, as did the Masālīt unified under Hajjām.[19]

Hajjām Ḥasab Allāh, Sultan of the Masālīt

The unification of the Masālīt was by no means the logical result of, or natural response to the fall of the Ancien Regime. There is no evidence that throwing off the Fūr yoke was a long-cherished pan-Masālīt dream, or that Hajjām was raised to the leadership on a wave of Masālīt national feeling. Oral tradition leaves no illusions about the way in which the unification came about. Hajjām's strategy consisted of inviting different feuding Masālīt clans to a banquet of bull's meat held somewhere in a *wādī* under a big tree. When the members of each clan – unaware that they were not the only guests invited – showed up, they had no choice but to be shot on the spot or to share in the meal of reconciliation, and to forget and forgive the bloodshed of the past.[20]

The anecdote also throws some light upon Hajjām's personality, for he is remembered as a strong and courageous man, who was 'not even afraid of the devil'. Yet it might create the false impression that Hajjām was above the different parties rather than deeply involved in clan politics as he was. The first major political move in his career had been to take the *firsha*ship of the Mistereng from a close relative under the threat of violence.[21] This occurred towards the end of the Ancien Regime, after the Mistereng had broken away from the Nyerneng. There are indications that the Mistereng were a rising clan, i.e. were extending their power in this period. The conflict with the Nyerneng had ended favourably for the Mistereng, and Hajjām's attempt to make the Kusubei (of Arara) subject to him failed only as a result of Fūr intervention.[22] Yet there was one *firsha* who was traditionally senior to Hajjām and more powerful. This was Isāgha Donkotch of the large clan of the Fukkunyang. Even after the beginning of the Turkiyya the Fukkunyang *firsha* had 'a separate *daftar*', that is to say dealt with the new regime independently from Hajjām, tradition says. Moreover, Hajjām did not accept the position which the Turco-Egyptians offered him until he had consulted *firsha* Isāgha, and when he did, it was Isāgha who confirmed him in his position.[23] A final indication that the latter may have been more qualified to become the leader of the Masālīt is the fact that the Mistereng deemed it necessary to invent the story that, during a visit of the four Masālīt *firsha*s to al-Fāshir, Isāgha was officially replaced as chief *firsha* by Hajjām.[24] Yet there is no memory of rivalry or armed conflict between the Mistereng and Fukkunyang. When Hajjām became the ruler of the Masālīt, Isāgha Donkotch became his deputy (*khalīfa*), and together they ruled nearly the whole of the Masālīt homeland.

Why Hajjām took priority over the *firsha* of the Fukkunyang cannot be explained in terms of the internal balance of power. The determining factor in Hajjām's rise to the leadership was his 'Turkish' connection. Although the sources disagree about its details, one element stands out clearly. In 1876, when a group of soldiers was sent into Dār Masālīt to collect taxes, Hajjām clearly tried to ingratiate himself with the new regime by assisting the tax collectors. He made his house available to them as their headquarters, supplied interpreters and accompanied them when they made a tour of the area within a radius of two whole days of his residence at Mogornei.[25] In the eyes of the soldiers who operated in Dār Masālīt, Hajjām was merely 'one of its kings',[26] but for the Masālīt, Hajjām's assistance to the Turco-Egyptian tax collectors had important political implications, as is evident from the following tradition. When al-Nūr ʿAnqara came to Dār Masālīt the four *firsha*s of the Nyerneng, Fukkunyang, Minjiri and Mistereng prepared to resist. However, *faqīh* Ismāʿīl ʿAbd al-Nabī, leader of the *khalwa* of Dirjeil, wrote a letter in which he listed the number of cows and slaves which the Masālīt promised to pay as tribute (*dīwān*) in return for peace. The 'Turks' accepted this, made a camp at Mogornei, and sent for Ismāʿīl asking him to bring what he had promised. 'Ismāʿīl was a *faqīh* and had nothing of course', the informant said, 'so he went to Hajjām, who collected the *dīwān*, took it to the "Turks", and was made head of the Masālīt in return.'[27] The fact that this tradition is most probably a later rationalization of *faqīh* Ismāʿīl's rise to power does not detract from the value of its message; Hajjām earned Masālīt recognition of his leadership by taking on the responsibility for dealing with the new regime on their behalf. *Vice versa* Hajjām owed Turco-Egyptian recognition of his position to dealing on its behalf with the Masālīt. Fraccolari hit the nail on the head when he characterized the *shaykh* as the one who pays to the government all the taxes payable by his subjects – to be reimbursed by the latter later on.[28] Masālīt tradition stresses one other element of Hajjām's 'Turkish' connection which was crucial to his career, namely his role in rooting out Fūr resistance personified by the 'shadow sultan' Harūn. When the new regime rewarded Hajjām with the title of bey and Hārūn's kettledrum, this was in Masālīt eyes equivalent to recognizing him as ruler, even sultan, of the Masālīt.

How long Hajjām had been *firsha* before he became a bey in 1880 is not known, but after his promotion he ruled for another four years. With the exception of *malik* Kurra of the Amunong in the extreme northeast, and the Amm Būs clans on the western frontier who continued to play hide and seek with the rulers from both east and west, he ruled the whole of the Masālīt homeland.[29] Memories of internal resistance against Hajjām are vague and not very numerous. There seem to have been some minor disturbances by youngsters of several clans who refused to take his authority very seriously until they were taught a lesson by Hajjām's 'Turkish' friends. In a similar vein his move from Wādī Nyala (just west of the modern El Geneina) to the government post at Mogornei was ascribed to the fact 'that he could not get along with the people.'[30] In general, however, his authority, in combination with that of the *firsha* of the Fukkunyang, seems to have been effective. Oral sources emphasise that Hajjām's administration did not have to start from scratch, for all along 'there were *maliks* who were used to obeying the orders of their *ḥukkām*.'[31] Hajjām's relations with the Turco-Egyptians continued to be good, but there were some conflicts with his neighbours and former overlords, the Fūr. After Sultan Ibrāhīm's defeat many Fūr had fled to the west. Some had entered Dār Masālīt and had settled near Fōra. There they fought at least two battles with the Masālīt, who after an initial defeat drove them out singing:

> Jaktūre has come, we will enter the fight with our hands,
> Jaktūre has come, we will enter with big poles,
> Jaktūre has come, we will enter with spears.[32]

Hajjām did not take part in the fighting, but when *shartay* Ibrāhīm Bōsha of Kerne, one of the traditional overlords of the Masālīt, invaded the same area a few years later, Hajjām was in command. Driving the *maliks* who had invited the *shartay* to come and make an end to his rule before him, Hajjām gave battle. He defeated the Fūr and beheaded their *shartay*, tradition says. His military band sang his glory:

He was killed, he was killed
Brāhīm Bōsha was killed
Fartāk, son of Kunji, cut off his head and he was killed.[33]

Thus Hajjām drove home to both the Fūr and his *maliks* that the days of the Old Regime had gone, and that the new ruler of the Masālīt was not to be trifled with. On the western border there were problems as well. When von Slatin met Hajjām in Kabkābiyya in 1881, he commented that 'the Massalit Sheikh . . . was constantly at war with the tribes on the frontier.'[34] The 'tribes' of the quotation were probably the elusive Masālīt clans called Amm Būs, which were mentioned above. There is no evidence that Hajjām waged war with either the neighbouring Marārīt, Awra, Erenga and Jabal, or with the Wadaians, who were holding their breath out of fear of a 'Turkish' advance.[35] In spite of the two episodes of armed conflict, Hajjām's reign is remembered as a period in which relations with the outside were peaceful, and in which Dār Masālīt faced east both politically and commercially. The main market was Mogornei, 'the bey's market'; tea, coffee, beads, imported cloth, interesting seeds like that of radish, some rifles and coins – almost exclusively for the rulers – reached Dār Masālīt mainly from the east.[36]

Hajjām is hardly ever referred to as sultan. He was addressed and is remembered as bey, and is regarded as the precursor, not the founder of the sultanate founded by the Gernyeng in 1884. Yet he behaved as a sultan. To begin with he had a kettledrum, the symbol of sultanic authority. Moreover, while the power over life and death had been the prerogative of the Fūr Sultan, Hajjām 'killed on his own authority.' Hajjām killed people even for small offences such as minor dishonesties, oral sources say, and 'when Hajjām attended a legal dispute, it was inevitable that one man would die.'[37] This is significant because dealing summarily with human life is a recurring element of the mystique surrounding the sultans of the eastern Sudanic belt.[38] In at least one case Hajjām took the right to make and unmake local rulers. He deposed the ruling *malik* of the Torong of Mogornei, and appointed a new *malik*, Adam Kebberre, instead. Masālīt criticism of his act was expressed in a song:

Listen to Hajjām Bey
how could he give Kebberre his high rank (*daraja*)?
the Torong are busy ruining the country.[39]

By granting the Borno *faqīh* Ayyūb Dā'ūd the right to administer the village of Maymerre, Hajjām trespassed upon another old prerogative of the Fūr Sultan. A real break with tradition was the favour which he did to the Manggere at Tirei, who lived on Dīseng land and therefore paid taxes to the *malik* of the Dīseng. Hajjām owed them a debt of gratitude, and when they complained to him of their situation he made them the truly royal gift of the land on which they lived.[40] Thus far only the Fūr Sultan had been able to grant land, and by arrogating this right to himself Hajjām clearly put himself in the ranks of the sultans. The Dīseng were so indignant that they were still suing the Manggere thirty years later. Although the Masālīt do not recognize the right (in contrast to the power) of sultans to alienate land, the later rulers of Dār Masālīt regarded Hajjām's grant as valid and never revoked it. The above example shows that Hajjām sometimes caused conflicts between the clans rather than solving them.

However, Hajjām deserves his reputation as unifier of the feuding clans because he built up a position which was strong enough to force the clans to keep the peace and to preserve the newly-found unity. The fact that the most enterprising young men could satisfy their ambition by other means than raiding their neighbours, namely by going east to Kulkul, where they were kept busy learning how to shoot a gun, and could earn the *riyāl*s and *tōb*s (*thawb*s) which would impress the home front, may well have facilitated Hajjām's task. Even the civil war which was fought to overthrow Hajjām was not a revival of old feuds, but a rebellion of almost all Masālīt against an oppressive ruler. The Gernyeng, Lereng, Komore, Dīseng, Gonykokong, most of the Fukkunyang and other clans all combined to depose Hajjām, while the southern clans, 'those who had been born and bred together with Hajjām', held themselves aloof.[41] In 1882–3 Hajjām was attacked at his residence in Mogornei. Several of his children, among whom his son Makkī, perished when his house was set on fire, but he himself escaped. However, when he heard his attackers beating his kettledrum behind his back, he retraced his steps and recovered it, thus earning a last praise song:

> Those who said: Hajjām will not come back
> where are they now?
> they dug holes and crept into them [to hide]
> he came thundering back like a thunderstorm.[42]

Hajjām fled to the southeast. On the way he was attacked by the Ajumung and Kusubei, who killed his brother ʿAlī Dunyuru, but he finally found asylum with the sultan of Dār Silā.[43]

Local tradition associates Hajjām's unpopularity and fall with the excessively high taxes which were levied during his reign. The Masālīt remember that they paid millet, *tukkiyyas*, horses, cows and other livestock, nuts, ghee and honey. They remember that the 'Turks' visited their country and took up residence with local rulers such as the *firshas* and *sambei*. The latter slaughtered bulls and killed game for them to eat; summoned the village youth to come dance and be merry, and made them 'presents' of grain which were delivered in Kulkul.[44] How much was collected in taxes is remembered neither by the Masālīt nor by the tax collectors. The Egyptian *bikbāshī* ʿAbd al-Salām who collected taxes from the Masālīt in 1876 wrote in 1913:

> The exact amount of the tribute which I collected I cannot now remember, but it included horses, cows and corn. The corn was loaded on hundreds of camels, donkeys and bulls.[45]

The impossibility of pleasing both his Masālīt subjects and his 'Turkish' overlords at the same time was one of the reasons for Hajjām's fall. However, his own cruelty and injustice were an important factor as well. 'Hajjām killed too many people' is the general opinion of the Masālīt. Even people of his own clan and subclan (the Mistereng Jodeng) admit this, for Hajjām also killed his closest relatives, ordering them to be tied up and thrown into the fast-streaming Wādī Kajja.[46] The standard story which is told to illustrate Hajjām's cruelty and sadism is that he forced men and women to walk all the way to Kulkul carrying loads of millet on their heads. Not only that, but he even sent his men to force them to walk through the loose sand of the *wādī* – which makes for very heavy going – so that he could come out to watch them, muttering, 'surely a lot of donkeys have come out today.'[47] To what extent Masālīt indignation about the novelty of having to pay more grain than the tax collectors ate on the spot, and of having to transport it over a relatively long distance, made them exaggerate Hajjām's cruelty, is hard to say; Hajjām fell when the regime with which he had identified himself was overthrown by the Mahdiyya.

Hajjām did not stay in Dār Silā for long, but long enough to assist the Dājū Sultan in chastising the Sinyār once again. Then he made his way back to Kabkābiyya or al-Fāshir, passing through the country of the Banī Ḥalba and avoiding Dār Masālīt. Once more he tried to make a comeback, but at Gorāse, east of Dirjeil, he was again defeated by a Masālīt army commanded by a Fukkunyang *faqīh*, Isāgha Choko. The Fukkunyang were most instrumental in defeating Hajjām and received credit for this in a song:

> Listen to Hajjām Bey
> in Mogornei, in thick bush
> Isāgha said 'surrender'
> and took his high rank.[48]

However, although Isāgha Choko won the day in the battles of both Mogornei and Gorāse, he was killed at Gorāse. Since the Fukkunyang *firsha* had fled (together with the *sambei* of the Gernyeng), the Fukkunyeng were temporarily left without a leader. This paved the way for the accession of *faqīh* Ismāʿīl ʿAbd al-Nabī of the Gernyeng.[49]

Chapter 4

The rise of the Masālīt Sultanate from a regional perspective (1883–1898)

Western Dār Fūr and the Mahdist State (1883–1890)

For the outlying parts of Dār Fūr such as the western frontier the Mahdiyya did not really begin until 1883 when the *anṣār* conquered El Obeid and won the battle of Shaykān. Only then did the Mahdī put a cousin of his, Muḥammad Khālid Zuqal, in charge of Dār Fūr. The Commander-General arrived in al-Fāshir in January 1884, replacing the Turco-Egyptian governor of Dār Fūr, Rudolph von Slatin, who had surrendered to the Mahdī in December 1883. In the period following the conquest of El Obeid and the occupation of al-Fāshir representatives of many of the ethnic groups of Dār Fūr came to El Obeid to swear allegiance to the Mahdī.

The Mahdiyya was a millenarian movement for the revival of Islam, or more particularly, for the restoration of the true Islamic community of the Prophet's days, at the end of time. It took the form of a *jihād* or holy war of independence against the Turco-Egyptian occupation and led to the establishment of an independent 'Sudanese' state (1885–98). To the rulers and commoners of the western Sudan the Mahdiyya presented itself not only as a religious message – a summons to swear loyalty to the 'divinely guided one', the Mahdī, and to join him in fighting the 'Turks' – but also as a new regime, as yet another central government interfering in local affairs and making new and burdensome demands. The new regime split Dār Fūr (and Sudanese) society as deeply as the French revolution had split western Europe. One was either for or against it; for a middle position there was –

particularly as the decade progressed – little room. It was in this period that the sultanate of Dār Masālīt emerged.

The rise of the sultanate cannot be studied in isolation. The present analysis will therefore deal with the developments which led to the emergence of the sultanate on three levels or scales, as if three concentric circles are drawn around Dār Masālīt, each one narrower than the previous one. It will deal with the history of the western frontier and its relations with the central government of the Mahdist state (the widest circle); with the western frontier itself, particularly the relations between Dār Masālīt and the other states and chiefdoms of the frontier area; and with the internal developments in Dār Masālīt itself (the narrowest circle). The latter will be analyzed in Chapter Five.

The Mahdist Sudan was divided into metropolitan and military provinces. The former were at the heart of the Mahdist state. They were administered from Omdurman and were fiscal areas rather than administrative units, while the latter formed the periphery and shielded the core-area.[1] The governors of the military provinces – who were increasingly taken from the Taʿāyisha, the tribesmen of the Khalīfa, were military commanders in charge of large standing armies. Dār Fūr was such a military province, and the two governors who ruled it between January 1886 and 1896 were relatives of the Khalīfa, and spent most of their time preparing for, or recovering from military expeditions. The military nature of their function is reflected in, and to a large extent determined the nature of the Mahdist documents dealing with Dār Fūr.[2] These documents consist mainly of letters exchanged between the Khalīfa – who succeeded the Mahdī in June 1885 – and the military governors in al-Fāshir, but also include the letters exchanged between the latter, their sub-commanders in the field, and the *shaykh*s and sultans of the frontier area. Finally they include a number of letters written by the rulers of the western frontier to each other – letters which were captured by the Mahdist armies and subsequently sent to Omdurman.

Western Dār Fūr was never effectively subjected or administered by the Mahdist state. Muḥammad Khālid Zuqal, who was governor of Dār Fūr from January 1884 to January 1886, was far too busy elsewhere in Dār Fūr to concentrate on the western frontier. Firstly he had to fight the Fūr 'shadow sultan' Dudbanga

Abū Bakr, who was succeeded as leader of the Fūr resistance against the Mahdist regime by his brother Yūsuf in September 1884. Secondly, he had to persuade the Baqqāra cattle nomads of southern and southwestern Dār Fūr to join their kinsman, the Khalīfa, in Omdurman.[3] Zuqal had orders not to fight the western sultans or treat them harshly; he did not go beyond trying to persuade them to submit to the Mahdist cause at least nominally, or beyond exchanging polite letters and presents with them.[4] If he was an administrator and general elsewhere in Dār Fūr, in his relations with the western frontier he was only an ambassador of the Mahdist state. Diplomatic correspondence was not new to the western sultans. In following years they would demonstrate abundantly that they had understood that paper was patient and that in diplomacy sincerity did not always have priority. However, side by side with dissimulation and flattery, one finds remarks of almost shocking sincerity. In a letter written to Zuqal by Sultan Yūsuf of Wadai in August 1885, Yūsuf (and his *ajāwīd* or advisers) – in spite of the glowing rhetoric and suave words in which they repeatedly professed their belief in the Mahdiyya – really refused to commit themselves to the Mahdist cause before they had received further orders from the *shaykh* of the Sanūsiyya in Libya. That the western sultans understood how revolutionary the Mahdist revolution was, is evident from this same letter:

> We believe in all the strong arguments which you brought in your letters. It is true that the time is the time of Mahdia and not of a worldly kingdom. In accordance with your order we gave allegiance to our Lord Mohammed Yusef who has been nominated as khalifa to the Mahdi. . . . We obeyed his order as the Mahdi is the Sultan of his time and all the other Governors are his followers and it is not necessary that he should be Sultan and son of a Sultan.[5]

After Zuqal's recall to Omdurman in January 1886, the relations of the western frontier states with the Mahdist regime became even more tenuous. Dār Fūr was divided into five administrative districts, each headed by 'one of the sons of the country'. Yūsuf Ibrāhīm, son of the last Dār Fūr Sultan, Ibrāhīm, who had been defeated by al-Zubayr, became governor of the district of al-Fāshir and Kabkābiyya; a Masālīt *faqīh* and Mahdist agent, Ismā'īl 'Abd al-Nabī, became governor of the Masālīt and of the western regions as far as the borders of Dār Fūr.[6] However, this experiment in indirect rule was an emergency measure which did not last. Yūsuf Ibrāhīm did not enjoy the Khalīfa's favour for long. Accused of seeking to restore the sultanate of his ancestors and to make himself independent, he fell from grace with the Khalīfa.[7] The latter then sent a relative, ʿUthmān Adam or Jānū, to punish Yūsuf and to take over the administration of Dār Fūr. ʿUthmān entered al-Fāshir in January 1888. In March Yūsuf was defeated and killed. The hostilities which led to his death ushered in a period of more aggressive dealings beween the *anṣār* and the sultans of the western front, who sided with Yūsuf's brother and successor, the 'shadow sultan' Abū'l-Khayrāt (1888–1891).

During his first months in office ʿUthmān Jānū concentrated his efforts upon pacifying northern and central Dār Fūr, but he also prepared a more effective subjection of the west. In March 1888 he ordered troops campaigning in the west to bring the rulers of the Tāmā, Qimr and Maḥāmīd with them to al-Fāshir for a visit. In April he asked permission to send troops to what he called the virgin lands of the Bidāyāt and Qurʿān, and to those 'worshippers of pagan rites', the Zaghāwa.[8] In May of that year, however, relations between the governor and the frontier sultans were – or at least seemed – still reasonable. Ismāʿīl ʿAbd al-Nabī, the Mahdist agent for Dār Masālīt, had eventually obeyed the order to come to al-Fāshir; the Qimr Sultan was reported to be on his way; and the sultan of Dār Silā wrote a letter saying that he adhered to the Mahdiyya and would send his sons.[9] Soon after, however, the illusions were shattered and diplomacy broke down. The Wadai Sultan, it was discovered, had been conspiring with the defeated 'shadow sultan' Yūsuf Ibrāhīm, and was – according to pilgrims and professional spies – committing every possible sin against the Mahdist doctrine and cause. He blocked the road from Wadai to Dār Fūr; killed most of a party of 1,400 western pilgrims; was procuring arms and ammunition from the Fezzān; had left his capital for Murra to guard Wadai's eastern border against the *anṣār*; and enlisted the national establishment of holy men to pray for a complete Mahdist defeat.[10] The unequivocal hostility of the sultan of Dār Silā became obvious in the same month (August 1888), when Mahdist messengers sent from the country of the Taʿāyisha were unceremoniously turned out of Dār Silā. This happened, it was reported, in accordance with orders Sultan Abū

Rīsha had given to 'his tribes' (the Simiyāt, Sinyār and Fongoro) not to allow any *anṣār* into Dār Silā, to tear up all Mahdist letters, and not to patch their clothes, as *anṣār* should.[11] Ismāʿīl ʿAbd al-Nabī, who had been described as the Mahdiyya's most loyal adherent in western Dār Fūr a year before, and who had actually obeyed the order to visit al-Fāshir, was secretly accused of having a 'taste for power' (*ḥubb al-riyāsa*) and leanings towards independence, and was deported to Omdurman. The Zaghāwa had been uncooperative all along and became the first victims of a Mahdist punitive expedition, which was soon followed by another one against the Qimr Sultan, Idrīs, who was conspiring with the new 'shadow sultan' Abū'l-Khayrāt.[12] One month later, in August, the *anṣār* invaded Dār Tāmā, whose sultan was exiled to Omdurman. ʿUthmān Jānū had changed his diplomatic frock for a military uniform, and soon the whole of western Dār Fūr rose in open rebellion against the *anṣār* in what is called 'the movement of Abū Jummayza', which lasted from September 1888 to February 1889 (see below).

The nature of Mahdist administration as a cause of local resistance

The precise causes of the deterioration of the relations between the governor and the rulers of the western frontier – or rather what was cause and what result in the chain of repressive measures and rebellion acts – is hard to establish. About the Mahdist routine of daily administration in western Dār Fūr little is known. There was a rudimentary judicial system with Mahdist judicial representatives residing in the administrative centres or garrison towns, and accompanying the armies in the field.[13] However, the available evidence does not suggest that the westerners resented the presence of these Mahdist judges amongst them. There was also a system of taxation. The subjects of the Mahdist state – including the recalcitrant inhabitants of western Dār Fūr – had to pay the Islamic dues of *fiṭra* and *zakāh* (the *ḥuqūq Allāh* or 'rights of God'), which were collected by the local authorities in cooperation with tax collectors from the central government.[14] In October 1891 some of the western rulers (those of Dār Masālīt, the Banī Ḥusayn, and Dār Qimr) were reported to be busy collecting taxes for the *anṣār* (*mashqūlīn* [*mashghūlīn*] *bi khadāmāt al-zakāwāt li'l-anṣār*), but how often and how much grain and livestock was paid by the western rulers to the central government is unknown. When they, in January 1893, were ordered to prepare grain stores and *lubūs* (quilted cotton covers for horses) for the approaching Mahdist army, the sultans of Dār Masālīt and Dār Qimr fled their capitals, while those of Wadai and Dār Silā prepared for war.[15]

If the extent of western resentment against the official Islamic dues demanded from them is not fully clear, the resentment about the abuses associated with these demands is well documented. Not included in the legal dues was all that the various Mahdist armies ate, drank, wore and stole when on campaign, or the movable and immovable goods they confiscated as booty (*ghanīma*) whenever their demands met with resistance. Evidence of how disastrous the movements of the armies often were for the areas through which they passed or in which they had their camps (*dayms*) is abundant. Moreover, the number of soldiers and followers who made up the armies, and who are all known to have lived off the countryside, leave little doubt about the impact of their presence on any particular locality.[16] In November 1888, at the climax of the Mahdist campaign against the western front led by Abū Jummayza, the army at al-Fāshir counted 36,419 soldiers; this was an exceptional, even unique, concentration of soldiers, most of whom were usually dispersed over the garrison towns of Dāra, al-Fāshir, Kabkābiyya, al-Uḍayya and Umm Ballā. In times of relative peace such as November 1892, there were just under 3,000 soldiers in al-Fāshir, 239 in Kabkābiyya and 338 in Kuttum. What numbers the camp-followers of a major Mahdist army could (but in western Dār Fūr rarely did) reach is illustrated by the extreme example of Maḥmud Aḥmad's army in November 1896, just before it left El Obeid for al-Fāshir; the women, slaves and children in its train numbered 20,000.[17] In June 1890, a famine year, ʿUthmān Jānū visited a detachment of soldiers in Jabal Kūnū (Kongyo) and reported:

> We found them in straitened circumstances as a result of the lack of grain, for they 'cleaned' [i.e. ate all the grain available in] the whole area of Kongyo and had travelled all over. The same is true for the other areas such as the *dār*s of the Banī Ḥalba . . . All these areas the *anṣār* 'ate' without leaving anything, little or much; only the district of the rebellious Masālīt – which is extremely prosperous – remains.[18]

In August 1895 the Zaghāwa complained that the Mahdist armies had confiscated absolutely everything they had found on their way; they had even deviated from the normal routes, it was said, possibly with the implication that the local people had not even been given a fair chance to flee.[19] In an undated letter of the same period Sultan Idrīs of Dār Qimr lodged a complaint against the soldiers of the garrison of Kabkābiyya, who had taken away without right 88 cows, many donkeys, seven free girls and one boy.[20] Apparently these practices were the rule rather than the exception, and often occurred against the wishes of the central administration in al-Fāshir. However, for the inhabitants of western Dār Fūr the Mahdist regime was not so much embodied by the governor and the administrative establishment in al-Fāshir, but by the armies which passed through their *dār*s peacefully, invaded them by force, or set up semi-permanent camps in their midst. These plunderings and arbitary confiscations by the Mahdist troops were a major cause for discontent.

Even more than tax demands and tax abuses, the western sultans resisted the Khalīfa's policy of *tahjīr*, in this context best translated as 'forced migration' or 'deportation'. The documents suggest that the forced migration to Omdurman was the lynchpin of the relations between the Mahdist administration and the frontier sultans. The governor's laments that the western sultans always promised to come, but never did, are as numerous as explicit statements by the sultans that they – in spite of their loyalty to the Mahdist cause – were afraid, and refused to be sent to Omdurman.[21] The Khalīfa ordered not only the western sultans to come and visit him in Omdurman for an indefinite period of time, but also other local authorities and even complete ethnic groups from all over the Sudan. Experience soon taught that the majority of those who made the *hijra* never came back to their home areas again.

What the Khalīfa hoped to achieve through this policy of *tahjīr* has not as yet been satisfactorily established.[22] One of his aims was probably religious; the *hijra* was among other things a refresher course in Mahdist beliefs and doctrine, but political aims seem to have been as important. After the death of the Mahdiī in June 1885 the Khalīfa wanted the *anṣār* to renew the oath of allegiance to himself. He also wanted stability on the frontiers of his state, and therefore demanded guarantees for the absolute and complete loyalty of the local rulers. The latter's readiness to perform the *hijra* to Omdurman became a symbol for absolute loyalty – as had been the case under the Dār Fūr Sultanate before 1874, and as it would be again after the Mahdiyya, under Sultan ʿAlī Dīnār. Moreover, the *hijra* of a local ruler and his close relatives and trusted followers – who formed the core of the local armies – took the fire out of any smouldering resistance movement, and provided the hostages needed to guarantee the loyalty and obedience of those who stayed behind. Irrespective of the fact whether the Khalīfa acted from the conviction that the end of time was approaching, or from fear that he would lose control, he made the Mahdist state into a Taʿāyishī autocracy, in which there was no room for strong local authorities with a traditional – and hence by definition independent – power base.[23]

The first reference to a summons from the Khalīfa to a number of Dār Fūr leaders to make the *hijra* to Omdurman dates from 26 August 1885, two months after the Mahdī's death. The Dervish Proclamation Register for 1302 H. (1884–5) gives the full text of the summons which was addressed to the governor, Zuqal, 'and all Amils and Nekibs in his company',[24] but adds that copies were sent to 28 local rulers or Mahdist agents, among whom:

> 1. El Amil Yusef, son of Sultan Ibrahim, head of the Fur and all his men.
> 2. El Amil Ismail wad Abd el Nebi, head of the Masalit and all his men.
> 3. Sultan Ibrahim, son of Sultan Suleiman of Dar Tama and all his men.
> 4. Sultan Ishak Abu Risha, Sultan of Dar Sula and all his men.
> 5. Sultan Yusef, son of Mohd. Sherif, Sultan of Borgo and men.
> 6. Sheikh Hayati, son of Osman Fodi (of Sokotto) and men . . . .
> 9. Amils of Zeghawi, Hajar wad Bahr, Adam Bosh, Saleh, Nur wad Bakr, Ali Taher Keru Keru and men . . . .
> 14. El Amil Tirja [Turjūk] and all Beni Hussein, Taalba and Hottia of the west . . . .
> 19. El Juma and Mararit Sheikhs . . . .
> 21. Amils of Mahamid Arabs.[25]

The Khalīfa's message was very clear:

> As you are of the loyal companions who give support to the faith . . . and as you know the excellence of the Hugra [*hijra*] and the forsaking of the homes in the name of God, you should therefore, hasten to come here with your grand Amil (Governor General) Mohd. Khaled (Zogal) with high energy and pure heart . . . . Keep to your vows and do not postpone the fulfillment of these vows by showing love of homes . . . The object of your coming is to renew your vow and in order to converse on the subject of God and acquire the recompense of the Hugra. He who fails to come after receiving this letter will be considered as a traitor and is bound to fall one day into our hands, even if he ascended to heaven on a ladder.[26]

Ignoring the summons was regarded as a hostile act, but only in the long run; ignorance of Arabic and living at a long distance from the capital were accepted as valid reasons for delay, as Sultan Abū Rīsha of Dār Silā discovered to his luck. While Abū Rīsha ignored the summons, Ismāʿīl ʿAbd al-Nabī, *ʿāmil* of the Masālīt, followed a slightly different tactic. He announced his willingness to make the *hijra*, but then procrastinated and played for time, finding various excuses why he could not leave his *dār* just yet. His first excuse, in February 1888, was that the road between Dār Masālīt and al-Fāshir was obstructed by the Fūr rebel leader Yūsuf Ibrāhīm, who had fled to Jabal Karōma and was then still at large; allegedly Ismāʿīl had to wage war upon Yūsuf before he could come. ʿUthmān Jānū accepted his excuse, but was not deceived by the second one in April 1888, when Ismāʿīl pretended that he had to stop the invading armies of the sultans of Wadai and Dār Silā before he could make his visit to al-Fāshir. 'We wrote to him', ʿUthmān Jānū reported to the Khalīfa, 'that he should come here at once with all his men, horses and fire-arms, and that he should pay no attention to the Borqāwī and Silāwī.'[27] By May 1888 Ismāʿīl had arrived in al-Fāshir. On 11 September 1888 he was deported to Omdurman in the company of the Mahdist commander al-Bishārī Rīda. He arrived in Omdurman in the same month, never to see Dār Masālīt again.[28]

In September also the sultan of Dār Tāmā, attacked in his capital by the Mahdist commanders al-ʿAṭā Uṣūl and Ḥāmid Majbūr, was deported to Omdurman.[29] It was no coincidence that the movement of Abū Jummayza (see below) began immediately afterwards, that it originated in Dār Tāmā, and that it counted the Masālīt among its earliest and most fervent supporters; Ismāʿīl's son and successor, Sultan Abbakr (1888–1905), from hindsight described his motive for breaking with the *anṣār* as follows:

> From the Servant of his Lord *amīr* Abbakr Ismāʿīl ʿAbd al-Nabī, *ʿāmil* of the Mahdī – peace be upon him – in the district of Masalāh . . . .
> Know that the Mahdī revealed himself as the Prophet of God did – God's peace and blessings be upon Him. In the past my father went to our Lord the Mahdī – peace be upon him. The latter gave [him] proclamations and he [my father] came [back] to our people of Masalāh. They submitted to the Mahdī's cause and continued in this state until Lord ʿUthmān came to us in Dār Fūr. We rejoiced about this and said: 'this is what we desired' . . . .
> My father Ismāʿīl left of his own free will and was not carried off by force or compelled [he went] for the sake of the religion. He proceeded to al-Fāshir, and never came back to us again. Therefore we took fright, and when you [Maḥmūd Aḥmad] came to Dār Fūr I did not look up or ask you anything; we were just afraid [because] of what happened to my father.[30]

According to oral tradition it was anger about Ismāʿīl's confinement in Omdurman, rather than fear, that caused Abbakr to turn against the *anṣār*, but the two sentiments may well have gone together.[31]

A similar fear of the *hijra* to Omdurman is evident from a letter written by the Qimr Sultan to Maḥmūd Aḥmad in the 1890s. The governor had persuaded Sultan Idrīs to come back from Wadai, where he had taken refuge from the *anṣār*, and to take up residence in his old capital again. In a frank letter Idrīs explained why he had fled:

> As for myself, the fact that I have been fleeing from you for all these years does not mean that we refuse you or refuse to follow the Mahdī – God's peace be upon him and upon his Khalīfa – but we dislike the journey to Omdurman; for all [ordinary] people and sultans like myself whom you cut off, you cut off [once and for all]; and whom you sent off on a trip to

> Omdurman, you sent off [once and for all]; therefore we hate to come to you, and therefore I flee from you My Lord.[32]

Idrīs assured the governor that he was full of good intentions, but that his attitude towards the *hijra* remained the same and was not negotiable. The governor should realize, he argued, that he had come back to Dār Qimr only because of his letter and for his sake – adding rather rudely: 'so don't let me hear you again.' In view of the above there is no doubt that the Khalīfa's policy of *tahjīr* was another cause for the westerners' revolt against the Mahdist state. What the Mahdist doctrine – that political legitimacy was not based on heredity but on divine election and religious vocation – had stated on the level of ideology, the taxes demanded from the western rulers, the abuses they had to put up with, and the forced visits to Omdurman imposed upon them, drove home in practice: that there was no place for the hereditary rulers in the new order.

The movement of Abū Jummayza, September 1888–February 1889

The movement of Abū Jummayza, which in a few months time mobilized the whole of western Dār Fūr against the Mahdist state, began to figure in the Mahdist correspondence in September 1888. Within two months the *anṣār* had suffered three defeats at the hands of the western armies, and the very existence of the Mahdist administration in Dār Fūr had been brought into jeopardy. The movement of Abū Jummayza therefore represents a specific and violent stage in the relations between the Mahdist state and western Dār Fūr, but it represents at the same time a stage, and even a climax, in the history of the relationships between the western frontier states themselves. The latter dimension has so far been ignored by historians, but is indispensable to a proper understanding of the movement. Its prehistory, its origin and development, its end and aftermath, give a view of the western frontier states at a moment of rapid change at which the old order showed both its potential for change and its limits. The initial success of the revolt demonstrates how traditional loyalties and alliances were mobilized and activated, and how traditional fears, feuds and other obstacles to cooperation were overcome. Its failure shows among other things how the old competition and mutual distrust proved too persistent to be more than temporarily suppressed. The failure of the revolt was followed by a strong but short-lived Mahdist offensive in the west. This offensive wrought much destruction and might have triggered off a new pan-western alliance, if it had not petered out in a natural disaster, the cholera epidemic of 1890, which killed off a large part of the invading army. More far-reaching were the changes which took place within the western frontier, where the emergence and consolidation of the sultanate of Dār Masālīt brought about a new balance of power.

The events of the revolt

The events of the revolt have been best described by Mūsā al-Mubārak, the only defect of whose account is that he at times overlooked the fact that even the intelligence system of a theocracy can be misinformed.[33] These events can be summarized by saying that the western front won most of the battles but lost the war. The first victory of the western front – called in the documents the battle of Tāmā – took the *anṣār* by surprise. It took place on 9 September 1888 and caused the death of twenty-four *anṣār*, among whom the commander Ḥāmid Majbūr.[34] The reinforcements brought by ʿAbd al-Qādir wad Dalīl and al-ʿAṭā Uṣūl, who were still in Dār Tāmā, came too late. The Mahdist army was ordered to move its camp back from Dār Tāmā to Abū Qurayn (in Dār Erenga), which was centrally located at about an equal distance from Dār Masālīt, Dār Qimr, Dār Tāmā and Dār Banī Ḥusayn, and had an abundant grain supply. At Abū Qurayn, the *anṣār* were joined by the detachment of the commander al-Khatīm Mūsā, and by elements of the local population, who were settled around the camp so that friend and foe could be more easily distinguished.[35] Either by chance or by strategy Abū Jummayza attacked the camp at a time when most of its soldiers had gone out to attack the rebels *via* another route; he defeated the garrison which had been left behind, and put the camp to fire. This new victory at Abū Qurayn in October had serious results; Abū Jummayza not only captured a large number of firearms and eleven boxes of ammunition, but also gained enormous prestige.[36] Until then his followers had consisted only of Tāmā (among whom the movement had originated, but who had dropped out of it as a result of the heavy casualties of the first battle), and Masālīt.

At the time of the victory at Abū Qurayn the governor reported to the Khalīfa that Abū Jummayza's following consisted 'completely of Masālīt, the people of Ismā'īl 'Abd al-Nabī the Maslātī', and added: 'his son, called Abbakr, is himself with this impostor, and of all the tribes only they [the Masālīt] flocked to him.'[37]

After the battle of Abū Qurayn the western front began to take shape. By November 1888 several groups of Fūr (led among others by 'shadow sultan' Abū'l-Khayrāt), the Tāmā, Asongor, Jabal, Zaghāwa, Bidāyat, Tarjam, Banī Ḥusayn, Banī Ḥalba, Borqū (or Wadaians), Dājū (of Dār Silā) and the rank and file of the Masālīt had flocked to the banner of Abū Jummayza, giving the revolt the character of a mass movement.[38] In al-Fāshir 'Uthmān Jānū now sounded the alarm. He sent for fresh ammunition and called most of the *'āmil*s of Dār Fūr, with their men, to al-Fāshir. He was determined 'to bring about the destruction of the Masālīt country and to kill the immoral impostor'. 'With God's help,' he wrote to the Khalīfa, 'we will leave the west a huge empty space where only ostriches will graze.'[39] The leader of the new Mahdist offensive in the west was Muḥammad Bishāra, who left Kabkābiyya for the west on 26 October 1888, at the head of an army of 16,253 men. He marched on Kulkul and Tineat and made his camp at Amm Dukhn, which was close to both Dirjeil, the capital of Sultan Abbakr of the Masālīt, and to Ḥarāza 'Abdille, the headquarters of Abū Jummayza.[40] Even this huge army was, however, defeated by the western front on 11 November 1888.[41] So great was the panic of the *anṣār* that the Kabkābiyya garrison fled to al-Fāshir even before the survivors of Muḥammad Bishāra's army had made their way back to it.[42] 'Uthmān Jānū, however, did not lose his head. He concentrated all the troops of Dār Fūr in al-Fāshir and, while he was waiting for more men and ammunition, he played for time. He made peace overtures to the western front and organized daily parades west of the capital to make the enemy believe that a new Mahdist offensive was close at hand, and to bolster the sagging morale of his men.[43] The western front – racked by internal conflict after Abū Jummayza's death from smallpox – hesitated and procrastinated until 'Uthmān Jānū had received a new supply of ammunition, the morale of the soldiers was high again, and until the Fūr between Kabkābiyya and al-Fāshir, who had taken to the bush to join Abū Jummayza's approaching army, had grown tired of waiting and had gone home.[44] When the westerners finally attacked on 22 February 1889, the Mahdist army numbered 36,419 men, of whom 7,656 had firearms and 3,591 horses. In the battle outside al-Fāshir the western front was defeated and destroyed.[45]

Who was Abū Jummayza?

All sources – written and oral – confirm that Abū Jummayza had been the unifying factor in the revolt of the western front. It had taken ʿUthmān Jānū quite some time before he had found out who the leader of the western front was. In his letters to the Khalīfa he had therefore used a stereotype and referred to him as 'the deceiver' (*al-shakhṣ al-muḍill*) or 'the one who is bound to be defeated' (*al-makhdhūl*). He continued to do so even after his intelligence service had provided him with more data. The name and ethnic identity of the man who made history as Abū Jummayza remained initially a mystery, although it was suggested that he might belong to the Qurʿān. How he looked and behaved, however, was soon reported in some detail: he was a beardless young man, of dark complexion, and – in contrast to the westerners, it was said – fluent in Arabic. He wore copper and silver rings on all fingers of his right hand – as many as six on each finger – not unlike a *dumbāri* or locust charmer. He lived like an *anṣāri*, reading the *rātib* and the proclamations of the Mahdī, and led the people in prayer.[46] The governor reported that the ignorant westerners believed that their leader had come out of a *jummayza* tree, but the name Abū Jummayza, by which the *faqīh* came to be known in the Cairo Intelligence Office, does not occur in the Mahdist documents of that time.[47] In western Dār Fūr he is remembered both as Abū Jummayza and as Muḥammad Zayn, his real name.

Before he had manifested himself Muḥammad Zayn had lived among the Mahriyya, a nomadic people of northwestern Dār Fūr, making a living as a *faqīh* by writing amulets (*waraq*) for women and children. When the Mahriyya had been attacked by the *anṣār* he had been standing on an *ʿanqarīb* (local bed), throwing dust at the *anṣār*; when they were defeated he went to Dār Tāmā to live in the desert. After the Mahdist occupation of Dār Tāmā and the deportation of its sultan, he had gone to the Tāmā princes, saying: 'I am the son of the Sanūsī, and I have been brought here by the wind; the time that I must follow my vocation has come; if you will fight the enemy you can be certain of victory.' He then performed all kinds of magic for them.[48] Whether Muḥammad Zayn claimed to be the son of the Sanūsī *shaykh*, or the deputy of that son, is not clear. In a letter to the Khalīfa he claimed to be what ʿUthmān ibn ʿAffān had been to the Prophet. It was this honorific function and title, the *khalīfa*ship of ʿUthmān, that had been offered by the Mahdī to the *shaykh* of the Sanūsiyya, who had ignored the offer. Muḥammad Zayn's claims and aims were expressed explicitly in the two letters which he wrote to ʿUthmān Jānū and the Khalīfa, known to us only through the summary given by ʿUthmān and the response of the Khalīfa. In these letters he claimed to be an adherent of the Mahdī, and to have sworn allegiance to the Khalīfa. He claimed the *khalīfa*ship of ʿUthmān ibn ʿAffān (the third *khalīfa* of the Prophet), and compared the conflicts between himself and the *anṣār* with those which had occurred between the Companions of the Prophet. He summoned ʿUthmān Jānū to surrender the administration of Dār Fūr so as to prevent further bloodshed. His letters must have been written shortly before his death.[49]

If the Mahdist government was fairly well informed about Abū Jummayza's movement, the Cairo Intelligence Office under General Wingate was not. It was there believed that Abū Jummayza was 'the sheikh of the Masalit', whose father had been deported to Omdurman, and who therefore thirsted for revenge. According to Wingate the belief that 'the Great Sanūsī' – as he also called Abū Jummayza – was on the point of overthrowing the Mahdist state, caused great panic and happy expectations even in the distant Nile Valley and in the eastern Sudan.[50] This was not confirmed, however, by any other source. According to *shāyib* al-Dūm of Sirba, who claimed to be Abū Jummayza's oldest living relative, Muḥammad Zayn was a descendant of a *faqīh* of the Ḥawāzma of Kordofan, who had come to Dār Tāmā and had settled on a spot called Jilme, in a *wādī*. Since he was a great *faqīh* with many students the Tāmā Sultan gave him an estate. The *faqīh* stayed on, took a local wife and begot a son called Wādī (because he had been born in a *wādī*). Wādī's descendants were called Tāmā Jilmese, after Jilme, their dwellingplace. Muḥammad Zayn Yiḥyạ Ādam Muḥammad Aḥmad . . . Wādī, one of Wādī's descendants, was born in Wāra, in Dār Erenga, but after he had studied the *Qur'ān* there, he went to Jummayza al-Ḥamra in Dār Tāmā. There he eventually manifested himself as the leader of the *jihād* against the Mahdist regime.[51]

Causes of the revolt

To what extent the nature and excesses of the Mahdist administration in western Dār Fūr were responsible for the revolt has been discussed above. The political dimension was as crucial to the movement of Abū Jummayza as Abū Jummayza himself. 'Abū Jummayza had seven sultans on his side,' one informant said, 'the Borqāwī, Tāmāwī, Qimrāwī, Zaghāwī, Dājāwī, Maslātī and Furāwī (Abū'l-Khayrāt).'[52] All these sultans temporarily buried their old feuds and jealousies, but rivalries remained strong. It is not at all certain that they would have submitted to the leadership of anyone of their own number. Abū Jummayza, however – as a religiously inspired leader – fell outside all normal categories. Without any prominent political status in any *dār*, and belonging to a politically insignificant ethnic group, he had no longstanding enmities, did not form a threat to the political ambitions of the rulers of the west, and did not directly endanger the balance of power between them. Finding a religious leader to raise mass support for a programme of political activism was part and parcel of the politically frustrated of all ranks of western Dār Fūr society, as will be seen below. An extreme example was the young man arrested by British Condominium officials in the 1920s for inciting people to the *jihād* against the French conquerors of Wadai. When interrogated, the young *faqīh* was quite perplexed, and answered that he had just been sitting under a tree when people came to him and told him that he was their prophetic leader.[53] What happened to self-proclaimed prophets and otherwise religiously inspired *faqīh*s whose call was not convenient to the temporal rulers of western Dār Fūr is abundantly documented. In February 1892, for example, it was reported to the Khalīfa: 'A Maslātī proclaimed himself in Dār Masālīt; he was executed through the good services of Abbakr the Maslātī.' In 1922 a later Masālīt sultan warned his subjects 'that there are a lot of ill-famed bad Fikkis [*faqīhs*] who . . . have been on several occasions killed by Masalit kings on account of their audacity in having falsely represented themselves as Prophets or Agencies of Heavenly Powers.'[54]

If there was any economic motive behind the revolt it was not recognized by either Abū Jummayza's enemies or the rank and file of his followers. That Abū Jummayza waged war against the Mahdist regime in order to open the route to Mecca (which was also a trade route), and that he was accompanied and advised by twenty-five Tripoli merchants who had been robbed of their possessions by the *anṣār*, is a story which was brought into circulation by the Cairo Intelligence Office, has been repeated by later historians, but has not been confirmed by primary sources.[55]

The Mahdist governor, 'Uthmān Jānū, realized that it was the combination of the political frustrations of the frontier sultans and the religious charisma of Abū Jummayza that made the revolt so dangerous. However, in none of his many letters to the Khalīfa did he give a proper analysis of the background or internal dynamic of the movement. There is no trace of self-criticism or introspection in these letters, and the question whether administrative measures or demands, or the (mis-)behaviour of the troops might have been responsible for the revolt is neither asked nor answered. Instead 'Uthmān explained the revolt in terms of Abū Jummayza's devilish inspiration and magic-mongering, and the ignorance and limited mental abilities of the westerners. He called Abū Jummayza 'a master of fraud and deceit', 'a deceitful magic-monger and a suspected devil', 'someone who was helped by the devil and helped the devil', etc.[56] The enormous popular support Abū Jummayza found among the common people 'Uthmān explained from the fact that 'the people of the west have no intelligence; people like the Tāmā and Masālīt, and the nomads, are the weakest in mental ability.'[57] The social and religious indignation, still audible in the oral traditions of the movement preserved in western Dār Fūr, was completely ignored by the Mahdist authorities. It is referred to in only one written source, namely R. von Slatin's *Fire and Sword in the Sudan*. After the defeat and death of the 'shadow sultan' Yūsuf Ibrāhīm, Slatin related, 'Uthmān Jānū's troops raided the country in all directions, perpetrating acts of violence and cruelty, and dragging thousands of women and children to al-Fāshir as booty. When Abū Jamayza – a young man who was reading the *Qur'ān* under a large *jummayza* tree in Dār Tāmā – was confronted with one such act of violence, he incited the local male population to offer resistance and to gain paradise by defending their women and children. Their victory over the Mahdist soldiers sparked off the rising of which Abū Jummayza became the leader. 'People adored him as a saint and looked upon him as the liberator,' Slatin wrote.[58] Although Slatin's account was probably exaggerated, unlike the Mahdist documents, his interpretation took Abū Jummayza's personal indignation and the oppression of the local population by the *anṣār* into account as causes of the western revolt.

All sources agree that Abū Jummayza was not – and did not claim to be – either a new Mahdī or a Prophet Jesus, and that he did not preach a new religious message. He did not fight the *anṣār* because they were *anṣār*, but because – in his eyes – they were not true *anṣār* and could not be regarded as true representatives or even adherents of the Mahdiyya. Abū Jummayza fought the *anṣār*, one informant said, 'because they did not fear God; because they took away people's possessions; and because they confiscated things without right.'[59] The misbehaviour of the *anṣār* came up in many oral accounts from Dār Masālīt: the *anṣār* used to enter people's houses and to take away anything that took their fancy; they felt superior to the Masālīt and showed no respect for their sultan; they showed no mercy towards the poor ladies who brewed beer in spite of the ban on alcohol, and broke all pots and jars of the houses where alcohol was found.[60] The arbitrary confiscation of property was unacceptable to the Masālīt, it was said, 'for after all the Masālīt had not taken all that trouble to rid themselves of Hajjām and the Turco-Egyptians for nothing.'[61]

In the songs of the time the *anṣār* are nicknamed *Kubbū Kullu* (Arabic for 'Pour out everything') since the *anṣār* – whenever they would smell beer or get wind of the presence of any other drink or dish – would peremptorily order people to 'pour out everything' for them. Those who lived close to the Mahdist camp at Ereije (Dār Erenga) in about 1888 lamented in a song:

Kubbū da humma jū
fī Ereije dammarū
darb Shalāl biqa lanā mudda
miskīn jahjahū.

'Pour out that' have come
and made their camp at Ereije
the road to Shalāl now seems long to us
they have bewildered the common people.[62]

Not all memories are negative. People remember that the *esprit de corps* of the Mahdist soldiers was high and was sustained by communal singing on the road:

> Allāhu dāyim, bāqin
> yā jalāla, dāyim sīdī Allāh.
>
> God is everlasting, eternal
> Oh majesty, God, my Lord, is everlasting.

However, many of the soldiers, particularly the *jihādiyya* or slave soldiers, were mainly concerned with filling their stomachs and changed the religious songs into mocking appeals for food to the local population:

> Allāhu dāyim, yallalāhu dāyim
> maʿragat al-jidād al-ṭaʿim
> iddihū li'l-zōl al-ṣāyim.
>
> God is everlasting, Go-o-od is everlasting
> give the broth of the tasty chickens
> to the one who is fasting.[63]

The Mahdist soldiers and administrators are in western Dār Fūr often referred to as Taʿāyisha, the name by which the ethnic group of the Khalīfa is known, and not as *anṣār*. It is possible that Abū Jummayza – who claimed to be a loyal adherent of the Mahdiyya, but fought its representatives in Dār Fūr as polytheists – saw the same contrast between the rightly-guided theocracy of the Mahdī and the Taʿāyishī autocracy of the Khalīfa. However, the *anṣār* whom Abū Jummayza fought are also referred to as 'Turks' and confused with the soldiers of the Turco-Egyptian regime, which preceded the Mahdiyya. This is hardly surprising, for there was a striking continuity between the Turco-Egyptian and Mahdist administration of Dār Fūr; the military camps of the *anṣār*, their military personnel, and the behaviour of that personnel in western Dār Fūr were to a large extent the same as before 1882. In one of its aspects, therefore, the revolt was – even on the level of the common man – a revolt against (yet another) central government forced upon the westerners from above and from the outside.[64]

The mixture of religious and social indignation ascribed to Abū Jummayza offers a clue to both his personal motivation and the overwhelming support his movement found among the common people. An analysis of the latter, however, must also take into account Abū Jummayza's religious charisma. The miracle stories associated with his name reveal more about the psychological make-up of the followers than about that of the leader, and seem to be rooted more in the ecological environment and cultural tradition of those who tell them than in the real qualities of him about whom they are told. The miraculous power to change dust into grain ascribed to Abū Jummayza is a familiar theme in the miracle stories of western Dār Fūr; its modern variant – changing sand into sugar – is still one of the most popular tricks of jugglers visiting Dār Masālīt from Khartoum.[65] The miracle of the *wādī* is another stereotype. It was said that once, when Abū Jummayza had spread his *farwa* (an animal skin used as prayermat) under a big tree in a *wādī* and was leading his followers in prayer, the *wādī* suddenly filled up with water, which came rushing down, dragging with it everybody and everything on its way. When the torrent reached the place where Abū Jummayza was praying, however, it changed its course and left the spot dry.[66] The same thing happened, it is said in al-Fāshir, to the spot where 'shadow sultan' Abū'l-Khayrāt lies buried.[67] Abū Jummayza could always be seen from afar; however big the crowd he was in, he always seemed a bit taller than the other people in his company. After he had died, his grave radiated light in the dark.[68] The prohibition against killing wild animals since they were created by God, and taboos on certain kinds of food – ascribed to Abū Jummayza by both oral and written sources – are familiar from both Islamic tradition and popular indigenous beliefs.[69] There is one miracle story which is associated with Abū Jummayza's prohibition against killing game:

> It happened that a Maslātī [in spite of this prohibition] killed a partridge; so he tied it under his underpants [so as not to be found out]. It reached noon and the *muezzin* called for prayer. However, the *imām* [Abū Jummayza] said: 'there is a corpse among us; we will not pray until we have buried it'. The people then asked: 'where is the corpse?' Abū Jummayza said: 'Sultan Abbakr, is it amongst your people?' Sultan Abbakr said: 'no, no, we don't have one', and the Masālīt began to ask each other: 'who has died? Who has died?' Then *faqīh* Muḥammad of the Amburtchung said: 'yes, there is a dead body; let everybody who has a *tukkiya* tied around his waist or a piece of

string [holding up his underpants] untie it'. They untied their underpants and the partridge appeared. They buried it and then they prayed. From that time onwards Abū Jummayza was angry with the Masālīt and began to sit with the Erenga.[70]

Abū Jummayza's followers were not alone in their belief in his supernatural powers. The emphatic and recurrent assurances that the *anṣār* were not afraid of the devil and magic-worker Abū Jummayza that appear in 'Uthmān Jānū's letters to the Khalīfa, make one suspect that the *anṣār* shared this belief. They not only called Abū Jummayza a devil, they actually believed that he was one, and were in terror of him. The Khalīfa's order to stop calling Abū Jummayza a devil, and to refer to him only as 'the deluder' or 'the one who is bound to be defeated', was an attempt to counter the general belief in his supernatural qualities.[71]

The late nineteenth century (the Mahdist period) was an age of faith in the Sudan. The argument that, in an age of faith, political, intellectual, social and economic issues tend to be expressed in religious terms is a platitude, which nevertheless contains much truth. Although the nature and history of Mahdist faith in the Sudan deserves to be studied in its own right, the present study examines Mahdist faith only as an ideology for social and political change. The Mahdist faith of Abū Jummayza and his followers – both rulers and commoners – was among other things a form of social and political protest. It gave the revolt against the Mahdist state the sanction of religion; personified in Abū Jummayza, it enlisted the support of the masses for the revolt; and it temporarily unified the jealous and ambitious rulers of western Dār Fūr. Its success was superficial and short-lived. Although Abū Jummayza succeeded in becoming a rallying point for the sultans and their bands of warriors, he was less successful in disciplining them and in leading them in war. Authority in military affairs, it seems, remained with the sultans among his following, in particular with the independent-minded and imperious Masālīt Sultan Abbakr and the Fūr sultan-in-exile Abū'l-Khayrāt.[72] The story that Abū Jummayza was throwing dust at the *anṣār* who attacked the Mahriyya, and his prohibition of hunting (which would have facilitated the problem of feeding his enormous army), suggest that he was not a practical man. He himself seems to have made a distinction between the warriors and the 'saints'; when Abbakr came to him to take the oath of allegiance, Abū Jummayza said to him: 'you are sultan'; to the Erenga he said: 'every clan has a banner and I am with you; you will enter paradise, for you do not take things unlawfully; you are *faqīhs*'.[73]

The 'saints', however, could not keep the warriors in hand. Abū Jummayza was able to unify the western front only temporarily. The political ambitions and jealousies of the western rulers, which were one of the strongest forces behind the movement, also contributed to its disintegration. It is the struggle for power within the western front, and particularly the role played in it by the Masālīt, that will be analyzed below.

The new balance of power in western Dār Fūr

The cooperation between the western sultans dated even from before July–August 1888, when ʿUthmān Jānū had opened the offensive against western Dār Fūr. The Fūr sultan-in-exile Yūsuf had been in constant communication with the sultan of Wadai, as became clear from their correspondence, which was captured together with the former's luggage on his defeat by the *anṣār* in March 1888.[74] In August of the same year, the new 'shadow sultan', Abū'l-Khayrāt Ibrāhīm, was in Dār Qimr, conspiring against the *anṣār* with Sultan Idrīs. At the approach of the Mahdist armies of ʿAbd al-Qādir wad Dalīl and al-ʿAṭā Uṣūl, Sultan Idrīs fled to Wadai, where he was received by Sultan Yūsuf in his own house, while Abū'l-Khayrāt fled to Sultan Isḥāq Abū Rīsha of Dār Silā, who 'treated him as his own son' and gave him a piece of land to live on.

The only discordant note in the harmony which existed between the rulers of the western frontier was the behaviour of Sultan Abbakr Ismāʿīl of the Masālīt. When Abū'l-Khayrāt fled from Dār Qimr, he camped first at Juruf al-Aḥmar (on the Masālīt–Wadai border) and then at Attamur Sanā (on the Silā–Wadai border). Only when he was expelled by Abbakr did he take refuge in Dār Silā.[75] It is possible that Abbakr was at this point still loyal to the Mahdiyya and that he rid himself of the local Mahdist garrison after the incident with Abū'l-Khayrāt.[76] However, even after the Masālīt had joined the western front in the movement of Abū Jummayza they remained troublesome and reluctant allies, trying to gain advantage over their fellow combatants as much as over their common enemy. Three incidents remembered by Masālīt tradition are evidence of this. The first incident occurred after what is locally remembered as the battle of Ereije in Dār Erenga (the first or second defeat of the *anṣār*):

> They [the Masālīt] clashed with the *anṣār* on a spot called Ereije, and defeated them. They took the kettledrums of the Taʿāyisha, their horses and rifles. Of the rifles they made three piles, for Abū Jummayza said: 'one third is for Sultan Abbakr, one third is for the *firsha*s and those who know how to use firearms, and one third is to be burnt'. The Masālīt heard this. They knew that the Erenga knew nothing about rifles. They therefore put all the superior rifles on the pile they kept for themselves. Then they put a large heap of straw on fire, and during the panic which this created they took possession of the other two piles of arms and clothes as well. They fought over the clothes, so that they ended up by all having a little piece each, which they tied around the hair-tufts [Masālīt: *totoke*] on their heads. Abū Jummayza was angry, because not a single Erengāwī had anything.[77]

The second incident occurred just after Abū Jummayza's death from smallpox. Apparently the Erenga who formed Abū Jummayza's immediate entourage tried to conceal his death, either because they feared that the western front would disintegrate when the truth beame known, or because they were afraid that they would lose their last shreds of political authority. The ruse worked for a while. Whenever Sultan Abbakr came to greet Abū Jummayza, he was told that the *faqīh* was asleep and indisposed to receive him. Eventually Abbakr learnt that the *faqīh* was unlikely ever to wake up again. He became so angry that he cut Abū Jummayza's tent into two with his sword, and revealed his corpse. In the skirmishes between the Erenga and Masālīt which followed, the Masālīt were victorious.[78] The third incident took place when the huge western army marched against al-Fāshir in December 1888. The major elements in the army were the Fūr, led by Abū'l-Khayrāt (whom the *anṣār* regarded as the leader); the Dājū, led by Bakhīt Abū Rīsha; the Wadaians, led by *faqīh* Wābī the Fallātī; and the Masālīt led by Abbakr. During the march the Masālīt treated their allies arrogantly and unjustly and took everything that caught their fancy: a waterskin here, a pair of sandals there, a good horse elsewhere etc. Abū'l-Khayrāt protested against this behaviour, and it was decided that the army would split up. The Fūr, Dājū and Wadaians were to take the southern route to al-Fāshir *via* al-Tawīla, while the Masālīt would take the northern route *via* Ṣarafāya, Konge and Kurma. According to Masālīt tradition this turned out to be to the advantage of the Masālīt. When the *anṣār* and the western front gave battle just outside al-Fāshir, the Masālīt were not there. While their allies were slaughtered, they plundered al-Fāshir, it is claimed, and returned home laden with booty.[79]

The western army was defeated on 22 February 1889, partly as a result of internal divisions, but mainly as a result of the military superiority (in arms, training, leadership) of the *anṣār*. Abū Jummayza's movement thus ended in failure. However, in the period between this defeat and the Mahdist occupation of Dār Masālīt, namely between February 1889 and July 1890, the western sultans tried to patch up the alliance and to bring the Masālīt back into line. The most serious rift in the western front was still that between Sultan Abbakr and 'shadow sultan' Abū'l-Khayrāt. Even ʿUthmān Jānū came to know of it, and reported thus to the Khalīfa in January 1890.[80] The sultans of Wadai, Dār Tāmā, Dār Qimr and Dār Silā all wrote to Abbakr trying to persuade him to reconcile himself with Abū'l-Khayrāt and to cooperate with him (and them) against the *anṣār*.[81] Abū Rīsha's letter was particularly patronizing:

> And you, my son, have become so ambitious that you have proclaimed the sultanate, in spite of the fact that the Fūr Sultanate has not had any of its subjects aspiring to this for a very long time, except for you. Don't allow aggressors such as the *baḥḥāra* and the Turks and their likes such as Zuqal and Jānū to infect you with their dissension (*fitna*). Abandon your ambitions and abandon the foolishness which is in your heart. How can you, my son, because of the first difficulty with your sultan Abū'l-Khayrāt proclaim a sultanate and inform him of this; and cause Muslim blood to be shed on your and their side?[82]

Abbakr's outright hostility towards Abū'l-Khayrāt and his uneasy alliance with his other neighbours cannot be understood without reference to his peculiar position among the rulers of the western frontier. With the exception of the Masālīt Sultanate, whose basis had been laid in 1884 and which Abbakr was trying to consolidate, all the powers making up the wstern front were sultanates and *shaykh*doms of long standing and sanctioned by tradition. During the Ancien Regime, which the western front tried to restore, Dār Masālīt had not formed a political or administrative unit, and had been subject to the Fūr Sultans, of whom Abū'l-Khayrāt was the living and legitimate representative. Abbakr himself had no hereditary status or traditional legitimacy. He was the son of a *faqīh* who had derived his political authority from the Mahdist regime, the sworn enemy of the western front. 'The Mahdi is the Sultan of his time . . . and it is not necessary that he should be Sultan and son of a Sultan,' the Wadai Sultan had written in 1885.[83] It was according to this principle that Ismā'īl 'Abd al-Nabī, and Abbakr after him, had risen to power. As long as they represented the Mahdist regime, there was nothing irregular in their position. However, when Abbakr broke with the *anṣār* and joined those who fought for the restoration of the Ancien Regime, there was no justification for either his position as sultan or for Dār Masālīt's status as a sultanate. In the letter quoted above Sultan Abū Rīsha stated quite unambiguously that Abakr had no business setting himself up as a sultan; that he had always been subject to the Dār Fūr sultanate, and should therefore support Abū'l-Khayrāt, then in exile in Dār Silā. Both oral and written sources confirm that it was Abbakr's legitimacy as a sultan that was at stake in his dealings with his neighbours.[84] The latter denied this legitimacy, and considered Abbakr as an upstart. Since Abbakr could not be a sultan *de jure*, he set out to become one *de facto*. Throughout his reign (1888–1905) Abbakr demonstrated that he was ready to use force to attain his aims. Under the circumstances, one might add, he had little choice but to use force.

The aftermath of the revolt

To what extent the western front was restored is unknown. After the victory of February 1889, 'Uthmān Jānū concentrated the Mahdist war effort upon the Fūr of Abū'l-Khayrāt (who again fled to Dār Silā), and the cattle nomads of the southwest, the Banī Ḥalba, who also fled to Dār Silā, which the *anṣār* were not authorized to enter.[85] In June 1890 'Uthmān Jānū decided to invade Dār Masālīt in order to punish the Masālīt for their disobedience and to obtain food for the soldiers.[86] The months of June and July, the beginning of the rainy season, were always a hungry period in Dār Fūr, since last year's crop had usually been eaten, while the new crop was not yet ripe. Moreover, 1306 H. (1888–9) had been a famine year. The Mahdist troops had eaten all they had been able to seize in the country of the Banī Ḥalba, where they had campaigned, and in the region of Kongyo (near Zalingei), where they had their camp. Only the Masālīt still had supplies of grain. At the end of July 1890 the *anṣār* moved from Kongyo to Chibuke, in Dār Masālīt. From there they trekked through the whole *dār* to collect booty and food, of which they obtained plenty.[87] After their defeat in battle, many Masālīt fled to Dār Silā or Wadai, or hid in the bush and the hills.[88] Abbakr himself fled to Wadai. However, the success of the *anṣār* was short-lived. To the hardships of the rainy season were added the fatal effects of a cholera epidemic. On 29 August 1890, ʿUthmān Jānū wrote to the Khalīfa:

> We inform you, Sir, that since we entered Dār Masālīt, the rains here have not ceased by day or night; the sun is hidden from sight and the cold here is fierce. It rains more than twenty times a day, for each cloud which comes by brings rain. The ground is therefore always wet, the dampness by night is like rain, and the mud is indescribable . . . . One gets bogged down and stuck in the clay up to one's thighs. During our stay here the *anṣār* encountered indescribable hardships; among others the rain which keeps pouring down upon them at all times, to the extent that it falls two days and two nights in a row, and that, when it stops, the sky is overcast; [secondly] the wood which is wet, so that no fires can be lit because of the dampness; [thirdly] the *wādī*s found on the way, which run so fast, are so deep, and keep running so long after the rains have ended, that they resemble rivers; and furthermore the trees, which grow so close together that no road can pass through them, so that some of them must be cut root and branch. These *dār*s are gloomy during the rains and their hardships numerous. . . . Nevertheless, the *anṣār* are perfectly content and vigorous, as if nothing is bothering them. However, the *anṣār* have been afflicted by a serious disease, which struck the *jihādiyya*, the

> Arabs and their families. As a result many *anṣār* died, as many as two hundred, three hundred or more a day. The army has been seriously affected, but we leave the matter to God – Elevated is He – and hope to be rewarded for this in the hereafter by God – may He do what He wants and chooses.[89]

While ʿUthmān Jānū held the harsh natural circumstances responsible for the physical and psychological collapse of the *anṣār*, Masālīt tradition believes in supernatural forces. The *anṣār* were either poisoned by eating a black bull sent to them by the Masālīt or Wadaians, or cursed by the *faqīh*s of Wadai, who prayed for their destruction.[90] The Mahdist army withdrew in disorder. The survivors reached al-Fāshir on 5 October 1890. ʿUthmān Jānū himself died four days later.[91] In the west the Masālīt returned to their *dār* and Sultan Abbakr resumed his efforts to consolidate the Masālīt Sultanate.

Western Dār Fūr and the Mahdist State: (1891–1896)

ʿUthmān Jānū was succeeded by another relative of the Khalīfa, Maḥmūd Aḥmad, who governed Dār Fūr from January 1891 to February 1896 – five years, of which he spent nearly three years outside Dār Fūr.[92] He is remembered as Maḥmūd ʿAsal – *ʿasal* or 'honey' standing for all that is sweet and pleasant – in contrast to his predecessor, who was called ʿUthmān Baṣal – *baṣal* or 'onion' standing for that which is bitter and unpleasant. Maḥmūd indeed dealt gently with the people of Dār Fūr, and in his early and optmistic reports to the Khalīfa he showed not only an interest in law and order, military security and loyalty to the Mahdist regime, but also in the economic wellbeing of the people who had been seriously affected by the famine. From August 1890 to July 1892, the tone of Maḥmūd's reports remained optimistic. Dār Fūr was reported to be quiet, its roads safe, its people once more busily cultivating their fields and rebuilding their villages. In a letter dated 25 November 1891 Maḥmūd looked back on his period of office until then:

> Since I reached these districts, which include Dār Fūr, I have been sparing no pains in discharging my duties regarding religious matters, the spreading of Islam and the settling of

> affairs in the Western district. Thanks to God this was done and the peace reigned everywhere, so that fugitives came back, reinhabited the places they have deserted and went on improving in righteousness and obedience. The said districts flourished.[93]

In order not to jeopardize the economic recovery of Dār Fūr the Mahdist government decided to remit all taxes for the year 1309 H. (August 1891–August 1892) in the whole of Dār Fūr:

> because of our sympathy for you, we today ordered the honorable ʿAbd al-Qādir wad Dalīl, the acting governor of the administrative centre of al-Fāshir, to relieve you of the above-mentioned tax obligations [in cash, grain and *tukkiyyas*], and also to withdraw the *anṣār* soldiers from your country; to treat you gently and friendly, and to regard you as special supporters [of the Mahdiyya], since you, by the grace of God, belong to the pioneers of the Mahdiyya, and have persevered in true love and sincere intentions [towards it].[94]

The situation in the west was politically satisfactory, as it always was when words, not acts, were expected from the western rulers. It was reported that the roads were open and that the Qimr and Tāmā were trading with the *anṣār*. On 26 October 1891 Maḥmūd reported to the Khalīfa:

> As for the tribes of the west, the road leading from them to al-Fāshir is open; all profess allegiance to the Mahdiyya and are fully in touch with us; but Abbakr the Maslātī is the most submissive and obedient [of all], followed by Turjūk the Ḥusaynī, and then the Qimrāwī. All are at present busy collecting the *zakāh*, and after this has been completed they will come to al-Fāshir. At present the *anṣār* appointed by . . . ʿAbd al-Qādir are with them, and several letters from them both to ʿAbd al-Qādir and myself have been received.[95]

Maḥmūd Aḥmad probably measured the different degrees of loyalty of the western rulers by the letters they sent, the promises they made, and the diplomatic and trading missions which were received in al-Fāshir. The rulers of the Qimr and the Banī Ḥusayn sent news that they wanted to trade with Kabkābiyya;[96] Abbakr of the Masālīt tried to ingratiate himself with the new governor by sending two of his brothers to offer Maḥmūd a pact of loyalty, which bound not only the Masālīt, but also – Maḥmūd naively reported – the Qimr, Banī Ḥusayn, Jabal, Girga and other ethnic groups; according to the messengers all these peoples 'were subject to the above-mentioned Abbakr and adhering to the same pact of obedience.'[97]

However, Maḥmūd was not deceived by the promises of the western rulers. As early as 27 May 1891 he complained to the Khalīfa:

> As for the people of the west such as the Maslātī, the Qimrāwī, Turjūk and their like, in accordance with their earlier reluctance *vis-à-vis* the Mahdiyya, they are not inclined to come, although they are the first to send letters and messages. There is no end to waiting for them, although their letters and promises keep coming. Nevertheless we do not despair of their coming, since we know that [in dealing with] people like them [we] require patience and forbearance towards what they do, until they get into hand. Therefore we continued to write to them and to request them [to come], and with God's will they will soon come to us so that their submission will be complete.[98]

When one of the rulers of the western front – the new 'shadow-sultan' ʿAlī Dīnār – eventually did come to al-Fāshir and actually requested to be allowed to make the *hijra*, Maḥmūd Aḥmad's reaction was one of outright surprise:

> ʿAlī Dīnār's request to come is extraordinary and unprecedented for a person like him; his actual coming is even stranger.[99]

Maḥmūd's departure from Dār Fūr was in a way a test of loyalty to the rulers of western Dār Fūr. The Masālīt, Qimr, Banī Ḥusayn, Tāmā and Jabal all remained in touch with the Mahdist administration,[100] but Maḥmūd's prolonged absence did not remain without effects. The sultans of Wadai and Dār Silā resumed their eastward expansion into Dār Fūr; the former established a military base in the country of the Zaghāwa Kobbe, while the latter attempted to bring the Banī Ḥalba and the *shartay*s of southwest Dār Fūr into his sphere of influence.[101] Maḥmūd's absence also allowed old and new conflicts within the western front to come to the surface. The Mahdist correspondence gives only glimpses of these, but for the period from March 1891 to April 1893 there is reference to: a Wadaian invasion of Dār Silā, a Masālīt–Qimr conflict involving the *shaykh* of the Banī Ḥusayn, a Qimr–Tāmā and Qimr–Zaghāwa conflict, and a conflict between the Dājū of Dār Silā and the *anṣār* of the old Fūr leader and Mahdist commander Saʿīd Burūs, which was reported to be the resurgence of an old pre-Mahdiyya feud.[102] Only when Maḥmūd Aḥmad returned to al-Fāshir in March 1893, and when the news of an impending military expedition to the west put a new strain on Mahdist relations with the western frontier, was the western alliance temporarily restored. In June 1893 the western rulers reacted negatively to the request to prepare grainstores and *lubūs* (cotton quilts for horses) for the approaching Mahdist army. The sultans of the Qimr and Masālīt prepared to flee, while those of Dār Silā and Wadai prepared for war.[103] The western rulers had reason to be nervous, for the Mahdist army had its own candidates for the thrones of Dārs Qimr, Tāmā and Masālīt in its train: brothers of the reigning sultans for Dār Tāmā and Dār Qimr, and for Dār Masālīt, Hajjām Ḥasab Allāh, the old rival of Sultan Abbakr's father.[104]

In March 1894 Abbakr broke openly with the *anṣār* and took bloody action against the Mistereng, Hajjām's kinsmen, who were suspected of conspiring with him.[105] In July a Mahdist army expelled the Wadaians from Dār Zaghāwa, defended the Zaghāwa against the Qimr, but suffered a minor defeat at the hands of the latter. This resulted in January 1895 in a new Mahdist offensive, led by Maḥmud Aḥmad himself. The *anṣār* occupied Dār Qimr and Dār Tāmā and put puppets on their thrones. The Mahdist offensive called into being a new defensive alliance of the western rulers, as always engineered by the Wadai Sultan, who did his utmost to provoke the *anṣār* to war. However, the Khalīfa – afraid that another army would fall victim to the hardships of the rainy season in west Dār Fūr – forbade Maḥmūd to attack either Wadai or Dār Masālīt, and ordered him to withdraw to al-Fāshir, where he arrived on 2 September 1895.

Maḥmūd's optimism and patience did not survive this campaign. In January 1896 – after another absence from Dār Fūr – he obtained the Khalīfa's permission to settle the problem of the western frontier once and for all, and even to fight the Wadaians in their own *dār*. In July 1896 the whole Mahdist army of Dār Fūr, stationed in different camps throughout the province, was in readiness and waiting for orders to move against the western front.[106] In the west the sultans bordered on panic. Sultan Abbakr was nervously concentrating and disbanding his army, and Sultan Abū Rīsha had come to the eastern fringe of Dār Silā, probably to guard his frontier against a Mahdist attack.[107] However, the Mahdist campaign never materialized. In the Nile valley the Anglo-Egyptian Reconquest had begun. In November 1896 Maḥmūd Aḥmad was recalled to Omdurman, leaving the administration of Dār Fūr to three *wakīl*s or acting-governors: Umbadda al-Raḍḍī in al-Fāshir, Sinīn Ḥusayn in Kabkābiyya, and Faḍl Allāh al-Daghūr in Dāra. The cancellation of the Mahdist campaign did not restore peace and quiet in the west. On the contrary, the mobilized armies of Dār Silā, Wadai and Dār Qimr, fell upon the Masālīt to punish Abbakr for his lack of support.

Between the Mahdiyya and the western front: Sultan Abbakr's dilemma

Whem Maḥmūd Aḥmad became governor of Dār Fūr, Abbakr had been one of the first to establish friendly relations with the *anṣār* (19 January 1891). In the most significant single event of that year, the 'shadow sultan' ʿAlī Dīnār's surrender to the *anṣār*, Abbakr had no direct part, although his hostility to the pretender to the throne of a restored Dār Fūr Sultanate was no secret to the *anṣār*.[108] When Abbakr finally broke with the latter in March 1894, it was out of annoyance with Mahdist support to Hajjām Ḥasab Allāh, the claimant to the Masālīt throne.

Abbakr's break with the Mahdiyya did not make him automatically a staunch supporter of the western front. Both before and after, he committed acts of aggression against his neighbours. The Masālīt Sultan was notorious enough to be used as a bogey by Sultan Yūsuf of Wadai, when he tried to bully the Banī Ḥusayn into recognizing his overlordship; and he was so feared by his neighbours, that the Tāmā Sultan preferred to face a Mahdist invasion on his own than allow Abbakr into his country to assist him.[109] Not even the Mahdist offensive of January 1895 could bring Abbakr into the western camp. When Maḥmūd Aḥmad invaded Dār Qimr in March 1895, Abbakr only agreed to receive Sultan Idrīs in his country to despoil him of everything and everybody he had with him, his wives, horses, arms and kettledrums. Sultan Idrīs gave a shocked and indignant account of this treacherous act in a letter to Maḥmūd Aḥmad: Abbakr had attacked him in spite of the letters they had exchanged; in spite of the *amān* (promise of safety) Abbakr had given; in spite of the fact that they were related by marriage; and in spite of the fact that Abbakr had made a pact with the Qimr by swearing on the *Qur'ān*:

> We entered his country. My people all dispersed inside his country and we remained with only a few; Abbakr could then get the better of me, and decided to . . . kill me. However, I refused to die a death without honour, and escaped with only my life. I escaped with only a few horses. All that I possessed was taken by Abbakr; my kettledrum and all my movable and immovable goods were taken by Abbakr. I myself went to Dār Borqū.[110]

Abbakr did certainly not rob Idrīs to ingratiate himself with the *anṣār*, for in the same month he managed to raid the Mahdist soldiers in Dār Qimr, to capture the cows they had collected as booty, and to kill the Mahdist commander sent out to recover the animals. Masālīt tradition does not realize that the main thrust of the Mahdist army was not directed against them, but against the Zaghāwa, Qimr and Tāmā; that the soldiers of commander 'Dardama' (Muḥammad Jūda Fāt) did not form the main body of the Mahdist army, but were just a detachment; and that the Mahdist army withdrew to al-Fāshir without avenging Dardama's death not for fear of the Masālīt but by order of the Khalīfa. Abbakr himself seems to have overestimated Masālīt importance as well; hardly had Maḥmūd Aḥmad's returning army reached Dār Zaghāwa, when Abbakr expelled the Mahdist nominee to the Qimr throne, thus clearing the way for his own candidate, Abūkōra walad Nūr.[111]

At this point Wadai Sultan Yūsuf turned the western alliance against the Masālīt to punish Abbakr for his treachery and to force him to give up the goods captured from Idrīs. Wadaian and Dājū troops invaded Dār Masālīt. Abbakr's brother, Tāj al-Dīn, was defeated at Mogornei, the sultanic residence at Dirjeil was reduced to ashes, Abbakr's mother captured in Dār Jabal, while Abbakr himself fled to the eastern fringe of his *dār*. Even there he was pursued by Sultan Abū Rīsha's troops. Help came from an unexpected direction, namely from the Mahdist commander ʿAbd al-Qādir wad Dalīl, who was campaigning in the country of the Banī Ḥalba, to the south of the Masālīt. ʿAbd al-Qādir's approach together with rumours that Maḥmūd Aḥmad himself had left al-Fāshir and was heading for Dār Silā, caused panic in the ranks of the Dājū and Wadaian troops in Dār Masālīt. The invading army hurriedly retreated. However, Abbakr himself feared those who brought relief from the invaders as much as the invaders themselves. Instead of joining the *anṣār* at Keibe or Kabkābiyya, as requested, he returned to Dirjeil. From there, at a safe distance, he composed polite and stylish letters to the *anṣār*, professing his loyalty to the Mahdist cause, and announcing his impending arrival.[112] Formally he remained on good terms with the *anṣār* until Maḥmūd Aḥmad was recalled to Omdurman, and until the Mahdist regime was overthrown. In reality he turned to the Sultan of Wadai for mediation in the war with his neighbours.

Abbakr's situation in January 1896 was the result of a trend which had begun in the late 1880s. During the governorship of ʿUthmān Jānū, Abbakr had managed to steer between Scylla and Charybdis and to stay out of harm's way. During the rule of Maḥmūd Aḥmad, his policy of independence from both the *anṣār* and the western front became so reckless that Abbakr came close to being crushed by both. Only sheer luck saved him from immediate ruin, and only the protection of the sultan of Wadai enabled him to keep his place in the sun. The events of late 1895 confirmed Abbakr's basic dilemma, namely that the enemies of his enemies could not be his friends. His father's deportation, the arbitrary confiscations and arrogant behaviour of the Mahdist garrison in Dār Masālīt, the order to make the *hijra* to Omdurman, while his rival Hajjām Ḥasab Allāh was kept in readiness west of Jabal Marra to take his place, made it impossible for Abbakr to remain in the Mahdist camp. However, he could not wholeheartedly join the western front because of the problem of his legitimacy as sultan. This problem, which was discussed above, lay at the back of the ideological combat which Abbakr waged with his neighbours before and after their invasion of Dār Masālīt. In the letter in which he asked for Mahdist military assistance against his neighbours, Abbakr wrote:

> In this year the Borqāwi and Silāwi came to me, both sharing the same cause. They tried to delude me by saying: 'Enter our

> religion and leave the religion of the Mahdi.' I said: 'No; we follow the Mahdiyya earnestly, while you are sultans of people adhering to traditional religion (*salāṭīn ahl al-ʿādāt*). We shall follow neither your words, nor your religion.'[113]

While himself posing as a properly Muslim, for Mahdist, sultan, Abbakr depicted his neighbours as pagans or nearly so. With the Mahdist administration, for whom anybody who did not adhere to the Mahdiyya was an infidel, this argument might have been valid, but not with the frontier sultans, who prided themselves upon being Muslim rulers and even descendants of the Prophet, as is evident from the long list of self-proclaimed honorary titles with which they introduced themselves in their letters. Even a fanatic Mahdist might have hesitated to put the label of 'adherent to traditional religion' on a ruler like Sultan Abū Rīsha who called himself: 'Commander of the faithful, offspring of the warriors of the Lord, descendant of the noble, comfort of the Muslims, founder of the pillars of religion . . . , who listens to the Lord of the two worlds and follows both the *Sharīʿa* and the *Sunna*.'[114] From the pen of Abbakr, who had himself left the Mahdist camp and waged war against it this was an unforgivable affront. Lacking traditional status himself, Abbakr tried to bring this status into disrepute by associating it with superstition, traditional religion and lack of proper Islamic standards.

This same disdain for the traditional rulers of the western frontier is evident in the anecdote oral tradition associated with the beginning of the invasion of Dār Masālīt towards the end of 1895. It is said tht Sultan Abbakr of the Masālīt deliberately insulted Sultan Abū Rīsha of Dār Silā and provoked him to war by sending him a razor-blade – suggesting that he should circumcise himself – and a *kamfūs* or cache-sex – a garment suitable for women and slaves. No wonder that the one who called himself 'the Commander of the faithful . . . the comfort of the Muslims and founder of the pillars of religion' 'flew into a rage and wept tears of blood', invaded Dār Masālīt and captured and 'married' Abbakr's mother, to let her see for herself whether he was circumcized or not.[115] Although this version of the Dājū–Masālīt war does probably not represent 'wie es eigentlich gewesen', the fact that people have chosen to remember it this way is sufficient to illustrate the present argument. According to another version of the same incident, the war broke out when Abbakr refused to comply with Abū Rīsha's demand for a share of the firearms captured from the *anṣār* by saying: 'You are a sultan and I am a sultan, so why should I give you anything?'[116]

The ideological and political weapons used by Abbakr in the external consolidation of the sultanate were Mahdist faith (*versus* traditional legitimacy), force of arms, and clever political manoeuvring. Abbakr exploited the conflict between the western front and the Mahdist regime for his own ends, and enhanced his own importance to both parties by functioning as an important but unpredictable and undependable factor in the balance of power. Abbakr was the *enfant terrible* of the western front, an unreliable member, but yet a member. His power base at home – the numerical strength of the Masālīt, their access to firearms, horses and slaves, the personality of their sultan and the ways in which he organized the Masālīt state to increase his (and its) power – will be analyzed separately in Chapter Five. However, no matter how strong the Masālīt were at the time of the rise of their sultanate, Wadai was the dominant power of the western front. It is this dominant position which will be discussed below.

Western Dār Fūr and Wadai: informal political dependence and its economic dimension

Wadai and the Mahdist State; rivalry for the western frontier

The Khalīfa's reign, which has been called 'the Taʿāyisha autocracy'[117] was a period of centralization which made itself felt even in the remote western province. The Khalīfa may not have controlled his military governors as effectively as he wished, but the correspondence suggests that his interference in small and big matters was continuous. The governor of Dār Fūr looked for military and political instructions to Omdurman, received much advice and many strict orders from the Khalīfa, and had to send in full and frequent reports – in times of crisis as many as two or three a week. Another element of this centralizing policy was the reorganization of the judicial system in Dār Fūr in 1891–2. Although the new system left considerable powers to the governor, the judicial deputies (*nā'ib sharʿī*) at al-Fāshir and in the outlying districts were examined and evaluated by a committee sent out for that purpose from Omdurman; their appointment or confirmation in their positions was subject to the approval of the Khalīfa and his supreme court. As early as 1885 the Khalīfa had taken cases involving bloodshed out of the governor's jurisdiction; at times even minor cases such as that of the lady who claimed to have been beaten by her husband and therefore asked for divorce, were referred from al-Fāshir to Omdurman.[118]

The Mahdist state, which was in many ways a successor state to the Turkiyya and was, moreover, a state at war, was also centralized economically. The Khalīfa's residence, Omdurman, became not only the administrative but also the economic capital of the Sudan. The Forty Days Road between al-Fāshir (Kobbei) and Egypt was again closed down, Kobbei destroyed, and the goods of the *jallāba* who still traded along the road were confiscated.[119] Dār Fūr's export trade was now completely diverted to the east, to Omdurman. Of the goods sent from al-Fāshir to Omdurman, consignments of salt, lead from the mines at Kutum and Kafōd, cloth (for flags), ostrich feathers, slaves and money are documented in the official correspondence. Omdurman supplied ammunition – the empty cartridges were often sent back to be refilled – and firearms. That it also supplied the Fāshir market with the 'luxury' goods the well-to-do could not do without, is evident from the governor's complaint in March 1891 that there was a shortage of clothing and perfumes on the Fāshir market, and from his request that the Khalīfa open the road to any trader who wanted to come.[120]

Al-Fāshir's relations with Wadai were limited. Like the *shaykh* of the Sanūsiyya in southern Libya, who had ignored the Mahdī's offer to become his fourth *khalīfa*, Sultan Yūsuf of Wadai ('the Borqāwī') had no intention of joining the Mahdiyya and being incorporated into the Mahdist state. After an initial exchange of presents and letters with the first governor, Zuqal, Yūsuf continued to write occasional letters in which he protested his allegiance to the Mahdiyya and denied the accusations levelled at him by Zuqal's successors. However, diplomatic relations went from bad to worse. The second governor, 'Uthmān Jānū, had orders not to start hostile actions against Yūsuf and to continue sending him friendly letters; but both before and during the revolt of the western front in 1888–9 the scarcely veiled hostility and fear of the Wadai Sultan developed into active propaganda for, and involvement in war against the *anṣār*. In letters to the Khalīfa written in August/September 1888 ʿUthmān accused Yūsuf of all possible hostile and irreligious acts, including smoking, drinking, refusing to patch his clothes and preparing for a war. In November 1888, during the revolt of Abū Jummayza, ʿUthmān reported that the enemy used Wadaian horses and a peculiar type of rifle. In February 1889 he sent the Khalīfa the written proof of Yūsuf's hypocrisy: a letter from Yūsuf to Abū'l-Khayrāt, congratulating the latter with his victory over the *anṣār*. Yūsuf's involvement in the revolt was once again proved by the seventy letters ʿUthmān found in the house of Sultan Abbakr of Dār Masālīt in August 1890; Yūsuf had actively campaigned to reconcile the divisions within the western front, encouraging its members to unite against the *anṣār* and promising them moral and military support. The Khalīfa, however, repeated his order not to invade Wadai and to make friends with its sultan.[121]

ʿUthmān's successor, Maḥmūd Aḥmad, added his voice to that of ʿUthmān in denouncing the Borqāwī as the evil genius behind the rebellion of the sultans of the west. Yet, although he received permission to chastise the western front, he had no permission to force the issue with Wadai. In April 1895 he wrote Yūsuf a letter with friendly advice and politely veiled threats:

> We have arrived [in Dār Tāmā], and if we were far away [before], now we have come close; if the road was closed [before], now it is open; and if the Qimrāwī and Tamāwī were determined to wage war upon us before, now their weakness has become obvious. Know that we have not come to destroy or confiscate goods . . . . but to win people for the Mahdiyya.[122]

Two months later Maḥmūd had lost patience with Yūsuf and assured him that only the lack of permission had prevented him from invading Wadai, and that he would not wait even one hour before doing so, once permission came:

> You say 'I don't want them [the *anṣār*] in my *dār*', but the *dār* belongs to God, who said . . . : the land belongs to God and it is inherited by whom he wishes. You incite the people of the west; your messengers are sent out and your letters succeed each other in all directions. Is the region of Dār Fūr perhaps subject to Borqū, and are you not satisfied with your own *dār*s?[123]

However, when Maḥmūd eventually obtained permission to invade Wadai, the Anglo-Egyptian 'reconquest' of the Sudan was on its way, and the Mahdist armies were recalled to Omdurman.

Under these circumstances trade between Wadai and al-Fāshir was not feasible. The roads were officially closed for most of the period 1885–98, but groups of pilgrims and a trickle of traders and spies continued to cross western Dār Fūr from Wadai – as the government found out in 1891, when it cracked down on western immigrants and arrested all of them.[124] In general, however, al-Fāshir faced east, both politically and commercially, while Wadai faced north, towards the Sanūsiyya, which dominated the trade route linking Wadai with Benghazi, Tripoli and Egypt.

After the Turco-Egyptian conquest of Dār Fūr Yūsuf, fearing that Wadai would be invaded next, had remained on the defensive. When the Mahdiyya replaced the Turkiyya, his fears remained the same, but his strategy changed; for the revolt of the western front, which formed a useful buffer between Wadai and the Mahdist state, gave him the opportunity to attack the latter indirectly and to extend his influence further east at its expense. According to the Wadaian *ʿaqīd*s interviewed in 1910:

> Lorsque le Mahdi eut enlevé le Dar For aux Turcs (1884), le Dar Guimr et le Dar Massalit refusèrent la domination Mahdiste et demandèrent la protection du sultan du Ouadaï, notre Seigneur Youssef-el-Chayeb . . . . Notre sultan les prit sous sa protection et chaque année, du vivant de Youssef, ils envoyèrent des présents. A sa mort, ils continuèrent à agir de même avec ses successeurs Ibrahim et Ahmed-El-Gazali. Avec Doude Mourrah, les sultans du Guimr et du Massalit se relachèrent de plus en plus et n'envoyèrent presque plus rien. . . . Il n'y a jamais eu entre le Ouadaï et les sultans Guimr et Massalit aucune convention écrite. Les sultans du Ouadaï y compris Youssef n'ont jamais eu droit de suzeraineté sur les diours [*dār*s] et les sultans de ces pays n'ont jamais été vassaux des sultans ouadaïens. Aucune imposition, aucune redevance ne leur a été fixée par le sultan Youssef. Les sultans du Dar Guimr et du Dar Massalit lui envoyaient ce qu'ils voulaient et comme ils voulaient; ils faisaient bien les choses, parce qu'ils avaient en grande estime notre sultan Youssef, qui leur avait accordé généreusement sa protection et sans condition aucune. Cela nous pouvons le jurer.[125]

The Masālīt also remember that Yūsuf was their sultan's protector, but add that this protection had its price, and that they paid a tribute consisting of horses and slaves. The Masālīt Sultan did not pay a fixed number of each, but the very best of all horses and slaves of the *dār*. For example, Abbakr's horse Marfaʿīn ('the hyaena'), *ʿAqīd* Mudda's horses Sesebān and Fundōqa'l-bint ('the girl's bottom'), and the favourite horse of Abbo Badawī, of whose existence Yūsuf was informed by nomads, were all demanded and paid as tribute or *dīwān*. Another favourite horse could only be retained by blinding one of its eyes and by subsequently writing to Yūsuf whether he really wanted a one-eyed horse? Two prize slaves of Abbakr, Amm Nabūd and Ab Runga, commanders of the *jihādiyya*, were also demanded as tribute. Yūsuf's representative in eastern frontier affairs was the *ʿaqīd al-Maḥāmīd*, Muḥammad Bishāra, who drew up and signed the demands for tribute, which was collected by Abū Āja, or by his successor as regular envoy to Dār Masālīt, *faqīh* Wābī.[126] Sultan Abbakr did not pay much, it was said, but he certainly felt the loss. The Qimr, Zaghāwa and Tāmā were said to have paid a similar tribute, and this is confirmed by written sources.

A number of (undated) letters written by Yūsuf and the *ʿaqīd al-Maḥāmīd* to the sultans of the Tāmā, Zaghāwa Kobbe and Qimr have been preserved. They were probably brought back by Maḥmūd Aḥmad's expedition to western Dār Fūr in 1895, and may therefore well date from the early 1890s.[127] The twenty letters are certainly but a fraction of Yūsuf's correspondence with the frontier sultans, but it is striking that more than half of the letters concern material demands which Yūsuf made upon them. Seven of the eleven letters addressed to Tāmā Sultan Sulaymān Ibrāhīm deal with the latter's reluctance or refusal to send Yūsuf the horses – the number ranges from one to five! – he sent for. The tone of the letters varied from only just polite to very angry, and four of them contained ultimata which allowed the sultan four to six days to pay up, before relations between the two countries were severed.[128] Sending worthless 'presents' was apparently as serious an offence as sending none; the *ʿaqīd* conveyed Yūsuf's displeasure to the Tāmā Sultan because he had sent 'such a worthless and imperfect horse that [even] my slave would not mount it.'[129] Although the standard of living of the western sultans was a far cry from that of the sultans of *1001 Nights*, it was not only the physical possession of a few (superior) horses and slaves that was at stake. The *ʿaqīd* was in fact quite explicit that this was not so in his letter to the Tamāwī: 'I asked you for it [i.e. a good instead of a bad horse] not because we have a shortage of horses, but for the sake of brotherly friendship.'[130] The refusal to pay may well have been a matter of principle as well.

Yūsuf not only demanded *dīwān*, he also functioned as an arbitrator in Abbakr's disputes with other frontier sultans. Sometimes he intervened to Abbakr's disadvantage, e.g. when he ordered Abbakr to give up the kettledrums and wives he captured from the Qimr Sultan in 1895. However, when in the same year the Dājū Sultan Abū Rīsha invaded Dār Masālīt and captured and 'married' Abbakr's mother, Yūsuf intervened in Abbakr's favour. The Queen-Mother was sent back to Abesher, where she was collected by the Masālīt.[131] Yūsuf even had enough authority to order Abbakr to go and fight Sinīn Ḥusayn, the Mahdist governor of Kabkābiyya, it was said, which he did without success.[132]

All this suggests that the ties binding the frontier sultans to Yūsuf were less voluntary than the bond of gratitude and respect mentioned by the Wadaian *ʿaqīd*s interviewed by the French in 1910. Apparently Yūsuf exploited the unrest on his eastern border to extend his political authority eastward. This is how Maḥmūd Aḥmad interpreted Yūsuf's political activities in January 1896:

> He [Yūsuf] has been tempted into something which could not be held against him before, or against his ancestors who have been at the head of the Borqū, namely, taking possession of the western districts which are integral parts of Dār Fūr.[133]

Sultan Abū Rīsha of Dār Silā was certainly doing the same. At the fall of the Dār Fūr Sultanate in 1874 he had annexed Dār Sinyār. During the Mahdiyya he tried to bring the whole area southwest of Jabal Marra into his sphere of influence. Two (undated) letters from his hand to a number of *shartay*s and *malik*s of the area leave no doubt about his political ambitions, 'Know that you were formerly subject to the people of the east [Dār Fūr], but subsequently I took possession of my whole *dār*,' he wrote in the first letter, and in the second:

> We inform you that my son ʿUlmā is coming to you with my letter. Don't ever trouble him, for he is the go-between

> between me and you. You know, my sons, that this is how it goes in this world; formerly you had your own sultan, that of Dār Fūr, but now things have fallen apart and you have become kingless like goats without a shepherd. Everybody is raiding you, the Masalāt, the nomads, and our own people as well. Now I have chosen you for myself; you have the *amān* [promise of security] of God, the Prophet and myself. No one will interfere with you, and if anyone attacks you, you must let me know, for I can deal with him. However, on the arrival of my messengers, you who are mentioned in the letter and all the people of the *ḥākūra*s close to you who are with you, summon everybody and read them my letter. All of you without exception must rise and come to me together and without delay, if you want peace and quiet. By God's will you will find complete tranquillity. If you refuse to come to me and disobey my present order my sons, don't blame me, but blame yourselves. Beware of disobedience and hardheadedness, and greetings as a conclusion.[134]

In April 1892 Maḥmūd Aḥmad reported to the Khalīfa that Abū Rīsha had appointed a man called Ādam Mīr Yaʿqūb of the Fūr as sultan of the area west of Jabal Marra, and that he had written to the inhabitants that he had taken possession of the area.[135] Nevertheless, even Abū Rīsha had to recognize Yūsuf's overlordship. When he refused to give Yūsuf his share of the firearms and horses captured from the fugitive Fūr Sultan ʿAlī Dīnār in early 1891, Yūsuf's troops invaded Dār Silā, drove its sultan from his *dār*, and did not withdraw until he had given up all the spoils of war.[136]

The economic dimension of political domination

Wadai owed its political dominance in this period to many factors of varying significance. Internal factors such as its size, the size of its population and army, the maturity of the state, the power mechanisms by which it maintained itself etc., cannot be studied here. External political factors, namely the defeat of its main rival, the Dār Fūr Sultanate, in 1874, and the power vacuum which resulted from the failure of the Mahdist state to control its western frontier, have been discussed above. It is an external economic factor, the fact that Wadai had better trans-Saharan trade relations with the markets of the Mediteranean and beyond than any of the frontier sultanates, that will be discussed here.

The northern desert route which linked Wadai with Benghazi, Tripoli and Egypt, and led *via* the oases of Jālū and Kufra, dated from long before the period 1885–1900 under study here.[137] It had been discovered in 1809, was further explored between 1809 and 1818, unsafe between 1820 and 1835, and reopened after 1835 by Wadai Sultan Muḥammad Sharīf. Trade expanded after 1850, when the religious brotherhood of the Sanūsiyya became a real power in the Libyan desert and the main organizer and supervisor of the trans-Saharan trade along this road. Trade flourished during the reign of Sultan ʿAlī of Wadai (1848–1876), and reached a climax in the period 1875–1900, partly because the western route from Kanem to Tripoli became unfeasible, and partly as a result of the establishment of the Mahdist state and the closure of the Forty Days Road in the east. The main carriers of the trade were the Majābra and the Zuwayya – called in western Dār Fūr the Fezzān traders – and the main transit ports were the oases of Jālū and Kufra, which were the headquarters of the Sanūsiyya. According to Cordell, the goods carried to Wadai from the north were similar to items traded on other desert routes and included 'arms, ammunition, English cotton goods . . . , Muslim clothing, woollens and draperies from Trieste, silks from France and the Middle East, loaf sugar from France, tea, coffee, drugs, hardware, spices, perfumes, jewellery and many varieties of beads'. Exports consisted mainly of slaves, ivory and ostrich feathers, which became popular in Europe after 1875. Although the exact volume of the trade is unknown, in the period 1890–1900, 200 to 300 camels weekly passed through Kufra.[138]

Before the Mahdiyya, the rulers of the frontier states had obtained import goods either *via* al-Fāshir, which traded with Egypt along the Forty Days Road, or by way of Abesher, which also traded with Egypt either *via* al-Fāshir or along the northern desert route. During the Mahdiyya this changed. The western frontier's political isolation from the political and commercial centre of the Mahdist state led to a relative economic isolation as well. It is true that the *jallāba* residing with the western sultans continued to trade through Kabkābiyya and al-Fāshir for most of the period, but trade followed the vicissitudes of war and politics.

Open warfare made trade impossible, while political rapprochements with the *anṣār* were accompanied by a temporary revival of trade.[139] Yet most import goods of value – in terms of both their price and significance to the western sultans – came from the west and northwest. They included prestige goods and war material, which the sultans must have needed more than before because of their wars with the *anṣār*, and because a new balance of power was being worked out among the frontier sultanates themselves. This was certainly true for the young sultanate of Dār Masālīt.

In the eastern Sudanic belt international or long-distance trade was an affair of state. There were three major factors which determined the organization of foreign trade and enabled the sultans to control it: the problem of insecurity, constraints on the internal market for import goods, and the customary sultanic rights to indigenous products which were – among other things – valuable export goods.

The problem of insecurity

With the possible exception of *faqīh*s and pilgrims, no one could travel outside his homeland and away from his kinsmen without risking to be robbed of possessions, life or freedom.[140] The protection of the rulers (both central and local *ḥukkām*) – it was argued above – was therefore indispensable even in regional trade, and more so when foreign trade and traders were involved. The protection which the sultan offered to foreign traders within the borders of his state was comprehensive. Nachtigal wrote in 1874:

> When in Wadai the time has come for the departure of a caravan to the north, and some of those who want to travel have not succeeded in collecting their debts, they turn to the king who does not delay in announcing clearly to the negligent debtor, whether a high official or a slave, 'If you have not satisfied your creditor by such and such a date, you will go with him as a slave as a substitute for the money you owe him.'[141]

If traders were robbed inside the sultanate, they were fully compensated by the sultan, who would subsequently settle his account with the robbers and their relatives.[142] Of Wadai Sultan Dūd Murra (1902–1909) it was said: 'If a merchant is killed the Sultan is sure to revenge him, and should the merchant kill a native the Sultan himself would pay the bloodmoney.'[143] The obverse of royal protection was royal control and regulation. It was this protection that was at stake when traders refused to play according to the sultan's rules. Those who broke the rules became outlaws and almost certain victims of what may be called licensed banditry. This is implied in the polite letter written in 1901 by ʿAlī Dīnār, the first Dār Fūr Sultan who tried to trade with a European government, to which the principles of foreign trade were alien:

> If you have to send trade goods to my country, I want you to appoint from your side special people, who must come to us for that particular purpose. Impress upon them that they must not sell their trade goods anywhere until they have reached me. If God wills, I will meet them and treat them with respect. Whether they bring little or much, we will buy it from them to their satisfaction, and we will send them back to you while they are full of praise and gratitude towards us, with the necessary letters . . . . However, if they linger on the country roads, which are unsafe, we fear that mishap may befall them from the hands of wrong-doers, and it would be painful for us to have this attributed to our country.[144]

That the mishap referred to in this letter would befall the unauthorized trader by order of the sultan is evident from a letter ʿAlī Dīnār wrote in June 1900 to a subordinate who was supposed to watch the road to Omdurman, *in casu* the head of the Simiyāt:

> We have noticed that you have left the way of obedience and have come to regard yourselves as independent, acting at your own discretion. This is impossible; you cannot act this way. You have ignored our injunction; we impressed upon you with the necessary emphasis not to open the road to those who, without a license, cross your country on their way to Omdurman with slaves and other goods. This matter will shorten your life and cause your destruction, if God wills, for you ignored our injunction. You committed an offence, so prepare yourselves to die if, from this moment onwards, you allow anybody to pass through your country without a license. When a traveller comes to you, stop him. If you find a license on him, fine; if not, arrest him with all he has with him and send him back to us, to be detained. Greetings.[145]

The ideal towards which the sultan strove was to have known merchants, with known goods, travelling along known roads, coming to him in his capital, where they sold and bought under his eyes, until he gave them permission to leave and letters protecting them on the road. Even if sultanic ambitions were not always in keeping with reality, state regulations left only a narrow margin for smuggling, breaking royal monopolies and stubbornness and shrewdness on the part of the merchants.[146] Yūnis Bādis, who traded in Dār Silā in the 1890s, admitted openly that he had little choice but to comply with Sultan Abū Rīsha's urgent 'request' to return a fine slave woman he had just bought to her previous owner:

> The woman did not want to return, nor did I want to give her up, but as the Sultan was the only man through whom I could sell my merchandise, I thought it best to give way.[147]

The sultan regulated the movements of the traders by issuing (or refusing to issue) what amounted to entry- and exit-visa to the caravans and their individual members.[148] He controlled the flow of trade by opening and closing the trade routes at will, either for political reasons (e.,g. a succession crisis in a neighbouring sultanate) or for rather selfish reasons (e.g. to insure a good price for royal goods sent abroad with a private caravan by preventing other caravans from leaving before it).[149] He also directed the flow of trade to the outside by issuing *laissez-passer*s to caravans and traders.[150] These were written requests or orders to neighbouring rulers to protect the merchants; in reality they also prescribed the route the caravan was to take. Outgoing caravans were led by people who were appointed by the sultan and whose function resembled that of ambassadors, 'agents of the state's authority beyond its borders'.[151] In the small sultanates these were usually close relatives of the sultan; in Wadai and Dār Fūr they were usually foreign traders (*jallāba*), who bore the title of *khabīr*.[152]

Inside the sultanate the foreign traders were divided into two categories: those who were residents and those who were not. Both had their own representative – himself a foreign merchant or relative of the sultan – appointed by the sultan for that purpose. The fact that Sultan Muḥammad Sharīf of Wadai (1835–58) ousted all non-resident foreign merchants from the kingdom may imply that resident traders were preferred.[153] The presence of their families and possessions in the capital certainly gave the sultan an extra lever to compel the merchants to obey his rules. The Fezzānī trader who ignored ʿAlī Dīnār's economic boycott of Wadai in 1910 learned this by bitter experience.[154]

There were also restrictions as to whom the merchants could sell their goods. Sometimes the goods imported by each caravan and merchant were recorded at their arrival on the border and/or capital. After their arrival – dramatically announced by gunshots – the traders first had to report to the sultan.[155] The latter always had the first choice of the import goods, samples of which were given to him as 'greeting presents', and the price of which he established himself, usually in a way which pleased the merchant.[156] After the other notables had made their choice, the remaining merchandise might be brought into the marketplace. Some imports, particularly firearms, gunpowder and ammunition, were royal monopolies; they could only be sold to the sultan or with his permission, and could under no circumstances be offered for sale in the market.[157]

Constraints on the internal market for import goods

If the custom which gave the sultan the first choice of imports was one constraint on their distribution, their price was another. In Dār Masālīt of the 1890s for example, a rifle with one hundred bullets cost three slave women; one *wagga* (72.22 grs.) of tea with ten heads of sugar cost five slave women; a medium size bottle of sandal oil cost one to two slaves.[158] A more important constraint on the sale of imports were the sumptuary laws which governed the appearance and behaviour of rulers and ruled, and which made firearms, exclusive clothes etc., the prerogative of the ruling class.[159] Traders who succeeded in evading the royal regulations – as occurred, for example, when indigenous merchants such as the camel nomads of the northern desert participated in the trade – would therefore still have difficulties in finding buyers other than the ruling elite, or even to enjoy the imports in public. If all else failed, the sultan could control their distribution by confiscating them by force. Sultan Abbakr of Dār Masālīt had no qualms about robbing those who were rivals to his power or prestige.

Sultanic rights to the most valuable export goods

A third determinant of the organization of foreign trade was a combination of two factors: the organization of the surplus extraction (taxation in kind) inside the sultanate, and the kinds of goods in which the price of imports had to be paid. Since the desert route was long and arduous, and transport primitive and costly, the number of products which were valuable enough to make their export worthwhile was limited. In general the foreign traders therefore only accepted ivory, ostrich feathers, rhinoceros-horn, slaves and coined money in return.[160] Although the regular (Islamic) taxes levied by the central governments of the eastern Sudanic belt yielded mainly grain and cattle (and in some cases slaves), there existed a host of customary dues by which the sultan obtained all the local produce of which he and his household were in need, and a part of those products for which a particular community was famous. He had moreover customary rights to certain products which not only gave prestige and power at home but were also highly valued as export goods abroad.[161] For example, all the sultans of the area had a right to one of the two tusks of every elephant found dead or killed within the state's boundaries.[162] Royal monopolies on exportable goods existed, but were not a general practice. Sultan ʿAlī of Wadai, for example, who reigned from 1858 to 1874, exercised a monopoly over the ivory of Dār Kūtī; the slaves of Dār Kibet were reported to be a royal monopoly as well.[163] As for slaves, official state-sponsored slave-raiding expeditions were organized both in Wadai and Dār Fūr, and – between 1888 and 1905 – in the Masālīt Sultanate. In the sultanate of Dār Fūr these expeditions were a royal monopoly farmed out by the sultan to high dignitaries of state, while in Wadai the sultan exercised more direct control.[164]

For the larger sultanates whose capitals became secondary distribution centres, state control of long-distance trade and traders was a significant element not only of their internal but also of their external policy. By favouring one route over another, or by closing certain routes, the sultan could control the access to imports – including firearms and ammunition – of the smaller kingdoms on his border.

In the period 1885–1900 the frontier sultans obtained goods imported from Egypt and Benghazi through three channels: as diplomatic presents from Sultan Yūsuf; from Fezzān traders *via* Abesher; and from Fezzān traders directly from Kufra. Obligatory gift-giving was an important element of diplomatic relations both between rulers of junior status and their overlord, and between rulers of equal status. The diplomatic exchange of presents was a function of political relations. It is therefore not surprising that there is hardly any mention of presents exchanged between the Mahdist government and the western frontier states, and that Sultan Abbakr of Dār Masālīt, who was still fighting for a place in the sun, was very sensitive to the kinds of presents he received; a present of 'old slaves, bad horses and broken rifles' from the Qimr Sultan in March 1896 was a *casus belli.*[165] The presents exchanged between the frontier sultans usually included some import goods, but were not very large. Those exchanged between them and their overlord Yūsuf were substantial enough to deserve the name diplomatic trade.[166] It is noteworthy that Yūsuf himself referred to his written demands for tribute both in terms of gifts made for the sake of friendship and brotherhood, and in terms of commercial transactions, *al-bayʿ wa'l-shīra'* (purchase and sale). For example, when the Tāmā Sultan had eventually complied with his demand, he wrote back:

> Your people have arrived and we have received the two horses and camels. May God bless you and reward you for this. You have not been unfair to us. We have always expected you to be a brother and friend to us, for our country is one, and we are one in spirit. That is why we demanded the horses from you. You have treated us fairly, so that if you are in need of anything, we will obtain it for you, if God wills. I have only one demand from you, that is, whenever there is a horse which I fancy, to buy it from you; but there is no debt between us. That is my opinion in regard to you, but you do not understand [the meaning of] brotherhood and friendship. May God assist us [in our dealings] with you. Furthermore, coming your way for friendship's sake are two garments (*thawb*s), *sūl* and *salam*, a double piece of *ʿalaj*, a piece of cloth number seven, drawers of *jōkh*, a double piece of *dabbalān*, and clothing for the owner of the horse, for that is our custom when a horse is sold.[167]

Gifts of import goods were the obverse of the payment of tribute. On another occasion Yūsuf sent the Tāmā Sultan a fully equipped horse – an extremely valuable present – two burnooses and high-quality cloth of the types *shīt*, *dabbalān*, *'alaj* and *jōkh*. To the sultan of the Zaghāwa Kobbe he sent an even more substantial gift of high quality imported cloth and five camel loads of gun-powder.[168]

The volume and value of diplomatic trade was small compared to the trade carried by the Fezzān. The majority of the Fezzān traders traded through Abesher, their main trading-partner, and proceeded from there to the frontier states to sell what was left over. Some, however, traded directly with the frontier sultans. In the 1890s as after the Mahdiyya Sultan Abbakr of Dār Masālīt, for example, had his own Fezzān traders and a direct route to Kufra, which avoided Abesher and led through the Tāmā Sultanate, which was small and weak:

> The son of the Sanūsī is at a place called al-Kufra at a distance of twenty-five days from Borqū. The Borqū are sending [people] to him; the Qimrāwī has forbidden [his subjects to use] the road from his country [to Kufra]; as for the Maslātī, his people are constantly coming and going to them, and the road between the two is open.[169]

The Sultan of Dār Silā further south depended more directly on Abesher for access to import goods. He therefore attempted to diminish his economic dependence on Yūsuf, or – as the source said – to obtain firearms from Libya without interference from Yūsuf, by attempting to open a trade route to the north *via* Dār Tāmā. The Tāmā, who feared the consequences of such a move, refused, and *faqīh* Ḍalma, the envoy of the Dājū Sultan, received a merciless beating and became the laughing-stock of the whole western frontier:

> faqīh Ḍalma daqqūh, daqqūh
> Lammā ḥārat wa bālat, khallūh.
>
> *faqīh* Ḍalma was given a severe beating
> not until he began to shit and piss
> did they let go of him.[170]

Two of the three channels through which the frontier states obtained imported goods could be closed by Yūsuf immediately and effectively, if he chose to do so. As for the third route, if the occasion arose, Yūsuf had enough leverage over the bulk of the Fezzān traders to effect a boycott of the smaller states. That the political use of economic weapons was not foreign to the sultans of this area and time-period is evident from Yūsuf's ultimatum to the sultan of Dār Tāmā. If the latter would not immediately hand over the three slaves with their slave wives and rifles, 'no one from your *dār* will enter ours and *vice versa* . . . and if anybody from you or from your country will come here, you will have to blame yourselves for the consequences.'[171] That an economic boycott of the frontier states was feasible was demonstrated by ʿAlī Dīnār in the years following 1909, which will be discussed below.[172] Sultan Yūsuf never went as far as ʿAlī Dīnār. The frontier states, harried by the Mahdist armies for almost a decade, needed his protection and had to pay the price, namely, some of their most valuable military resources. Yūsuf, for his part, needed them as a buffer against the same Mahdist armies.

Sultanic control was never absolute. Yet, since trade was in principle administered trade, economic issues were intertwined with political issues. Wadai's formal ascendancy over the frontier states was reinforced by Sultan Yūsuf's dominant position in the long-distance trade of the area. How important this foreign trade was to the smaller states will – with regard to Dār Masālīt – be discussed below.

Chapter 5

The rise of the Masālīt Sultanate from within: Sudanic tradition re-enacted

The previous chapter contained an analysis of the connection between the rise of the Masālīt Sultanate and the Mahdiyya (both as a faith and a centralizing state). The rise of the sultanate coincided with and was connected with the overthrow of the Turco-Egyptian regime by the Mahdist state. The founder of the Masālīt Sultanate was an agent of the new Mahdist regime. His son and successor, involved in an ideological battle with the neighbouring sultans, defended his country's (and his own) new status by referring to his Mahdist faith. Moreover, the wars of the Mahdiyya – the struggle between the western front and the Mahdist state, and the precarious balance of power which came into existence as a result – enabled the Masālīt to consolidate their sultanate through power politics and clever diplomacy.

The present chapter deals with the internal consolidation of the sultanate. An analysis of Ismā'īl 'Abd al-Nabī's rise to power is followed by a description of the administrative system which developed during the reigns of Ismā'īl and his successor, and which was patterned on an old Sudanic tradition. The chapter concludes with a discussion of the impact of the foundation of the state upon social stratification in Dār Masālīt.

Ismā'īl 'Abd al-Nabī, founding father of the Masālīt Sultanate

The overthrow of Hajjām Ḥasab Allāh, it was argued in Chapter Three, was the result of a combination of internal and external factors. Hajjām was deposed because his rule was experienced as oppressive, and because the regime to which he owed his leading position was overthrown by the *anṣār*. Since the *firsha* of the Fukkunyang – the most important clan after that of Hajjām – was compromised by his association with Hajjām and the Turks, the Masālīt turned to a local *faqīh* who had joined the Mahdiyya at an early stage, Isma'īl 'Abd al-Nabī of the Masālīt Gernyeng.

From the written sources it is known that 'Ismā'īl 'Abd al-Nabī al-Maslātī' was appointed Mahdist agent 'for the western region as far as the borders of Borqū [Wadai]', by the Mahdist governor, Zuqal, when he left al-Fāshir in January 1886.[1] Zuqal only confirmed Ismā'īl in a position he already occupied, for already in August 1885 Ismā'īl ranked on the list of Dār Fūr authorities who were summoned to make the *hijra* to Omdurman as 'al Amil Ismail Abd al Nabi, head of the Masalit'.[2] According to Masālīt tradition Ismā'īl ruled for four years, i.e. came to power in 1884. Although Ismā'īl's loyalty to the Mahdiyya was called exemplary, and although he received a letter of praise from the Khalīfa in October 1886, he was ordered to come to al-Fāshir. After excuses and delays Ismā'īl finally arrived in al-Fāshir in May 1888. There he fell ill, but on 16 September 1888 – without having been allowed to return to Dār Masālīt to collect his followers – he was sent to Omdurman in the company of the Mahdist commander al-Bishārī Rīda.[3] Because of Ismā'īl's popularity among the westerners, the governor, 'Uthmān Jānū, had been obliged to give him a splendid welcome. 'Uthmān himself did not press the Khalīfa to retain Ismā'īl in Omdurman indefinitely. Another Mahdist agent in the west, however, explicitly referred to Ismā'īl's *ḥubb al-riyāsa* ('love of leadership' or 'taste for power') and requested the Khalīfa to personally invite Ismā'īl to make the *hijra* to Omdurman because 'his presence here only causes trouble.'[4] From September 1888 onwards the Mahdist correspondence is silent about Ismā'īl; only the letters of his son and successor Abbakr, written in January 1896, make it clear that Ismā'īl never returned.

While the Mahdist documents provide a rough outline of Ismā'īl's career, the details are provided by the oral sources. According to the essay written by Ismā'īl's grandson, 'Alī Ḥasan Tāj al-Dīn, Ismā'īl was a descendent of the Khuzzām Arabs, who had come to Dār Masālīt from Tunis by way of the Batḥa area in Chad. One of his ancestors, Muḥammad Sāja came to Dirjeil and established a *khalwa*, which owed its importance to its location on the route to Mecca and to the western pilgrims it thus attracted. The direction of the *khalwa* passed from father to son, until it fell to ʿAbd al- Nabī, Ismāʿīl's father, in the fourth generation. ʿAbd al-Nabī wanted to learn more than just memorizing and reciting the *Qur'ān*, so he went to El Obeid, where he was initiated into the Ismāʿīliyya brotherhood (a branch of the Sammāniyya), by Ismāʿīl al-Walī (1793–1863). After finishing his studies, ʿAbd al-Nabī returned to Dār Masālīt. He named his son from this period after his teacher in El Obeid, Ismāʿīl. When Ismāʿīl was fourteen years old, he had memorized the *Qur'ān*. Badly treated by his older half brother, he picked up his slate and travelled westwards in search of more knowledge. After three years of peripatetic studies in Wadai and Borno he decided to make the pilgrimage to Mecca. However, when he passed through Dār Masālīt his brother Ibrāhīm persuaded him to come to Dirjeil and to take over the direction of the *khalwa* at Ibrāhīm's death.[5]

Although ʿAlī Ḥasan's essay has the advantage of being based on oral sources, its concern to prove Ismāʿīl's Arab descent, high standard of learning and saintly character makes it an unreliable source. According to oral sources collected by the present author Ismāʿīl was born in Dirjeil, where his father ran an important *Qur'ān* school (*masīk* or *khalwa*). Ismāʿīl became a *faqīh*, like his father, and in this capacity he travelled to Dār Silā, Wadai, Dār Jabal and Dār Erenga, earning a living by writing amulets and *maḥāya* for the people. For some years he settled in Dār Jabal where he had a wife. During a drought in the late 1870s, however, he left the wealth in goats he had accumulated in someone's care and went to Wadai. There he studied religion and survived the drought by offering his services to the local people. During this period the *khalwa* of Dirjeil was run by Ismāʿīl's halfbrother Ibrāhīm Burām, and it was not until the latter's death that Ismāʿīl took over. Although the *khalwa* did not specialize in any specific Islamic science, many students, *faqīh*s and pilgrims visited it. They were hospitably received, Masālīt tradition says, by Ismāʿīl and his many wives.[6]

When the Mahdī proclaimed himself, Ismāʿīl – together with some colleagues and relatives – went to visit him either in Gedir or – which is more likely – in El Obeid.[7] He came back with a new religious message. One of the texts he brought back is still remembered today:

Allāhumma 'nṣur al-Dīn
wa ayyid al-Mahdī al-amīn
wa ahlik al-kuffār al-mushriqīn
aʿdā'aka aʿdā' al-dīn
yā rabbanā (al-)ʿalamayn
amīn

Allāhumma 'nṣur dīn al-Islām
wa ahlik al-kuffār al-li'ām
bi-ḥurmati nabīka wa mahdīka
afḍalu ṣalāti wa salām
dhū al-jalāla wa'l-ikrām

Allāhumma baddid shamlahum
wa farriq jamāʿatahum
wa zalzil aqdāmahum
wa nakkis aʿlāmahum
wa-'qtul aṭfālahum
hum wa-awlāduhum
ghanīma li'l-muslimīn
amīn

. . . .
istajib duʿā'anā
wa-lā taruddanā khāyibīn
yā arḥam al-rāḥīmīn
amīn.

Oh God, make the religion victorious
and support the true Mahdī
and destroy the unbelieving polytheists
your enemies, the enemies of religion
oh Lord of the two worlds
amen

Oh God, make the religion of Islam victorious
and destroy the ignoble infidels
in the honour of your Prophet and your Mahdī
the most excellent prayers and blessings
[You are the] Possessor of Majesty and Honour

O God, disperse their gathering
and scatter their crowd

and make their feet stumble
and bring down their banners
and kill their children
they and their sons
are booty for the Muslims
amen

. . . .
Answer our prayers
and do not turn us back unsuccessfully
Oh most merciful of the merciful
amen[8]

The Mahdī had asked Ismāʿīl whether the Masālīt knew the *shahāda* (profession of faith). When Ismāʿīl replied that they knew it in their hearts but could not read or recite it, the Mahdī had instructed him to teach the people of the west how to recite both *shahāda* and *jalāla* (praise songs) in choruses.[9] Apparently Ismāʿīl and his colleagues succeeded in doing this at an early stage. When the Masālīt in 1883–4 marched against Hajjām, Hajjām heard them coming and sneered at those 'who bleat like sheep whose lambs have been taken away'.[10]

Ismāʿīl also conveyed the Mahdī's prohibition against fermented drinks and tobacco, as is illustrated by a popular jingle:

Sayyidnā jāb jawāba
khallū al-khamr wa'l-tāba
yā Allāh
nasīrū ʿand al-imām nazūrū
yā Allāh.

Our lord brought a letter
abandon liquor and tobacco
oh God,
we will go to the *imām* to visit him
oh God.[11]

Ismāʿīl's role in the overthrow of Hajjām was only indirect. The army which attacked Hajjām in Mogornei was led by the Fukkunyang, although it included many other clans of northern Dār Masālīt. Ismāʿīl himself did not take part in either the battle of Mogornei, in which Hajjām was put to flight, or the battle of

Gorase, in which his return with Turco-Egyptian assistance was frustrated. Yet Ismāʿīl's role in mobilizing the people and in raising the morale of the warriors is well attested:

> Ismāʿīl collected an army, appointed *ʿaqīd*s (captains) and lined them up, each *ʿaqīd* with his own men. He called *faqīh*s, who said prayers (*duʿā'*) and washed *Qurʾān* texts written on wooden slates off into a water jar (*zīr*). Then he summoned each *ʿaqīd* with all his men to come and dip the tips of their spears in this water. When all had done so, the water jar broke. Ismāʿīl blessed them with his rosary, saying: 'Victory comes from God'.[12]

After the battle of Mogornei the Fukkunyang war leader Isāgha Choko offered the leadership to Ismāʿīl, it was said, because the Fukkunyang had too few powerful men and lived too isolated to give the Masālīt a sultan.[13] The story may well be a later rationalization, invented by the Gernyeng, for there is evidence suggesting that there was competition between Ismāʿīl and the Fukkunyang. The latter had not only borne the brunt of the battles with Hajjām, but had also been the leading clan during the Ancien Regime. When Isāgha Choko was killed in the battle of Gorase, Ismāʿīl's reaction was: 'today our authority (*ḥukm*) has been consolidated.'[14]

Ismāʿīl reigned for four years. He ruled the Masālīt homeland and the area inhabited by the Arab groups to its northeast. To what extent he ruled Dār Jabal and Dār Erenga is not clear. It was said that he won a military victory over the Erenga at Ṣarafāya, and that he replaced the *firsha* of Dār Jabal with his own candidate. However, it was not until 1889 that Abbakr effectively and permanently incorporated the two areas into the sultanate.[15]

Ismāʿīl left Dār Masālīt in May 1888. The Mahdist correspondence suggests that he had become too powerful and independent to be left in place. According to Masālīt tradition Ismāʿīl was summoned to Omdurman because Hajjām Ḥasab Allāh had lodged a complaint with the Khalīfa, saying that Ismāʿīl was just 'a *faqīh* and the ṣon of a *faqīh*', and had usurped his authority. Hajjām was put in the right, it was said, because he could call to witness a number of ex-officials of the Turco-Egyptian administrative establishment of Kulkul and Kabkābiyya: ʿUmar wad Tirhō, Abbo Jiddo Saʿd, Ḥasan Umm Kadōk and others.[16] Ismāʿīl was imprisoned and died in Omdurman. For a while, it seems, the *anṣār* put their hopes in Abbakr, Ismāʿīl's son and successor. However, from August 1890, at the latest, they were grooming Hajjām Ḥasab Allāh to replace him.[17]

When Ismāʿīl left for al-Fāshir in May 1888 he was still loyal to the Mahdiyya. Even if he went reluctantly, he went of his own accord, and was given a resounding welcome in al-Fāshir. While in al-Fāshir, it was said, Ismāʿīl grew disappointed with the changes which had taken place since the Mahdī's death – changes, so he believed, which had replaced the religious ideals of the Mahdī with the aspirations for power and temporal gains of the Khalīfa. He was probably disappointed as well that he was not allowed to go back to Dār Masālīt to collect his followers.[18] To his son Abbakr, who was sent back, he gave the advice 'to stay in peace with those who keep the peace with you, to make war upon those who make war upon you; but if the Baqqāra [i.e. Khalīfa's clansmen] come, do not submit.'[19] Abbakr was sent back from al-Fāshir to rule Dār Masālīt during his father's absence. It was said that he was sent in the company of the Mahdist commander ʿAbd al-Qādir wad Dalīl, who went out to the western frontier to collect livestock for the *anṣār*. When they reached Kabkābiyya and were told that 'shadow-sultan' Abū'l-Khayrāt was in the southwestern part of Dār Masālīt, Abbakr was ordered to go and fight him. In the meantime the other *anṣār* marched against Dār Tāmā. Abbakr allegedly sent an army, but returned to Dirjeil himself.[20]

Until then the Masālīt had not openly broken with the Mahdist administration, but now they did. The story of how this occurred is remembered in colourful detail. At the time there was a Mahdist garrison in Dār Masālīt. Its 'behaviour was very bad, like that of Hajjām', it was said. 'They entered the village and confiscated grain etc. The Masālīt refused to accept this, for that was not what they had driven out the Turks for.'[21] The sign for the revolt was given by Ḥasan Kunji – Ismāʿīl's servant and later Abbakr's *wazīr* – whom Ismāʿīl secretly sent back from Omdurman to tie the 'ribbon of authority' around Abbakr's wrist, and to convey Ismāʿīl's message 'to kill the Turks, but not to kill the *anṣār*'. The Masālīt then summoned the *ra's miyya* (commander) of the *anṣār*, who bragged to his men: 'Is that black calling me? This very moment I will go and cut his throat.' The Masālīt grabbed him, took his arms, and soon made him pipe down. When the whole force had been disarmed, all – except for the slave soldiers, who were retained – were provided with sandals and waterskins and ushered out of the country.[22] Thus the Masālīt left the Mahdist camp and joined the opposition that was gathering around Abū Jummayza.

Ismāʿīl's qualifications for leadership

Ismāʿīl's main qualifications for leadership stemmed from his being a *faqīh*. First of all Ismāʿīl was a *faqīh* under a new regime which had been brought into being by a *faqīh*, the Mahdī, whose agent Ismāʿīl was. Secondly, Ismāʿīl was a scion of a local 'holy family' of long standing. Ismāʿīl belonged to the Dōlong section of the Gernyeng. The ancestor of the Gernyeng Dōlong, it was said, was *faqīh* Ṣāliḥ, a powerful *faqīh*, famous for his ability to make rain by means of the *amm dallu* – a charm consisting of an Islamic text put in a calebash (*dallu*) which was hung in a tree. *Faqīh* Ṣāliḥ's son, Muhājir, was a famous healer. When people who were ill were washed with water containing the ink of his prayer texts, they were cured. Their skill and prestige brought Ṣāliḥ and Muhājir considerable wealth (including grain, livestock, slaves and wives) and in the end, *ḥukm* or administrative authority, for Muhājir was allegedly appointed as *sambei* of the Gernyeng Dōlong by the Dār Fūr Sultan or his representative in the west. The drumchiefs (*malik*s) of the Gernyeng of the area were subordinate to the *sambei*, who was in turn subordinate to the *firsha* of the Fukkunyang.

One informant suggested that the *ḥukm* of Ismāʿīl, Abbakr and their successors, was a continuation of the *ḥukm* of the *sambei*, which had its origin in religious prestige.[23] However, this interpretation is problematical; Ismāʿīl was not a direct descendant of the *sambei* and he did not inherit the authority or power of the *sambei* (and *malik*s) peacefully, but took it by force. The last *sambei*, Sulaymān Kijikinang, was executed for having allied with Hajjām and probably – since none of Hajjām's other supporters were killed – for being a rival and threat to Ismāʿīl's own power. Ismāʿīl also curtailed the power of the *malik*s, although the right to collect the *zakāh* of the Dirjeil area was not taken from them until the reign of Abbakr, 'whose kettledrum (*naḥās*) broke their *dinggars*.'[24] Ismāʿīl attempted to associate the sons of the *sambei* and *maliks* of the Gernyeng with the new regime by incorporating them into the new elite. However, their opposition to Abbakr suggests that they regarded the Masālīt Sultan as an usurper of, rather than heir to their *ḥukm* over the Gernyeng. Rather than regarding Ismāʿīl heir to the *ḥukm*, prestige and power of the *sambei* and the *faqīhs* Ṣāliḥ and Muhājir, one might regard his and their rise to a position of political authority as parallel developments, demonstrating once more the opportunity for social mobility inherent in the position of *faqīh* in the Sudan. One might argue that Ismāʿīl came to power not because he succeeded to a line of traditional hereditary rulers, but because he missed such a traditional, ethnically defined power base, and was hence less entangled in Masālīt inter-clan rivalries. Ismāʿīl's great-grandson took this interpretation *ad absurdum* by arguing in his essay that Ismāʿīl came to power after a general democratic election.[25]

Ismāʿīl is mainly remembered for his religious activities. He taught the Masālīt to chant the *shahāda* and *jalāla*; he ordered the people to make mosques (*masīks*) and appointed *imāms* for them.[26] He ordered them to pray and to observe the fast. The latter is illustrated by a story about the people of Konyose, the area around Gokor, south of El Geneina, which is Nyerneng territory:

> When Ismāʿīl succeeded Hajjām, he ordered the people to pray and fast, but the people of Konyose did not want to hear about fasting. Then it was rumoured that Hajjām was once more advancing against Ismāʿīl and an army gathered to fight him. When the rumour proved false, Ismāʿīl diverted the army from its original purpose and ordered it to give a sound beating to the people of Konyose, who refused to observe the fast. The punishment was followed by a decree that everybody who broke the fast again must pay a fine of one cow for every day he did not fast.[27]

Ismāʿīl also prohibited the use of tobacco and *marissa* (local beer), and implemented another proclamation of the Mahdī by reducing the brideprice from ten cows to two cows for a virgin wife and one cow for any other wife.[28] Until today the ladies of the extended royal family are very proud of having been married off according to Mahdist practice and regard this as another proof of their superior Islamic standards. The commoners, in contrast, often paid the rest of the bridewealth in secret.[29] The reduction of the bridewealth was a serious financial setback for the mothers of desirable daughters such as Rafa, the Meidob girl living in Dirjeil in the 1880s. When the new law came into force, Rafa had just refused a suitor who had offered a substantial bridewealth in the hope of finding an even better match. She expressed her regret in a song:

> Mahdiyya ẓahar
> takākī biqā baqar
> yā ammī tijārnā inkasar
> sīd khayrī yijīb majīdī ḥajar.
>
> The Mahdiyya has appeared
> *tukkiyya*s have come in place of cows
> oh mother, our trade has been destroyed
> my lover brings stone dollars.[30]

Other social practices Ismāʿīl prohibited were the traditional religious ceremonies which have been labelled 'pre-Islamic survivals'. These ceremonies were held at specific shrines – usually stones, hill tops, caves or big trees – to ask God for rain (when the millet was in the fields), for wind (when it was winnowing time), for the change of heart of an unresponding beloved, for children, for a prosperous reign, etc. That these 'pre-Islamic survivals' had been islamized is evident from the song used during the rainmaking ceremonies held at Ḥajar Jarkonei, close to Dirjeil:

> Mundīmini dīri nāganong
> bararōk nirāgo kei keirendong
> lā illāhi illā'llāh
> Muḥammad rasūl Allāh.
>
> Our God, listen to the noise
> of the he- and she-camel
> There is no God but God,
> Muḥammad is the Prophet of God.[31]

Ismāʿīl forbade these practices and blocked the path leading to the shrine of Ḥajar Jarkonei. He did not have much success, and even Sultan Baḥr al-Dīn (1910-51) still thought it necessary to cut down a sacred tree in Beida to put an end to the pagan rites performed at its foot.[32]

The image of Ismāʿīl preserved by oral tradition is a lively one, showing many details. It shows Ismāʿīl's two protruding front teeth, which gave one of his brides such a bad scare; it shows his ring and his nice, clean *jallābiyya* of *kalkaf*, which went with the status of *faqīh*, and which were reason enough for the Masālīt Majarang to attack and rob him.[33] Yet the image is idealized and presents Ismāʿīl in pastel colours, as a saintly, just, humble and peaceloving man. The image is maybe not false, particularly if Ismāʿīl is compared with his more ambitious, powerful and tyrannical son. However, it is incomplete, for Ismāʿīl was certainly interested in power. By conscious political acts and a definite administrative policy Ismāʿīl laid the foundation and determined the basic features of the Masālīt state, which reached full development during the reign of Abbakr.

Founding the state

In the documents Ismāʿīl called himself – and was called – *ʿāmil al-Mahdī* (Mahdist agent) in Dār Masālīt.[34] The title of *ʿāmil* came into use in May 1884, replacing that of *amīr* used until then. Whether Ismāʿīl had originally adopted the title of *amīr* is unknown. It is not unlikely, for his son Abbakr styled himself in a letter to the Mahdist administration in 1896: '*amīr* Abbakr Ismāʿīl, Mahdist agent in the district Masalāh'.[35] Ismāʿīl is remembered as *sayyidnā* (our Lord), the common way of addressing a learned *faqīh*. However, his contemporaries used to refer to him as well as *jubbāy*, 'the one to whom people bring whatever he demands', used as an equivalent of sultan in most of the frontier area and Wadai.[36] Although Ismāʿīl's influence, before he became sultan, rested mainly on his prestige as a *faqīh*, after 1884 he laid the foundation for the basic institutions of the Masālīt Sultanate. The three groups of people who became the pillars of his regime were: his own Gernyeng kinsmen; those Masālīt who came home after employment by the Turco-Egyptian administrators of Kulkul and Kabkābiyya; and a network of *faqīh*s.

That Ismāʿīl understood the truth of the saying that 'no one can sit alone and be a chief' is evident from his policy towards his own clansmen, the Gernyeng. From the very start Ismāʿīl made himself their undisputed ruler by suppressing the power of the *sambei*, who was executed, and of the *malik*s of the Gernyeng of the Dirjeil area. At the same time, however, he had to absorb the power of these traditional local rulers by recruiting their sons into the new ruling elite (through grants of administrative estates) and the new royal family (through intermarriage). Not only the Gernyeng of the Dirjeil area were closely associated with the new regime. The Gernyeng Asumang, who had their *dinggar* in Duwei (now in Chad), were summoned to Dirjeil and were settled there. Of the Gernyeng Salāmī, who had a *dinggar* on the Fūr side of the Wādī Azūm, a number of individuals were given important administrative positions. Thus the Gernyeng became the core of the new central government.[37]

When the Turco-Egyptian regime had conquered the Dār Fūr Sultanate and had established an administrative centre at Kulkul (later Kabkābiyya), a number of Masālīt youths entered their service. Most of them became soldiers and learned military discipline and new fighting techniques, including the use of firearms. Even before the surrender of Slatin and the fall of the Turco-Egyptian regime in Dār Fūr, Muḥammad Khālid Zuqal had come to the soldiers in Kulkul with the message 'that the Mahdī had manifested himself in Khartoum, that the world had become Islam, that they should not obey the Turks, and that everybody should go home, should pick up his gun and go home to his relatives.'[38] Those who returned to Dār Masālīt attached themselves to Ismāʿīl, bringing both their rifles and their skill to use them. Although they had been ordinary soldiers in Turkish service, they became important figures at Ismāʿīl's court, and a source of strength for the new sultan. Some of them received important administrative positions. Ḥasan Kunji became Abbakr's *wazīr*, *bāsī* Aḥmad ʿUmar Abū Lafta (of the Gernyeng Dōlong), who had earned his nickname in the service of ʿUmar wad Tirhō, governor of Kabkābiyya, became governor of the district of Kajenggessa. *Faqīh* Arbāb Barsham (of the Jabal) was one of the sultan's envoys to the sultan of Wadai. *Bāsī* Bukhārī (whose mother was related to Ismāʿīl's mother), became governor of the district of Indirrabirro. *ʿAqīd* Mudda Ab Zokko and his brothers (Masālīt-Lisang), Bakhīt Kurjūk (Masālīt-Mandara) and others fulfilled more purely military functions. Although these men were free Masālīt, their function was that of slaves; that is to say, they were comparable to the *jihādiyya* (professional slave soldiers trained in the use of firearms) in the armies of the *anṣār* and – in the 1890s – in the army of Ismāʿīl's son and successor Abbakr.[39]

Other men and women who had been associated with the Turco-Egyptian regime came to Dār Masālīt as refugees, or were brought to Ismāʿīl as captives. *Faqīh* Abāy, for example, a *jallābī* who had been a judge (*qāḍī*) under the Turco-Egyptians (and possibly under the Ancien Regime), was one of those who fled to Dār Masālīt and was captured and brought before Ismāʿīl. Because of his religious knowledge and prestige he was not enslaved; he entered Ismāʿīl's service as a scribe and judicial adviser, and was given an estate on the Wādī Barei. Ab Mondokōra, who had been the keeper of the bell (*mondokōra*) with which the governor of Kabkābiyya had summoned the people, came to fulfill the same function at Ismāʿīl's court. Some of the *ḥarīm* (wives, sisters, daughters) of the Turco-Egyptian personnel of western Dār Fūr were captured as well. They were married off to Ismāʿīl's sons and other close relatives, to produce more kinsmen and to help provide the hospitality befitting the status of the new rulers.[40]

Another group of people who had been associated with the Turco-Egyptian regime were those *ḥukkām* who had traditionally been representatives and appointees of the Dār Fūr Sultanate, but had been left in place by the 'Turks' and Hajjām. Some of these were maintained in their positions by Ismāʿīl. Others were eliminated. ʿAbd al-Qaffā, 'the sultan of Roro', who was the brother of the *shartay* of Kabkābiyya and administered the area of Dirjeil Siminyang, was attacked and killed by a force consisting of the Gernyeng (Ismāʿīl's clansmen) and the Diseng (his in-laws). The possesions of ʿAbd al-Qaffā, including his horses, slaves and rifles, came to swell Ismāʿīl's treasury and boosted his military power.[41] Thus Ismāʿīl increased his power by absorbing slave and free elements of the Turco-Egyptian establishment into his administration, by eliminating those who posed a threat to his own power, and by confiscating their material wealth.

A third pillar of Ismāʿīl's regime was a group of *faqīh*s who either lived at court or had *Qur'ān* schools in the countryside. Some of these were relatives of Ismāʿīl; others had been fellow students and colleagues before Ismāʿīl's rise to power, or had offered their services at a later stage.[42] The *faqīh*s aided Ismāʿīl in spreading Islam in its Mahdist guise, and in implementing the Mahdi's prohibition of *marissa*, tobacco, high bridewealth, etc. In a letter to the *faqīh*s associated with *faqīh* Makkī of Murle, Ismā'īl described *faqīh* Makkī as 'sent by me as representative in religious affairs, so as to make the country prosperous, to call God's mercy down upon us and his blessings upon all our acts, and [so as to bring] victory over our enemies and peace in our fatherland.' The letter also contained an order – namely 'to assemble at his [*faqīh* Makkī's] place every Friday in order to recite the entire Book of God' – and the threat of punishment to anyone who absented himself or fell behind in reading.[43]

The *faqīh*s functioned as Ismā'īl's ministers in religious affairs. They did not usually receive high administrative posts or administrative estates. Yet, it was said: 'Ismā'īl strengthened the *faqīh*s and drew them close.'[44] He did so in several ways. First of all he gave his own sisters and daughters in marriage to *faqīh*s. His eldest daughter, Arsho, was married to *faqīh* Ḥanafī (of the Gernyeng Dōlong). 'Asha Shaddo, another daughter, was married to *faqīh* Muḥammad Tigil Abyad ('the white monkey'); Ḥawā' Dumballa was married to *faqīh* 'Alī al-Tamtam (son of Ismā'īl's halfbrother, Ibrāhīm); and Ismā'īl's sister Khadam Allāh was married to *faqīh* Yūnis Kirdī (of the Tāmā).[45] The children from these marriages all became *abbonga* (princes) and *ammonga* (princesses), with all the privileges and paraphernalia of royal status. Ismā'īl bestowed other privileges upon the *faqīh*s as well. He occasionally gave them clothes, horses and slave women, and provided them with estates of privilege.[46] A number of *faqīh*s received the right to administer the village or area in which they lived, and from which they were allowed to collect and keep taxes and other revenues. In the letter to the *faqīh*s of Murle, Ismā'īl ordered the addressees to pay the *fiṭra* they collected from the commoners to their leader, *faqīh* Makkī.[47] *Faqīh* Makkī also received the *zakāh* and customary dues from the people of Murle, who were his clansmen. Murle was thus taken out of the sphere of authority of the traditional local *ḥukkām*, i.e. the *malik*, who received a special warning from Ismā'īl: 'let no one of the *malik*s or others oppose him.'[48] In a similar way, *faqīh* Ḥanafī administered his own people, the Gernyeng Dōlong of Kibiri, Tirei and Ab Sōga (near Dirjeil), over whom his father had been *malik*. However, *faqīh* Abāy, the *qāḍī*, received taxes and dues from the Turūj (on the Wādī Barei in the northeast), with whom he had no ties of kinship, and whom he rarely, if ever, visited. By granting these *faqīh*s estates of privilege Ismāʿīl provided them with the means to maintain their families and the students of their *khalwa*s. He did not usually replace *malik*s with *faqīh*s or superimpose the *faqīh*s upon the local nobility. *Faqīh* ʿId, the travelling companion and fellow student of Ismāʿīl's youth, who was appointed *firsha* of Dār Jabal, seems to have been an exception.[49]

Ismāʿīl ruled for four years (1884–1888). Although he laid the basis for the sultanate's internal administration, it was his son and successor Abbakr who, in the first decade of his reign, consolidated the sultanate both internally and externally, and developed its institutions.

Abbakr Ismāʿīl: consolidation and centralization (1888–1905)

Like other Sudanic kings Sultan Abbakr embodied and employed two sets of ideological beliefs; one, Islam, represented the corporate identity of his polity *vis-à-vis* the outside; the other, which may be called Sudanic tradition, outlined the relations between the ruler and his subjects.[50] While the sultanate was presented to its neighbours as a miniature Mahdist state, internally it came to be organized as a Sudanic state, patterned on the pre-1874 Keira Sultanate of Dār Fūr. Hajjām Ḥasab Allāh had been a representative of the Turco-Egyptian regime. Ismāʿīl ʿAbd al-Nabī had been an agent of the Mahdist state. Abbakr, however, established himself as a full-fledged sultan of equal status to the neighbouring frontier states – even if junior to Wadai. Internally he consolidated the new central government, following the lines already laid out by his father Ismāʿīl, and made himself its undisputed head. He did this in four ways:

(i) by patterning his own position on the traditional Sudanic kingship as represented by the Keira Sultan of Dār Fūr;
(ii) by creating a new ruling elite and a network of administrative estates;
(iii) by creating a professional slave army to guarantee the military superiority of the state and to reduce the sultan's dependence on his new ruling elite;

(iv) by exercising some control over Dār Masālīt's foreign trade.

Sudanic kingship: impressing the subjects with his own grandeur

In contrast to his father Ismāʿīl, Abbakr is remembered as an imperious, short-tempered, arbitrary and cruel sultan. In the early days of his reign he was still a man of the people, visited in his home by people of all social ranks, and greeted with a congenial *Abū Azzata, kornanga* ('good-morning, father of ʿAzza').[51] In the course of time Abbakr withdrew more and more into his *danga* or mud tower, which overlooked the capital and its environs. In the decade 1888–98 Abbakr acquired all the outward signs and symbols of a sultan, including the personnel traditionally associated with this rank. Instead of the bell or *mondokōra* of Ismāʿīl's days Abbakr beat the kettledrums or *naḥāsāt*, which he had captured from the *anṣār*.[52] Abbakr's palace not only possessed the *danga*, or two-storied mud tower, typical of the royal palaces of the eastern Sudanic belt, but also the *warra bāya* and *warra deiye*, familiar from the Keira court at al-Fāshir. The *warra bāya*, the narrow or women's gate, was guarded by Ab Tarbūsh, who was famous for the headgear (*kalamshiyya*) he wore in the old style, and notorious for giving anybody whose right or reason to enter the palace was not obvious at best a shower of insults, and often a sound beating. The *warra deiye* or men's gate was guarded by Abba Maṭar, the ex-gatekeeper of the Keira Sultan Ibrāhīm (1873–4). At his death Abba Maṭar was succeeded by another slave, Ab Sinān Jīr, who owed his nickname to his 'chalkwhite teeth' (and by implication pitch black face), and whose son – sitting on top of the hill overlooking El Geneina – still guards the present sultan's palace today.[53] Those who managed to be admitted into the sultan's presence took off their sandals and turban, and – kneeling, and clapping their hands softly – murmured, with averted eyes: *Allāh yanṣurak, yā sulṭān*; *Allāh yanṣurak, yā sulṭān* ('oh sultan, may God grant you victory').

The sultan acquired innumerable wives and concubines, many of whom were slave women. They lived in the women's quarters and were guarded by eunuchs. During Abbakr's campaign against the *anṣār* in 1889, not only the women of al-Fāshir fell to his share, but also the syphilis with which they were afflicted; during

Abbakr's reign, it seems that this disease was still an attribute of royalty as well.[54]

The sultan was surrounded by a number of titled officials, of whom the *wazīr* had the highest rank. Although the title of *wazīr* was an indication of high status rather than of a narrowly defined function, in Dār Masālīt the *wazīr* advised the sultan in military affairs and had the leadership in war. Whether Ismāʿīl had a *wazīr* is not certain. During Abbakr's reign the *wazīr* was Ḥasan Kunji (of the Masālīt Dājū). It was Ḥasan Kunji who advised Abbakr to get rid of the Mahdist garrison in 1888. It was the *wazīr* who – in the war of Ab Saddara – decided that the Masālīt cavalry was no match for that of the nomad enemy and should therefore leave the scene to the riflemen surrounding the sultan. It was he who advised Abbakr against making peace with the Fūr in 1905, and against keeping the Masālīt army together to fight the Fūr as one force.[55]

The sultan also had in his service a number of *amīn*s, court officials and trusted personal servants with rather ill-defined functions. Apart from performing a variety of services in the palace, and being sent out for all kinds of errands and missions, the *amīn*s were a status symbol; having a number of people with no obvious function hanging around or trailing behind one, was (and is) an unmistakable sign of importance in the area. Junior in age and importance to the *amīn*s were the errand boys called *ṭuwayrāt* (little birds) and the stable-boys (*korāyāt*), counterparts of those who had been attached to the Keira court in al-Fāshir. Like the Keira Sultans also, Abbakr obtained a Fūr court poet (*mōgāy*), who composed praise songs for the sultan and performed for his entertainment.[56] There was a prayer leader or court *imām* and a muezzin, who called the people to prayer. Even the *qāḍī* (Islamic judge) was a court, rather than a state official; he was the sultan's secretary, scribe and judicial adviser. From Abbakr's reign until the 1930s the office of *qāḍī* was occupied by (two families of) Borno people.[57]

The creation of a new ruling elite and the estate system

Consolidating and extending his own position and power was only one element of Abbakr's policy. To make the state function he needed a central government and a ruling elite to run it. Although the foundation of the sultanate and the creation of the ruling elite affected the traditional system in many ways, the new central administration was to a large extent imposed on top of the existing *mulūkiyya*s and *furūshiyya*s, which continued to exist and function throughout this period. The administrative set-up of the Masālīt Sultanate resembled a patched quilt. Each new central government had left its traces, but the background colours of the traditional network of drumchiefs and clans remained visible both in between and under the patches. Since the central government officials, from Keira times to 1900, were often chosen from among the people they were to administer, the patches themselves often had the same colour as the area they covered. An important exception to this rule was formed by the Gernyeng, who came to dominate the central government of the Masālīt state from the late 1880s onwards.

Of the three pillars of Ismāʿīl's administration (the *faqīh*s, Turco-Egyptian personnel, and Gernyeng), the Gernyeng had been most significant. During the reign of Abbakr they continued to be the major element of the new ruling elite, which consisted of *bāsinga* (sing. *bāsī*), *maqdūm*s and traditional local rulers.

The *bāsinga*

The people who, with the emergence of the sultanate, came to be called *bāsinga* were first of all close relatives of Ismāʿīl (brothers and uncles), and secondly – by extension – the descendants of the traditional rulers (*sambei*, *malik*s) of the Gernyeng.[58] The term *bāsī* came to be used as well for individuals who became closely associated with the sultan without being Gernyeng. They became *bāsinga* because they were men of great prestige and natural authority in the Dirjeil area at the time of Ismāʿīl's rise to power, and lent him their support from the very start.[59] *Khalīfa* Riziq, for example, who was important enough to become Ismāʿīl's *khalīfa* (deputy) and governor of the districts of Kododol and Konyose, was of the Gufā Arabs of the Dirjeil area. He was known as a strong man and a skilful hunter, who would never perform the ritual ablution before prayer in a proper way, it was said, since that would affect his luck and success in hunting. 'Ismāʿīl brought him together with his children', it was said, and *khalīfa* Riziq became one of the most important *bāsinga*. *Bāsī* Arbāb Barsham, who became Abbakr's ambassador to Wadai, belonged to the Nyumuri (Jabal) of Gorase, a village near Dirjeil, and had been a fellow student of Ismāʿīl before the latter's rise to power.[60]

There were *bāsinga* without and with administrative estates. The '*bāsinga* without a *dār*' were of different types. Some simply became *bāsinga* because they were the sultan's relatives, others because they combined local authority and prestige with influence and goodwill at court. *Bāsī* Abū Rō, of the Masālīt Gonymorong of Kanāre, a village close to Dirjeil, was mentioned as an example of those

> who are called *bāsinga*, [but] have no *ḥukm*, and are not *malik* or whatever. [A *bāsī* of this type] is an ordinary commoner, [but] strong, important, loved by everybody; when he rides out [e.g. to war] everybody rides out with him; when he speaks, his orders are carried out; when he goes to the sultan, his words are listened to. They call him *bāsī*.[61]

Bāsinga of this type lived a short distance from the sultan and were the first to come to his aid in emergencies. Although they did not have the duties of the *bāsinga* with administrative estates, they did share their standard of living; fine horses, expensive clothes, slaves etc. Some of the '*bāsinga* without a *dār*' had become *bāsinga* not because they possessed, but because they lacked local prestige and local ties. Those who joined the sultan as refugees from justice and outlaws from their own clans were incorporated into the sultan's slave establishment (*jihādiyya*), but could be styled *amīn* or *bāsī*.[62] Being *bāsī* almost seems to have been contagious, for those free Masālīt who left their clans and villages to attach themselves to a powerful *bāsī*, often became *bāsī* by association. *Faqīh* ʿAlī al-Tamtam, *Khalīfa* Riziq, and others had their own free Masālīt retainers, who were their brothers-in-arms and participated in the daily meat and *marissa* parties.[63] All those who became *bāsinga* without being Gernyeng, became Gernyeng by association. It is probably for that reason that informants often use the term *bāsinga* and Gernyeng indiscriminately.

In contrast to the titles of *amīn*, *maqdūm* etc., that of *bāsī* was restricted to the generation of Ismāʿīl and Abbakr, that is to say, to those who were adult men in the 1890s. The royal scions of the following generation, that of Tāj al-Dīn and Andōka, were called by the name of *abbonga*. The most important *bāsinga* were those who had been granted administrative estates, the '*bāsinga* with a *dār*', or district governors (see Table 1).

Table 1 The *bāsinga* with a *dār*

Name	Tribal affiliation	Governor of
1 *Bāsī* Nyarmōl son of *sambei* Nyānūle	Gernyeng Dōlong	the Karyeng and Mistereng, now partly in Chad
2 *Bāsī* 'Alī al-Tamtam, son of Ismā'īl's half-brother Ibrāhīm	Gernyeng Dōlong	northeastern Dār Masālīt, the districts of the Masālīt Amunong and various Arab groups
3 *Bāsī* 'Abd al-Qādir	Gernyeng Salāmī	Tenni, Fofo, Kebbere, on the Masālīt/Fūr border in the east
4 *Bāsī* Bukhārī, related to Ismā'īl through his mother	Masālīt Dājū	Duwei, west of the present El Geneina, and the district of the Amburtchung of Indirrabirro
5 *Bāsī* Aḥmad 'Umar Abū Lafta	Gernyeng Dōlong	Kajenggessa (Masālīt Gamang)
6 *Bāsī* 'Umar Ismā'īl, Abbakr's brother	Gernyeng Dōlong	Jabal Fukkum (before his death in 1888)
7 *Bāsī* (*khalīfa*) Riziq Qāsī	of the Dirjeil area	Kododol (Fukkunyang) and Konyose (Nyerneng)

The maqdūms

A second element of the new ruling elite was that of the *maqdūms* (agents or representatives). There were two types of *maqdūms*. Those of the first type resembled the *bāsinga*. They were district governors, not of royal blood, but (often) of the same ethnic group as the people they were to administer on behalf of the sultan. For example, *maqdūm* Bashīr was governor of the Masālīt-Lereng, his own clan – an appointment he had held since Keira times; *maqdūm* Dūdū Somītkilō was *maqdūm* of the Masālīt-Mandara of Ḥajar Jabōk; *maqdūm* Riziq Batanjān (of the Maḥādī) became governor of the Maḥādī and Dārōk of Dādī in the northeast.[64] The only difference between the *maqdūms* and the *bāsinga*, it seems, was the fact that the former were not Gernyeng. Whether the *bāsinga* had more influence at court, while the *maqdūms* had a stronger local power base, cannot be established with certainty.

Like the *bāsinga* most of the *maqdūm*s who were governors had at least one wife and house in Dirjeil, or were at least regular visitors at court.

The second type of *maqdūm*s consisted of slave officials of the sultan or the governors. They acted as a liaison between the central government and the local rulers and represented the former to the latter. They belonged to the *jihādiyya*, and only indirectly to the ruling elite. For example, ʿAbd al-Khayr Ab Faḍḍāy (son of a slave woman presented to Abbakr by the Wadai Sultan) was Abbakr's *maqdūm* or representative at Amm Zuwayfa, the residence of *shartay* Bukr of Dār Erenga; Jimme Tindil, also a slave, was frontier guard against the Fūr and government representative at Ṣaraf ʿUmra; Somīt Abarranjāl, a third-generation freed slave of *bāsī* Aḥmad Abū Lafta, was the latter's *maqdūm* in the Kajenggessa district; *maqdūm* Ab Daqdāq, a slave and allegedly the murderer of the fugitive Fūr Sultan Abū'l-Khayrāt, was *bāsī* ʿAlī al-Tamtam's executive agent in the district of Ḥajar Kajja, among the Marārīt.[65]

The traditional rulers

A number of traditional rulers were so strong, efficient and loyal that they did not need to be subordinated to a governor. In the administrative pyramid, there was no level of officials separating them from the sultan. Instead of dealing with a *bāsī* or *maqdūm*, they dealt directly with visiting *amīn*s of the sultan. Whatever this may have meant for the power and prestige of the *firsha*, the commoners preferred a governor to *amīn*s; the irregular, but frequent visits of the *amīn*s, who had to be given *ḍiyāfa* (hospitality) whenever they came, were more burdensome than the more regular and fixed demands of one district governor.[66]

Of the three groups making up the new ruling elite, the *bāsinga* were closest to the sultan and, therefore, probably more influential than the other two. They were the sultan's councillors, lived in Dirjeil and spent their days in the sultan's company; only in the rainy season would they go to one of their villages outside the capital, to farm and supervise farming. In war they formed the cavalry and fought in the front line, closely watched and imitated by the commoners. In peacetime they were sent on diplomatic and trading missions to neighbouring sultans. When Sultan Abbakr was in need of a new *qāḍī* who was proficient in Arabic, he sent two *bāsinga* to the sultan of Dār Tāmā to recruit one. To negotiate the release of his mother, who was captured by the sultan of Dār Silā in 1895, Abbakr sent *khalīfa* Riziq. When the *ʿaqīd al-Maḥāmīd* came to Dirjeil to discuss this same matter, Abbakr hid in a backroom because he feared treachery, while *khalīfa* Riziq conversed with the guest from Wadai.[67] The *bāsinga* could take command and act for the sultan in any kind of emergency, but their main function was administrative; they were granted administrative estates, that is to say, districts which they administered on the sultan's behalf.

Administrative estates and estates of privilege

The creation of a new central administration and a new ruling elite required a redefinition of the existing division of land, people and other resources. Ismāʿīl and (after him) Abbakr therefore allotted different areas of land and groups of people (villages, *mulūkiyya*s, *furūshiyya*s) to different members of the new ruling elite. Their objective was twofold: to provide the new elite with an income, and to have the country properly and efficiently administered on the sultan's behalf. The areas so allotted may be called estates. Although the Masālīt themselves rarely distinguish between different types of estates – they usually use the term *dār* – two types of estates can be distinguished. The small estates, granted primarily to provide the grantee with a living, will be called estates of privilege. The larger estates, granted as much with a view of their proper (and profitable) administration as to the necessity to provide the governors with an income, will be called administrative estates.[68]

An estate of privilege was a small area of land (usually one to three villages) granted by the sultan to a *faqīh* or close (female) relative, so that the grantee could maintain himself and his dependents from its revenues (taxes, fines, labour services, etc.). Estates granted to *faqīh*s had existed in the area long before the rise of the Masālīt Sultanate. The Borno people of Konge, who gave the Masālīt a series of judges, claim (and are said) to have received Konge as an *hākūra* (estate) from the Keira Sultan Muḥammad al-Ḥusayn (1838–73). Tamr Ab Jiddo, in this same area, was another Borno estate, originally granted to a Borno pilgrim during the Ancien Regime. Two villages, Adada Borqū and Adada Sharīf, had been given to the Borqū (the people of Wadai) by the Keira Sultan Muḥammad al-Faḍl (1803–38), when the Wadai prince and future sultan Muḥammad Sharīf, on his way back from Mecca, fell ill and camped there. Maymere, near Mogornei, was granted by Hajjām Haṣab Allāh to his scribe and adviser, *faqīh* Ayyūb al-Sanūsī, a relative of the Borno of Tamr Ab Jiddo.[69] After the rise of the Masālīt Sultanate Ismā'īl and Abbakr continued the practice of giving estates of privilege to *faqīh*s. *Faqīh* Ḥasab Allāh of the Banī Ḥusayn had an estate at Kereinik, where he had a big *khalwa* and cotton plantations on the bank of the *wādī*. When he died during the war the Masālīt fought with Sinīn Ḥusayn of Kabkābiyya, the estate was given to his children, who later abandoned it during the Fūr invasion of Dār Masālīt in 1905. *Faqīh* Abāy, Ismā'īl's judge, had an estate among the Turūj on the Wādī Barei, and the Borno judge who succeeded him received Shinggilba, in the same area, from Ismā'īl.[70]

All the above-mentioned were strangers, i.e. not indigenous to Dār Masāḷīt. This is striking, but not surprising. Masālīt *faqīh*s were less in need of sultanic support for they had a right to land by the very fact of being Masālīt, and had a right to certain dues such as the *fiṭra* by custom. However, during the reign of Ismā'īl and Abbakr, even indigenous *faqīh*s, residing amongs their clansmen, were given estates of privilege. The privilege consisted of the fact that the estate was exempted of government taxes, and that the Islamic and customary dues could be collected and kept by the grantee.[71] The estates granted to the *faqīh*s had a number of features in common. They were small and they were fertile, being usually situated on a *wādī* and often possessing palmtrees. They were granted as a privilege to the grantee with the object of providing him and his dependents (family, slaves, students, visitors) with a living. They were exempted from government taxes, and they were owned by *faqīh*s who were usually resident on the estate and who were often strangers.

The estates granted to close (particularly female) relatives shared most of these characteristics. Sultan Abbakr's sister Khadam Allāh, for example, resided at Amm Shibayḥa, where all the Islamic and customary dues were paid to her. She did not herself administer justice, but received part – the sultan's part – of the fines which were paid. Moreover Amm Shibayḥa was a sanctuary for people fleeing from the law or from vengeful enemies. Khadam Allāh's men (slaves) would keep the pursuers out, and she herself would try to settle the problem amicably and to the advantage of the refugee, either by ordering those who had been wronged to let the matter rest, or by interceding for the refugee with the sultan. In serious cases the refugee might need her protection permanently and would settle at Amm Shibayḥa.[72] *Iya* Sandukka, one of Abbakr's wives, was given an estate and packed off when she showed the first symptoms of leprosy; she received the right to the government's share of the *zakāh*, *fiṭra*, fines and customary dues in the village of her relatives.[73]

Most *bāsinga* had one or more wives in villages outside, but not far from Dirjeil. These villages consisted, apart from the *bāsī*'s compound (with his wife, concubines, other slaves and children), of commoners who had lived in the village before the *bāsī* had settled there, or had attached themselves to him afterwards. In his village the *bāsī* collected (and kept at least half of) the taxes, administered justice and pocketed the fines, and had a right to labour services (also called *kumal*). According to oral sources the *bāsī* was like a sultan in his village, and superseded the *malik* or *firsha* to whom the village (-land) belonged. In the absence of indigenous administrative documents it is impossible to determine how formal the grants of estates were, and whether there was a clear dividing line between the estates of privilege given to *faqīh*s, the royal villages, and the informal tax privileges enjoyed by the many royal relatives, state officials and favourites of the Dirjeil area, whom the sultan did not normally ask for his share of the *zakāh*.[74]

Two significant exceptions to the general pattern were the estates granted to Abbakr's mother Ḥabība and his younger halfbrother, the future Sultan Tāj al-Dīn. Tāj al-Dīn received the government's share of taxes and fines from the Awra of Kafānī (who also maintained his horses), but was not resident at Kafānī. Abbakr's mother Ḥabība, of the Diseng, received the revenue from Dār Jabal, possibly for the sake of her younger son Sharaf al-Dīn. Ḥabība herself did not reside at Dār Jabal and hardly ever visited it. The day-to-day administration was in the hands of the *firsha*, who was regularly visited by Ḥabība's slave *maqdūm*s and supervised by her brother *bāsī* Mokony. Dār Jabal was moreover an exceptional estate because of its size; in the 1920s it consisted of about sixty villages. As a result Ḥabība did not keep all the revenue from Dār Jabal for herself, but passed part of it on to the sultan.[75] In fact, the estate of Dār Jabal was – in spite of the fact that it was given to a close female relative to provide for her maintenance – an administrative estate, rather than an estate of privilege.

Administrative estates were larger than the estates of privilege; they might consist of an important *furūshiyya* or up to ten *mulūkiyya*s. They were again grants of *ḥukm*, of administrative and judicial authority over the people of a specific area. However, the grant's object was not so much to provide the grantee with a living – although that was automatically and amply provided for – but to establish the central government's authority over the area in question.

The creation of a network of administrative estates (or the division of the country into districts) was part of a conscious administrative policy which was typical of all states of the eastern Sudanic belt. It was perceived as the key to a properly functioning central government, as is evident from one informant's rhetorical question: *balā ḥākūra btitmassak?* ('Can [a sultanate] be held without estate[s]?')[76]

The *ḥukm* of the owner of an administrative estate or district governor consisted of the right (and duty) to administer justice and collect taxes. Since the governors spent their days in the company of the sultan, minor offences and minor disputes continued to be settled by the local rulers, who were supervised or spied upon by the governor's slave *maqdūm*. Only if the settlement was disputed or glaringly unjust was the case referred to the governor in Dirjeil. If the governor presided over a lawsuit in person – either when it was referred to him or when he visited the estate – the fine imposed was completely his. The fines of cases settled on the spot were shared between the local ruler and the governor. The latter's share was paid into a local public treasury – containing mainly grain, goats and *tukkiyya*s – which was at the disposal of the governor. Normally the sultan did not demand a share of the judicial revenue.[77]

As for the *zakāh*, its collection locally remained the responsibility of the local rulers. The governor, through his *maqdūm* and *jihādiyya*, supervised the collection and – after having consulted the sultan – gave orders for its division and redistribution. Of the total amount of millet collected as *zakāh*, one half was divided among the village *shaykh*, the *malik* (or *firsha*) and the governor, while the other half went to the sultan. The sultan gave orders to distribute part of his share among certain relatives, *faqīh*s, royal slaves, and poor and needy commoners. The remainder of his share he left with the local ruler, in a special grainstore, as a store of reserve food.[78]

The arrangements concerning the *fiṭra* were different. The men paid their *fiṭra* to the *faqīh* who led them in prayer on the Feast of Fastbreaking at which the *fiṭra* was to be paid. The women and children paid to local rulers. During Ismāʿīl's reign the *midd* or measure of grain with which the *fiṭra* was measured out, consisted of five and a half times two hands full of grain, i.e. a rather small amount. However, Abbakr increased the size of the *midd* in which the *fiṭra* was assessed. If the governor sent his *maqdūm*, people had to measure out grain with whatever size *midd* the *maqdūm* would bring.[79] The commoners greatly resented the inflated size of the *midd al-fiṭra*. When Tāj al-Dīn Ismāʿīl, after the battle of Shaway in which Abbakr was captured by the Fūr, put himself at the head of the Masālīt army, he had to cajole both *firsha*s and commoners into supporting him, by promising to reduce the *midd al-fiṭra* to its original size.[80]

The animal tax called *zakāt al-bahāyim*, *ʿushūr*, or *khidmat al-māl*, was another source of income for sultan and governor. When the Condominium officials came upon the scene in the early 1920s they reported:

> A tax known as ʿushr is taken off cattle, sheep and goats. In theory, as its name implies, it is a tenth of the herd. In practice nothing is taken for three years, but in the fourth year, one mature female is taken for every five animals in the herd. The owner of only two or three heads of cattle can clear himself by a payment of sheep and the owner of only a few sheep by a payment of takaki. . . . Of horses the Sultan appears to have the right to take a colt every three or four years from the offspring of each brood mare. He does not take fillies.[81]

Oral sources confirmed the existence of an animal tax during Abbakr's reign. However, how regularly or systematically it was collected is not clear, for oral sources gave different rates and rarely specified the lapse of time between one collection and the next. The district governor was responsible for collecting the animal tax. He received the major share, since the sultan only received the number of animals he specifically asked for. The rates of the grain and animal taxes were fixed. However, when a mild governor determined the amount of grain tax to be paid, he would leave the grain eaten by the people during and immediately after the harvest out of account. Similarly, a mild governor would not take into account the calves which were less than one year old, when collecting the animal tax.[82]

The amount of *zakāh* and other grain and animals which the sultan physically removed from the local public treasuries varied according to the circumstances, increasing sharply when there were emergencies. Sultan Tāj al-Dīn, Abbakr's successor, who had many Zaghāwa wives, requisitioned grain whenever there was a drought or acute grain shortage in Dār Zaghāwa. In 1910, when Wadai Sultan Dūd Murra took refuge in Dār Masālīt, he was given the *zakāh* grain of the Gernyeng, which otherwise might not have been demanded.[83] Only rarely did the sultan requisition *zakāh* grain for the use of his family or court, for the sultan had his private fields, called *kirsh al-fīl* ('the elephant's belly'), which were cultivated by his subjects. The *bāsinga* who owned administrative estates were each responsible for the cultivation of a part of 'the elephant's belly', and organized the labour required by summoning the people of their estates. The name given to this labour service rendered to the sultan was *kumal*, a Masālīt word denoting primarily the labour services owed by the bridegroom to his parents-in-law.

One of those responsible for the cultivation of the *kirsh al-fīl* was *bāsī* Aḥmad Abū Lafta, governor of Kajengessa in southern Dār Masālīt. Just before the rains *bāsī* Aḥmad requested *malik* Barre of Kajenggessa to send people to clear the (roughly) four *mukhammas* (or three hectares) of 'the elephant's belly' for which he was responsible. About ten people or so, all young men, led by their *warnang*, then came from Kajenggessa to Dirjeil to cut the small trees, to burn the shrubs, and to smoke the snakes, rabbits, foxes etc. out of their holes and burrows. After the plot had been cleared they went back. With the first rains some thirty men came back to sow, and when the millet had come up, a large number of people came to Dirjeil to weed. The communal weeding of 'the elephant's belly' was a festive social occasion. The workers were accompanied by their *malik* or *firsha*; they brought gifts of clarified butter and honey, and the goats and bulls which represented the governor's (or sultan's) share of the judicial revenues. The sultan himself came out to meet them, to participate (symbolically) in the weeding, and to give presents of cloth and red salt to the *warnang*s, *malik*s and *firsha*s. Finally, at harvest time, the people of Kajenggessa came again to harvest the millet, to thresh and winnow it, and to transport it to the sultan's grain stores.[84]

Kumal for 'the elephant's belly' was, apart from warfare, the largest single labour service which the Masālīt owed their sultan. However, there were many other minor labour services expected from them. When a swarm of locusts laid its eggs near Dirjeil, *bāsī* Aḥmad summoned the people of Kajenggessa to come and bury them; the hole which was dug for this purpose was so big that it became a lake. When the sultan's house or the fences of his compound needed repair, the people of Kajenggessa and other districts came to Dirjeil to mend them. Even during the 1920s people came from as far afield as Indirrabirro to repair the sultan's palace.[85]

The customary dues, referred to as *khidmāt* or *khadāmāt* ('services'), constituted another important source of revenue. While *zakāh* and *fiṭra* were collected once a year, *ad hoc* demands for (varying amounts of) clarified butter, honey, straw mats, *tukkiyya*s etc. were made at intervals. Whenever the sultan needed something, he informed his governors, who sent their *maqdūm*s to the *malik*s or *firsha*s of their estates to collect what was required. The following is an account of the collection of *tukkiyya*s from *malik* Barre of Kajenggessa by Somīt, the *maqdūm* of *bāsī* Aḥmad ʿUmar:

> (Narrator): Somīt goes. As soon as he comes to *malik* Barre [the *malik*] says: 'well?'
> (Somīt): Abba [*bāsī* Aḥmad] says that they want *tukkiyya*s.
> (Barre): How many?
> (Narrator): When he would say forty, fifty, a hundred, whatever, they called the people. The *nuqāra*, Amm Kabāyir, was beaten: kung, kung, kungkungkung.
> (The people): What is the news?
> (Barre): Somīt has come. In Dirjeil, it is said, they want *tukkiyya*s to clothe the *jihādiyya* and to make tents.
> (The people): Fine.

> (Narrator): Everybody contributes five *rubṭa*s; every child even contributes five *rubṭa*s. They complete the number of *tukkiyya*s demanded and make the warp for *tukkiyya*s of eight or nine *rubṭa*s . . . They weave *tukkiyya*s from these *rubṭa*s, put them on transport animals, and take them to *bāsī* Aḥmad's house. Then the sultan says: 'bring me x number of *tukkiyya*s to make tents and to clothe the children [slaves].'[86]

The rest was kept for the governor and stored in his house. In the same way everybody had to produce a calebash of honey or a jar of clarified butter, whenever the sultan or governor sent for it.

Some customary dues, such as the greeting gifts (*salām*) presented to the sultan on the occasion of the two Muslim festivals, were taken to the sultan by, and at the initiative of the local rulers. Spontaneous (or quasi-spontaneous) also was the hospitality (*ḍiyāfa* or *ikrām*) offered to royal relatives or state officials whenever they passed through an area. The 'movable *ḍiyāfa*', i.e. those gifts the royal guests did not consume on the spot, were transported for them to their houses.[87] The right to all stray animals or runaway slaves captured in the governor's estate (the *hāmil*) was another irregular, but not unimportant, source of revenue for governor and sultan. The local ruler was obliged to inform the governor or sultan of the *hāmil* found in his territory and to pass on at least part of the animals or slaves. Apart from the *hāmil* the local rulers had to take all the ivory, ostrich feathers and rhinoceros-horn obtained in his territory to the governor. One tusk (and possibly part of the feathers and horn) the governor passed on to the sultan, but the rest he disposed of at his own discretion. The *malik* and hunters were compensated by the governor from the local public treasury in goats and *tukkiyya*s. In practice the local rulers might be able to evade state control of these products, particularly if the *malik* was popular with his people and was confident of not being betrayed. However, if the local ruler was caught keeping back what was Caesar's, the consequences might be serious. A *firsha* of Dār Jabal was deposed when the sultan discovered that he had kept a number of runaway slaves and cattle raided from the nomadic neighbours to himself.[88]

The creation of a number of administrative estates, assigned to a relatively small group of trusted members of the new ruling elite – many of whom were Gernyeng – was one way in which the Masālīt sultans consolidated the authority of the central government. The estate system provided the government with a substantial and regular income and, at the same time, provided for those 'new rulers' who were constantly on the sultan's side to advise him, act for him, and – in case of emergency – defend him.

The creation of a standing slave army

A third major element of Abbakr's policy of consolidation and centralization was the creation of the *jihādiyya* – slave soldiers skilled in the use of firearms. Slaves, firearms and people who had the expertise to use them were not a new phenomenon in Dār Masālīt in the 1890s. However, until the Masālīt captured a large number of firearms and slaves during the wars of that decade, there was no body of professional slave soldiers. The core of Abbakr's *jihādiyya* was formed by those slave soldiers who had been retained when the Mahdist garrison had been expelled from Dār Masālīt. Initially these *jihādiyya* served as Abbakr's bodyguard, but in time their numbers increased so much that they formed three separate villages and were headed by three (slave) commanders (*ra's miyya*s), Ab Julla, Ab Runga an Amm Nabūd.[89]

As instruments of external or foreign policy the importance of the jihādiyya was limited. In cases of a general war against a foreign enemy the *jihādiyya* were far outnumbered by the levies of Masālīt footmen and were equalled, if not exceeded, in military importance by the mounted nobility. Their position in battle was at the centre, in front of the sultan; defending the latter at all costs, rather than joining the offensive and helping the Masālīt to win the day, was their main military task.[90] Nevertheless, in checking all outside aggression short of a general war, the *jihādiyya* played a major part. Thus they were a source of strength for the sultan in the fulfillment of his primary obligation, that of protecting his subjects against outside aggression.

More important was their role as an instrument of internal policy. Since the sultan and his *bāsinga* lived in Dirjeil and administered the country from the capital, they were represented in the countryside by agents and liaison officers. The latter, called *maqdūm*s, were chosen from the *jihādiyya* or slave soldiers, and in a way it was they who made the system work. Although they had no judicial authority, they closely observed and reported on the administration of justice by the local rulers. They played a crucial part in the collection of taxes. During the Ancien Regime and the Turkiyya, taxes had always been collected by central government representatives, rather than brought in automatically. During Isma'īl's reign there had been no systematic and efficient collection of taxes by the central government, although many people had voluntarily brought in the Islamic dues of *fiṭra* and *zakāh*. During Abbakr's reign this changed. Partly this was the outcome of the new estate system, but partly it resulted from the fact that the sultan and *bāsinga* had a force of well armed professional slave soldiers at their disposal. It was the *jihādiyya*, led by *maqdūm*s chosen from their midst, who knew how much grain had been harvested and how large the herds were. They supervised the division of the tax grain collected by the local rulers. They transported the sultan's share of the grain to the capital, to a *mayram*, a *faqih*, or other favourites and protégés of the sultan. Confronted with the firearms of the *jihādiyya*, the commoners had little choice but to obey the central government's orders. The *maqdūm* of *bāsī* Aḥmad, it was said, 'frightened the people with his rifle, so that they became really disciplined.'[91]

Abbakr used the *jihādiyya* not only to enforce the central government's policies in the countryside but also to keep the new ruling elite he had created subordinate to himself. By claiming the bulk of the slaves captured in war for himself, by confiscating the best male slaves owned by commoners and *bāsinga*, Abbakr made his own *jihādiyya* the strongest single military unit in the country.[92] Even free Masālīt – one type of the '*bāsinga* without a *dār*' discussed above – came to join the sultan's *jihādiyya*, usually after problems of some kind had made their stay in their home areas impossible or undesirable. The sultan gave them a rifle, a horse, and – in time – a house and the bridewealth with which to find a wife. Like the other *jihādiyya* they were under the sultan's direct orders; they were 'the sultan's hands'.[93] Although they were of free birth, they belonged to the sultan's *jihādiyya*, his private and independent source of strength; as such, and in spite of the fact that they were often called *bāsinga* themselves, they belonged to the sultan's major weapon to keep the 'real' *bāsinga* in check. Abbakr certainly gave his *jihādiyya* many privileges. He allowed them to take home part of the *zakāh* grain and livestock which they collected as taxes. Hence they never farmed in the rainy season, it was said, in contrast to the *jihādiyya* of the other *ḥukkām* and the slaves of the commoners. 'Who would eat the grain of the *zakāh*, if they did not?' an informant said; 'who would eat the goats, rams and bulls brought to the sultan as greeting presents, if they did not?' However, this was not all. The *jihādiyya* began to act as if they were their own masters. They grabbed whatever came their way without being called to order or punished by the sultan. It was this privileged position of the *jihādiyya*, and particularly the way in which they abused this position that gave Abbakr the reputation of being 'the sultan of the slaves', and his rule that of being oppressive.[94]

Not only the commoners resented the power given to the *jihādiyya*. The Gernyeng too were resentful. They felt that Abbakr refused to share power with the Gernyeng; that he had reversed Ismā'īl's policy of co-opting powerful Gernyeng in the ruling elite, rather than eliminating them; that he began to depend more on his slaves than on them. In reaction a number of *bāsinga* came together in an opposition party, which included *bāsī* 'Alī al-Tamtam and *abbo* Tāj al-Dīn, and prepared a *coup d'état*.[95] Abbakr had indeed little patience with those members of his new ruling elite who became so powerful that he perceived them as a threat to his own position. These were either summarily executed, as in the case of Dūdū Somītkilo of the Mandara, or robbed of all their possessions (particularly slaves, firearms and horses), as happened to *bāsī* Nyarmōl and *bāsī* 'Abd al-Qādir.[96] However, although Abbakr used his *jihādiyya* to centralize the sultanate and to make himself its undisputed head, he never gave his *jihādiyya* *ḥukm* or major administrative positions. It is possible that Abbakr might have tried to do so, if he had not been forced to depend on both the Gernyeng and other able-bodied Masālīt to fight the sultanate's many wars, and if the state's internal revenue (rather than revenue from foreign trade) had not been all-important. As it was, there was no Masālīt parallel for the developments in the Keira Sultanate of Dār Fūr, where, according to O'Fahey, the traditional Fūr titleholders were partly ousted by an elite of slaves and foreigners depending on the sultan.[97] The Gernyeng, the *bāsinga*, may have been more subordinate to their sultan than they wished (and then they would be under Abbakr's successors); but, in spite of their complaint that Abbakr had become 'the sultan of the slaves' rather than of the Gernyeng, they remained the dominant element of the ruling elite.

Control of foreign trade

The fourth element of Abbakr's policy of consolidating the power of the state was his control of foreign trade. It has been argued above that in the eastern Sudanic belt foreign trade belonged to a separate economic sphere and was to a large extent controlled by the state. Developments in Dār Masālīt in the last two decades of the nineteenth century confirm this. During the Ancien Regime, the Masālīt had not really participated in the trade along the major route between the Wadai and Dār Fūr sultanates, which passed just north of their homeland. When Nachtigal travelled along the road in 1874, the only stop on the Dār Fūr stretch of the caravan route which was more than just a place to spend the night was Tineat, the residence of the *shartay* of Dār Fia. There the caravan paid a greeting gift of a few slaves to the *shartay*'s deputy, but even here the caravan did not do any business except for exchanging some amber beads for food. Nachtigal noted, however, that:

> Tineat lies on the one great road that connects the capitals of the two countries [Wadai and Dār Fūr], and [during the reign of Wadai Sultan Muḥammad Sharīf] almost daily there passed through it small and large caravans, as well as single travellers, all of whom . . . Jellaba.[98]

Apart from raiding the caravans, the Masālīt had participated in the caravan trade only marginally and indirectly: as suppliers of some slaves, ivory, ostrich feathers and rhinoceros horn; and as buyers of beads, cloth, tea and sugar for the happy few. The middlemen with whom they dealt were the *jallāba* peddlers who travelled through Dār Masālīt, and possibly with those *jallāba* who resided in the administrative centres along the trade route between Wadai and Dār Fūr.

With the emergence of the Masālīt Sultanate this changed. During the reigns of Ismāʿīl and Abbakr, the new capital of Dirjeil became a centre of long-distance trade. Since the trade between Egypt and Dār Fūr and between Dār Fūr and Wadai had been interrupted by the outbreak of the Mahdist revolution, Dirjeil became one of the southern termini of the trans-Saharan trade from Benghazi. The shift of the trans-Saharan trade from the Borno–Tripoli to the Wadai–Benghazi route, and the interruption of the trade along the Forty-Days-Road from Dār Fūr to Egypt certainly favoured this development.[99] However, a more important factor was political developments in Dār Masālīt. There is no evidence to suggest that long-distance trade contributed to the rise of the sultanate. On the contrary, the sultan attracted foreign trade because he needed its products for his court and his ruling elite; because he could accumulate sufficient quantities of the desired export goods; and because he could provide the security the traders needed.

When the Fezzān traders first came to Dār Masālīt oral tradition does not remember. In Nachtigal's caravan in 1874 there was one 'merchant from Tripoli travelling to Darfur to dispose there of some of the luxury articles which he had been unable to sell in Wadai'.[100] However, there were no Fezzān traders with Hajjām Ḥasab Allāh in Mogornei; in that period imports such as tea, sugar and beads came from the east, from Kobbei and possibly Kabkābiyya. Yet from Ismāʿīl's reign onwards, Fezzān traders visited and resided in Dirjeil. Apart from the fact that their *shaykh*, *faqīh* Ramla, was apparently close enough to Ismāʿīl to be forgiven when his son made Ismāʿīl's unmarried daughter pregnant, little is known about the Fezzān until the reign of Abbakr (1888–1905).[101]

The *jallāba* had come to Dār Masālīt long before the Fezzān. During the Ancien Regime Dār Masālīt had been visited by *jallāba* peddlers, while some *jallāba* had lived in Tineat, a minor administrative centre and stop on the Wadai–Dār Fūr highway. The *jallāba* settlement at Karrak probably dated from the Turkiyya, when Karrak became a Turkish camp (*daym*). The major concentration of *jallāba*, however, at Wiḥayda, near Dirjeil, dated from the 1890s and was founded by those *jallāba* of ʿUthmān Jānū's army who contracted cholera in Dār Masālīt, but eventually survived. The *jallāba* were mostly small traders. During the Mahdiyya (Abbakr's reign) they continued to trade with al-Fāshir, but they obtained most of their goods from Fezzān traders in Abesher. During this period the foreign trade was almost exclusively in the hands of the Fezzān.[102]

Abbakr controlled the foreign trade first of all by controlling the traders, that is, the Fezzān, *jallāba* and the trader-*cum*-diplomats from Wadai. There is no evidence that Abbakr gave out written entry or exit visas or *laissez-passers* like his sultanic neighbours, but parallels between Dār Masālīt and the neighbouring sultanates are not lacking. No caravan could enter Dār Masālīt without the sultan's (oral) permission and promise of protection. No caravan could leave before the sultan had decided that the time to pay his debts had come.[103] In Dār Masālīt, as elsewhere, the foreign traders had their own, separate, quarters, and were administered by their own *shaykhs*, who were directly responsible to the sultan. The *jallāba* of Karrak were administered by their *shaykh* Khalīlo; those of Wiḥayda by the more powerful *shaykh*, Kuttūk. The Fezzān lived in Dirjeil. *Faqīh* Ramla was their *shaykh* and landlords since all Fezzān were lodged in his compound. Each *shaykh* was responsible for all the traders of his ethnic group. He tried them, when they committed an offence. He collected whatever dues had to be paid. He was their spokesman at court and the sultan's mouthpiece at home.[104] Although the *shaykhs* did not belong to the sultan's council like the *bāsinga*, they were in direct and continuous contact with the sultan, who – through them – had full knowledge of and a firm grip upon the trading community.

The sultan's control over the traders, it has been argued above, entailed both rights and duties. That protection was the obverse of control is, in the case of Dār Masālīt, illustrated by the way in which the sultan guaranteed the payment of debts owed to the foreign traders. When the sultan received a complaint that his brother, *abbo* Badawī, had refused or failed to pay his debts, he took immediate action. He sent for Badawī, gave him a scolding, and, before Badawī was aware of what was happening, settled the debt on the spot by handing Badawī's concubine over to the creditor.[105] When the Fezzān in Dirjeil were robbed of a large quantity of beads, the sultan – furious – ordered all *bāsinga* and *firshas* to search their districts. When nothing was found the sultan fully compensated the Fezzān by paying the full price of the beads. However, at the same time he ordered *malik* Kajjam, the tax collector (*jabbāy*) of the market of Dirjeil, to look out for everybody who had a suspiciously large quantity of beads to spend. Time passed. Then, one day, Kajjam saw Zaynaba, the wife of *bāsī* Bukhārī, in the marketplace. She was accompanied by a slave woman who carried a basket (*rayka*) on her head as shopping bag. Zaynaba bought every possible thing in the market (*nabaq*, *ḥimayd* nuts, *jakhjakh* etc.), and paid in beads. Kajjam immediately informed the sultan, who sent for Bukhārī and ordered his slaves to go and search Bukhārī's house. When the beads were found, Abbakr became so furious that he killed Bukhārī on the spot with an axe, and had his body flung on a rubbish dump. Bukhārī was related to Abbakr through his mother. He was moreover a *faqīh* and much respected by the Masālīt.[106] However, like his sultanic neighbours, Abbakr protected the foreign traders and guaranteed their financial security – even at the expense of his close relatives.

Abbakr not only exercised control over the traders but also over the distribution of the import goods. By doing so he made import goods the prerogative of the ruling class, that is to say, he made them status symbols, badges of royal status and administrative rank, and rewards for loyal service. The types of the trans-Saharan goods imported have been discussed above. They fall into two categories, firearms and prestige goods (mainly fine clothes, fancy articles of use, horse furniture, exclusive food stuffs), which were the indispensable status symbols of the ruling elite. Rifles called *Ab Zīnāt* were for the sultan. *Abū Lafta*s and *Ab Ruḥayn*s (double-barrelled guns) were sold to other members of the ruling class, the standard price being three slave women for a rifle plus one hundred bullets. However, although foreign trade was an important source of firearms (and hence of military power) for the sultan, the firearms captured by the Masālīt in war were at least as important. The prestige goods included fine quality cloth of many types. For the women the traders brought *firka baysūn*, *firka ridhā'* and *shīt* (which cost one slave for a *firka* of twelve yards). For the men they brought shawls, ready-made robes of *jūkh* (which could only be bought for ivory, rhinoceros-horn or ostrich feathers), the multi-coloured silky material called *'alaj* (sold in exchange for slaves), *khaytam*, *shāhī*, *dabbalān* (a strong type of cotton cloth) and *kamar*s (silk belts of four yards, which cost one to two slaves). For the ladies the traders brought moreover a large variety of beads and perfumes (which cost one to two slaves per bottle). Fancy horse furniture, popular with the noble horsemen, was expensive as well. A *bishit* (a saddle pad consisting of seven layers of coloured cloth with golden fringes), for example, cost as much as five slave women. Tea, sugar and other delicacies not locally available were also a prerogative of the ruling class. Except for the latter – and its slaves, who were allowed to suck the tealeaves and sugar left in the teapots – no one in Dār Masālīt ever tasted tea.[107] The foreign traders also imported some cheaper goods such as lower quality perfumes and the rough cotton cloth called *rāḥat al-khayyāṭ* ('the comfort of the tailor') and *raqabat al-kunjul* (a shiny material) sold in units worth one cow each.[108]

The distribution of the foreign goods was limited by several factors. When gunshots had announced the arrival of the Fezzān caravan and when the traders had come to greet the sultan in his palace with the most exclusive goods as greeting gifts, the sultan was given the first choice of the merchandise. After the sultan, it was the turn of the *bāsinga* and other members of the ruling class. The Fezzān did not offer their goods for sale in the marketplace, but kept them in their compound. They supplied everything on credit; only when they had almost exhausted their stock and were preparing for the return trip, did they begin to put pressure on the sultan and other buyers to pay their debts.[109] The most expensive and exclusive robes, rifles etc. were for the sultan's private use. Moreover, his store-rooms were always full of import goods, for it was with presents of high quality cloth and other foreign goods that he rewarded the members of his ruling elite and distinguished them from the commoners. An example of royal status being rewarded by gifts of import goods is that of the daughters of Ismāʿīl, whom Abbakr dressed in *firka*s called *jāz* 'so that people would know who they were.' That administrative rank was rewarded in this way is evident from the presents of fancy robes which the traditional rulers received from the sultan on the occasion of the annual Feast of Fastbreaking. The presents to the *faqīh*s were rewards for religious services. The rifles and smart clothes given to the sultan's *jihādiyya* 'so that people would be afraid of them', were rewards for loyal service and heroic deeds.[110] Abbakr's conscious use of both firearms and prestige goods to reward his ruling elite and to distinguish it from the commoners was one guarantee for the exclusiveness of import goods. It was complemented by the sumptuary laws which ruled out the possession of fancy clothes and other prestige goods by the commoners.[111] The high price of foreign goods, finally, was a third factor which made most import goods inaccessible for the commoners. The limitations on the distribution of foreign goods thus strengthened the military power and *esprit de corps* of the central government and tied it more firmly to the sultan.

Most foreign goods were sold in Dirjeil for ivory, ostrich feathers, rhinoceros-horn, and animal skins. Since the range of exportable goods was limited, controlling the access to export goods could be an effective, indirect way of controlling the access to imports. The control exercised by Abbakr was never absolute. Yet there were old and new institutions which put a large part of the exportable goods at the disposal of the sultan and his ruling elite. Ivory was a monopoly of the central government. Whenever an elephant was found dead or shot, the *malik* of the area had to inform the district governor and transport the ivory to the latter's house. While the *malik* and the hunters were recompensed with gifts befitting their status, the governor and the sultan shared the ivory. The smoothest tusk (called *al-ʿarūs*, 'the bride') was for the sultan, while the tusk which the elephant had used most (called *al-khaddām*, 'the servant') was the governor's. Ostrich feathers and rhinoceros-horn too had to be sold through the governor (and hence, most probably, through the market of Dirjeil), but this is less well documented.[112] If the local rulers could keep the small bonanzas of ivory and feathers a secret from the governor, they might be able to sell directly to the traders. However, the acquisition of new clothes or other luxury goods would be easily detected and raise suspicion. The sultan and *bāsinga* not only passively waited for their share of the exportable goods to be brought in from the countryside, they also engaged actively in producing export goods. For example, they sent out hunting parties (led by *ʿaqīd* Mudda) to procure ivory, ostrich feathers and rhinoceros-horn, and raised tame ostriches, whose feathers fetched about half the price of the wild birds.[113] There is, however, no evidence that the sultan and *bāsinga* put any pressure upon their subjects to increase production for exports.

Another major export item were slaves. After the rise of the sultanate, the new ruling elite came to own the bulk of Dār Masālīt's slave population. The sultan himself obtained more slaves than anybody else, as war booty, as *hāmil* (runaway slaves), and as the royal share of slaves brought back from raids. Abbakr also confiscated slaves owned by his subjects, but in doing so his main objective seems to have been to create a strong slave army and to check potential rivals, rather than to procure slaves for export. More directly geared to the export trade, oral sources suggest, were the raiding parties which set out from Dirjeil to raid slaves from the Kongyo area (near Zalingei) and Dār Qimr. The Masālīt were of the opinion that the Fūr had become Fartīt (i.e. enslavable) after the fall of their sultanate in 1874. The Qimr were not Fartīt, but the Masālīt do not seem to have had pangs of conscience about selling them; even persons claiming to be *faqīh*s were sold.[114] All the sultan's newly acquired slaves were lodged in the huge compound of *maqdūm* Marjān Dinggayre until the sultan had decided their fate. Then they would enter his *jihādiyya* or his *ḥarīm*, would be presented to a favourite, or sold to the Fezzān and exported.[115] The sultan did not interfere with the slave trade inside Dār Masālīt or between Dār Masālīt and Dār Silā. Everybody could buy and sell slaves freely. The sultan did not have private slave traders and did not put pressure on the Masālīt to produce slaves for the Dirjeil market. However, he did allow the Fezzān traders to visit the *malik*s and *firsha*s in order to buy up 'high quality', that is to say Masālīt-born slaves, for whom they paid a high price in cows.[116] It seems that the sultan had so many slaves at his disposal from other sources than trade, that he did not have to interfere with the slave trade, for which Dirjeil had in any case become the nearest major market. In the period of the Mahdist wars, an informant said, 'the place was teeming with slaves' (*al-waṭa' kullu 'abīd*).[117] By providing the new ruling class with material rewards, the foreign trade became a source of strength for the new central government.

The rise of the sultanate: its impact upon the commoners, local nobility and slaves (1888–1905)

So far the analysis has concentrated on the foundation and organization of the Masālīt state. The main features discussed above were the creation of a (Sudanic) ideology of state, a professional slave army and new elite, and the establishment of an estate system and control over foreign trade. The impact which the creation of the new central government had upon the commoners, traditional rulers and slaves of Dār Masālīt had thus far been referred to only in passing, e.g. in the discussion of Abbakr's taxation system and the privileged position of the *jihādiyya*. It is this impact that will be analyzed below.

The sultanate and the local nobility

The new central government was to a large extent imposed on the traditional ruling class of *malik*s and *firsha*s – 'as a *rakūba* (straw roof)'.[118] The local rulers kept their jurisdiction in minor cases and continued to collect taxes, but their power and privilege were negatively affected by the rise of the sultanate. Their judicial authority was seriously curtailed in the following ways:

— they lost judicial authority over the inhabitants of both the estates of privilege and the villages which were the residence of members of the royal family.
— they were spied upon or supervised in the administration of justice either by the slave officials of the governor, or by the slave officials and *amīn*s of the sultan. The fact that many central government agents were slaves was an extra source of resentment.
— they had to share their judicial revenue with the governor, who could take over any case that promised to be profitable.

In the field of tax collection the local rulers had increasing duties and decreasing returns:

— they could not collect taxes from the estates of privilege or the royal villages.
— they received a smaller percentage of the taxes collected, although their real income – as a result of the regular and efficient tax collection and royal gifts – may not have decreased.
— they were supervised by slave agents of the central government, who also collected the taxes and treated the local rulers peremptorily.
— they lost the authority to establish the *midd* (or measure of grain) in which taxes were paid. The tax collectors could (but certainly not always did) bring their own *midd*.
— if the governor or sultan decided to collect the *fiṭra*, the local nobility lost this source of revenue as well.
— the local rulers lost the right to redistribute the surplus which

was extracted through taxation. It was the sultan (and governor) who decided to whom the surplus was redistributed.

— the administrative duties of the local rulers increased, since more customary dues and *ḍiyāfa* were to be paid, more labour services to be performed, more wars to be fought.

— the local nobility lost the right to the *hāmil* (stray animals and runaway slaves).

— they also lost the right to (a share of) exportable goods such as ivory and ostrich feathers, and hence lost independent access to import goods. Since the right to ivory, for example, was a right emanating from ownership of the land, the local rulers in a way lost their rights to land, of which the government could dispose whenever and as it wished. The loss of independent access to imported prestige goods was in practice compensated by the presents given by the sultan, the presence of long-distance traders in nearby Dirjeil, and the opportunity to obtain export slaves during the wars of the sultanate.

— the military power of the local rulers decreased as well, at least relatively, i.e. in comparison with that of the new ruling elite. Before the rise of the sultanate the local monopoly of the legal use of force had rested with the local rulers (their *warnang*, the age group of the young men, and slave and free hangers-on). After the rise of the sultanate the new ruling elite, armed with rifles and served by well-armed *jihādiyya*, superseded the local nobility as the superior military force inside Dār Masālīt.

— finally, as in Keira and Turco-Egyptian times, local rulers could be deposed by the central government. Since the government was now residing in their midst, opportunities to fall foul of it increased. The frequency with which local rulers were deposed and replaced may well have increased accordingly.

It cannot be denied that the Keira state of the Ancien Regime had theoretically possessed many of the rights which now came to be exercised by the central government of the Masālīt Sultanate. However, in practice, the Keira government had left the local rulers a large degree of autonomy, interfering only in major disputes and the collection of taxes. The new central government, constituted by Masālīt and residing in Dār Masālīt, was much more ambitious. Faced with the familiar ideology of the Sudanic state and with superior military force, the local rulers had little choice but to obey. Some of the local rulers became distinguished and wealthy members of the new ruling class, while others became lesser – but still – members. However, the process by which small *malik*s became indistinguishable from the commoners in anything but their claim to an ideological obsolete status, probably set in this period.[119] Most of the local rulers continued to belong to the ruling class, but lost power, prestige and revenue. That they resented 'big government' is known – indirectly – from the attempts of some of them to reattach themselves to the restored Fūr Sultanate (after 1898), and from their desertion during the battle of Shawai (in 1905), which will be discussed below.[120]

The sultanate and the commoners

The commoners were most affected by the new taxation system which came into force during the reign of Abbakr. The commoners came to pay more taxes than before for many reasons. Taxes were levied more regularly and collected more efficiently than before. The size of the *midd* – the unit in which taxes were assessed and paid – came to be determined by the central rather than the local government. Demands for customary dues and hospitality (*ḍiyāfa*) increased, as did the demands for agricultural labour and for military service in the many wars of Abbakr's regime. Added to this were the extortions by the *jihādiyya*, whose privileged position was in itself a thorn in the commoner's flesh. Local produce had always left the local communities. After the rise of the sultanate, however, more local produce was channelled out of the local community to the central government than before.

The uses to which the local produce extracted through taxation was put, were to a large extent traditional. Part of it was consumed conspicuously by the ruling class. The rulers ate richer food and provided food to a larger number of wives, slaves, children, hangers-on and guests, than a commoner could maintain.[121] Part of the extracted surplus was stored locally, as reserve food for times of need such as wars and droughts, which abounded in the nineteenth century. Part of the local produce extracted by the central government was redistributed by the sultan to his administrative personnel, his *faqīhs*, his dependent relatives, to the poor and needy of the commoners,[122] and – to an increasing extent – to his *jihādiyya*. A small part of the revenue from taxes (for example horses and cows) were traded (locally and regionally) for products of neighbouring regions. Both the ways in which the local agricultural surplus was extracted and the uses to which it was put were therefore largely as they had been during the Ancien Regime. However, it was the new ruling class, not the foreign government and traditional rulers, that controlled and allocated the surplus. Since the central government had come to reside in the country itself, and since the ruling elite had increased in size and included a privileged, dependent slave element, that part of the surplus that was distributed among the commoners decreased, at least relatively.

In the field of law the commoners could now appeal against the sentences of the local rulers in the nearby courts of governor or sultan. However, oral accounts suggest that the multiplication of rulers alarmed rather than reassured the commoners. The threat to take the case to Dirjeil was usually enough to make the parties in the lawsuit accept the decision of the local ruler.[123] Finally, while the commoners resented the privileges given to the *jihādiyya*, they chafed as well at being dominated by the Gernyeng.

Of course the new regime had redeeming features as well. First of all there were loopholes. The southern part of Dār Masālīt was never as tightly administered as the northern part; popular local rulers had a large measure of autonomy, might still determine the *midd* locally, and be able to withold runaway slaves, stolen cattle, ivory etc., from the central government. Secondly, the new system was a very personal one, in which new and traditional rulers, commoners and slaves, all dealt with each other in face-to-face relationships; they worked, hunted and fought side by side; worried equally about locust plagues and poor rains (which would not, of course, equally affect them); and – if one looks beyond the golden varnish of royal status – lived very much the same kind of life. The sultan and the governor posed as fathers of their people – another aspect of Sudanic ideology. The sultan knew everybody by name, oral sources say; asked his visitors about their relatives, knew who was in need of tax grain to get by, etc.[124] Moreover, the new sultanate brought commoners and traditional rulers the pride and prestige of belonging to an Islamic state and – at least for a time – independence. The new sultanate certainly had the advantage of offering protection against aggression and material demands from the outside. Even if the rise of the sultanate itself was the cause of much aggression from the outside, it strengthened the position of the Masālīt *vis-à-vis* their neighbours, and made them a powerful, aggressive and expansive force. Their raids into Dār Fūr and Dār Qimr, their expansion into areas which traditionally belonged to the Fūr and Dājū are evidence of this.[125]

An undeniable indication, however, that the commoners and traditional rulers resented the new regime, is the fact that they deserted their sultan in battle. In 1905, when the Fūr army of Sultan ʿAlī Dīnār invaded Dār Masalīt and gave battle in Shawai, Sultan Abbakr was deserted by 'the Masālīt', oral sources say, and left alone with his slaves and relatives.[126] He was captured by the Fūr, imprisoned in al-Fāshir, and eventually executed. Oral sources ascribed Abbakr's unpopularity to many factors. Heavy taxation, particularly the animal tax and the outsize *midd al-fiṭra*, was one of them. Another factor was Abbakr's greed, for people resented that Abbakr took most of the spoils of war for himself and confiscated people's slaves without right or good reason. People resented the extortions and the privileged position of the royal *jihādiyya*, who did not even have to farm; the fact that Abbakr recruited free Masālīt into his *jihādiyya*;[127] and his harshness and cruelty in administering justice. As for the latter, in 1894 Abbakr executed all the leading men of the Mistereng, who were suspected of having harboured Hajjām Ḥasab Allāh. With his own hands he killed his 'brother' *bāsī* Bukhārī, found guilty of robbing the Fezzān traders, and sentenced Bukārī's brother to having his hand cut off. Abūlonggo, of the Turūj, who was Abbakr's keeper of the kettledrums, was beaten to death and left in the sun for all to see, when he tried to abscond with one of the drums. Riziq Batanjān, of the Awlād Māna, was summarily executed when he was found with one of the sultan's wives. The same fate befell *firsha* Mōmad Nyitirre of the Nyerneng for retransferring his allegiance to the Fūr after the restoration of the Dār Fūr Sultanate in 1898; he was thrown into a pit and killed with an axe. Although none of these crimes was belittled in the oral sources, the sultan's lack of pity was looked upon with disfavour.[128]

The sultan was blamed as well for another feature – his increasing inaccessibility. Sitting in his *danga*, screened off from his people by mud walls and gatekeepers who were not to be trifled with, Abbakr could in the later years of his reign only be approached through his *amīn*s and according to protocol.[129] The growing gap between the sultan and the commoners is well illustrated by the following anecdote:

> Towards the end of his reign Abbakr only appeared in public at the time of the Friday prayer. Since it was so difficult to penetrate into the sultan's presence, someone who had a complaint or had been treated unjustly (a *maẓlūm*) would cry out loudly after the Friday prayer in order to attract the sultan's attention. Once a man cried out because the *abbonga* had taken all his hens. Abbakr was annoyed with the man for making such a fuss about such a trifle. When he said so he was criticized by *faqīh* Makkī of Murle, who asked him whether he did not realize that hens were the cows of the poor man. For Abbakr this was reason to break off all relations with the *faqīh*. When the *faqīh* was in his turn criticized by his son for having antagonized the sultan, he answered mysteriously: 'You and your horse are young and strong, and Abbakr and his horse are young and strong, but wait and see what tomorrow has in store for you.' The next day news was brought that the Fūr army was approaching. In the battle which ensued Abbakr was deserted by his men and captured.[130]

The most striking feature of the list of grievances informants presented as explanations of Abbakr's unpopularity is the fact that his right to act as a sultan was neither questioned nor criticized. It was for transgressing the limits of sultanic authority, and for not living up to the expectations which he himself, by adopting the ideology of Sudanic kingship, had created, that Abbakr was rejected by his people. The criticism of Abbakr voiced in the oral sources and the later history of the sultanate – particularly the way in which the Masālīt defended their independence against the Fūr and French – suggest that the Masālīt resented the excesses of Abbakr's rule, rather than the sultanate itself.

New masters and new slaves

As a result of the rise of the sultanate and the many wars of the last quarter of the nineteenth century, both the major slave-owning group and the slave population of Dār Masālīt changed. As for the latter, during the 1880s and 1890s, many of the slaves who lived in Dār Masālīt fled and never came back.[131] The new slaves who were acquired in this period were to a large extent acquired in the same ways and from the same sources as before, but in much larger quantities. In the oral sources they are referred to as 'the real slaves', or 'the slaves of the sultanate', that is to say, first generation in contrast to Masālīt-born slaves (*muwalladīn*). Oral sources suggest that there had never been as many new slaves as in the period 1884–1905: 'the place was teeming with slaves.'[132]

The slave-owning group changed as well. The traditional rulers, who had owned most slaves in Dār Masālīt before the 1880s, were replaced as the main slaveholders by the new ruling elite, headed by the sultan. Ismāʿīl ʿAbd al-Nabī had depended on his clansmen because he had no slaves. In the course of his reign he acquired slaves, e.g. those who fled westward at the fall of the Turco-Egyptian government, and those he captured during his military expeditions against *maqdūm* ʿAbd al-Qaffā and the Qimr. However, most slaves came to Dār Masālīt during the wars against the *anṣār* and the other frontier sultanates during Abbakr's reign. In these wars the *bāsinga* bore the brunt of the battle. It is therefore not surprising that the bulk of the slaves who were captured became theirs.

The new rulers acquired slaves to a large extent for the same purposes as other Masālīt, i.e. to obtain domestic and agricultural labour and to expand their kingroup. In the palace the heavy domestic work was done by slaves, as it was in the compounds of the commoners. Male and female slaves fetched wood and water for the sultan's household. Male slaves took care of the horses, guarded the gates etc. Inside the compound lived the sultan's legal wives, who each had five to eight slave women (*surriyya*s) living with them and working under their supervision. The royal women (both free and slave) were responsible for the food of the sultan and his many advisers and guests. Apart from that, they acted as the sultan's lovemates and were mothers to his children. Particularly the slave concubines – so much more numerous than the free and legal wives – expanded the sultan's kingroup most spectacularly; Abbakr is said to have fathered more than fifty children, mostly from slave concubines, who 'were given the *fāṭiḥa*', that is to say, were legally married, when they bore the sultan a child.[133] 'We really lived in the shade,' a slave woman of the court of al-Fāshir said;[134] in reality the *dolce vita* at court was probably harder than it may seem from hindsight. One of the Sultan Abbakr's concubines was paid to the Fezzān traders to settle a debt, before she had had time to find out that she was bearing the sultan's child. The other royal ladies were many a time forced to flee in front of invading armies, losing most of their possessions and often their freedom.[135]

Except for the sultan's *jihādiyya*, young wives and concubines, all slaves farmed during the rains. A number of slaves did agricultural labour throughout the year, tending vegetable gardens near the wells of the *qōz* and in the *wādī*s. All *ḥukkām* had their own fields, farmed by their slaves, relatives and – either in the capacity of overseer or farmer – by themselves. They also had a share of the grain tax and had a few fields cultivated for them by their subjects. They did not, therefore, depend on slave labour to produce their family's needs, but to produce a grain surplus befitting their status. This surplus was normally not marketed, but used to provide for dependents (relatives, slaves and free commoners), i.e. to maintain and increase the rulers' political power.[136]

Yet some important changes did occur. After the rise of the sultanate, slaves came to be used for more specialized types of work (and idleness) than before. First of all – as was explained above – they were employed as professional slave soldiers (*jihādiyya*), thus assuring the new ruling class control of the means of destruction. Secondly, they were used as eunuchs. Abbakr had at least seven eunuchs, who had been castrated locally by his *wazīr* Ḥasan Kunji, who had seen the operation performed when in Turco-Egyptian service. The eunuchs were go-betweens between the sultan and his *ḥarīm* in matters ranging from taking the food from the women's quarters to the sultan's guest-chamber, to escorting the ladies chosen for that night to the sultan's bedroom. During Abbakr's reign slaves were not given major administrative positions.[137]

Another change resulting from the establishment of the sultanate was an increase in the export of slaves. One reason for this was the availability of more export slaves than before. The power vacuum created by the collapse of the Ancien Regime in 1874 and only temporarily and incompletely filled by the Turco-Egyptian regime and the Mahdist state, had made warfare and raiding within western Dār Fūr a more important means of acquiring slaves than ever before. In combination with the slave trade from Dār Silā, Wadai and southern Dār Fūr, these wars and raids brought more new or 'unintegrated' slaves to Dār Masālīt than ever before. At the same time, the emergence of Dirjeil as a transit port and terminus of the long-distance trade with North Africa, where slaves were in demand, made the export of slaves easier and more attractive. Moreover, as a result of the presence of a sultanic court in Dār Masālīt and the proliferation of *ḥukkām*, the need for arms and prestige goods – imported from North Africa and payable in slaves – increased substantially. One indication for the increased export of slaves in this period is the sale and export of Masālīt-born, second generation slaves, who were bought up by the Fezzān traders in the Masālīt countryside. The slave raids into the Kongyo area of Dār Fūr is another indication. Numerical data on the volume and value of the slave trade from Dār Masālīt is not available for either the Masālīt or the North African end of the trade. Yet the provisional conclusion proposed here points in the same direction as Cordell's about the slave trade between Wadai and Benghazi: that it grew throughout the latter part of the nineteenth century, and still expanded in some regions after 1900.[138]

How these changes affected the position of the slaves can only be guessed. Although the *jihādiyya* enjoyed certain privileges, for the other slaves the threats and realities of sale must have been effective means of disciplining them. The abundance of new slaves and the ease with which they could be obtained must have made domestic and agricultural slaves less dear to their masters, who may have treated them accordingly.[139] However, until more research has been done, nothing conclusive can be said.

Chapter 6

'The sultan is like a buffalo in the fight':[1] struggle for independence and prelude to colonial rule

The period 1898–1916 was a period of dramatic political change in the Wadai–Dār Fūr region. The present chapter attempts to tell this complicated story from a regional perspective but with special reference to the Masālīt Sultanate. The first section gives an analysis of the relations between the frontier states and the head of the restored Dār Fūr Sultanate, 'Alī Dīnār (1898–1916). The story of the interaction between the French colonialists (who came upon the scene in 1909), 'Alī Dīnār and the frontier states is the subject of the second section. The Masālīt were conquered militarily and lost part of their territory to the French. They did not, however, pass under French colonial administration, because it was internationally agreed in 1921 that they fell into the British sphere of influence. The political events of the period intensified certain structural features of the Masālīt state and reactivated the Mahdist faith of its subjects, which became the ideology of popular revolt against the royal family of the Gernyeng and their informal French overlords. These internal developments in Dār Masālīt are analyzed in the third section of this chapter, 'Factionalism and popular revolt'.

'At sunrise our horses will drink blood':[2] The Masālīt *versus* 'Alī Dīnār, 1898–1905

The end of the Mahdiyya coincided with the death of Sultan Yūsuf of Wadai (1898). The restoration of the Dār Fūr Sultanate by the Fūr prince 'Alī Dīnār and the civil war which followed Yūsuf's death in Wadai, rang out the period of Wadai's domination of western Dār Fūr. Muḥammad Ṣāliḥ, nicknamed Dūd Murra ('the lion of Murra', his place of birth), maintained close political and commercial relations with the Sanūsiyya in the north, and was soon preoccupied with the French advance upon his western border. Dominant in the period 1898–1909 was ʿAlī Dīnār, the new sultan of Dār Fūr. Having left Omdurman just before or after the decisive defeat of Khalīfa ʿAbd Allāh by Anglo-Egyptian troops, he took al-Fāshir and declared himself sultan of Dār Fūr before the new Sudan Government had found time to concentrate on this distant province. When it did, ʿAlī Dīnār became first the government's agent managing Dār Fūr affairs, and was later recognized as a quasi-independent sultan paying a nominal tribute to the Sudan Government.

In everything he did ʿAlī Dīnār claimed to be restoring the sultanate of his ancestors. Condominium sources – to a large extent intelligence collected in preparation for the occupation of Dār Fūr in 1916 – describe his method of government as 'highly personal, centralized and authoritarian', and 'despotic, sometimes cruel, but surprisingly effective'.[3] To what extent ʿAlī Dīnār restored the sultanate, and to what extent he modernized it, has not been studied yet. O'Fahey's thesis[4] of the increasing centralization and bureaucratization of the Old Sultanate and the increasing importance of the long-distance trade may suggest that ʿAlī Dīnār's reign was a continuation of earlier trends. This also applies to the increasing literacy of his administration and his control of trade; no trader could travel in Dār Fūr without a pass stating his name and destination, or without paying the various tolls and other dues.[5] Yet a comparison with the Mahdist state, (which was itself bureaucratically a continuation of the Turco-Egyptian government), suggests itself as well. The assessment (not necessarily the collection) of taxes in coins, the use of money in the conventional sense by the traders with whom ʿAlī Dīnār dealt in al-Fāshir, and the minting of his own coins were a continuation of Turco-Egyptian and Mahdist practices, and like them, a response to closer contacts with the Mediterranean and the European world beyond.

For the states of the eastern Sudanic belt there were two main distribution centres of manufactured goods, Egypt and Northern Libya. Traders from Tripoli and Benghazi followed the desert route *via* the Sanūsī lodges (*zāwiya*s) and oases of Jālū and Kufra, and travelled from there to Dār Fūr, either directly or *via* Abesher. Traders from Egypt sometimes followed this same desert route, but they often came to Dār Fūr *via* the Nile valley and the Anglo-Egyptian Sudan, returning either by the same road or *via* the north. From the beginning of his reign ʿAlī Dīnār traded with the Anglo-Egyptian Sudan, and through it with Egypt, for example with the international company of ʿAbd Allāh Kaḥḥāl.[6] His commercial and political relations with the Sanūsiyya in Libya seem to have been more limited. ʿAlī Dīnār's early years (1898–1902) coincided with the height of the influence of the Sanūsiyya, which had centres in Fezzān, Tibesti, Borku, Ennedi, Bagirmi and Wadai. However, in contrast to his neighbour Dūd Murra, ʿAlī Dīnār's attitude towards the Sanūsī leaders seems to have been one of caution and suspicion. In 1900 he politely refused to let the Sanūsī leader Muḥammad al-Mahdī travel to Mecca through Dār Fūr or establish a *zāwiya* in al-Fāshir, and the Sanūsī presence on his northwestern border worried him enough to establish a frontier post in Dār Zaghāwa. Yet he exchanged letters and presents with the Sanūsīs, and managed to maintain good relations with them. When the exchange of presents developed into trade, is hard to say, but it must have occurred between 1902 (the death of the Sanūsī leader Muḥammad al-Mahdī) and 1909 (the occupation of Wadai by the French). After 1909 ʿAlī Dīnār's political and commercial relations with the Sanūsiyya became more intensive.[7]

In spite of the fact that the period 1898-1902 was a period of civil war in Wadai, ʿAlī Dīnār was in close contact with his western neighbours. Ibrāhīm, sultan of Wadai from 1898 to 1901, tried to shake off the Sanūsī yoke and may well have looked upon the eastern route through Dār Fūr as an alternative to the northern one. His present of fifty magazine rifles, three boxes of ammunition, six horses and two concubines, is a good example of diplomatic trade, although the clothing, coffee and kettle sent by ʿAlī Dīnār did not reach him before his deposition and death. His successor Aḥmad al-Ghazālī (February 1901–2) issued at least one *laissez-passer* to a caravan going east through Dār Tāmā, while al-Ghazālī's successor Dūd Murra (1902–9), immediately after his accession to the throne, received and sent back a caravan of *jallāba* led by 'Abū Takiyya, servant of ʿAlī Dīnār'.[8] The tradegoods reaching Dār Fūr from Wadai consisted mainly of livestock (horses, camels and cattle) and probably slaves. Ivory was not normally exported *via* Dār Fūr, but *via* the northern route to Egypt and Benghazi, which were the major sources of manufactured goods, Dār Fūr being a secondary one. The major caravan route between Abesher and al-Fāshir was in this period the one leading through Dār Qimr, Dār Zaghāwa and Dār Tāmā, and lay slightly north of the one skirting Dār Masālīt, which had been the highway in the nineteenth century.[9] However, in August 1904 Dūd Murra closed the road to al-Fāshir because ʿAlī Dīnār 'illtreated the merchants from Wadai forcing them to sell their goods at prices fixed by him, which were less than their cost price.' In 1906, after ʿAlī Dīnār's raid into Wadai to punish the raiding Maḥāmīd, Dūd Murra imprisoned everybody suspected of going to Dār Fūr, but was more preoccupied with the French presence on his western frontier. Apparently ʿAlī Dīnār intended to make peace with Dūd Murra, for in 1908 it was reported in Khartoum that he had sent twenty delegates to the Sanūsī leader to ask him to mediate between the two sultans, and to exchange ivory for firearms and ammunition. But it was already too late, and just as the sultans of Wadai and Dār Fūr had been unable or unwilling to form an alliance in order to stop the advance of the *baḥḥāra* in 1874, so Dūd Murra and ʿAlī Dīnār failed to combine their forces to stop the French advance from the west.

There were many ties which bound ʿAlī Dīnār to the rulers of Wadai and the sultanates of the western frontier. In the words of the sultan of Dār Silā:

> We and you are today neighbours in God, and neighbourliness is sacred. Between us is the Book of God, and the Book is sacred. We are related by marriage, and relationship by marriage is sacred. [Moreover] we are sultans, and being a sultan is sacred.[10]

ʿAlī Dīnār undoubtedly agreed with that, but he believed that there was one more bond, that of lord and vassal. Acting upon this belief, ʿAlī Dīnār set out to restore the western border of the Old Sultanate of Dār Fūr. To the frontier sultans who had fended for themselves for more than twenty years the prospect of incorporation into ʿAlī Dīnār's kingdom was not at all attractive. The fact that ʿAlī was not the son of a sultan but one of the many grandsons of Sultan Muḥammad al-Faḍl (1803–38), may have been a useful ideological weapon in their resistance. As the sultan of Dār Silā put it in a letter to the French conquerors of Wadai:

> Si vous demandez des renseignements sur Ali Dinar, (sachez) qu'il n'a pas obtenue le sultanat de son père; mais au contraire depuis le sultan Yaacoub Bok Doro les sultans (du Sila) se sont succédés de père en fils jusqu'au Sultan Bakhit. Ainsi donc, ne suis-je point un des fils des sultans qui se sont successivement succédés? Comment voulez-vous que je suive le fils d'un pauvre diable (meskine)?[11]

Western Dār Fūr ranked high on ʿAlī Dīnār's list of military priorities, as is evident from the fact that his attempts to defeat Sinīn Ḥusayn, the Mahdist *amīr* of Kabkābiyya, began as early as 1900. His relations with Dār Silā were initially good. He married a Silā princess, called Amm Raqīq, and the trade routes between the two countries were open. In April 1903 a pilgrim reported in Khartoum that 'he passed a merchant at Keila, one day west of Fasher with 350 head of cattle and about 80 slaves, who had been brought from the south of Dar Sila for sale at Fasher.'[12] Diplomatic exchanges of goods are only documented for the second decade of the twentieth century, but were probably common in the first decade as well. On 6 February 1915, for example, Sultan Bakhīt of Dār Silā and his son sent ʿAlī Dīnār among other things a present of a horse and two male slaves, a sword to be ornamented with silver, and a number of slaves to be exchanged for women's clothes in the market. In exchange for slaves and an occasional horse, ʿAlī Dīnār sent mainly imported manufactures (particularly high quality *jibba*s and drawers), products of the workshops in al-Fāshir (such as silver-ornamented spears and, occasionally, rifles), and mules and donkeys of superior quality.[13] In the documents ivory, ostrich feathers and rhinoceros-horn are conspicuous by their absence; there is evidence that Bakhīt sent these items east to the Nile as early as 1901. In that year he wrote to ʿAlī Dīnar to complain about the Maʿāliya of southern Dār Fūr, who had intercepted a caravan carrying twenty large pieces of ivory and two hundred bundles of feathers to *dār sabāḥ*, i.e. the Nile valley.[14] In 1906 relations broke down. It was reported in Khartoum that the people of Dār Silā were raiding into Dār Fūr and that Bakhīt refused to obey ʿAlī Dīnār's order to give up the possessions and relatives of the Masālīt Sultan who had been defeated and captured by ʿAlī Dīnār in 1905.[15] In 1908 Alī Dīnār plundered Bakhīt's *mahmal* which passed through Dār Fūr on its way to Mecca, and in al-Fāshir traders and pilgrims from Dār Silā were branded as slaves and enrolled in ʿAlī Dīnār's army.[16] In December of the same year Bakhīt requested the Sudan Government to open the roads from Goz Beida to Kafiakingi and from Goz Beida to the Nile *via* southern Dār Fūr and Kordofan, and complained of ʿAlī Dīnār's blockade.[17] In 1911 Bakhīt still expressed his concern about the two roads to the east, and assured the Sudan Government that he could meet the demands of ivory, ostrich feathers, rhinoceros-horn and livestock of any trader the government would send.[18] However, by 1912 Dār Silā had signed away its independence to the French.

Idrīs Abū Bakr of Dār Qimr ruled a small and poor country. He was known as Idrīs 'Sirayjuh Barra' ('whose saddle is outside') because he always had a horse saddled and ready to flee. Apart from taking flight in due time, Idrīs's external policy consisted of serving as many overlords as necessary, and marrying off his daughters to important friends and potential enemies. Although all the sultans of the area married each other's sisters and daughters – thus acquiring valuable spies and a safe refuge at neighbouring courts – Idris had been longest at the game and was the real expert in strategic marriages. When ʿAlī Dīnār married a Silā princess, he considered it politic to offer ʿAlī a daughter of his own. However, when ʿAlī Dīnār failed to defeat Sinīn, the Mahdist *amīr* of Kabkābiyya, he changed his mind, possibly for fear that he was betting on the wrong horse. His advice to ʿAlī Dīnār, that he should first show himself a real man before he could marry a Qimr princess, was not well received. The invading Fūr army plundered Dār Qimr and took many captives, including princess ʿAzza, her brother Hāshim, and other members of Idrīs's family. It goes without saying that the sultan himself had fled in time.[19]

At the end of the Mahdiyya the Masālīt Sultanate was at the height of its expansion and reached beyond the Wādī Azūm into areas which belonged to the Fūr homelands. When ʿAlī Dīnār took power, he sent out Adam Rijāl to take this area – the area of Kongyo or modern Zalingei – into Fūr possession again. Sultan Abbakr showed himself cooperative; *bāsī* ʿAbd al-Qādir who governed the district of Gernye and Burobaranga was withdrawn and recrossed the Wādī Azūm to Fofo and Tenni on the Masālīt side.[20] This did not satisfy ʿAlī Dīnār, who believed that the Masālīt had no *dār*, and that their sultanate had been just a temporary arrangement, 'something in between'.[21] Soon Adam Rijāl was summoning Abbakr's *malik*s (those who had belonged to Dār Kerne), presented them with robes of office, and reconfirmed them in their positions as servants of the Dār Fūr state. Abbakr punished his *malik*s, but remained defensive towards ʿAlī Dīnār.[22] When the Masālīt persistently refused to submit, ʿAlī Dīnār decided to use force. He sent out two armies commanded by Adam ʿAlī and Maḥmūd ʿAlī al-Dādingāwī. At their approach, Sultan Abbakr divided his army and sent his brother Tāj al-Dīn with one half of the men to the northern front, while he himself led the half which was to defend the *dār*'s eastern border. Ill-advised by his *wazīr*, Abbakr engaged in battle with the Fūr before the northern army had returned. In Shawai, just south of the confluence of the Wādī Bāre and Wādī Azūm, the Masālīt were defeated. Abbakr, unlucky enough to fall from his horse when the saddle slipped, was identified to the Fūr by a deserter, who pointed him out shouting 'see the buffalo, see the buffalo' (*dāk al-jāmūs*). He was captured together with many other Masālīt and large numbers of livestock, and taken to al-Fāshir, while the horn played:

ʿAyyāl Masālītke
ma ʿandukum nafaʿ
Sulṭān Abbakr
al-Fūr masakūh.

Sons of the Masālīt
you are good for nothing
Sultan Abbakr
was captured by the Fūr.[23]

Abbakr entered al-Fāshir on 12 May 1905 riding a white camel. It is said that his path crossed that of *mayram* ʿArafa, the daughter of the late Fūr Sultan Ḥusayn, who mocked him:

Yā Abbakr, jābūk?
rakkabūk fī qaʿūd
zayy Amm Zayn shaqqūk al-sūq?

Say Abbakr, did they bring you?
Did they put you on a camel

and show you around the marketplace
like Amm Zayn [any common slave girl]?

Abbakr answered proudly: 'I was brought by men' (*rijāl jābūnī*).[24] ʿAlī Dīnār reported his victory to the Sudan Government and listed as spoils of war 1800 horses, shields, cotton-quilted horse armour, and 500 rifles. 'As it is our custom, and the custom of Kings and Sultans to pardon and forgive,' he wrote on 12 May 1905, 'I have therefore forgiven him [Abbakr] and covered him with our favours,' meaning that he would keep Abbakr in al-Fāshir as a hostage as long as there was any doubt about the attitude of the Masālīt.[25]

In the meantime the Fūr armies, from their camps at Chibuke and Mogornei, plundered the country. After a second defeat at Kunjuldei large numbers of Masālīt fled to Dār Silā and Wadai. A number of *malik*s submitted and were reinstated, while the places of fugitives were filled with more cooperative relatives.[26] ʿAlī Dīnār wanted to break the Masālīt Sultanate up into its constituent parts. In a later invasion in March 1910, the Fūr armies were accompanied by the son of Hajjām, the old sultans of the Awra and Marārīt, and relatives of the *firsha* and *shartay* of the Jabal and Erenga.[27]

Whether ʿAlī Dīnār really intended to restore Dār Kerne and Dār Fia is not known, for the Masālīt refused to submit and rallied to the banners of Tāj al-Dīn, Abbakr's brother. Tāj al-Dīn had fled to the western border, to Tumtuma, from where he appealed to Dūd Murra for help. Dūd Murra, who could not afford an imbroglio with the Fūr on his eastern border, refused.[28] Tāj al-Dīn, recruiting soldiers as he went, then toured the western fringe of Dār Masālīt (Charow, Iffene, Gurun, Misterei) and made a camp at Gilānī. There he spent the rainy season and was joined by those who had fled to Abesher, including Andōka, Abbakr's eldest son and future sultan. According to Masālīt tradition Tāj al-Dīn whipped up the fighting spirit of his men by asking them: 'Who of you has not lost his cows? Who of you has not lost his children? If you want to become slaves, sit down [idly]; but if you want to be free, I will free you.' The kettledrum was beaten and the young men danced and sang: 'If God wills we will die; in our *dār* we will die happily.'[29] At the end of the rains the Masālīt ambushed the Fūr in Gilānī and defeated them. They drove them out of the camps at Chibuke and Mogornei and pursued them deep into Dār Fūr, singing:

> Ḥarbatnā kajam
> fī ra'āsnā 'l-ʿijam
> maʿā ṭilʿit al-sham[s]
> khaylnā yisharb al-dam
> wa ṭayrnā yākul laḥam.
>
> Our warband is invincible
> We may chatter like barbarians,
> but at sunrise
> our horses will drink blood
> and the vultures will eat [human] flesh.[30]

Probably in December 1905 Sultan ʿAlī Dīnār sent another army against the Masālīt. It was defeated at Kejkeje, and one of its commanders, a Bertāwī called Qamr al-Dīn ʿAbd al-Jabbār, who had come to battle dressed up as a bridegroom coming to take his bride, was killed in Duwei. Irate Masālīt soldiers who could not forgive him his taunting war-cry 'slaves, where is your father' (*ʿabīd abūkum wayn*?) slaughtered him as a goat, it was said, and all made off with a small piece of his silken *jibba* as war trophy. The hornblower took the bad news back to al-Fāshir: 'Qamr al-Dīn, the precious *firka*, has been ruined by the Masālīt.'[31] In revenge ʿAlī Dīnār executed Sultan Abbakr. His brother Tāj al-Dīn's stoic reaction was: 'one head of millet from a heap does not make it smaller.'[32]

According to the Masālīt it was ʿAlī Dīnār who in the end took the initiative to make peace. Tāj al-Dīn, who had been warned that ʿAlī Dīnār had not sworn on a real *Qur'ān*, but on the case of one filled with cotton, hesitated. ʿAlī sent back a reassuring message: that he did not fear Tāj al-Dīn, but God; that he had sworn on seventy *Qur'ān*s, and that Tāj al-Dīn should send *faqīh*s so that he could take the oath in front of them. This was done, and a delegation led by *faqīh* Yūnis, Tāj al-Dīn's brother-in-law, was sent to al-Fāshir to conclude peace, probably in 1907. ʿAlī Dīnār received them well and prepared a big banquet. *Faqīh* Yūnis, who had his heart in his mouth and feared for his life, hardly touched the food until ʿAlī Dīnār urged him to 'fall to' in perfect Masālīt, which he had memorized for the occasion. 'We are all Masālīt,' ʿAlī allegedly said, and '*la grande bouffe*' made the fraternization complete.[33] The homefront was jubilant, teased *faqīh* Yūnis with his timidity, and praised ʿAlī Dīnār for his generosity towards the members of the delegation:

Tukkiyya sirwāl,
tukkiyya ra's māl,
tukkiyya baddid ḥumār,
barrak Allāh fi Dīnār,
jāb sajanjābū, khawwaj al-fugrān.

One *tukkiyya* to wear as pants,
one *tukkiyya* to invest,
one *tukkiyya* to spread over the donkey's back,
God bless Dīnār,
who sent us silk and made poor devils into *khawāja*s
[light-skinned foreign traders].[34]

The precise contents of the agreement is not known, but Alī Dīnār undertook to return part of the captives and Tāj al-Dīn probably to pay a tribute. On the latter's exact status apparently no agreement was reached, for according to the Intelligence Office in Khartoum the Fūr referred to Tāj al-Dīn as *ra'īs* (head), but not sultan of the Masālīt, and in a letter of February 1910 ʿAlī Dīnār referred to the Masālīt *ḥukkām* as 'our people, our slaves governing Dār Masālīt'.[35] The Masālīt claim that they preserved the independence which they had so dearly won on the battlefield, and which they were soon after to defend again against French aggression from the west.

'A brief slaughter of Frenchmen': prelude to colonial rule

> [Dār Masālīt] has contributed nothing to the sweep of history beyond a brief slaughter of Frenchmen, nothing to philosophy beyond a rough habit of contentment, nothing to politics but a short and latter-day shadow of the mediaeval empires from Sennar to Songhay.[36]

On 2 June 1909 the French occupied Abesher. Dūd Murra fled to the north and was replaced by the French puppet, Adam Asīl, a grandson of Sultan Muḥammad Sharīf. The French conquest of Wadai was the realization of a policy decided upon in 1906, when the French abandoned the defensive policy they had been pursuing towards Wadai and began to push steadily eastward. The factors behind this decision were numerous; among them were the consolidation of French authority in the rear areas; the instability of the border which the Wadaians frequently 'violated'; fears of a joint Ottoman–Sanūsī occupation of Wadai from the north, or an economic occupation of Wadai and the diversion of its trade to the north and east by respectively the Ottomans and the British.[37]

After the conquest of Abesher the French disarmed the inhabitants and invited the subjects and tributaries of the Wadai Sultanate to submit. On 5 June 1909 Asīl wrote to the frontier sultans announcing that he was the new sultan of Wadai. The first to respond to his letter was 'Uthmān, sultan of Dār Tāmā, soon followed by Bakhīt of Dār Silā, who promised to obey Asīl as his ancestors had obeyed Asīl's ancestors. Idrīs Abū Bakr of Dār Qimr, Tāj al-Dīn of Dār Masālīt and 'Alī Dīnār all sent congratulations. Those of the latter, however, contained a clear warning:

> il y a quelque chose que tout le monde connait, à savoir que le Tama, le Zaghawa, le Guimr, le Massalit, le Sila son mes vassaux; si tu le sais et si tu t'entiennes là nous serons amis, au cas contraire, tu entendras parler de moi.[38]

Tāj al-Dīn's letter was a disguised declaration of independence:

> Louange à Dieu qui t'a enfin fait rentrer dans le pays de tes pères, et qui t'a donné le thrône de tes ancêtres au Ouadai, comme il m'a donné celui du Massalit.[39]

Asīl was probably well aware of what 'Alī Dīnār and Tāj al-Dīn meant, but the French were not, and immediately pushed on east. Aside from that, the instructions of Colonel Fiegenschuh, the new governor of Wadai, were quite explicit: to confirm French sovereignty over Wadai's vassal states, to give letters of protection to the sultans of all frontier *dār*s and to all heads of the villages lying astride the border with Dār Fūr. Thus the French hoped to strengthen their hand in the Anglo-French negotiations about the Dār Fūr/Wadai border.[40] By the end of September 1909 the French had raised the tricolor in Dār Tāmā, where 'Uthmān (who fled to 'Alī Dīnār) was replaced by the French nominee Ḥasan. In November the French visited Dār Qimr which was in a state of mobilization after a threatening letter from Tāj al-Dīn to Idrīs saying:

Tu as appelé les *Kirdis* dans ton pays et tu es la cause qu'ils viennent chez nous. Tu n'es q'un *Kirdi* toi-même et je me vengerai sur toi et sur ton pays.[41]

Idrīs was happy to sign a treaty with the French, by which Dār Qimr became a protectorate of the French (not Wadai), undertook to pay one thirtieth of its annual grain crop and animal wealth and to abolish the slave trade.[42] The column which visited Dār Silā in October was given a less warm welcome and hurriedly sent for reinforcements from Abesher. Bakhīt was forced to sign a similar treaty to that signed by the other frontier sultanates. Its text ran as follows:

From the Commander of the Faithful, Sultan Muḥammad Bakhīt, son of Sultan Isḥāq Abū Rīsha. The reason for this document comes from the French: between us and them peace (*amān*), a treaty and covenant have been concluded. There will be no war between us and them ever. All this [has been agreed upon] with Governor Captain (*Qābitayn*), the *wazīr* of France. The condition or conditions which exist between us and them are: to refrain from war with the tribes, except with the one which attacks us, and [even then] with their [French] permission. To rule justly as God – Elevated is He – has ordained; we will abstain from deceit. The French will be the protectors and we the rulers in our country. The roads will be open for the traders and for all the commoners. Slaves will not be sold anymore. We will keep the firearms in our own possession except when they are needed to kill a thief or aggressor. Whenever we are harmed by neighbours we will not attack them unless with their [French] permission. Whenever [the] Captain wants to count the people, he has my permission to do so.[43]

The tribute was not specified in the treaty. It was fixed in money (francs and *riyāl*s) and paid mainly in livestock and sometimes in grain or ivory.[44]

This was the situation in the frontier area when the governor, Colonel Fiegenschuh, decided to take Asīl for a tour of the frontier *dār*s. He announced his visit as follows:

Salut – Dans un mois j'irai voir les sultans de l'Est avec mon ami le sultan Acyl. Notre intention est à apporter le paix, de

> connaître les sultans et de finir les luttes fratricides. Les musulmans sont libres de pratiquer leurs croyances. Nous venons seulement pour assurer la libre circulation par le commerce à tout le monde. Préviens les habitants de ne pas abandonner les villages sur notre passage. Le Sultan Asil ne vient pas pour te commander, mais pour te voir en ami.[45]

Since no Wadai Sultan ever left his kingdom except to wage war (or to go on pilgrimage to Mecca), the impact of this letter was enormous. Eventually Fiegenschuh was persuaded to leave Asīl at home and to reconnoitre the frontier (to start with Dār Masālīt) on his own, but even then the difference between 'une simple promenade militaire' of 582 men and 129 horses and a military invasion may not have been clear to the Masālīt. Since the western fringe of Dār Masālīt had not been cultivated in the rainy season which had just come to an end, it is possible that the Masālīt had planned to fight the French all along. Yet Tāj al-Dīn had given Fiegenschuh a clear warning:

> Tu dis que le Ouadai est à toi, c'est bien. Tu dis que le Tama, le Guimr, le Sila te sont soumis, c'est bien. Je ferai de même. Mais le Ouadai est au couchant et le Dar Massalit est au levant. Tu veux venir me voir? Ne viens pas encore, mes gens sont sauvages, ils auront peur de tes tirailleurs qu'ils ne connaissent pas encore. Remets donc à plus tard ton voyage.[46]

On 4 January 1910, in the battle of Kirinding ('the wild figtree') or Wādī Kajja near the present El Geneina, the French were ambushed and totally defeated. They left 280 dead, of whom five Europeans (including Fiegenschuh), on the battlefield.[47] Even in Abesher people sang jubilantly:

> Anā Tāj al-Dīn
> sayfī tarīn
> wa jawādī badīn
> najāhid al-kufur nammā'l-mahdī yibīn.
>
> I am Tāj al-Dīn
> my sword is sharp
> and my horse is stout
> we will fight unbelief until the *mahdī* appears.[48]

'Alī Dīnār had meanwhile become increasingly alarmed by the

French activities on his western border. The Sudan Government's only answer to his complaints about the border violations was the advice to be patient and to be reassured that the French Government would respect its agreement with the British Government, and consequently the western border of Dār Fūr. When the French invaded Dār Masālīt ʿAlī Dīnār's suspicions about French intentions proved right. He sent a boasting letter to the Sudan Government that 'our slaves in charge of Dār Masālīt' had killed the French down to the last man. In reality however, his feelings about the defeat of his rivals at the hands of rebels against his authority were very mixed. Tāj al-Dīn's gift of a number of horses and firearms captured from the French was interpreted (and undoubtedly intended) not so much as a share of the spoils of war presented by the humble vassal to his lord, but as a subtle boast: see how we defeated the enemy you have been afraid of all this time.[49] The Fūr generals who had excused their defeat by Tāj al-Dīn by saying that the latter was their peer, were now challenged to prove this and to defeat the French and capture their arms as Tāj al-Dīn had done. However, the army which left for the western frontier marched not only against the French, but also against the Tāmā and Qimr collaborators and the Masālīt, who were to make an act of submission and give up all the firearms captured from the French.[50] The Fūr army first invaded Dār Qimr, replaced Idrīs with a relative, Aḥmad Bayḍa, and made a *daym* at Abtar.

In the meantime Dūd Murra, who had initially fled north to his spiritual lord, political advisor and major trading partner, the Sanūsī, had returned to the Kapka mountains northeast of Dār Tāmā. He was accompanied by adherents of the Sanūsiyya (*ikhwān*) and members of the northern desert tribes, and began to organize resistance against the French from his new hide-out.[51] In the south, Bakhīt of Dār Silā had secretly joined the anti-French camp. After the battle of Kirinding he sent an angry letter to Asīl blaming him for his advice not to fight the French, and a letter of congratulations to Tāj al-Dīn promising support.[52]

For the French all this portended little good. Hopelessly understaffed even before the defeat at Kirinding they now faced four enemies who might well make common cause. While Paris furiously debated whether they should or should not have been where they were, the garrison hurriedly fortified Abesher. Reinforcements were under way. Although the imperialists in

Paris praised their work as 'une oeuvre noble et grande, une oeuvre de haute humanité, une oeuvre éminemment française',[53] the people of Abesher, particularly the women, openly jeered at the French and insulted them in the street. The situation was indeed quite serious. Even the Wadaian allies of the French, including Asīl, were suspect. In March 1910 a number of Wadaian dignitaries fled to Dūd Murra in Kapka. Asīl continued to support the French. After the battle of Kirinding in January he had received two letters from Tāj al-Dīn advising him to get rid of the remaining French as soon as possible:

> Ils sont venus blasphémer chez nous et il est arrivé ce qui devait arriver entre nous et eux par la grâce de Dieu. . . . Si la religion de tes pères et ancêtres te convient toujours . . . connais ta ruse avec le chrétien qui est auprès de toi. Nous te protégerons alors sans profit à cause de la religion Mahométane s'il plaît à Dieu.[54]

The French (and Asīl) realized that Tāj al-Dīn 'in his ignorance of things European thinks that France is just a village from which small groups of people come to look for fortune in Africa just like the people of Fezzān and Benghazi';[55] Asīl therefore replied to Tāj al-Dīn:

> Il ne faut pas perdre la tête et être trop orgueilleux parce que tu as tué le Capitaine. Les blancs (Français, Anglais, Allemands) ont tout conquis. Tu seras vaincu par les Français. On ne peut arrêter leur marche, tous les sultans ont été vaincus. Tu n'as pas encore fini de faire la guerre aux Français. . . . Si le Massalit était fort, je le saurais. Tu n'es qu'un petit sultan. Tu seras responsable devant Dieu de la mort des 'meskines'. . . . Si tu es Mahdi il faut te battre car tu es le joint de la volonté de Dieu. Mais tu n'es qu'un sultan et tu seras vaincu.[56]

While the French were waiting for reinforcements (which arrived in February 1910) their enemies prepared for attack. Yet they first had to come to terms with each other. The Masālīt for example were not planning an advance on Abesher, but a defence against the Fūr in Dār Qimr. Afraid that the Fūr and Tāmā would jointly descend upon Dār Masālīt, French sources say, Tāj al-Dīn tried to provoke a French attack in Dār Tāmā in order to divert Fūr attention from the Masālīt. In February he invaded Dār Tāmā, replaced the French puppet Ḥasan with Shūsha, his own nominee, and returned to Dār Masālīt laden with booty. The French moved fast. Seven days later, on 25 February, they restored Ḥasan and returned to Abesher. Thereupon the Fūr moved into Dār Tāmā and gave the Tāmā their third sultan in two weeks, namely the old Sultan ʿUthmān, who was installed on 5 March. At this point Tāj al-Dīn submitted to ʿAlī Dīnār and contacted the Fūr generals to plan a joint attack upon Abesher.

The Fūr had in the meantime been intriguing with Wadaian dignitaries in Abesher. Rather than supporting Dūd Murra they had written to the *ʿaqīd al-Maḥāmīd* (who had so far remained in the French camp) to join them and to bring with him a Wadaian prince as the Fūr candidate for the throne. This plan failed since the *ʿaqīd* instead joined Dūd Murra in Kapka.[57] It was only then (March 1910) that the Fūr decided to make common cause with Dūd Murra and invited him to join them at Gereida (85 kilometers southwest of Kapka and 50 kilometers east of the capital of Tāmā). Dūd Murra declined the offer, for – as his *ʿaqīd*s explained in their letters – his army was too large and consisted of too many different kinds of people, including the *Ikhwān*, the Kinīn (Tuareg), the Arabs of Kānem, the Zuwayya, Bidāyāt, the Qurʿān or Tubu, and others. Instead Dūd Murra suggested that each would attack the French from his own side.[58] According to a French report the date for the general attack was fixed on 15 April 1910, but the will or ability to coordinate the attack must have been lacking. A small raiding expedition by the Fūr led to a French punitive expedition and a battle at Gereida in which the Fūr were defeated. One week later (on 14 April) Dūd Murra's men, possibly not aware of the Fūr defeat, were repulsed at Biltine and returned to Kapka. Only the Masālīt were jubilant that 'God had brought the French to rid them of the Fūr'.[59] Until today the Masālīt remember with a grin how Badāwī, Tāj's brother, returned to Dār Masālīt with captives, horses and cows as spoils of a war in which he had not lifted a finger.[60]

The French greatly exaggerated the importance of the battle of Gereida for propaganda purposes. In reality it was a minor victory which did not restore French prestige or break the strength or purpose of their enemies. Its only significant (indirect) result was Dūd Murra's flight to Dār Masālīt,[61] which was an even better base for operations against Wadai, and whose ruler was a more congenial ally than the Fūr. As long as Dūd Murra was so close to

Abesher, and as long as his men, together with the Masālīt, continued their raids into French territory, there was no chance that eastern Wadai would find peace.

Before the French conquest Abesher had been, according to Boyd Alexander, 'the refuge of all the bad hats under the African sun', attracting those 'who have had no use for the new [colonial] Africa'; after Kirinding it was Dirjeil that became the centre of rebels against, and refugees from, the French.[62] In October 1910 the new governor Colonel Moll, who had instructions to punish the Masālīt at the first possible occasion, decided to take action. While he sent one column to Dār Masālīt *via* Dār Tāmā and Dār Jabal, he himself took the direct route east and gave battle in Darōtī (close to the present El Geneina) on 9 November 1910. Of the 20 Frenchmen 8 were killed (including Moll) and 5 wounded. Of the 310 Wadaian and Senegalese soldiers, 28 were killed and 69 wounded, while 14 disappeared. In spite of this, Darōtī was a French victory, even if a Pyrrhic one.[63] Tāj al-Dīn was killed together with about forty of his close relatives and hundreds of commoners. 'That day the vultures of the *dār* ate their fill,' the Masālīt say, and all 'the children of the *Gōz* became orphans.'[64] While the remainder of the French troops limped back to Abesher the Masālīt lamented their dead:

Kuma Darōti dulunga tiringa
Gernyent indānong sawiyei
Masākīnte deinong ōriyei
Mbelije Ab Tōra tonōrong.

Ḥajar Darōti remained a deserted site,
the Gernyeng are desolate,
the commoners groan like cows,
the young men have been finished off
by the Ab Ṭayra (rifles).

and:

Darọti is left a deserted site
O Tuja how great a guilt have you borne!
O people of the Sultan run swiftly
the Christian has no milk [sc. of human kindness]
make no turning of the head.[65]

The French followed up their victory with a punitive expedition in January/February 1911. The Masālīt fought three more battles with them, but then all people and livestock retreated to the hilltops, while the French – crossing the *dār* in all directions – executed their policy of 'repression méthodique' in the valleys and on the plains. Dirjeil was burnt and over 2,000 head of cattle were captured. The Erenga and Jabal made (a separate) peace, but no Maslātī came in to offer submission. The leader of the expedition, Colonel Maillard, noted in his report that the Masālīt were awesome and courageous enemies and that their resistance was a truly national resistance; he concluded with some practical advice: that the troops should not take any artillery, since there were too few buildings to haul down.[66] The two sultans, Dūd Murra and Andōka (Abbakr's son who had succeeded Tāj al-Dīn), fled to the east in the direction of al-Fāshir. However, at the Wādī Azūm they turned around; the imperious Fūr Sultan ʿAlī Dīnār was not a feasible alternative to the French.[67]

Although the back of Masālīt resistance had thus been broken, eastern Wadai remained turbulent and Dūd Murra was still at large. In June 1911 the whole of eastern Wadai rose in rebellion against the French. The Kodoi rebellion, as the French call it, which began in Dār Tāmā and consisted of a series of risings in different areas, seems to have been a popular rebellion directed against foreign and non-Muslim rule and in particular the tax demands of the new regime. Although Dūd Murra may not have instigated the rebellion, he was certainly involved, and from their base in Dār Masālīt he and his *ʿaqīd*s made dramatic appearances upon the scene and successfully raided the villages of collaborators of the French. The repression of the rebellion by the French in August 1911 marked the end of serious resistance against the French in eastern Wadai. In October Dūd Murra and Andōka gave up the fight. Dūd Murra surrendered and was pensioned off to Fort Lamy.[68] Andōka wrote to Asīl in the same month:

> From . . . Amīr Muḥammad Andōka, son of Amīr Abbakr [son of] Faqīh Ismāʿīl ʿAbd al-Nabī to the Commander of the Faithful, our father Sultan Adam Asīl, son of Maḥmūd, [son of] Sultan Muḥammad Sharīf the Abbasid . . . God . . . has appointed me in the place of my fathers and grandfathers after the death of my paternal uncle Tāj al-Dīn. Every man rules and

> acts in a way which is of benefit to his country and subjects.
> Amīr Tāj al-Dīn acted in his reign as he saw fit; but as for me, there will be absolutely no enmity between me and any of God's creatures, in particular [not] with your lordship; for my grandfather lived [in peace] with your fathers, and my father with your brothers. Thus we will live [in peace] with you.
> I ask *amān* (promise of security) from God, from you and from the French, for my country is ruined and our means of subsistence have gone up in flames. My people are suffering extreme hardship and keep to the *wādī*s. You are my father, in the place of a father to me; relieve us from the warfare, so that we can find peace of mind.
> Whatever is demanded from us, we will not disobey you or the French.[69]

In a similar vein he wrote to the French commander ('we do not have the strength to fight the government'), adding that while Tāj al-Dīn had made common cause with the Fūr, he had nothing to do with them. On the contrary, 'if the people of the east, the Fūr, come to us, we will inform you immediately so that you can come to us.'[70]

By this time the French had realized that Dār Masālīt and Dār Qimr had been integral parts of the Old Dār Fūr Sultanate and the Turco-Egyptian Sudan and would hence eventually fall to the Sudan Government. Yet they felt that they had a right to both *dār*s as compensation for the losses in men and money they had suffered while pacifying the area, and were determined to use their presence in the frontier *dār*s to force their interpretation of the traditional border between Wadai and Dār Fūr (and hence the new border between French and British territory) upon the British. In this interpretation that part of Dār Masālīt that lay west of the Wādī Asunga and Wādī Kajja had never belonged to Dār Fūr.[71] When Andōka submitted, therefore, ceding this area to the French became a condition for peace. Andōka was not in a position to refuse. By allowing a French column to collect the mortal remains of the last Frenchman who stil rested in Masālīt soil, and by returning to the French eighty of the rifles captured at Kirinding, Andōka had fallen afoul of ʿAlī Dīnār, who wrote to him in January 1912:

> A l'honorable Emir Mohammed Bahr Eddine (Andoka) fils de

l'Emir Ab Beker. Salutations. Nous avons compris tout ce que vous mentionnez dans votre lettre au sujet de la présence des Français chez vous, de l'accueil que vous leur avez fait et de la remise des armes que vous leur aviez prises et que vous leur avez livrées. Nous n'approuvons pas cette restitution et vous devez être sévèrement blâmé pour cela, vu que les sus-mentionnés ne sont venus au Massalit que pour prendre les corps de leur morts et les objets qu'ils avaient cachés dans votre pays; mais lorsqu'ils ont vu que vous les aviez accueillis avec une faiblesse manifeste et que vous étiez soumis à eux, ils vous ont demandé les armes. . . . Obéissez-nous et soumettez vous à nos ordres. Ne vous faites pas d'illusions; vous croyez que les chrétiens vous ont laissé tranquilles parce que vous leur avez remis les armes, non, par Dieu, c'est nous qui les avons écartés de votre pays et vous avons débarassés d'eux à l'aide des règlements (traités) et de la politique. Ils n'ont aucun droit sur vous. . . .'[72]

In the same way he wrote to the highest dignitaries of the Masālīt state:

Apprenez maintenant que le Massalit est le pays de mes ancêtres et de mes pères, qu'il est célèbre par mon nom et que je me suis fatigué à l'excès pour vous débarasser de l'oppression du Gouvernment Français. Je désire maintenant que vous suiviez mes conseils et la voie droite. . . . Vous serez tranquilles s'il plaît à Dieu, grâce à lui et au Prophète, et le Dar Four sera une capital unique (un mème gouvernement) comme il l'était.[73]

When ʿAlī Dīnār's letter reached Andōka he had just signed away to the French a substantial part of his kingdom in a letter dated 27 January 1912:

From (. .) Sultan Muḥammad Baḥr al-Dīn, son of the late Abbakr Ismāʿīl, to the ruler of the high and glorious French state, His Lordship Kunīl [Colonel], ruler of the overpowering state, sultan of the sultans of the land of the Sudan as far as Wadai and its periphery. . . . Your letter has reached us and we have understood all you have mentioned to us. . . . I hear and obey God and you. You blamed us with regard to the border from Wādī Asuna [Asunga]. By God and for God I have abandoned it and will never encroach upon it. I stand by the order which you have given me with the will of God – Elevated is He. Know that the whole *dār* is yours, even beyond the border you have mentioned. I have no objection. Everything, good and bad, is in your hand. I will never disobey the orders of the government and you will not have to blame me again. I merely ask from God and from you a complete pardon. Do not listen to the gossip of slanderers about us. I have only one word. . . Moreover I have abandoned all the land of Wādī Asunga which you demanded as far as you said . . . , and we will never encroach upon it.[74]

Although French justifications for chopping off the western part of Dār Masālīt were not very sophisticated, they were understandable to the Masālīt. While the French justified their action by referring to the loss of 12 European and 218 Senegalese and other lives, of 238 rifles, 92 horses, 70 camels, 20,000 bullets etc., the Masālīt believed (and believe) that they paid the area west of the Wādī Asunga as bloodmoney (*diyya*) for the French killed at Kirinding and Darōti.[75] Andōka seems to have regarded it as a condition for peace and for French military assistance against ʿAlī Dīnār. When Colonel Hilaire met Andōka at Todoronna (the confluence of the Wādī Kajja and Wādī Asunga) on 28 February 1911 to inform the *malik*s of the ceded area of their new status, Andōka seemed quite unconcerned about the cession and greatly worried about the intentions of ʿAlī Dīnār. He expressed his dismay at the fact that the British left 'the Fūr madman' in power and begged the French for a strong garrison (which he offered to feed) to protect the Masālīt against him. The French promised Andōka that in case of an attack by ʿAlī Dīnār 400 French riflemen would be sent to protect the country as far as (i.e. west of) Dirjeil. The French also restored Dār Erenga and Dār Jabal to the Masālīt Sultan, who promised to give the Erenga and Jabal chiefs a full pardon. Hilaire was pleased with the young sultan. 'Sans le passé sanglant qui nous éloigne,' he wrote to his superiors, 'il serait bien sympathique.' He presented Andōka as delighted with his new watch, impressed with the manoeuvres of the French troops, and happily chatting about recent history, French military strength and other topics.[76]

Like Dār Qimr, whose treaty the French had apparently decided to forget, and in contrast to Dār Silā and Dār Tāmā, Dār Masālīt had no fixed tribute. Eventually it was to be British. 'Le Massalit est certainement un pays où nous ne sommes entrées que pour en sortir au plus vite,' Colonel Largeau wrote in 1911, and the governor had instructions not to let French troops make an act of 'installation durable'.[77] Nevertheless, in the drought years 1913 and 1914 Andōka made for some time monthly deliveries of about one hundred camel loads of millet to the French garrison at Tumtuma; and the Masālīt remember the hundreds of cattle they sent to Abesher as tribute payments rather than restitutions of raided cattle, as the French claimed.[78]

In spite of the reconciliation with the French, the existence of a pro-Fūr and pro-French faction in Dār Masālīt (as in all frontier states), the presence of Fūr troops in the area, and the threat of Fūr invasion which remained real until 1916, did not give the Masālīt much peace. Andōka's cavalry at Dirjeil was kept in a state of preparedness, which elicited from his sister *ammo* Zahra the proud but anxious song:

> Khaylhum mulajjamīn
> suyūfhum mudarraʿīn
> Kinnaga al barḍū [byirḍaʿū] fī Ab Sōga
> Rabbī yidāriʿ li sulṭān Dirjayl.
>
> Their horses are bridled
> their swords are slung
> The King's children who drink from [the well] of Ab Sōga
> May my Lord shield the sultan of Dirjeil.[79]

In August 1914 Andōka became so concerned about an imminent attack by ʿAlī Dīnār that he decided to put the Wādī Kajja between himself and the Fūr and to move the capital closer to the French, to the present El Geneina. There was another reason why Dirjeil was abandoned for El Geneina: drought. When Colonel Julien visited Dirjeil in December 1913, he reported that it was half deserted and that people had to fetch water at a distance of 20 to 25 kilometers.[80]

The drought was another reason for the turbulence of the frontier area. It began in 1912 and lasted until 1915, and was the result of poor rainfall, warfare and continuous raiding. Thousands of people died, thousands fled to the south. While the northern areas lost as much as 65 per cent of their inhabitants, Dār Silā doubled its population, French reports say, and there were Wadaian refugees as far south as the heart of Dār Fongoro. In Abesher only the dignitaries, the merchants, and the big village owners were able to stay on. Those who were too old or young to flee died in the streets and in front of the mess of the French garrison, which eventually, in the first half of 1914, had to be evacuated itself. A large number of refugees formed bands of bandits (led by a 'Colonel' and *ʿaqīd*s), which terrorized the countryside.[81] French sympathy for the victims of the drought was only rarely translated into practical aid. In a drought of this proportion the French did not have the means for relief. Even the public granaries of the Old Sultanate would not have been adequate to the situation. Yet Colonel Largeau had no reason to be so smug about the new regime. He wrote in his report for February to April 1914:

> Des silos administratifs auraient évidemment un grand secours. En 1903 il en existait au Territoire; on n'a pu les maintenir parce que le budget local n'étant pas autonome, le Commandement ne peut établir ni suivre un programme de longue haleine.

Rather than admitting that the French in this matter could have learned from the old sultans, he wondered:

> ce que serait devenu le Ouadaï si un cataclysme de cette portée était survenu au temps que les sultans imprévoyants et désordonnés entretenaient autour d'eux des milliers des personnes oisives (. . .)?[82]

The fact that the sultan of Dār Masālīt which was also affected by the drought could still deliver one hundred camel loads of grain per month, should have tempered Colonel Largeau's harsh judgement of the sultans of the old type. The French even continued to collect tribute from Dār Tāmā, which had, according to their own estimate, lost two thirds of its population; even the Wadaian refugees in Dār Silā had to pay taxes to the French. The difference between the old and new regimes cannot have escaped the indigenous population: at the height of the famine Governor Julien was battening on his subjects' misery by selling at exorbitant prices public grain which had been paid as taxes.[83]

As a result of French aggression, Fūr irredentism and the

disastrous famine, the period 1909–1916 was one of near anarchy in the frontier area, in which old and new conflicts were fought out inside and between traditional political units. The frontier area suffered most from the border dispute which was at one level a diplomatic problem between the governments of France and Great Britain, and at another, rivalry between the French administration of Wadai and ʿAlī Dīnār. The occupation of Abesher *per se* had not alarmed the latter, but the speed with which the French began to plant the tricolor in what he considered western Dār Fūr, did.[84] The French did nothing to allay his fears. Only a few months after the occupation of Abesher they issued a proclamation which read in translation:

> République Française
> Liberté – Egalité – Fraternité,
> Province française de Ouadaï,
> Son Excellence le Lieutenant-Colonel Millot, émir du Territoire français de l'Afrique centrale du Chari au Dar For, aux gens vertueux qui suivent librement leur puitée. Ceci est pour les informer que les français sont les amis de Ouadaï comme les anglais sont les amis du Dar For. Le désir des français est d'administrer selon les coutumes et avec générosité. Leur but unique est de donner la liberté et la prospérité à tous leur sujets de toute race et de toute religion. Ils ne veulent ni le mal ni le mort de personne. Ils ne redoutent aucun obstacle et méprisent les menaces d'un imposteur. En conséquence, il ordonne que si le nommé Ali Dinar le Forien pénètre dans le pays du Ouadaï sans l'autorisation du gouvernement français, il devra être chassé comme un être malfaisant (. . .).[85]

To keep the French out of Dār Fūr ʿAlī Dīnār used three weapons. Since the Sudan Government did not allow him to deal directly with foreign European powers, he could use diplomacy only in his dealings with the Sudan Government, which continued to assure him that the border problem was being solved diplomatically by the great governments of France and Britain.[86] ʿAlī Dīnār had his doubts and decided to use his second weapon, his armies, against the French in Wadai. However, as has been explained above, the armies were sent out as much against the frontier sultanates as against the French. Even Dūd Murra refused to put his fate into the hands of ʿAlī Dīnār or his generals.[87] The armies proved therefore an ineffective weapon.

The third weapon ʿAlī used was that of economic boycott. After the French conquest of Wadai all roads between Dār Fūr and Wadai remained closed for three years. ʿAlī Dīnār confiscated the goods of all traders who wanted to go to Wadai. Those who tried to go anyway had to pretend to head for the north, and could only go to Abesher by a detour *via* Beskere (in Ennedi). However, the oases of the northern desert were held by the Sanūsiyya, which supported ʿAlī Dīnār's policy of 'cutting Wadai off from the sea' and forbidding all relations with the infidels. Sī Ṣāliḥ Abū Krīmī, lord of Beskere, blocked Wadai's northern route to the Mediterranean and forced all southbound traders *en route* to Wadai to go to al-Fāshir. The fate of those who tried to evade the boycott, and to outwit ʿAlī Dīnār and Sī Ṣāliḥ is evident from what happened to Ibrāhīm al-Ḥajj Muḥammad al-Maghribī of Benghazi. He had been established as a trader in al-Fāshir since 1905. In 1910 he wanted to make a trip to Wadai, and in view of ʿAlī Dīnār's boycott he pretended to go to Benghazi and travelled *via* Beskere. There he was stopped by Sī Ṣāliḥ, who delayed him for four months and charged him enormous prices for the food he and his company needed. Even the envoys of Asīl, who brought a written invitation to Ibrāhīm, could not mollify Sī Ṣāliḥ. Only after he had sworn on the *Qur'an* that he would not go to Wadai but to Dūd Murra in Dār Masālīt, Ibrāhīm was allowed to join a caravan of Majābra and Maghārba, which was for the occasion put under the command of the *imām* of the *zāwiya* of Beskere. Ibrāhīm got rid of his companions on the way and reached Abesher safely, only to find out that ʿAlī Dīnār had confiscated his wife, children, slaves and other possessions.[88] After the French victories in Ennedi and Sī Ṣāliḥ's flight to Dār Fūr in May 1911, ʿAlī Dīnār's boycott became less effective. In August 1911 Asīl wrote to the Egyptian trader ʿAbd Allāh al-Kaḥḥāl, the commercial agent of the Wadai Sultans in Cairo since the 1880s, that trade could be resumed now the route *via* al-Dūr and Beskere was open again.[89]

Whatever ʿAlī Dīnār's attitude towards 'infidels' – undoubtedly a negative one – may have been, fears for the security of his western border seem to have been the most important obstacle to good relations with the French. In August 1912, when he for some unknown reason believed that the border had been settled, he immediately sent a caravan to Abesher, which included his private merchandise and was accompanied by his son who carried letters to the governor of Abesher.[90] Yet, in spite of the fact that the border had not been settled, and in spite of the fact that the tricolor was flying in Goz Beida and Nieri, ʿAlī Dīnār lifted the trade boycott of Abesher towards the end of 1912. From then onwards caravans carrying blue and white cloth called *rubʿiyya*, sugar and gew-gaws of all kinds, visited Abesher regularly.[91]

As long as there is no study of ʿAlī Dīnār's economic policy one can only speculate on why he decided to lift the boycott. The French victories over the Sanūsiyya in the northern desert may have influenced his decision, as did probably the increasing popularity of the trade route *via* Kordofan and Baḥr al-Ghazāl (Kafiakingi), which bypassed Dār Fūr to the south.[92] It is unlikely that ʿAlī had resigned himself to the state of affairs on his western border. On the contrary, the opening of relations with the French may have been aimed against the frontier states, and may have been a new weapon in ʿAlī Dīnār's struggle to subdue them. It was certainly very threatening for Dār Masālīt, which counted upon French protection against ʿAlī Dīnār's wrath about its French connection. ʿAlī meant it to be threatening, as is evident from a letter he wrote to Andōka on 8 December 1912:

> (Sachez) que j'ai donné à ces derniers [the French] des biens précieux, que mes commerçants sont allés chez eux et que moi, s'il plaît à Dieu, je ravagerai votre pays.[93]

Although the trade between al-Fāshir and Abesher was now open, ʿAlī Dīnār continued to use the boycott against the frontier states. Although the route *via* Tumtuma and Dār Masālīt was used for a short period of time, during most of 1913 and 1914 the only official route between al-Fāshir and Abesher was that *via* Dār Tāmā, where the French in good Sudanic tradition had established a garrison to protect and control trade, and Dār Qimr, which continued its heart-rending attempts to be on good terms with French and Fūr at the same time.[94] While the French in 1913 regarded ʿAlī Dīnār's attitude as 'des plus correctes', the latter's hostility towards Dār Masālīt reached a new climax. Andōlia's complaints that ʿAlī was boycotting trade to and from Dār Masālīt were confirmed by Colonel Julien, who wrote in his report of August 1913: 'Le certain est que le sultan du Darfour a établi un barrage défendant entrée ou sortie vers ou du Massalit sous peine de mort.'[95] The Fezzānī trader Sanūsī al-Naffār, Andōka's close friend and adviser, was one victim of the boycott; he was imprisoned in al-Fāshir for trading with 'that slave of ours'.[96] Probably ʿAlī Dīnār's relations with the Masālīt were not at breaking point continuously in the period 1913–16. Yet up to ʿAlī's defeat by the Sudan Government in 1916 there were persistent rumours and fears that a Fūr invasion of Dār Masālīt was imminent. Only with Dār Silā did ʿAlī Dīnār's relations improve spectacularly, particularly after the French had temporarily evacuated Dār Silā in August 1914. In 1915, just before the conquest of Dār Fūr by the British and the reconquest of Dār Silā by the French, ʿAlī Dīnār declared the route to Dār Silā to be the only official road to the west.[97]

Factionalism and popular revolt: Dār Masālīt 1905–1916

The period 1890–1910 was Dār Masālīt's Age of Chivalry, the memory of which has been preserved in many tales and songs. Ater 1898 there was a period of relative peace in which the Masālīt knights or *fursān* (sing. *fāris*) showed off their courage and fighting skills in occasional raids on neighbours, and their horsemanship in front of the local belles who would break into ululations and songs. The song sung for *ʿaqīd* Mudda, who lost the horse called Bagersa (Masālīt for 'one-eyed') when he was out slave-raiding in Dār Fūr, captures the spirit of the times:

> ʿAqīdnā yā Mudda
> mālū sawwayti shayn?
> Bagersa fī medde
> kayf binaṭṭiṭ kay!
> Niḥna wa'l-banāt
> kullu ḥizinnā lay[k].
>
> Oh Mudda, our *ʿaqīd*
> why did you go wrong?
> How Bagersa used to dance
> in the sultan's train!
> We and [the other] girls
> are all sad for you.[98]

Another more militant song was sung by the female fans of

Abbakr's *amīn*, Aḥmad Duway of the Urmōk clan of the Qimr:

> ʿAyāl Urmōk wayn humman?
> Aḥmad sār maʿā minayn?
> Antūnī sayf nilāgī wayn?
>
> Where are the sons of Urmōk?
> With whom did Aḥmad ride out to war?
> Give me a sword! Where shall we give battle?[99]

Praise songs for the princes of the blood were particularly popular. The news that Tāj al-Dīn had recovered from his circumcision and had received two slave girls (Amm Gazza and Amm Ḍīfān) as concubines, spread in the form of a song:

> Al-ṣughayyar qām
> al-kārib al-ḥizām
> Sīd Jimme maʿā Mursāl
> Amm Gazza wa Amm Ḍīfān.
> Tāj al-Dīn sughayyar
> dōr al-sulṭān.
>
> The young one has grown up,
> the one who girds his loins,
> master of Jimme and Mursāl,
> of Amm Gazza and Amm Ḍīfān.
> Young Tāj al-Dīn has now become
> of the calibre of sultans.[100]

Abbo Tāj al-Dīn, like other *bāsinga* and *abbonga*, gathered around him a group of followers and hangers-on from both the commoners and the nobility (and including slaves), who never left his side and lived at his expense. These circles around prominent noblemen formed small beer-drinking and riding societies, which followed a certain code of honour and vied with each other in horsemanship, courage and military exploits. There were many of these small power centres, but that of the sultan, i.e. the government, was the most powerful one, followed by that around that son, brother or uncle of the sultan who was at any particular point in time his most likely successor. Usually the different groups combined into two opposing factions: those who favoured the *status quo*, and those who expected to gain from a change of regime. Abbakr had antagonized so many members of both the old and new elite that his opposition, led by *faqīh* ʿAlī al-Tamtam and supporting the candidature of Tāj al-Dīn, was strong and actively conspiring to overthrow him. Abbakr's fateful decision in 1905 to send half of the army to the northern front may have been inspired by his doubts about the loyalty of the opposition party. *Faqīh* ʿAlī al-Tamtam is said to have compared Abbakr's capture with the removal of a thorn stuck in his head.[101]

Although the opposition during Abbakr's reign may have been uncommonly strong, factionalism was structural in Sudanic kingdoms such as Dār Masālīt, since in principle any close male relative of the reigning sultan could succeed to the throne. Coups d'état instigated by the princes of the blood and succession disputes were therefore far from rare. The succession dispute between Tāj al-Dīn and Andōka after the defeat at Shawai may have been partly responsible for the second victory of the Fūr at Kunjuldei, after which most of the nobility, including Andōka, fled to Dār Silā and Wadai. Subsequently Tāj al-Dīn's role in rallying the Masālīt and driving out the Fūr earned him the sultanate. In the battles of Gilānī and Kejkeje the nobility firmly stood together, but after the victory Andōka, his brother Badawī and others made an abortive coup attempt which led to the imprisonment and near execution of Andōka, and exile in Wadai in the case of Badawī.[102] In contrast to Wadai, where all the brothers of the sultan were blinded at his accession, or Dār Fūr where they were pensioned off into obscurity, in the frontier sultanates the royal princes were the core of strength and the pillars of the administration, in spite of the existence of an important slave element.[103] Tāj al-Din's advisors pointed out to him the importance of the princes; he forgave his cousins, forcibly married them to his daughters, and eventually appointed Andōka as his successor.[104]

The structural factionalism was particularly dangerous when it was exploited by disgruntled overlords or outside enemies. In the 1880s ʿUthmān Jānū had tried to exploit Mistereng/Gernyeng rivalry by advocating the reinstatement of Hajjām. In 1910 the armies of ʿAlī Dīnār had a son of Hajjām in their train, as well as relatives of the rulers of Dār Erenga and Dār Jabal. In 1914 ʿAlī Dīnār gave a warm welcome to ʿAlī Sennān, uncle of the then reigning sultan Andōka, who had fallen from favour.[105] Andōka succeeded Tāj al-Dīn in very unfortunate circumstances, just after the battle of Darōti when the Masālīt were in shock and had scattered in all directions. Andōka himself was inconsolable at the death of his brother, and took courage only after a stern reproach by *abbo* ʿAlī ab Shanab, who told him to behave as a sultan and to stand up as a leader for his people. On Ḥajar Maymere, near Mogornei, he was invested in a simple ceremony by Sultan Dūd Murra with Tāj al-Dīn's turban, and probably sword.[106]

Andōka was a mild ruler, it is said. Yet factionalism was rife because he was young, and caught between the French and the Fūr, who vied for his allegiance and played on the divisions in the ranks of the nobility. When Andōka concluded peace with the French a strong war party emerged, which was led by his brother Badawī and was said to have Fūr sympathies.[107] A coup d'état led by Badawī could count on Fūr support. On 17 December 1912 ʿAlī Dīnār wrote to Andōka:

> Bref, voici ma réponse à vous: Fais à la tête suivant ton bon plaisir, ou bien suis nos ordres comme les sujets soumis au royaume du Darfour, et tout ce que nous te demanderons paye le en soumis, cela te reposera et reposera les gens. Ou bien quitte le pouvoir et laisse le à qui en est le plus digne de ta famille et qui nous reposera par la soumission à nos ordres.[108]

Andōka's attempt not to alienate Badawī alienated the French, who were irritated by Badawī's continuous raids into French territory. On 8 April 1913 the governor of Wadai wrote to Andōka:

> Et vous, vous ignorez la sortie de votre frère Bedaoui, à la tête d'une centaine d'hommes dont 30 fusils. Si réellement vous l'ignorez ou que votre frère ait le droit d'agir à sa guise sans avoir besoin de votre autorisation, c'est que le Sultan du Massalit serait votre frère Bedaoui et non vous; dans ce cas je voudrais savoir à qui m'addresser des deux.[109]

Two relatives of Andōka (ʿAbd al-Sharīf and ʿAlī Sennān) fled to ʿAlī Dīnār hoping they might overthrow Andōka with Fūr support. One relative, the son of *faqīh* ʿAlī al-Tamtam, tried to obtain French support to become sultan, but was found out and publicly criticized in a song:

> imbiyan igeinde kei
> nyemmu babanāto nyanyande

ʿAbd al-Karīm qādirte
sultana nasāratō ndide.

Although we let you share, you schemed on your own.
The oil of your father you did not eat.
ʿAbd al-Karīm how could you want to be
the sultan of the Christians![110]

Andōka had to face not only the discontent of a faction (and separate individuals) of the nobility, but also popular discontent.

The Masālīt had lost the battle of Shawai in 1905 for many reasons. The superior arms and numbers of the Fūr, the decision to fight with only half of the army, the deceit of the *wazīr*, were all instrumental in the defeat. Moreover, Sultan Abbakr had probably underestimated the enemy. When a *faqīh* offered to divert the Fūr armies from Dār Masālīt with prayers, Abbakr flew into a rage and – implicitly referring to the enormous wealth the state had obtained in the wars with the *anṣār* – he severely scolded the poor *faqīh* for trying to divert 'the public treasury' from his *dār*.[111] Abbakr certainly underestimated his unpopularity with the commoners, which has been discussed above. The commoners were tired of pulling chestnuts out of the fire for the Gernyeng and of the favouritism shown to the royal slaves, and they deserted Abbakr in battle.

When Tāj al-Dīn began to rally the Masālīt for another war the commoners and their *malik*s would join him only if he assured them not to take their booty away from them, and if he would reduce the *fiṭra* tax to what it had been under Ismāʿīl. Tāj agreed and undertook to pay compensation (in cows) for all rifles or male horses he had to confiscate for the war treasury.[112] When he, after the victory of Kejkeje, began to organize his administration, the commoners had again reason to be content; the governors were Tāj al-Dīn's *fursān* and brothers-in-arms who counted no doubt many Gernyeng but also included a man like *amīn* Dā'ūd Bōbale of the Nyerneng, who became Tāj al-Dīn's *wazīr* and governor of the districts of Konyosa and Mistere. Tāj al-Dīn won the hearts of his people for another reason. Like his father and brother he was an *anṣārī*. He wore the patched *jibba* of the *anṣār*, led the people in prayer and read the *rātib* of the *Mahdī*.[113] He presented the war against both Fūr and French as a war against infidels. 'If you kill an infidel you go to paradise,' he told his men, 'and if you are killed by an infidel you go to paradise as well.'[114] One simply could not lose in fighting for his cause. The Masālīt were proud of being *anṣār*, as is evident from the song they sang when they pursued the Fūr after the battle of Kejkeje:

> Ab shanab dūdkinna,
> anṣār shaylīn ngāchirre daqq al-ḥaddādī
> akhayr min daqq al-naṣāra al min sabāḥ jaybinnā.
> Qatalū shartay Zayn fī quṭun dāsinna,
> qatalū Qamr al-Dīn biḥarjinna.
> Kallim ʿAlı sulṭān Fūr, kam bijīnā khallīhu yijīnā,
> kam mā bijīnā, niḥna mā fāḍiyinna!

> Oh bewhiskered lion,
> the *anṣār* carry smith-wrought spears
> surpassing the Christian arms they bring us from the east.
> They killed *shartay* Zayn and hid him inside the cotton bush,
> they killed Qamar al-Dīn outraging us.
> Tell ʿAlī, sultan of Fūr, to come if he intends to come,
> if he doesn't, we will not be idle![115]

However, Gernyeng domination did not suffer a real setback. The first decade of the twentieth century was one of warfare, and in warfare the sultan depended on his relatives – the core of his cavalry – more than ever. Moreover, in this period Abbakr's many sons (about thirty or forty) began to reach manhood and to play an important political role.[116] In contrast to the sons of Abbakr's *bāsinga*, who grew up in the villages of their mothers somewhere in the *dār*, and married local girls for a bridewealth in cows, the direct descendants of Abbakr grew up at court and married without payment from among the slave girls. The children of these unions, having no maternal relatives, grew up in the capital as *abbonga*, while the children of the *bāsinga* merged with the commoners.[117] The princes of the blood, who regarded themselves as equally royal but less fortunate than Andōka, compensated themselves materially by living off – 'eating', the Masālīt say – the commoners. For the latter Gernyeng domination became in the course of Andōka's reign more and more oppressive. The *abbonga* became a terror to the countryside. Those who were given districts to govern became so oppressive, it was reported in 1921, that a general protest of the *malik*s in 1916 led to the dismissal of thirty *abbonga* governors.[118] Those who did not have districts toured the *dār*, demanding hospitality, taking without compensation the fattest bull, a handsome horse, a pretty girl, even the spears someone was carrying, and fining and punishing people at their discretion. Whenever an *abbo* came to a village, the people of the whole area brought presents, hoping that they could thus buy off a visit to their own villages; and far and wide people hid their livestock from the *abbo*'s greedy eyes. Complaining to the sultan was risky, people remember, for after all one would be accusing a relative. Moreover the sultan could only be approached through his *amīns*, and was too preoccupied with foreign affairs to care about the details of internal administration.[119]

It is impossible to say how acute a grievance exploitation by the *abbonga* was in the first years of Andōka's reign, but there is evidence that the exactions of the royal clique of *abbonga* and their adjutants had already become a social problem. When one of Tāj al-Dīn's cavalry commanders, called Kondojo, was killed by the owner of a fat goat Kondojo insisted to have for lunch, the commoners criticized him in a song: 'you Kondojo, commander of all those horsemen, for the sake of a goat – not even a sheep – you have left your children orphans.'[120]

Andōka's submission to the French and the burden of paying tribute in a period of drought and famine were more acutely resented by the commoners. The discontent expressed itself in the risings of *faqīh*s and prophets (particularly 'Prophets Jesus') who proclaimed the holy was against the infidels and their indigenous stooges. The coming of Prophet Jesus (*al-nabī* ʿĪsā) was an element of the Mahdist tradition, according to which Prophet Jesus would descend at the end of times to kill the Antichrist who had defeated the Mahdī.[121] The 'plague' of prophets which had been endemic in the area since the revolt of Abū Jummayza in 1888, affected not only Dār Masālīt but also Dār Tāmā and Wadai. In 1905 a Masālīt *nabī* ʿĪsā was executed in al-Fāshir. In 1911 the French reported the execution of a prophet called *faqīh* Abbo in eastern Dār Masālīt. In the drought years fighting *faqīh*s proliferated: in June 1913 a *faqīh* of Gorane (in French Dār Masālīt) led an attack on the Frenchpost at Tumtuma because the French heliograph on top of Jabal Gorane, so he believed, caused the failure of the rains. In November 1913 the post at Abesher, the capital of Wadai, was attacked by three *faqīh*s and a sorcerer, all of whom were killed. In

November and December the French reported the rising of two prophets in Dār Masālīt, remembered by the Masālīt as 'the war of the *faqīhs*'.[122]

A rising of this type usually began with the withdrawal of a *faqīh* to a hilltop or another isolated area, where he began to preach the evil of drinking beer and the necessity of fighting the infidels. Promises that the enemies' bullets would turn into water, and that sticks would turn into rifles in the hands of their followers, were often part and parcel of the message of the prophets. A typical meeting of anti-government *faqīhs* and commoners was described in 1921 to the British who, after their occupation of Dār Fūr, also had their share of prophets:

> A large concourse of fikis and other men, said to number a thousand, collected in the open air. Under the direction of the head fiki, the assembly repeated the 'Gelala', the 'Istighfar', the 'Salla ala El Nebi', the 'Bismillahi', the 'La hawla wa la quwata illa Billahi', and the 'Subhan Allah' each a thousand times. Then the whole Koran was allotted, a few suras to each fiki present, each board, when full, being washed clean with water which was carefully conserved. From this water, which contained, as it were, the whole Koran in solution, every man capable of bearing arms drank, in the belief that it would protect him from injury by the Government's weapons. All were then instructed to fast from Tuesday to Thursday.[123]

The Masālīt remember only two risings of this type in this period, the rising of *faqīh* Dugdug, who manifested himself as *nabī* ʿIsā in the area of Turmenung on the Wādī Barei, and the 'war of the *faqīhs*' in southern Dār Masālīt. Of the story of *faqīh* Dugdug the only known version is that of the government, i.e. Sultan Andōka and the people of Dirjeil. Dugdug rose in 1911 or 1912. He won wide support among both commoners and courtiers of Dār Masālīt who thought it not unlikely that God, who had sent Abū Jummayza to their part of the world, had now sent the Prophet Jesus. Many people in Andōka's direct environment, particularly the former followers of *faqīh* Sinīn from Kabkābiyya, secretly believed in the prophet, who thus became a real rival and threat to the power of Andōka. Yet, as most of his fellow-prophets, Dugdug came to a sad end. Sharaf al-Dīn Ismāʿīl, Andōka's uncle, rode out at the head of a warband and defeated

Dugdug and his followers in battle. Dugdug himself and many of his disciples were killed, while the livestock of the whole area was rounded up and taken to Dirjeil, where all the credulous of the capital were given a severe beating.[124]

Soon afterwards the whole southern part of Dār Masālīt (the areas of Misterei, Konyosa, Kunjunung, Ḥajar Jabōk, Bir Tābit, and Charow) broke into rebellion against the Gernyeng.[125] The leaders were *faqīhs*, first *faqīh* Isāgha Daldūm of Abun, and later – after Isāgha had surrendered without a blow and had been pardoned – ʿAbd al-Raḥmān of the Konjorong and Yaʿqūb of the Minyiki who hoped to become the new sultan. It reached the ears of the French in Abesher that *faqīh* ʿAbd al-Raḥmān contended that Ismāʿīl ʿAbd al-Nabī, Andōka's grandfather, had been nothing but an insignificant *faqīh* of Khuzāmī origin, and that he himself, a full-blooded Maslātī, had more right to be sultan.[126] The French did not realize that the rebels' main grievance was Andōka's submission to the French and the tribute (*jizya*) he paid to them. The rebels believed that Andōka, by submitting to the French against the advice of the late Tāj al-Dīn, had degraded himself and was degrading them, but they also had a more material grievance.[127] The southern areas, particularly Bir Tābit and Konyosa, it was said, were the only areas far and wide which had a reasonable grain crop in 1913. Andōka had therefore decided to levy a special, ferociously heavy, tax of six *waybas* (i.e. almost 200 kilos) millet per hut.[128] Most probably it was this millet that was sent by the ton to Tumtuma and Abesher, and people concluded that all the riches and reserves of the *dār* – in 1913 a matter of life and death – were being given to the 'infidels'. An additional grievance was the fact that Andōka began to tax the *faqīhs*, who had been tax-exempt until then.[129]

The revolt began with the murder of several slave soldiers of Badawī who were visiting the area of Kujunung, possibly to collect taxes. While the Gernyeng in Dirjeil discussed their strategy, the rebels gathered at Ngōbe (near Kujunung). Badawī and *amīn* Aḥmad Ab Shulūkh were sent out to subdue them. By following a tactic of attack and immediate withdrawal their horsemen lured the rebels from Ngōbe to Kudumule, where Badawī's riflemen were hidden in the bush. Those rebels who were not killed, like *faqīh* Yaʿqūb, dispersed in flight. When Colonel Julien visited Dirjeil in December (25–8 December 1913), Badawī came riding back from the front to pay his regards. He informed Julien that all was under control, at least until a new false prophet would rise, which happened all the time, he said, particularly among the Erenga and the people of Konyosa.[130] After the battle of Kudumule, Badawī made a camp at Charow and systematically laid the area to waste by burning villages and confiscating livestock and grain. The rebel area was declared *mubāḥ* ('ownerless') it was said, and all the 'Kaseyeng', the people of the *gōz* or northerners, as well as drought victims from Wadai and Dār Silā profited from the 'free for all' to come and plunder. Only after most inhabitants had fled, did the sultan call the punitive expedition to an end and recall Badawī to Dirjeil. The famine of 1913, which claimed so many deaths in southern Dār Masālīt, is remembered there as 'the famine of Badawī'.[131] Although sources collected in Dār Masālīt in the 1920s suggest that Andōka's uncle, ʿAlī Sennān, whose maternal relatives were from Konyose, had instigated the rising, this is not very probable.[132] The revolt was a popular movement, and in view of the arms of the rebels, was doomed to failure right from the start, as ʿAlī Sennān himself would have been the first to know.

The surrender of Dūd Murra and the submission of Andōka in 1911 had not put an end to the anarchy which prevailed on Dār Masālīt's western border. Raids and counter-raids alternated with punitive expeditions, while bands of robbers took up their abode in 'ce pays que nulle autorité n'a jamais tenu en main'.[133] As an informant in the southwestern tip of Dār Masālīt put it:

> Those were different times. We slept with our sandals on to get up at the first sound of the *dinggar*. Our spears and provisions were always ready, for there was no peace.[134]

The policy makers in Dār Masālīt were to a large extent responsible for the unrest, and were possibly following a deliberate policy. It is true that Andōka was in need of the livestock which the raids provided in order to send it to al-Fāshir (as presents for ʿAlī Dīnār or for sale in the market), and to pay to the French. The latter demanded livestock in restitution for livestock raided from French territory, but the restitutions required new raids, which called for new restitutions etc.[135] Yet there was more to these raids than the simple need for livestock. Although the French had the impression that Andōka did not give the cession of the land west of the Wādī Asunga a second thought, Masālīt policy towards the ceded territory suggests the opposite. In at least one case French records made it clear that the livestock which in their terminology had been 'raided', had been collected by Masālīt *abbonga* as taxes, and that the Masālīt inhabitants of French Dār Masālīt showed a 'manque absolu de loyalisme', and were accessory to the raids by failing to inform the French.[136] The Masālīt apparently still regarded the ceded territory as theirs, and their raids and tax demands suggest that they were determined to make French possession of the area a very mixed blessing.

Andōka's concern not only to preserve the Masālīt Sultanate but even to extend it is evident from the discovery made by the French governor of Goz Beida in November 1916; the Masālīt had silently taken over, and were collecting taxes from villages which belonged to Dār Silā but which lay on the east bank (i.e. Masālīt side) of the Wādī Asunga.[137] It is possible that the continuous raids into French territory were the work of the war party led by Badawī, and hence partly out of Andōka's control. However the prompt restitution of almost 400 cattle after an angry letter from Colonel Julien in 1913 suggests that Andōka was in control when he wanted to be. His feeble excuse for failing to attend the combined military expedition against the bandits in Iffene in that same year caused doubts of his sincerity even in the minds of the French, who nevertheless stuck to their opinion that Andōka, even if he was weak, was of good will.[138] After the Iffene incident Andōka paid his first spontaneous visit to the French and rode to the post at Tumtuma with only a few companions. Apparently he felt that he had pushed his luck too far. However, Masālīt aggression and expansion whenever and wherever the pressure on their western and eastern borders subsided – e.g. when 'Alī Dīnār's throne began to totter in 1916 – suggests that Andōka continued to push his luck to the very limit.[139]

Chapter 7

Some direct results of indirect rule: Dār Masālīt in the 1920s and 1930s

El Abid ligu hurria
El Awin ittefagia
El Eyyal effendia
El Sebian askaria
Wa El Gurush mahia
Zaman el Hakuma nazar kefaia.

The slaves found freedom
The women the right to ask for divorce
The children school degrees
The young men military careers
and money found salaries
The time of the Government . . . you can see for yourself.
(*baqqāra* song)[1]

The Condominium period (1898–1956), in which the Sudan came to be ruled by Great Britain as a dependency of Egypt, introduced changes which had a lasting effect on Sudanese society and economy. In most of the Sudan Condominium Rule had been established in 1898. Hence the process of change which resulted from the incorporation into the British Empire, with all that entailed, was well under way there when the Sudan Government conquered Dār Fūr in 1916. The object of this final chapter is not to study this process in detail in either Dār Fūr or Dār Masālīt (which was occupied in 1922), but to outline some immediate consequences of Dār Masālīt's incorporation into the Anglo-Egyptian Sudan – consequences which have dominated and hampered its development until today.

The occupation

With the occupation of al-Fāshir in May 1916 the delimitation of the boundary between French and British spheres of influence, i.e. of the old Dār Fūr/Wadai border, became both necessary and feasible. The Sudan Government was quite ignorant of the area west of Jabal Marra; in 1917, when it received complaints that Andōka was forcibly retaining members of ʿAlī Dīnār's *ḥarīm*, it requested the French governor of Wadai to persuade Andōka to let the ladies go.[2] That the French politely refused, and broke a lance for Andōka, was typical of the general pattern of their relations with the sultan, which had become cordial and close. Andōka was a regular visitor to the posts of Tumtuma and Abesher and mixed freely with the French officers, who dined and wined with him and made him gifts of whisky, wine and small wonders of western technology such as clocks and rifles.[3] As long as Andōka paid his annual 'presents' of millet and bulls, and as long as the raids into French territory remained within limits, the internal administration of Dār Masālīt was not interfered with, and the sultan had nothing to fear from the French. On the contrary, he leaned on the French to maintain his position at home. When in October 1917, for example, Badawī was stirring up trouble again, and groups of Masālīt, angry about the tribute demanded from them and armed to the teeth, were reported near the borders, Andōka rode to Abesher to protest his good will and – as the French shrewdly realized – 'dans l'arrière pensée de faire rentrer dans l'ordre les fauteurs de troubles en paraissant s'être assuré notre appui'.[4]

Although French and British officials on the spot had instructions to do nothing that might affect or complicate the final decision about the Chado–Sudanese boundary, in reality the French had abandoned their claim to Dār Masālīt and Dār Qimr. In June 1916 they wrote to the Qimr Sultan Idrīs to go and meet the British in al-Fāshir. Idrīs obeyed, and received a splendid reception from the governor, who presented him with two horses, forty garments of different kinds, a carpet, forty heads of sugar, forty pounds of coffee and other things. Andōka probably received a similar letter. In July he sent a letter of congratulations to the conquerors of al-Fāshir, requesting the repatriation of Masālīt captives there, and hinting that he was willing to reaffirm his allegiance to Dār Fūr.[5] The French were apparently tired of having to keep Andōka in power and the border area in peace all on their own, for in October 1917 they advised the British to establish a garrison on Dār Masālīt's eastern border until it would be decided whether Dār Masālīt was to be French or British. In February 1918, the British Foreign Office gave its approval. In March one company of infantry commanded by J. H. Hardy and accompanied by H. A. MacMichael as political officer established a post at Kereinik. The intentions of the Sudan Government had been explained to Andōka in a letter:

> After many salaams – I have heard from the French Commandant at Abéché that there is a party in Dar Masalit trying to upset your authority, and to cause trouble in your Dar. With the same object, i.e. to support your authority, and also to let your people see that we have no intention of permitting the peace to be broken on our frontiers, I have obtained permission also to establish a post on your Eastern border, and my wakil, MacMichael Bey, will be proceeding from here in about two weeks time to establish a post there. I wish you fully understand that I have no intention of interfering with your administration of your country, but that I am putting the post there solely to support your authority in case of trouble arising from persons wishing to upset your authority in the Dar, and that the French and Anglo-Egyptian Governments are prepared to work in conjunction in maintaining order on their borders.[6]

The instructions given to the commander of the garrison were in accordance with this letter. The border post was to be only that. It had no authority over the indigenous population, had to provide a guard of honour and present arms to the sultan, had to pay for the grain, milk, meat and labour it required, and had to keep away from the 'native women' to an extent which would 'protect the feelings of the inhabitants and preserve the health of the soldiers', but would not disregard 'the tendencies of human nature' and cause discontent.[7]

Andōka made the necessary arrangements to supply the post but made no secret of his hostility towards the British, and succeeded in making a very negative impression on the political officer. The latter reported their first meeting:

> Endoka himself is about 28 years old, small and gross-looking, with blubber lips, sagging mouth and negroid features, chocolate coloured and insignificant in appearance, addicted to drink, weak and irresolute in character. His manners are bad from any point of view, native or otherwise, being rough and blatant. He sits in a chair slapping the arms of it and throwing his legs about and lolling and rolling with yawning nonchalance. He affects rather a 'devil-may-care' attitude, and, having no natural dignity of his own, gives himself vulgar and pretentious airs, in the hope to impress the bystanders.[8]

When he was received by a guard of honour and the three Englishmen stepped forward to greet him, the sultan refused to come off his horse. When he eventually did, 'he gave himself insufferable airs, kept his face swathed up in linen, and would not condescend to utter a syllable beyond an occasional grunt or click.' In the evening the sultan became roaring drunk within sight of the British camp. MacMichael attributed Andōka's misbehaviour to his Francophilia, but also realized that it was locally believed that the troops had come to occupy and administer Dārs Tāma, Qimr, and Masālīt, and even Wadai. The Kereinik post immediately began to attract people who were discontented with the *status quo*: Tāmā, Wadaians, even a messenger from Dār Runga, and disloyal subjects of Andōka such as the local rulers of Dār Erenga, who wanted to break away from Dār Masālīt. The former sultans of the Marārīt and Awra (who were living in exile in Dār Kerne) and a pretender to the headship of Jabal Mūn (who lived near Kutum) began to make ready to move on Dār Masālīt.[9]

In spite of the fact that Andōka was hostile, imprisoned all those who contacted the post without his explicit orders – even to sell milk! – and hid his rifles, war horses and even wives outside the capital, the British officials were bound by their instructions to support him and choose his side. When the *shartay* of Dār Erenga came into conflict with the sultan's *maqdūm* there (a slave called Saʿīd Ab Dūdū), who had confiscated the *shartay*'s property on account of his British sympathies, they were forced to hand the *shartay* over to Andōka and swallow the latter's impudent letter.[10] For the Sudan Government officials in Kereinik incidents like these meant a loss of face; by the end of 1919 they were clamouring for immediate occupation, since the Masālīt interpreted the delay as weakness and as evidence that Dār Masālīt would become French after all. The Sudan Government refused to give permission for this until the results of the Anglo-French boundary negotiations would have become official.[11] When this came about in March 1921, the Government had already begun to prepare for the occupation of Dār Masālīt, and had formulated a set of proposals which were discussed with Andōka himself in al-Fāshir, in January 1920. The sultan was to pay to the treasury of al-Fāshir L.E. 500 in cattle to be sold in al-Fāshir. He was to provide free buildings for the Government's troops and personnel in Kereinik, and provide them with grain (which would be credited to the civil budget) and meat (which would be paid for on the spot). The sultan would not have power of death and his judicial powers would be defined. Slavery and the import of liquor were to be forbidden; fire-arms were to be surrendered, and taxes were to be collected by locally elected representatives. Finally, the sultan should realize that his continuance in power depended on obedience to the Government and his acceptability to his subjects. Andōka accepted most of the proposals, protesting only against the popular election of *maqdūm*s. He undertook to disband his army at the occupation of his *dār* by Anglo-Egyptian troops, but requested the return of some rifles for a small personal bodyguard and for his *maqdūm*s.[12]

However, the Nyala rising of 1921, which produced side-effects in Dār Masālīt, forced the pace of events. The rebels who – led by a *nabī ʿIsā* called ʿAbd Allāh al-Suḥaynī – stormed the government post at Nyala and killed a British official, had in their ranks many of the Masālīt inhabitants of southern Dār Fūr. The Masālīt of the west were in contact with their relatives in southern Dār Fūr, and prepared to attack the fort at Kereinik if the Nyala rising would prove successful. This time the commoners were not incited against, but by the royal family, and rumours spread that the Government intended to collect four years of taxes all at once, that it would draft the young men, and would tax houses and even dogs! Andōka himself was under suspicion as well. It was said that he had ordered his *faqīh*s to pray for an event which would prevent the Anglo-Egyptian occupation of his *dār*,and that he had ordered the commoners to keep their sandals, spears and water skins in readiness. Yet he was a restraining influence upon his brothers and uncles, ordered the dispersal of the armed assemblies of horsemen and footmen which gathered around them, and even came to live outside the fort for a while to prevent it from being attacked. Throughout October 1921 the Kereinik post was virtually in a state of siege, while 4,000–5,000 warriors were camping in a nearby *wādī* and bands of mounted noblemen came to stampede the market outside the post, making off only when the machine guns and rifles appeared over the walls. However, the Nyala rising was suppressed, *faqīh* al-Suḥaynī executed, and the Kereinik post reinforced. The Masālīt attack on the fort never materialized.

Yet the Sudan Government was determined to teach the Masālīt a lesson. The British Resident, Reginald Davies, fearing that he would lose his native administration team, counselled against a severe punishment of the ruling elite and argued that: ‘our moral claim to their [Masālīt] loyalty is nil’, and rests solely on ‘the verbal agreement made with the Sultan during his stay in Fasher last year’. It was therefore decided to pardon the sultan, his notables and important relatives, who were nevertheless all summoned to Kereinik and persuaded to swear ‘to loyally adhere to the agreement made between him [the sultan] and the Government for the future administration of Dar Masalit; [and] to abstain in future from all treacherous activities’.[13] It was deemed necessary that the troops should give a show of force in the *dār*; that El Geneina should be occupied immediately; that a general fine should be levied, and that exemplary punishment should take place.[14]

On 22 January 1922 El Geneina was occupied. Masālīt tradition remembers that ‘when the English came to El Geneina, they came in anger’.[15] Andōka, making a virtue of necessity, resigned himself to the occupation. ‘A trivial, but striking, symptom of this attitude was’ – Davies reported – ‘his coming, on foot, running through the soft sand of Wadi Kaja to meet the cars, and helping with his own hands to lay down branches and gusab [straw] for them to run over’.[16] At the end of February 1922 the sultan received a robe of honour. By 1923 he was reported to be a teetotaller and extremely religious. Apparently Andōka had decided to play the part the Sudan Government had chosen for him. The angry young man who had shocked H. A. MacMichael in 1918 evoked Davies' pity:

> When one sees his corpulent little figure standing, with a slight swagger, in the middle of a circle of his kneeling subjects, who

> clap their hands softly in unison and prefix their replies to his remarks with a "May God give you victory", it is difficult, comparing his political situation with that of his predecessors, to regard him as anything but a rather pathetic spectacle.[17]

In the meantime the Chado-Sudanese border had finally been settled, and the commission which was to delimitate the boundary on the spot had commenced its work. From their new fort in El Geneina the Sudan Government officials set to work to transform the administration of Dār Masālīt.

Indirect rule

As a result of the special circumstances under which the Sudan Government established its first contacts with the Masālīt Sultanate, the principles on which the administration of Anglo-Egyptian Dār Masālīt was set up was from the beginning that of 'indirect rule'. Dār Masālīt was treated as 'a miniature Lugardian emirate' and, at least from hindsight, as the laboratory for indirect rule in the Sudan. Lugard's ideas about indirect rule certainly had adherents in the Sudan Civil Service, and R. Davies, the first Resident of Dār Masālīt, was one of them. However, as G. N. Sanderson has pointed out, 'indirect rule' did not become general administrative policy in the Sudan until 1926, and down to 1924 'the official attitude to indirect rule was predominantly pragmatic and administrative rather than political and ideological.'[18] In 1924 Andōka received a brevet from the Governor-General of the Sudan and a letter which read:

> To El Sultan Mohammed Bahr El Din ibn El Sultan Abu Bakr, Sultan Dar El Masalit.
> After compliments etc. I write this to inform you, officially, of the alteration happened in Dar El Masalit after it had been occupied by the Sudan Government and an Agent had been detailed to represent it in that Country. As being President of the said Government and under this my letter, I, officially, confirm your position as Sultan of Dar el Masalit, taking power direct from me. Therefore I put the power in your hands to take the whole steps, which you desire, for the comfort and prosperity of your Country, subject to the approval of our

> Government Representative, residing with you, and the Governor Darfur Province.[19]

What the Government gave with one hand it took away with the other. With the occupation of Dār Masālīt and the assumption of sovereignty by the Government the sultan's authority was seriously curtailed. He lost control over the armed forces, lost his right to deal with foreign powers or settle external boundaries and his authority over aliens (i.e. most of El Geneina, which became an enclave differing from the rest of the *dār*).[20] In internal administrative affairs the sultan was supervised by a British Resident, whose authority was limited, but whose influence was pervasive. 'The Resident's duty,' A. J. Arkell wrote in 1926, 'is to know as much as possible (no easy task when he is not directly in touch with the people, a naturally reserved, fanatically inclined, race, many of whom do not speak Arabic) and to do as little as possible.'[21] He was not to give orders to the sultan, but only to advise him, and was the mouthpiece of the governor of Dār Fūr province, who did have the authority to give orders to the sultan, and in whose hands lay 'the control of the finances and policy of Dar Masalit'.[22] In practice the Resident was much more powerful.

The Sudan Government regarded its commitment to 'indirect rule' not as a commitment to abstain from changing Dār Masālīt, but to bring about change by using the method of 'indirect rule'. The implicit aims of its policy were to make the sultanate loyal, just and progressive, cheap and efficient, possibly in that order. By the time the Resident, R. Davies, started his 'experiment in genuine Nigerian-style, indirect rule', the Government had already formed a set of opinions and prejudices which were to be a guideline for the future. One of the fixed ideas of the policy makers was that Andōka was weak, 'something of a broken reed, in constant need of stiffening by the Resident'.[23] Even R. Davies, who grew quite fond of Andōka, described him as a weak and irresolute ruler, who was lacking in driving-power and whose clemency was untempered by firmness. That Andōka through his mildness was popular with the commoners was praised, but his failure to keep his brothers and uncles – 'merely jackals of varying degrees of rapacity' – in line was and remained a thorn in the flesh for the Sudan Government representatives from 1918 to 1940.[24] The latter maybe did not realize that this failure to control the princes of the blood was not so much a weakness of character, but a weakness of the constitution of a small Sudanic kingdom like Dār Masālīt, made more pronounced by the particular circumstances of colonial conquest.[25] In any case, their task was to change, rather than to understand this. The exclusion of the sultan's relatives (*abbonga*) and (ex-)slaves from the administration became the most consistent element of Government policy in Dār Masālīt.

The *abbonga*

The administrative system of the sultanate had undergone some changes since Abbakr's reign. Abbakr's *bāsinga* had been district commissioners who not only had rights but also duties, and were instruments of a policy of centralization. Grants of administrative rights (and revenues) entailing no, or hardly any, administrative duties had been limited in size and had been made mainly to *faqīh*s and an occasional (female) relative. The *bāsinga* of Ismāʿīl and Abbakr had been chosen mainly from the Gernyeng, their clansmen or relatives in a wide sense. They did not consist only, or mainly, of brothers and uncles of the sultan (who were not numerous), but had absorbed the sons of the old Gernyeng *malik*s and other powerful non-Gernyeng individuals from the Dirjeil area. Abbakr had realized that the interests of the state were not identical with those of the nobility it had created, and took no chances. Possible rivals to his power, however close or valuable to him, were killed or robbed of the horses, slaves and firearms which gave them their power. Abbakr built up a strong army of slave soldiers, who could be used against both nobility and commoners and were resented by both. Thus, oral sources say, Abbakr became the 'sultan of the slaves', not of the Gernyeng or the Masālīt. However, Abbakr had allotted two districts to close relatives: Dār Erenga to his brother Tāj al-Dīn and to his mother. Dār Jabal, which she, as a woman, was not expected to govern herself. Whether these close relatives had financial privileges over the *bāsinga* in general is not known, but the allotment of Dār Jabal to provide for a close relative, rather than for those who formed the pillars of the administration and the core of the army, set a dangerous precedent for the future.[26]

In 1905, when Tāj al-Dīn succeeded Abbakr, his major internal enemies were Abbakr's sons, who disputed his right to the throne, and who had inherited what was left of their father's slave army, horses and rifles. Their abortive coup gave Tāj the excuse to confiscate these, but his decision to pardon rather than eliminate them meant that they had to be absorbed into his administrative corps and provided for. Hence they were appointed as governors of districts.[27] After 1910, when most of the *bāsinga* and many of Tāj al-Dīn's cavaliers had died a natural death or in battle, the *abbonga* became politically all-important.

The *abbonga* consisted first of all of all Abbakr's sons, many of whom had slave mothers; secondly, of all those sons of his brothers, sisters, uncles and aunts, who grew up in the capital; and thirdly, of slaves brought up at court. When Andōka became sultan his close relatives began to act in their districts not as district commissioners who adminstered their districts on behalf of the sultan, but as grantees of districts like those originally granted to *faqīh*s. When the Sudan Government officials came on the scene in the 1920s, they looked upon a district of an *abbo* as 'a feudally-owned domain, the owner of which has right to certain dues from his vassals'.[28] According to a report of 1928:

> Such influence as the Sultan possesses himself is very small, and is confined to the neighbourhood of Geneina. The 'hakura' system is largely responsible for this. Under it they [the subjects] have little interest in Government beyond their overlords into whose control the Sultan does not enter. In other words, the Sultanate is divided into a number of small kingdoms, the overlords of which are obviously inclined to further their own interests rather than those of the Sultan.[29]

Oral sources confirmed that the *abbo* was like a sultan on the spot where he lived. No *firsha* or sultanic messenger interfered with him, and he was 'above taxes', i.e. did not pay taxes and 'ate' what he collected.[30] According to the Resident R. Davies, Andōka had tried to reassert the state's power over the nobility in 1916, when the fall of 'Alī Dīnār and the rapprochement with the French allowed him to concentrate on domestic affairs. The complaints made by the commoners and *malik*s about the injustice of the *abbonga* became so numerous that he abolished the *dār*-system almost completely and arranged to provide for his brothers from his own pocket.[31] Andōka's use of slaves as governors (alongside with and instead of close relatives and the usual free non-

Gernyeng officials) may have been another (vain) attempt to re-centralize the sultanate. British sources suggest that Andōka had the slave and free *amīn*s and *maqdūm*s far better in hand than the *abbonga*, for the former were described as 'merely executive agents of the Sultan, sent out to collect taxes or other requisitions', and the latter as the owners of fiefs, the revenues of which provided them with a living.[32]

The administrative reports of the Sudan Government officials dwelled at length on the evils of the *abbonga* and *amīn*s. In 1918 it was reported from Kereinik that 'the people are groaning under the maladministration of Endoka's tax-farmers and are looking to us to come and deliver them.' In 1920 the murder of a Hausa pilgrim by one of Andōka's brothers was reported as the sixth murder committed by the brothers in recent years. The proposals formulated in April 1919 included the proposal to have tax collectors locally elected, so that 'Endoka's harpies' could be done away with. In the belief that the *dār*-system had survived the abolition of 1916 only to a very limited extent the Sudan Government in 1921 abolished the *dār*s with one stroke of the pen: 'the system of allotting a dar to any individual shall be abolished; there will remain only the tribal and central organization.'[33] Only a few *abbonga* were recognized by the Sudan Government as officials of the sultanate's internal administration or native administration, as it came to be called. The judicial authority of *abbonga* and *amīn*s was not recognized, and as few as possible were appointed to the sultan's new advisory council and the tax assessment boards. Andōka's brother Badawī, his maternal uncle Ndili, ʿAlī Ab Shanab and Kajjām Zubayr (both Gernyeng born and bred in southern Dār Fūr), and *amīn* Aḥmad Ab Shulūkh of the Maddarong were the major exceptions to the anti-*abbonga* policy of the Government, and became the pillars of Davies' native administration team.[34] Immediately after the occupation harsh measures were taken against those *abbonga* and *amīn*s who had obstructed tax assessment in their district or village. Andōka's brothers ʿAlī Umm Belōlo and Yaʿqūba were sentenced to imprisonment in al-Fāshir, as was Ab Dūdū, the slave *maqdūm* of Dār Erenga, who resented his exclusion from the tax assessment board in favour of his subordinate, the Erenga *shartay*. A typical case was that of *amīn* Aḥmad Ab Shulūkh. *Amīn* Aḥmad had appointed a certain *shaykh*, called Mahdī, in return for a bribe.

This was resented by the commoners over whom Mahdī was appointed. When one of them lodged a complaint with the sultan, however, he was referred to the *amīn* himself. The latter tied the man up and, when ordered by the sultan to set him free, he only released him against the payment of a horse.[35]

However, both the administrative reports of later years and the oral testimonies of *malik*s and commoners of the Masālīt countryside leave no doubt that the *dār*s continued to exist, and that *abbonga* and *amīn*s succeeded each other in governing and 'eating' them with and without the sultan's knowledge. The fact that they were and could not be dispensed with completely in tax assessment and collection facilitated this. In 1928 the Resident still lamented the 'hakura' system which had officially been abolished in 1921. In the same year Badawī, who had failed to report the presence of a subversive *faqīh* in his district, was again deposed as lord of the *dār* which had been abolished in 1921.[36] In 1931 some three dozen-odd *abbonga* threatened to use violence against the sultan's maternal uncle Ndili, who had complained about their depradations in front of the governor of Dār Fūr. Two *abbonga*, a son of Abbakr and a son of Tāj al-Dīn, were exiled, while the other sons of the two sultans were forcibly settled in the environs of El Geneina for at least one year. The most notorious oppressors, moreover, were prosecuted for recent exactions.[37] It is not clear whether the *abbonga* really refused to compromise with the new regime or whether they never really got a chance. The Sudan Government seems to have had its conclusion that they 'failed to adapt' ready from the start, and had pinned its hopes on the next generation, namely on Andōka's sons, particularly *abbo* ʿAbd al-Raḥmān (the present sultan) and the late *abbo* Muḥammad Nimr, who attended the primary school in al-Fāshir and were absorbed into the native administration in 1928.[38]

The local nobility

The decision to exclude the *abbonga* and *amīn*s from the administration made it necessary to include the local rulers, the *malik*s and *firsha*s. However, since these lived in the countryside and sometimes did not speak Arabic they were even more out of the Resident's reach than the *abbonga*. The area outside the enclave of El Geneina and environs belonged to a different world, which was sometimes idealized, but mostly feared. In October 1922 the Resident wrote about the southern area: 'the people there are as wild as hawks. Unlike the northern folks, vast numbers of them speak no Arabic. Also we have had "incidents" there, people killed in resisting arrest, for instance, last summer; and it is from that region,if anywhere, that trouble might come.'[39] Moreover the Masālīt positively disliked the British. 'A Britisher is rarely ever given a smiling welcome,' the Assistant Resident, A. J. Arkell, wrote in 1926, and he quoted the remark of a subordinate: 'What is the matter with the nas [people] up here? They've all got faces like early Christian martyrs.'[40] Since the countryside was outside the Government's reach and since all change had to come about through the sultan, the 1920s were fully devoted to the development of an administration around the sultan; administrative activities outside the enclave were restricted to the collection of taxes and the punishment of crime.[41] For the *malik*s and *firsha*s this implied that their traditional position was recognized, defined and (hence) slightly, but increasingly changed. The Government officially recognized their authority to settle minor disputes, punish small offences and levy fines not exceeding 15 *tukkiyya*s or one bull, part of which they could keep. They were also involved in tax assessment and tax collection, which the Government hoped to make exclusively their responsibility. Of the tax assessment boards of 1922 at least seven had a *malik* or *firsha* as one of the three members. The 'taxpayers' strike' of 1934 drove home to the Government that the *amīn*s of the sultan and a few *abbonga* were indispensable in matters of taxation.[42]

Although the local rulers were left in place and incorporated into the native administration, the Resident deemed it necessary to tidy up the system of *malik*s and *firsha*s. The system was 'in a state of considerable confusion', he felt, because *dimlij*s called themselves *malik*s, and *malik*s *firsha*s, and because the administrative units were in a process of changing from tribal units (the *mulūkiyya*s) to territorial ones (*furūshiyya*s). He therefore persuaded the sultan to bring all *malik*s who were still independent under *firsha*s, and to reduce the number of *firsha*ships by dismissing 'the more useless firshas' and amalgamating their districts.[43] It was the aim to reduce the thirdy-odd *firsha*s to a list of only fourteen and to reduce the small *firsha*s to their original status of *malik*. 'Yet the score of firshas omitted from this list never submitted to the headship of those firshas under whom they were supposed to have been placed,' A. J. Arkell wrote in 1926. 'If the firshas of these physically separate clusters of villages do not each have their own tax-list, no tax can be collected.'[44] In 1936 there were still thirty-two *firsha*s and only in 1938 was their number reduced to twenty-six, seventeen of which were Masālīt.[45] The *malik*s, in contrast to the village *shaykh*s and *firsha*s, lost much of their power – even if not their traditional position as land 'owners'. The Sudan Government had no need for an extra level of officials between village heads and *firsha*s, who together collected and brought in the taxes. The *malik* disappeared from the *daftar* (cash-book), oral testimonies say, and became a relic of the older 'tribal' organization, as he still is today. There were suggestions to take the judicial authority away from the local rulers, but this was not practical.[46] Yet the trend to make them into mere tax collectors was not seriously criticized until 1934.

The sultan

As for the sultan, his authority was significantly curtailed in matters of internal administration as in external affairs. R. Davies's 'constitution' of 1921 neatly codified those elements of the judicial and of the executive power of which the Sudan Government approved, and wrote many authorities and offices which existed (and for some time) continued to exist out of official existence. As native administration officials the Government only recognized the deputy sultan (Badawī), the *wāzīr* (*amīn* Aḥmad Ab Shulūkh), the *qāḍī*, the *maqdūm* of Dār Jabal and Dār Erenga (dismissed in 1923), the sultan's representative attached to the Resident (a new office), three *amīn*s and six messengers. The sultan was the head of the executive, but could dismiss the members of his 'cabinet' only with the consent of the Resident. As local native administration officials the Government recognized – as was explained above – the *shaykh*s, *firsha*s and (to some extent) the *malik*s, who were dismissed and appointed by the sultan.

The judicial authority of the sultan was curtailed as well, for he no longer had the power of death, could levy only limited fines and pronounce limited sentences, and did not have his own prison. Cases involving aliens and slaves were reserved to the Resident or to mixed courts of representatives of both Sudan Government and native administration. The sultan, however, heard appeals from the legal decisions of the local rulers, and the *qāḍī* (or Islamic judge) was nothing more than the sultan's legal expert, dealing particularly with cases of inheritance and contentious divorce.[47] After 1923 the judicial system was elaborated and refined with the establishment of a travelling rural court and a border court. The *qāḍī* became gradually more important, while the sultan benefitted from the construction of the Government fort at Ardamatta (outside El Geneina) and the physical separation of the Sudan Government personnel from the native administration headquarters.

Although the Resident was in theory the advisor and supervisor of the sultan, in reality he initiated change, for the legislative authority lay with the Sudan Government, represented on the spot by the Resident. Nevertheless the Resident had to move cautiously and slowly so as not to alienate the sultan, who was his only handle, or channel, for change. The sultan was not fooled by guards of honour and 'indirect rule' rhetorics. In 1923 he bitterly remarked that 'the Government had stolen his dar as a man steals another man's wife.'[48] The Resident expressed his private views in a letter to 'my dear Colonel' (the governor of Dār Fūr) in March 1922, saying that he expected 'a good many thorns in the path of Indirect Administration' and doubted whether 'the show will be in a state to hand over to Redfern [his successor] by this time next year (unless the imperial family, Endoka included, has hanged itself by then in the rope given to it).'[49]

R. Davies was the first to realize that the handle by which change had to be brought about needed to be much stronger than it was. The sultan had indeed been given practically all the power the Sudan Government had not reserved for itself, but 'even to the most ignorant Maslati', it was admitted in 1924, 'the mere presence of a Government Post and Garrison at Geneina means a diminution of the Sultan's prestige.'[50] Apart from prestige and real authority the sultan had lost a substantial part of his revenues. One of the reasons for this was the introduction of minted money, particularly into the enclave of El Geneina, which was the residence of the Government-paid soldiers and police, and of the traders who had followed in the Government's train. In 1918 H. A. MacMichael had complained of the lack of minted money and the almost complete ignorance of Egyptian or French money among commoners and nobility, which made 'purchase for work and purchase of provisions' difficult.[51] At the end of 1923 the situation in and around El Geneina had completely changed. R. Davies wrote in 1924:

> For four years money had been gradually filtering into the country from the Post at Kereinik. Since the occupation of Geneina this process has been vastly accelerated. The immediate result has been a 50% depreciation in the cash value of 'tokaki'. It is now practically true that nothing can be bought here except for cash. The standard of living has completely altered. The households of the well-paid soldiers and police are examples which give rise, in the other inhabitants, to many 'wants', formerly unfelt, which the new market, with a score of foreign traders, can supply. Those who formerly wore homespun now call for Manchester goods. Tea, coffee, sugar and other foods are craved for by people who had barely tasted any of them a few years ago.[52]

This was not true for the commoners or – as Davies pointed out – for the countryside. 'The Masalit, Erenga and Fur have not yet learnt how to spend money,' it was reported in 1932. 'They clothe themselves in homespun and do not purchase sugar or tea.'[53] However, it was true for the nobility and particularly the sultan, who could not deny his household what every soldier and policeman provided for his wife and children, and who had to keep up a royal lifestyle.

The sultan's revenue from taxes had seriously decreased since the occupation. The graintax (*zakāh*) was taken by the Government. The value of the herd tax had diminished due to a slump in the animal market. The dues of *tukkiyyas* had only 50 per cent of their former purchasing power and the income of L.E. 200 which the sultan had earned by supplying meat to the regular troops in Kereinik fell away when these troops had become irregular troops, who did not have a formal commissariat, in January 1922. R. Davies noted that: 'the result of all this is that the Sultan is bankrupt and in debt', and illustrated the state of affairs with the story that 'Bedawi, the Sultan's eldest brother and Wakil, was reduced to pawning his drawers to obtain a burma [jar] of merissa [local beer].'[54] He warned the governor of Dār Fūr that the 'severe financial embarrassment', which had replaced 'the prosperity of a simple kind' for the sultan, his household, relatives and officials, made their hostility towards the government and their extortions from the commoners inevitable. Davies therefore proposed to pay the sultan a salary, which 'should be a generous compensation to him for his loss of sovereignty', and would make 'the idea of a return to the pre-occupation conditions thoroughly repugnant to him'.[55] The proposal to give the sultan a salary was linked to the plan to immediately, but gradually, introduce the collection of taxes in cash. In 1924 the sultan received his first salary of L.E. 425. In 1925 he received a salary of L.E. 975 to be increased to L.E. 1200 once the *fiṭra* tax would have been abolished completely. The salaries of the other officials were not paid from the sultan's Privy Purse, but from the native administration's income from taxes paid in cash (i.e. the cultivation, or poll tax, and half of the animal tax) and from the fees and fines of the *qāḍī*s court, the *marissa* or beer-brewing licences and the leases of the brick-stone stores in the El Geneina market. How high the sultan's salary was can be understood if one compares it with the salaries of the members of his 'cabinet', of which the highest, that of the *wazīr*, was only L.E. 120. The sultan's main expenditure was the maintenance of his sixty brothers and sisters, his twenty uncles and his innumberable collaterals, and also that of his two hundred horses, which had until then (together with rifles and slaves) determined the state's military potential, but which now came to be looked upon as the sultan's 'chief extravagance'.[56]

The year 1924, in which taxes were partially put on a cash footing and in which the sultan received his first salary, was a milestone in Andōka's career. The salary was part of the general trend to centralize the executive power in the hands of the sultan. The trend had been set by the decision to exclude the *abbonga* from political power and to facilitate the control over the local rulers by reducing their number and by making their districts more uniform. It continued in subsequent years. In 1927 the native administration received its own prison. In 1928 the mixed courts were replaced with 'native' courts. In the same year the Resident, his staff and the garrison moved to the fort at Ardamatta outside El Geneina Town. In 1929 the native administration accounts were fully separated from those of Dār Fūr province, and in 1930 the native administration received its own exchequer with a balance of L.E. 500.[57] The native administration had come of age, and its guardian-angel, the Resident, became more and more invisible. The powers which the Sudan Government increasingly delegated to the successful native administration were given to the sultan. Davies's enthusiasm for building up the position of his ward sometimes needed to be tempered. When he, in a discussion of 'landtenure by aliens in Dar Masalit' stated that all land was held by the sultan as trustee for his people, he received a curt answer from H. A. MacMichael that: 'no such thesis arises ipso facto from the practice of indirect rule.'[58] The fact that the sultan ended up by owning most of the land and shops of El Geneina Town suggests that Davies's views in the end prevailed.

According to the annual report of 1933 the sultan had become a different man. He had been:

> the hero of many campaigns, the saviour of his people, and the subject of their songs. A bull ruffled after many a fight and forced to answer to the coaxings of his trainers. Inwardly, fearful of the gibes that the girls might level at him, hateful of the foreign yoke, demoralised by the French, suspicious and uneasy in mind. Outwardly, docile, doing as he was bid and wishing someone else do it for him; childishly gauche.

By 1933 Andōka had become a man after the Sudan Government's own heart, not so different from an eccentric English country-gentleman, self-confident, fond of horses, and the proud owner of a two-seater Ford.[59] The sultan's attitude towards taxes also changed after 1924. In 1925, when the tax assessment boards proved inefficient, the sultan personally toured and reassessed a large part of the *dār*, substantially increasing the amount of taxes to be collected.[60] In 1932 it was reported:

> Whereas in the past he regarded it [his revenue] as Government Taxes, which he as a Native Chief was bound to collect for the Government, now he looks upon it as his own revenue which he knows his people can pay to him without hardship, and he insists on payment.[61]

Even the revenue from the licenses for beer-brewing, until then collected by the sultan's aunt – possibly because all beer-brewers were and are women – the sultan began to claim for himself. The sultan played the part chosen for him by the Sudan Government perfectly and was a willing instrument of its policy of centralization. In a way he played his role too well. In 1926 the Assistant Resident noted his 'jealousy of the Kadi exercising any initiative'. In 1929 the Resident noted that the sultan seemed unwilling to discuss matters of public interest with his sons, who had finished school and had been absorbed into the judicial and financial branches of the native administration. In the annual report of 1933 there was another indirect complaint of over-centralization. The Resident lamented the inefficiency of 'the Firshas, the local feudal chiefs . . . as their subjects prefer to deal with a kindhearted Sultan who is always ready to hear their complaints.'[62] The commoners had apparently sensed that the sultan was and wanted to be the centre of power more than ever before.

The first signs of disenchantment came in 1928, when the Resident reported:

> there is a 'cancer' gnawing at the vitals of the Dar Masalit Native Administration and endangering its future well-being. I refer to the miserly hoarding by the Sultan of his Privy Purse. At his court is no oriental splendour, no royal entertaining, no provision for needy relatives, no charity. His court is pictured in a man secluded in a 'garrety' house sitting up late counting his gold.[63]

Andōka even economized on shrouds for the dead; while Abbakr had provided his household and relatives with shrouds of fourteen cubits, Andōka gave only seven cubits of cloth, an innovation frowned upon by his entourage. In their criticism of the sultan the colonizers showed a surprising lack of insight into the changes they had brought about themselves. Gone were the days when the *jallāba* girls in Abesher praised Andōka in a song for throwing into their midst all the coins which the French had paid for his horses and for which he had no use at home.[64]

In 1934 the Sudan Government had a brief moment of truth. The Resident, Sandison, warned against 'the undoubted tendency of Indirect Rule to build up centralized African autocracies, disregarding the bases of former African constitutions and states which were decentralised and democratic.' His analysis of the sultan was that half of his personality was extremely progressive, e.g. easy to convince of the value of a proper system of accounts and the value of a cash basis for taxation, while the other half was that of a 'traditional African potentate . . . antipathetic against decentralization'.[65] The solution Sandison proposed was to foster the local rulers, who – he summed up – 'settle cultivation and domestic disputes, punish owners of animals which stray into standing crops, regulate the price of grain, construct and repair wells, interrogate suspicious strangers and perform a hundred and one humble yet necessary offices without reward or recognition from us.' Rather than training them as tax collectors Sandison proposed to educate *firsha*s and *shaykh*s in the field of justice.[66]

Educating the sons of local chiefs was not a new idea in 1934. From 1927 onwards the sultan had been ordered to put pressure upon his *firsha*s and *malik*s to send their sons to school, and four *khalwa*s had been opened in the sultan's palace in El Geneina, and in Tenjeke (Dār Erenga), Mabrūka (Mistere) and Chaffa. The Masālīt resented and resisted what they considered 'infidel' education. In 1927 there was a rumour that the *khalwa* was a trap to catch boys and send them to the Nile valley. In 1929 it was sarcastically reported that the *khalwa*s were in no direct danger of over-crowding. In 1930, however, more than half of the *firsha*s had sent sons to school. By 1939 their number had risen from seventeen to thirty-three, while fourteen sons of *firsha*s were on the sultan's staff, employed mainly in tax assessment.[67] It cannot be denied, however, that the education of the sons of the local chiefs (and those of the sultan) was a very slow and weak antidote against the centralization of executive power in the sultan's hands. The Sudan Government officials in Khartoum, who had in the meantime introduced 'indirect rule' throughout Dār Fūr, and had realized that the Masālīt Sultan was not so different from other tribal leaders who had been handled with less scruple, considered putting the Dār Masālīt native administration on one line with the other native administrations. The successive Residents, however, continued to defend Dār Masālīt not as an ideal native state, but as 'the one native state in the Sudan which has not been created by Government and . . . . deserves to be given the right to develop along its own lines.'[68] In 1946 the Sudan Government was still intending to carry out its plan, but agreed to wait until after Andōka's death. The sultan died in 1951, but then the Condominium Government was winding up its affairs in the Sudan. The new Masālīt Sultan apparently believed, or wished to believe, in the myth of the uniqueness of Dār Masālīt's status under the Sudan Government; when the Sudan prepared itself for self-government in the early 1950s, he made a short and vain attempt to regain his independence or at least to obtain special privileges.[69]

Colonial rule and the commoners

The impact of taxes in cash

The changes introduced by the Condominium Government did not leave the commoners untouched. They were affected most seriously and most directly by the new taxation system introduced by the new regime. The Government began to interfere with the traditional system as early as 1921, even before the occupation. It decided that the grain tax (*zakāh*) would be collected in kind for the benefit of the Government, while the sultan would keep the revenue from *fiṭra* and the herd tax (*zakāt al-bahāyim*), to be collected in kind in traditional manner. Together with the sultan the Resident created twelve tax assessment boards, chosen from 'the more suitable firash and dimalig, with a strong leaven of noted and respected elders – not the umana class – who would do useful propaganda in explaining the tax to the people, and by their mere presence on the boards, do much to make them submit to it quietly.' The notables (two per board) were chosen 'on the criteria of good character and intelligence', while the clerks in eleven of the twelve cases were *faqīh*s.[70] All crops were liable to taxation, and when it 'in spite of the Sultan's assurance . . . turned out that there was no exactly known midd in general use', the Resident accepted the *ardabb* and the ten-*raṭl midd* as units of measure. The boards were instructed to visit the villages and to call on the village head 'to show them the village's cultivation, about which they shall ride to get a clear idea of its size and the quality of the grain.' After assessing the crop the clerk was to record the one tenth that was to be collected in 1922, after next year's harvest.[71] The Resident was concerned 'to render less abrupt the transition from the existing light and haphazard taxation to the heavier regular taxation of the future.[72] He therefore decided to collect in *ardabb*s only half of the number of *rayka*s assessed; that is to say that he demanded only ca. 350,000 kilos of millet instead of the ca. 550,000 kilos assessed in *rayka*s. About 180,000 kilos were actually collected.

The Resident considered collecting the grain tax partly in cash, and to accept only so much millet as was required for the garrison, but there is no evidence that he actually did. While assessing the grain crop the boards were also to record the people liable to *fiṭra*. Since this was a poll tax, this enabled the Resident to estimate the population of Dār Masālīt (including Dār Jabal and Dār Erenga) at ca. 65,000 in 1924.[73] In 1923 2,984 *ardabb*s (ca. 570,000 kilos) of millet were assessed and almost completely collected. However in 1924 and 1925 taxes were put on a cash footing, among other things to provide the sultan with an appropriate income. In 1924 only half (namely the sultan's half) of the herd tax was collected in cash at rates of 10 P.T. per camel or horse, 5 P.T. per head of cattle and 1 P.T. per sheep and goat. It was reported that L.E. 700 was collected by the *firsha*s without any difficulty.[74] In 1925 both the grain tax and herd tax were renamed and assessed and collected in cash. The cultivation tax levied on all adult men and women i.e. 40,000 of the 65,000 inhabitants, it was said – was 7 P.T. per male and 3 P.T. per female cultivator, which was lower than elsewhere in Dār Fūr, where the rates varied from 10 to 16 P.T. for men and from 5 to 8 P.T. for women.[75] In 1925 'the Masalit paid up more taxes than ever before', namely L.E. 2,900. The village continued to be the unit of assessment. The amount of taxes for which it was assessed was based on the number of cultivators and animals it counted and on the official rates, but it was the *shaykh* who had to distribute the amount to be paid among the villagers.[76] In subsequent years the tax assessment was refined; the boards were reduced by two thirds, supervised and speeded up, and the sultan himself began to participate in the assessment. This led to a rising tax curve until the world depression made itself felt in Dār Masālīt in the early 1930s. In 1928 assessment became triennial. In 1932 the cultivation tax for women was abolished, that for men increased to 15 P.T., and in 1934–5 tax assessment was put on an individual basis.[77]

The innovations introduced by the Sudan Government from 1922 onwards made the tax burden of the commoners much heavier than it had been before – with the exception maybe of the tribute paid to the French in the drought years 1913–14. This is true even for the years 1922 and 1923, i.e. before taxes were collected in cash. One reason for this was that – through no fault of the new system – the old taxes continued to be collected alongside with the new, which were sometimes presented as *ghanīma* or spoils of war and not as the legal dues of *zakāh* and *fiṭra* prescribed by the *Qur'ān*.[78] After the taxes had been renamed these Islamic taxes continued to be collected by the *malik*s, *firsha*s, *abbonga* and *amīn*s of the sultan. 'Our present taxes do not, I imagine, replace Zeka on crops in the eyes of the people in that it should be paid in the actual kind of crop grown,' the Resident wrote in 1929; 'our tax is not assessed on the crop and the firshas and others who collect it do not participate in the distribution as they should in Zeka.'[79]

The 'hospitality' (*ḍiyāfa*) to the assessment boards, which made capital out of their vast new powers by accepting and expecting bribes in return for a reasonable or low assessment, may not have been a completely new phenomenon, but became a heavier burden than before. The Resident was aware of this, and among the instructions which the board members swore to carry out was a restriction on the *ḍiyāfa* they were allowed to accept: 'but no movable "diafa", in the form of animals, money, "tokaki", etc., may be accepted.' The Resident also discovered that at least one board 'had behaved as a travelling assize, hearing cases, imposing fines, and receiving what is euphemistically called *ḥaqq al-naṣr* ('the right of victory') from successful litigants.'[80] Reducing the number of boards must have eased the burden of *ḍiyāfa*, but the wife of a clerk who served on the boards for many years after 1927 still remembered how the fattest animals of the village flock would not survive the board's visit, and that they received a royal welcome wherever they went.[81]

The most serious innovation from the point of view of the commoners was the rigidity of the new system. First of all it did not exempt those who produced less than ten *rayka*s (or 120 kilos) of millet as had been the case under the old system. Secondly, by fixing the *midd* at 10 *raṭl* – which was rather high – the new system did not allow for the adjustment of the tax rate to unfavourable (natural or other) circumstances. This was in contrast with the old system under which the *midd* of grain had been fixed locally and had changed according to the quantity and quality of the area's grain crop and according to the season. Under the old system also taxes had been taken from the harvested crop. If the harvest failed no taxes were paid. This relation between what was produced and what was paid in taxes was severed when the Government began to base the amount of taxes to be paid on the probable yield of last year's crop. The old system's automatic famine relief – so necessary in an area which was regularly visited by man-wrought and natural disasters – went down the drain in 1922; the cattle plague of 1924, the drought, near-famine, and the epidemic of relapsing fever in 1926/7, the poor harvest of 1930, the locust plague and near-famine of 1932, the effects of the world depression in this same period, suggest that the need for such famine relief had not become superfluous.[82] In French Wadai and Dār Silā this innovation had been introduced about ten years earlier, and in a letter to the French in 1911 Sultan Bakhīt had voiced local indignation about it with inescapable logic: *al-kharāj mā yakhruj illā min al-mawjūd* ('taxes can only come from what exists'). An informant in Kajenggessa in 1978 reminisced: 'with the beginning of tax-listing people's troubles began.'[83]

A final fault of the system in the eyes of the commoners was that they did not understand it. Even the Resident admitted in 1927 that 'each year [since 1922] they have been told to pay something different.' Tax arrears were a foreign concept to the Masālīt, and even today they remember their bewilderment at the introduction of the new unit of measure called *ardabb*! That they were paying more every year cannot have escaped them.[84]

The introduction of money taxes created a whole new set of problems for the commoners:

> The piaster was very expensive at first. . . . The English refused to accept *rubṭa*s or whatever product after a while. They wanted cash and you had to take your products – millet, *rubṭa*s or animals – to the market and sell them for cash.[85]

That the piaster was indeed expensive for the common man is confirmed by the administrative reports. The arguments that 'cash is by no means unobtainable and the people are getting used to it', and that 'there is a great deal of money in the country', were used by the Resident in his plea for the introduction of a money tax in 1924 and cannot be taken at their face value. Even so the Resident qualified his statement by adding: 'if need be we can accept tokaki at somewhat less than their nominal value' – thus illustrating that the Government had its share in making the piaster expensive for the common man.[86] He also realized that cash was not *easily* obtainable outside the enclave of El Geneina and environs, and that levying taxes in money did not in itself lead to the circulation of money in the *dār*.

One solution to the lack of money with which to pay taxes in the countryside was to arrange the garrison's annual purchase of grain in such a way that the less monied regions of the *dār* would obtain some cash.[87] In the adjacent areas of Dār Qimr and the Zalingei area, which was called Western Darfur District, commoners and administrators faced the same problem of scarcity of money. In Dār Qimr the herd tax was put on a cash footing in 1928. The Resident noted that:

> it [this change] has not, however, caused circulation of coin in Dar Gimr because though the animal owners are compelled to exchange their animals for cash in Geneina or at Fasher, they only bring back sufficient money to pay their tax. The remainder is immediately exchanged for cloth, sugar etc.[88]

Therefore 'Sultan Idris should supply 100 Ardebs of grain to the Merkaz from the villages, with a view to causing the circulation of money in Dar Gimr', it was proposed in 1931. 'The price would be paid out to the village representatives on delivery of the grain.[89] In Western Darfur District it was reported:

> The Fur has no capital, and does not use money for his own purposes. He has however certain natural resources which he must obtain and sell to acquire the cash annually demanded by the Government, and which he would otherwise not require. Unlike Dar Masalit there is no military force in the Emirate with its concomitant distribution of cash so that the Fur is even more dependent on his neighbours for money.[90]

The Fūr therefore had to sell tobacco, salt and peppers in Zalingei or al-Fāshir, or earn five milliemes per day working on the roads for the Government. It was the same in Dār Silā, although there the problem was much older. As early as 1909 Colonel Millot had insisted on the payment of taxes in cash, since it was 'le moyen le plus efficace pour déterminer l'activité des transactions et stimuler la torpeur du contribuable'.[91] However, demanding that people pay taxes in money, did not give them money to pay, and eight years later it was reported that 'l'argent est encore rare dans le Sila, celui dépensé par les troupes étant presque entièrement drainé par les commerçants.'[92]

Alongside with regulating the annual grain purchase of El Geneina's garrison, the Government tried to stimulate the circulation of money by bringing in traders. As early as 1918 the political officer at Kereinik had stated that there was no minted money in Dār Masālīt, and that 'the need for a trader or two' was great.[93] The trades did come. In December 1926 it was reported:

> Geneina, the capital, is a town of recent growth having sprung up since the occupation, when it was a small village containing the sultan's residence. It is steadily increasing in size. . . . There is a market with about 30 red-brick shops and the merchants include 2 Greeks (one of whom has a liquor licence), 2 Syrians and various Gellaba.[94]

The presence of traders fostered new wants, particularly for factory-made cloth, sugar and tea, but provided in the 1920s and 1930s mainly for the inhabitants of the enclave, the garrison, the Resident and his staff, the sultan and his 'cabinet', who all received salaries and wages in cash. In 1934 it was estimated that 86 per cent of the money the Government brought into Dār Masālīt was lost by its immediate flight to pay for foreign imports. Since markets were remote, there was not much of an export trade, and prices of exportable goods, particularly livestock, ruled low.[95] The little money the local rulers or commoners could obtain above the money needed for taxes was spent on the same import goods. Rather than stimulating the circulation of money the traders drained the *dār* of all the money it contained. The result of this was that for the people of western Dār Fūr cash remained a commodity, not money in the conventional sense of the word:

> The Fur cannot exercise foresight and buy money for his taxes with his grain at the season when grain is at a premium. He waits until the lists are sent out and then, owing to the universal demand, he finds in grain-money, or salt-money, or cloth-money transactions that money is at a premium. In this way . . . by his hand-to-mouth barter economy he accentuates the almost daily and irresponsible fluctuations in the value of money. In short money acts more in Zalingei as a commodity than as a standard of value.[96]

The pull of the market forces worked slower than the colonizers sometimes wished:

> The Masalit, Erenga and Fur have not yet learnt to spend money. They clothe themselves in homespun and do not purchase sugar or tea; money obtained in the Geneina market is hoarded for the tax collector.[97]

That the market forces were doing their work became evident in the early 1930s, when the world depression made itself felt even in this remote corner of the British Empire. The depression also demonstrated the enormous impact of the new taxation system upon the local economy by magnifying and intensifying its effects.

There is no mention of the depression in the annual reports for Dār Masālīt until 1932. However, since the years 1930 and particularly 1931 were years of famine, its contribution to the general misery of the people may not have been recognized before that date. In Northern Darfur District the reduction of the taxpaying capacity of the people in 1931 was ascribed to both the 'heavy turn-over of saleable animals in exchange for grain' – a common phenomenon in times of famine – and to the scarcity and expense of money – the most significant effect of the world depression in western Dār Fūr – which led to a heavy fall in livestock prices.[98] In 1932 the end of the famine made the administrators optimistic: 'After two difficult years with famine in certain areas, and grain scarce and dear, there have been excellent crops,' it was reported from Dār Masālīt; 'the year has been most satisfactory in that despite the universal shortage of money the entire District has been relisted.'[99] From Northern Darfur District it was reported that there was enough grain and milk so that people's cash needs were limited to sugar, tea, clothes and tax payments. Yet, the report added, money is becoming more expensive every day:

> The importance of currency in terms of marketable commodities was still a new experience when the rising tide of money receded from their grasp.

What this meant to the common man was illustrated with an example:

> Last week the quarter of mutton was being sold in Fata Borno market for 5 m/m, i.e. 2 P.T. the carcase. The head and skin

> brought in 1½ P.T. The owner had paid an animal tax of 1 P.T. on that 3½ P.T. sheep – which was in excellent condition. Surely an inequitously unfair return to the producer on his labour – and his capital.[100]

In Dār Masālīt 1933 was reported as a bad year as a result of the world depression:

> the purely native concerns of the people, their food and drink, their work-a-day clothes, their barter marketing and their morale have remained comparatively unimpaired. But their routine conversion of primary commodities into cash for tax payments and purchases of luxuries has suffered, in their eyes, an unexplicable upset. They are selling, and are compelled to sell, an ardeb of grain for 2/6, a sheep for 1/- and a prime bull for 6/-. Two years ago these prices would have read 12/-, 7/7 and 21/- respectively. Money has fled their land.[101]

Of an assessed amount of L.E. 5,668 only L.E. 3,817 was realized as 'combined tax' (cultivation and herd tax combined). Rates were, however, not reduced. Some reports suggest that the common man was not alarmed at the situation, but at most surprised or even impressed:

> the average peasant, while God has kept his granary filled and his cattle in health, takes his financial troubles philosophically. Indeed this matter of money to his mind is purely a Government concern. He will say (and is he entirely wrong?) 'the Government brought money to our lands and the Government has taken it away. The Government is Shedid' [strong].[102]

The 'taxpayers' strike' of 1934 in Dār Masālīt, however, proved how serious the situation in reality was. There were several reasons why tax collections broke down in 1934. One of these was the fact that the tax collection had been left completely to the *firsha*s rather than to the *firsha*s and sultanic agents together, as had been customary. A more important reason was that the relisting of 1932 represented an increase in the amount of taxes to be paid which was not due to an actual increase in men and animals, but to the sultan's revision of the assessment lists. The higher assessment moreover followed rumours about a tax decrease, and the result was 'that considerable internal movement and some emigration culminated during the early months of 1934 in a virtual "tax-payers strike".'[103] The third reason for the strike was the world depression, and the scarcity and expensiveness of money, which magnified the hardships which the new taxation system imposed upon the commoners. This finally opened the Government's eyes. The Assistant Resident, Sandison, gave a lucid analysis of how heavily the tax burden weighed on the commoners, and why:

> From the point of view of monetary conditions Dar Masalit must be viewed in two sections, an enclave including the Government Cantonment and Geneina Town, and the Countryside. These two sections are not, however, complementary as in the majority of administrative districts in the country. Owing to the slump in animal and hides prices, Dar Masalit has practically no exports and the traders in Geneina Town have become retail shopkeepers and pandering to the desire of soldiers and police for tradegoods. At the present they perform no function for the countryman.
>
> The Government enclave receives some L.10200 annually in wages, excluding wages received and not spent locally, while the countryside gleans about L.1100 from grain purchase, animal hire and other services. The enclave spends at least L.8500 annually on imported trade goods, while at the utmost the countryside spends L.1000.
>
> The enclave pays in direct taxation L.250, and in indirect taxation perhaps L.1500, while the assessment of the countryside in 1933 was L.4800 in Combined Tax, and the collection totalled L.3500. This assessment represented 24% of the market value of all the listed animals of Dar Masalit, taking the animal values given by Mr. Campbell in his 1933 Report . . . and allowing a margin of one quarter for underlisting in the animal figures. Collection value represented 17.5% of their capital value.
>
> To emphasize the affluence of the enclave, and the stark poverty of the countryside, it may be noted that the two hundred soldiers of the S.D.F. [Sudan Defence Force] in Geneina receive more in wages than the 15552 [male] natives of the countryside have ever paid in taxation. But this wealth is not beneficial to the countryman for 86% of the total Government

> expenditure is lost by its immediate flight to pay for foreign imported goods. . . . It will be noted that no figure representing purchases for export of local commodities is shown. This is the actual position; a small trade in semn [ghee] persists, but it is practically all imported from French territory, and a hypothetical figure for Dar Masalit would be in the neighbourhood of L.250.[104]

Migration and Mahdist faith

The 'taxpayers' strike' of 1934 was an extreme response to the extreme hardship caused by the world depression. From the early 1920s the people of Dār Masālīt and elsewhere in Dār Fūr had responded to the new demands in different ways. Those commoners who had an agricultural surplus obtained the money for taxes by selling this surplus in the market at whatever price the particular circumstances of supply and demand would dictate. If they did not do this voluntarily, it was done for them, for tax arrears were collected by rounding up the whole village herd, and by selling as many young animals as was necessary to pay off the tax debt.[105] Another possible response to the new tax demands was to grow a money crop, e.g. cotton, chilis and onions, as the sultan encouraged his subjects to do.[106] Unfavourable circumstances might dictate another response, that of borrowing money from those who always had money, the traders, who were mainly outsiders. The story of Seidou, the Fallāta food and transport contractor for the French garrison in Goz Beida, shows how the penury of the indigenous taxpayers, who sought or were compelled to accept his services as a money lender, could make a trader very wealthy and politically all-powerful.[107] Lending money was not the only solution to a crisis situation. In 1931, when a locust plague ruined the crop and money was scarce, people tried to work for wages. A report on Dār Qimr made mention of: 'the flood of whole villages from Wadai (and this year from Dar Masalit) looking for khidma [a job] at 2 P.T. a day in order to pay their Poll-Tax'.[108]

Moving away was another extreme, but very common response to the tax demands of the new regime. From 1923 onwards refugees from French Wadai had been crossing the border into Anglo-Egyptian Dār Masālīt because of 'better conditions under our [Condominium] Government'. The immigration of no less than a thousand households in 1928 was ascribed to 'a "tightening up" of administration in general and a drastic tax collection campaign' in Wadai.[109] The Sudan Government officials had little sympathy for the French system of administration to which they derogatorily referred as 'système dé' (*débrouillez-vous*, i.e. 'shift for yourself'). Yet they took harsh measures against the refugees who caused chaos in Dār Masālīt because 'they knew no Sheikh or Government [and] were not themselves known', and could not be punished for their tax evasion or cattle thefts.[110] The French authorities invariably demanded the return of the refugees and sent endless lists of names of refugees whom the Government, that is to say the sultan, had to round up. The authorities in Dār Masālīt seem to have done what they could – they even burned the villages of refugees – but the French, rather than blaming their own administration, made Andōka their scapegoat and accused him of making propaganda for immigration to Dār Masālīt.[111]

Not only French subjects moved away to evade taxation. In 1928 'the lack of feudal spirit among the Masalit and their proneness to flitting about the Dar' was at least partly ascribed to the triennial tax listing, 'for a man may have lost his animals or so and yet be required to pay taxes for them.'[112] Moreover, since villages, not individuals, were assessed, village heads welcomed newcomers who would of course share the tax burden. The danger that taxpayers would flee rather than pay was so real that the tax arrears of 1926 had to be struck off, and that the sultan in 1934 refused to collect any taxes until the French had started their tax drive on the other side of the border.[113]

Many Masālīt did not move to another part of their *dār*, but – as so many in Dār Fūr – to the Nile valley. This emigration was the dominant feature of the period 1925–35 and remained important afterwards. One of the background factors of this emigration was that the new government, by uniting the Sudan politically, by improving communications and safeguarding the roads, facilitated movement. The swelling stream of pilgrims, who entered the Sudan *via* El Geneina and thus accentuated the fluidity of Dār Masālīt's population, illustrates this.[114] The Government also abolished slavery; in a few decades most of Dār Masālīt's slaves 'disappeared', either by taking the freedom road into greater anonymity in the east, or by merging with the commoners.[115]

Under the new regime slaves could take their claims and complaints to court, and undertook, or were compelled to undertake, the payment of their own taxes. Even the sultan was reluctant to pay taxes on his slaves, and ten of the villages known as *ahl warrai* (the people of the court), which consisted exclusively of royal relatives and (ex-)slaves, lost 41 per cent of their male cultivators in the year 1925–6.[116] Yet, although the establishment of Condominium Rule made it easier for people to move, more importantly, it made it necessary for people to move.

The present study cannot do justice to the variety of factors which pushed and pulled the emigrants, but two major factors can be singled out. First of all the Masālīt emigrated to the Nile valley – for shorter or longer periods of time – to work for wages in the cotton schemes developed by the Government in the Gezira. Thus they could earn the money they and their relatives needed to pay taxes, to pay as bridewealth now that raiding for cows had become less feasible, and to satisfy the new wants for factory-made cloth, tea and sugar, which became the major addiction of Sudanese (including Masālīt) society.[117] The second motive was religious. Those who resented the new 'infidel' government for religious reasons flocked to Aba Island, the residence of Sayyid ʿAbd al-Raḥmān al-Mahdī, the son of the Mahdī and one of the biggest cotton lords of the Gezira. Aba Island became the centre of what was now styled neomahdism,[118] the belief in the end of the world and the victory of Prophet Jesus (*nabī ʿIsā*), that is to say – in the eyes of many – Sayyid ʿAbd al-Raḥmān himself.

'Neomahdism' in western Dār Fūr was as old as the Mahdiyya itself. Some of it's 'outbreaks' had been directed against the Mahdiyya and the French, but in the 1920s its main enemy was the Sudan Government. As early as 1920 Andōka, torn between his antipathy towards subversive *faqīh*s and suspicion towards the new government, had written to the Sayyid for advice on what to think of those prophets who continuously proclaimed themselves. The Sayyid, who was trying to allay British suspicions about his political intentions – it was feared that he intended to proclaim himself king of the Sudan – wrote back that Andōka should beware of them, since they were false prophets and infidels.[119] The unrest of 1921, which led to the occupation of El Geneina, also had religious overtones. In 1922 it was deemed necessary to take precautions against 'fanatical risings' in Dār Fūr, and Andōka was instigated by the Government to issue a proclamation to all the *firsha*s and *malik*s of Dār Masālīt:

> I would bring to your knowledge that there are a lot of ill-famed bad Fikkis [*faqīh*s] who . . . have been on several occasions killed by Masalit Kings on account of their audacity in having falsely represented themselves as prophets or Agencies of Heavenly Powers. Now notice is hereby given to all Firash and Muluk that they are held responsible for any chaos or tumult that may occur in their Districts. Their responsibilities are extended to those acts of sedition that are often attempted by Fikkis or Dervishes who start insinuating their ruinous traditions by calling crowds to cluster round them, or taking up their abode in a hill and give medicines to their attendants and then gradually make known their actual intentions. On the immediate appearance of such seditious Fikkis the Government must forthwith be informed.[120]

Nevertheless, when *faqīh* Muhājir in 1927 started a holy war in the Zalingei area, the southeastern part of Dār Masālīt was actively involved, while the sultan himself was said to be accessory by silence. Muhājir's promises, that bullets would not harm his followers, that sticks would change into spears when thrown, that his followers would obtain clothes and other loot in Zalingei, and that they would be relieved of the Goverment taxes of that year, throw some light upon the grievances of the common people of the area.[121]

Until 1922 migration from Dār Fūr to Aba Island did not take on serious proportions, but after 1923 and particularly 1925 the stream of *muhājirīn* – as those who left their homes to join the Sayyid in Aba Island were called – seriously alarmed the Government. The latter was dismayed that the 'native chiefs' of the west, 'even though they realise that the spread of Mahdism is detrimental to tribal authority and discipline, which they represent', did nothing to counter the Sayyid's active propaganda, and shared the general belief that the Government was not there to stay and would be overthrown by the Sayyid as *nabī ʿIsā* as the Turkiyya had been overthrown by the Mahdī.[122] A. J. Arkell, who was regarded as the expert on neomahdism in Dār Masālīt, believed that Andōka was playing 'a double game' as far as neomahdism was concerned,[123] but this is doubtful, certainly after the occupation of Dār Masālīt. Andōka may, in spite of the fact that he was a Tījānī, not have been immune to the Sayyid's religious charisma, but he resented the political exploitation of that charisma at his own expense. In 1925, after he had called on the Sayyid during a visit to Khartoum, the sultan complained of the large number of Masālīt who were induced by the Sayyid to leave their *dār* and were settled at Aba or in the Sayyid's colonies in the Gezira and other provinces.[124] This resentment only increased in the course of time:

> The Sultan, piqued by being politically scored off by S.A.R. [Sayyid ʿAbd al-Raḥmān], who is robbing him of his men, expressed disgust that the religious leanings of his men should be exploited into providing slave labour for S.A.R. He states that at Abba, according to religious precedent, his people are divided into Muhagarin and Ansar but that their treatment is the same: forced labour from 6 a.m. to 3 p.m. with two rotls of grain as sole reward. The rest of the day they can hire themselves out and make a millieme or two to eke out their living. The conditions are those of forced labour without adequate payment.[125]

Andōka's analysis may not yet have been as lucid in the mid-twenties as it was in the 1930s, but his lack of enthusiasm for the Government's solution to the problem, i.e. forbidding the pilgrimage to Aba, listing all the Mahdist *masjid*s, *khalwa*s, *faqīh*s and villages of the *dār*, issuing orders to the *firsha*s – under threat of punishment – not to let anyone go east without permission, cannot be interpreted as secret support of neomahdism or the Sayyid's political ambitions. Andōka indeed protected his people against the British listing mania ('They shall measure the land grassblade by grassblade'); he denied that there were any Mahdists in his *dār*; feigned surprise when a *faqīh* was caught in the act of reading the *rātib* and was generally unhelpful. Yet he did make a list of the Masālīt *faqīh*s who were the Sayyid's main proselytizers. Among these were the ringleaders of the rising of Dugdug and the war of the *faqīh*s of 1914, who had all joined the Sayyid in the east and wrote letters of propaganda back to the *dār*.[126] The sultan denounced particularly the leader of the war of the *fuqarā'*, *faqīh* Yūsuf Ṣābir, as 'the chief means by which the Masalit were persuaded to emigrate from the dar and join the Sayyid in the east'.[127] Yet, to Arkell's indignation, the sultan hinted that the Government should tackle the problem at the other end, in the east, and regarded the 'witch-hunt' of the British as futile, since 'it was really impossible to tell who were going on pilgrimage and who in search of work.'[128] This was very true. Since religious and economic motives intermingled in people's minds, labour migrants and pilgrims or *muhājirīn* could not be distinguished. Those who became the Sayyid's 'slaves' were even more exploited than the other migrants, but they did find a point of identification and some protection, e.g. against the Government's taxes.

The British were certainly paranoiac with regard to neomahdism, and saw the Sayyid's spectre everywhere. Hence A. J. Arkell's belief that 'in Masalit nearly everyone is at heart fanatical', anti-Christian and a supporter of the Sayyid, cannot be taken at its face value.[129] Yet both intelligence reports and oral testimonies confirm that most Masālīt believed in the Sayyid and that many took the trouble to go to Aba and see for themselves. 'Sure I went to the east,' an informant said; 'they told me that the Prophet Jesus had risen, but when I arrived I found that it was only the son of the Mahdī.'[130] Another contended that 'except for Baḥr al-Dīn, who entered the Tījāniyya [brotherhood] because the English objected to the *ṭarīqa* [religious brotherhood] of the Mahdī, everybody else belonged to the *anṣār*. The *khawāja* [i.e. the Resident] told the Masālīt:

> awʿa min bushka al-ṭīn
> wa min ʿaṣā andarāb
> awʿa min ʿayyāl hijlīj
> awʿa min al-tamtarūn.
>
> beware of the mud pot [used as ablution vessel]
> and of the stick cut from the *andarāb* tree
> [which prophets' prayers might turn into spears or rifles]
> beware of the nuts of the *hijlīj* [used as rosaries]
> beware of the [Mahdī's] prayerbook.[131]

A (Sudanese) intelligence agent reported in 1926 that the belief in the Sayyid was not prevalent in El Geneina or among the troops, although over half of the latter were *anṣār*. However,

> the majority of the villages I found to be Mahdists and believers in Saiyid Abel Rahman's character as Prophet Jesus, whose

> time they believe to be near at hand. Before the usual prayers they perform two 'prostrations' in honour of Saiyid Abdel Rahman whom they designate as El Sadig (the Truthful). They daily repeat the Mahdist hymn.[132]

The emigration from Dār Masālīt and western Dār Fūr in general was the immediate and dramatic response to the incorporation of the area into the Anglo-Egyptian Sudan, and set a trend which has not been reversed until today. It is the most striking illustration of how Condominium Rule, by developing the central part of the Sudan, underdeveloped the periphery, including Dār Masālīt. The Government's response to the mass immigration into the Nile valley was strangely mixed. It did not object to the labour migration which provided the indispensable and cheap labour for the cotton plantations, but it tried to stop the migration of the religiously discontented – as if the two could be separated. By trying to contain neomahdism the British made a half-hearted attempt to keep the consequences of changes they had introduced themselves within limit. Both the British and the Masālīt saw a religious factor, namely Sayyid ʿAbd al-Raḥmān, as the clue to the solution of their problems. The fear of the British was the hope of the Masālīt, who turned to the man who combined traditional religious charisma with new economic power:

> The Prophet in whom the age puts its hope, follow him oh men of Islam. . . . Disobey not the Truthful one; he beareth the very burden of the Mahdi. I call upon you to turn to the pilgrimage (to Aba) with pure intention. Abdel Rahman the Truthful one in a vision has called upon his horsemen. . . . Our leader and refuge, behold the gates of mercy open before us. This is his time, behold the Mahdi and the Prophet before him. He is the seal of all prophets, fully sealed with divine secrets.
> The Prophet of mercy, the Lord of plenty, love for him has brought life to the Island. . . .
> The Truthful one has ordered his affairs, through thee I hope to attain salvation.
> Abdel Rahman the Truthful, may the Lord exalt his state![133]

Glossary

abbo (non-Arabic), plur. *abbonga*; honorific, in Dār Masālīt given to the male descendants of Sultan Abbakr Ismāʿīl (1888–1905). Compare O'Fahey (1980), 149.

ajāwīd (Arabic), plur.; elders, counsellors.

ʿāmil (Arabic), agent, governor; See Holt (1970), 121, note 1: 'The usual significance of *ʿāmil* in Muslim administrative terminology is "fiscal official". It had this meaning under the Mahdia but was used in a much wider sense to imply the Mahdi's, or later the Khalifa's agent in administrative matters.' In May 1884 the Mahdī ordered the title of *ʿāmil* to be substituted for that of *amīr*, used until then.

amīr (Arabic), prince; title adopted by the Masālīt Sultan Baḥr al-Dīn Abbakr (1910–51); see also under *ʿāmil*.

amīn (Arabic), personal servant, confidential advisor; the title was given to both important state officials and court officials who were the ruler's personal servants.

ammo (non-Arabic), plur. *ammonga*; honorific, given to the female descendants of Sultan Abbakr Ismāʿīl (1888–1905); the feminine of *abbo* (q.v.).

anṣār (Arabic), plur.; helpers, followers; this name, originally given to the Medinan followers of Muḥammad, was given by the Mahdī to his own followers.

ʿaqīd (Arabic), commander, leader of a warband. In Dār Masālīt this title was given to the leader of the young men of several villages and hamlets, who was the head of *warnang*s (q.v.). The title of *ʿaqīd* was also given to those who were chosen to lead the men in battle, during a hunting expedition or a raid. In Wadai it was a common (military) title of administrative officials, e.g. the *ʿaqīd al-Maḥāmīd*, who was the governor of northeastern Wadai and the Wadai Sultan's charg̣é d'affaires in relations with the sultanates of Wadai's eastern border. Compare Nachtigal (1971), 403 and O'Fahey (1980), 150.

ardabb (or **irdabb**) (Arabic), ardeb, a dry measure of 198 l.

baḥḥāra (Arabic); the people of the river, i.e. the Nile or Baḥr al-Ghazāl. This name was given to the ivory and slave traders who operated in the area south of Dār Fūr. Compare Nachtigal (1971), 406 (Baharina).

bāsī (non-Arabic), plur. *bāsinga*; In Dār Masālīt honorific, given to those members of the ruling class, who were either relatives of Ismāʿīl ʿAbd al-Nabī (1884–1888) or otherwise closely associated with him. It was restricted to the generation of Ismāʿīl and his son Abbakr (1888–1905). Compare O'Fahey (1980), 33, 150; Nachtigal (1971), 450; and Kropàçek (1971), note 56.

dala (Masālīt), drum chief; can denote *malik*, *dimlij* and *firsha* (q.v.).

dār (Arabic), country, land; frequently used in names, e.g. Dār Masālīt, the country of the Masālīt; Dār Fūr, the country of the Fūr; *dār sabāḥ*, the east or the land in the east, in western Sudan often referring to the Nile valley. Compare Nachtigal (1971), 406.

dimlij (non-Arabic); 'sub-district chief below a *shartay*' (O'Fahey, 1980, 150); see *malik* and see Chapter 2, note 86. Compare Nachtigal (1971), 406 (*dimilik*).

dinggar (non-Arabic), wooden drum, in Dār Masālīt symbol of authority of the *malik* (*dala*), the head of the land-owning clan. Compare O'Fahey (1980) (*dinger*).

dīwān (Arabic), tax or tribute. In western Dār Fūr the term seems to imply that people who paid *dīwān* to a ruler had a high degree of autonomy or were formally independent. See Chapter 2, note 79 and compare Nachtigal (1971), 406.

ḍiyāfa (Arabic), obligatory hospitality (a customary due or tax) to be provided to visiting members or representatives of the ruling class. Compare Nachtigal (1971), 406 (*difa*).

diya (Arabic), blood money, compensation for homicide or serious injury.

dumbāri (non-Arabic), locust charmer, who was to isolate himself on the top of a hill in order to divert (with his staff) the locusts menacing the community's crops. See Chapter 2, note 40.

falgo (non-Arabic), cone of salt, produced in the Jabal Marra

	area from saline soil; in Dār Masālīt used as a currency. See Chapter 2, note 53.
faqīh	(Arabic), anomalous plur. *fuqarā'*; Muslim holy man, *Qur'ān* teacher.
Fartīt	a generic name which the inhabitants of the Northern Sudan used to describe those non-Muslim tribes which lived south of the Dār Fūr Sultanate. See O'Fahey (1980), 73.
fātiḥa	(Arabic), opening chapter of the *Qur'ān*. 'To receive the *fātiḥa*' or 'to be given the *fātiḥa*' could in Dār Masālīt mean 'to be married' or 'to be manumitted'.
firka	(Arabic), piece of cloth which was smaller than a *tōb* (q.v.). In Dār Masālīt a *firka* was half the size of a *tukkiyya* (q.v.).
firsha or **fursha**	(possibly Arabic); (hereditary) district chief in command of several *maliks* (q.v.) and subordinate to the *shartay* (q.v.). Before 1874 the *firsha* was the highest indigenous authority in Dār Masālīt. See Chapter 2, note 102.
fiṭra	(Arabic), tax of one *midd* levied in Dār Fūr and Wadai at the Feast of Fastbreaking (*'īd al-fiṭr*). Compare *Encyclopedia of Islam*, iv, 1204 (*zakāt al-fiṭr*); and Nachtigal (1971) 407.
fursān	(Arabic), sing. *fāris*; knights, cavaliers, horsemen.
furūshiyya	(possibly Arabic); the office of *firsha* or the *firsha*'s district.
ḥajar	(Arabic), hill, rocky outcrop; frequently used in names of hills, e.g. *ḥajar* Jerkonei, the Jerkonei hill.
ḥākim	(Arabic), plur. *ḥukkām*; ruler, he who possesses *ḥukm*, i.e. judicial and administrative authority.
ḥākūra	(Arabic), used in Dār Masālīt usually as an equivalent of *dār*; for example *ḥākūrat al-Mistereng*, the land of the Mistereng. In other parts of Dār Fūr it means 'an estate granted by the sultan', 'a delimited area of land, granted by the sultan to individuals of lineage groups to use it for productive activities, to profit from its tax revenues, and/or to rule it politically on behalf of the sultan' (definition by La Rue, unpublished 1980). Compare Nachtigal (1971), 408–9 (*hawakir*); and O'Fahey (1980), 51–62.
hāmil	(Arabic), (the obligation to hand over) runaway slaves and stray animals (to the ruler); a customary due owed to the ruler.
ḥarīm	(Arabic), harem, the female part of the household, consisting not only of the wives and concubines, but also of the daughters, female servants, resident aunts, grandmothers etc.
hijra	(Arabic), emigration, departure; term applied to the

emigration of the Prophet Muḥammad from Mecca to Medina in 622 A.D., and also to the emigration of the adherents of the Sudanese Mahdiyya, who were ordered to leave their homes to join the Mahdī and (later) his Khalīfa.

ikhwān (Arabic), sing. *akh*; brothers; in the context of this study denoting the members of the Libyan religious brotherhood, the Sanūsiyya.

imām (Arabic), imam, Muslim prayer leader.

īya (non-Arabic), mother; a title prefixed to the name of married women. Compare O'Fahey (1980), 150 (*iiya baasi* and *iiya kuuri*).

jallāba (Arabic), sing. *jallābī*; travelling merchants; in Dār Fūr used particularly to indicate merchants from the Nile valley. Compare Nachtigal (1971), 409 (Jellabi).

jallābiyya (Arabic), galabia, a loose, shirtlike garment; the common dress of the male population in Egypt and the Northern Sudan.

jibba or **jubba** (Arabic), a short *jallābiyya* (q.v.). The patched *jibba* was the prescribed dress of the followers of the Mahdī.

jihād (Arabic), holy war (against infidels); in certain circumstances a duty for Muslims.

jihādiyya (Arabic), professional slave soldiers, normally foot soldiers, skilled in the use of firearms.

jubbay (Arabic), the equivalent of sultan, commonly used in the frontier sultanates and Wadai; 'he to whom people bring whatever he demands'; not to be confused with *jabbay* (Arabic), tax collector.

khalīfa (Arabic), deputy, vicar. 'The Khalīfa' refers to Khalīfa 'Abdullāhi, the successor of the Mahdī (1885–98).

khalwa (Arabic), *Qur'ān* school.

khidmāt or **khadāmāt** (Arabic), sing. *khidma*, *khadāma*; in Dār Masālīt generic name for customary dues (of e.g. honey, ghee, cloth). Compare O'Fahey (1980), 104, who gives 'obligatory labour for estate holder or chief'.

Kirdī generic name given in Wadai and Dār Fūr to the non-Muslim tribes living south of the Wadai Sultanate.

kumal (Masālīt), 'bride labour', the labour services which the bridegroom owed to his parents-in-law for two or three years. The term is also used to indicate labour services performed for the ruler.

maḥāya or **maḥḥāya** (Arabic), potion made of the ink of a *Qur'ān* text or prayer, mixed (or washed from a slate) with water; often used as medicine.

maḥmal (Arabic), a richly decorated litter sent by Islamic rulers to Mecca as an emblem of their independence.

malik (Arabic), plur. *mulūk*; drum chief; clan head and title-holder to the clan's land; head of a number of village chiefs. See Chapter 2, note 86.

maqdūm (Arabic), 'commissioner or viceroy appointed for a fixed term or purpose' (O'Fahey, 1980, 152). In Dār Masālīt the title was given to members of the ruling class who had the rank of *bāsī*, but were not of the royal clan, and – more commonly – to those slaves who functioned as go-betweens between the district governors and the local rulers. Finally there were *maqdūm*s whose title dated from the Ancien Regime, during which they had been agents of the Dār Fūr Sultan or one of his *shartay*s. The '*maqdūm* of the west' was a slave official who was the Dār Fūr Sultan's direct representative in western Dār Fūr between approximately 1840 and 1870.

masjid (Arabic), place of worship, a small mosque; 'In Darfur the prayer place of a village, often an open area marked out by stones, to which were attached a verandah and a hut used as an elementary' (Nachtigal, 1971, 412).

mayram (non-Arabic, possibly in origin a Kanuri word) = princess.

midd or **mudd** (Arabic), plur. *amdād*; a standard grain measure of varying size. In Western Dār Fūr the *midd al-zakāh* or *midd al-madaq* (the *midd* of the threshing-floor) varied normally from about 8 to 12 *raṭl*s, i.e. from about four to six kilos. The *midd al-fiṭra* (the *midd* by which the *fitra* tax was measured) was much smaller. See Chapter 2, note 32, and compare Nachtigal (1971), 413 (mudd).

miskīn (Arabic), plur. *masākīn*; commoner, ordinary (free) subject.

mulūkiyya (Arabic), the office of *malik* (q.v.), or the *malik*'s district.

nabī ʿIsā (Arabic), 'the prophet Jesus'. According to Mahdist traditions the prophet Jesus would descend at the end of times to kill the Antichrist (*al-dajjāl*), who had defeated the Mahdī. See Holt (1970), 23. Since the French and British colonialists were often regarded as the Antichrist, opposition against them often gathered around a 'prophet Jesus'.

nafīr (Arabic), (in Dār Fūr) a communal labour party.

qāḍī (Arabic), Islamic judge.

qūz or **qōz** (Arabic), stabilized sand dune.

rātib (Arabic), supererogatory exercises of devotion; in the

	Sudan often referring to the *rātib* of the Mahdī, a collection of prayers and verses from the *Qur'ān*, compiled by the Mahdī.
raṭl	(Arabic), rotl, a weight; in Egypt and the Sudan 449,28 g.
rayka	(Arabic), open wicker basket, a standard measure (of grain) equivalent to 30 *midd* (q.v.).
Resident	Condominium official, the Sudan Government's representative in 'indirectly ruled' Dār Masālīt.
riyāl	(Arabic), generic name for silver coinage, exemplified by the (Austrian) Maria Theresa dollar, the (Egyptian) Majīdī dollar, and the silver coin struck by Sultan Alī Dīnār of Dār Fūr (1898–1916).
rubṭa or **rabṭa**	(Arabic), unit of cotton thread, locally spun; in western Dār Fūr used as a currency.
salām	(Arabic), greeting-gift; a customary due paid by subjects when visiting their ruler, and by traders when arriving at the ruler's residence.
sambei	(non-Arabic), in Dār Masālīt a district chief ranking between *firsha* and *malik* (q.v.). See Chapter 2, note 110.
shartay	(non-Arabic), district chief in the Dār Fūr Sultanate; head of a number of *firsha*s. While some *shartay*s were directly responsible to the sultan, others were subordinate to higher ranking provincial governors or *maqdūm*s. The *shartay*'s office and district were called *shartāya*. Compare Nachtigal (1971), 415.
shaykh	(Arabic), (in Dār Masālīt often) village head.
tahjīr	(Arabic), of the same root as *hijra* (q.v.); inducement to emigrate; term used to describe the Khalīfa's policy of forced or compulsory emigration (to Omdurman).
tōb	(Arabic, *thawb*), outer garment; piece of cotton cloth which served as a currency in Dār Fūr and Wadai. In Dār Masālīt a *tōb* of native cloth was the size of two *tukkiyya*s (q.v.); sometimes used as name for imported white cloth (see e.g. Felkin, 1884–5, 250). See Chapter 4, note 167.
tukkiyya	(Arabic), plur. *takākī*; strip of local cotton cloth, varying in width, but (in Dār Masālīt) usually about ten cubits long. See Chapter 2, note 36. Compare Nachtigal (1971), 417 (*toqqiyya*).
wādī	(Arabic), dry riverbed or seasonal stream.
wakīl	(Arabic), deputy.
warnang	(non-Arabic), leader of the village youth; subordinate to an *'aqīd* (q.v.). See Chapter 2, note 82 and compare O'Fahey (1980), 152 (*ornang*).

wayba	(Arabic), whiba, a dry measure of 64 *raṭl* or approximately 32 kilos.
wazīr	(Arabic), 'an honorific rather than a specific office' (O'Fahey 1980, 153). In Dār Masālīt one of the most important state officials and the leader of the army in war. The *wazīr* did not belong to the royal clan of the Gernyeng.
zakāh	(Arabic), the legally required alms or tax. Although it was often referred to as *'ushr* in Dār Masālīt, it was in reality one thirtieth of the grain crop and a varying (but even smaller) percentage of the animal wealth. Compare Nachtigal (1971), 417; and *Encyclopedia of Islam*, iv, 1202–4.
zāwiya	(Arabic), a small domed mosque erected over the tomb of a Muslim saint, with teaching facilities and a hospice attached to it, usually the establishment of a religious order. In Dār Fūr it often referred to the lodges of the Libyan religious brotherhood of the Sanūsiyya.

Notes

Introduction

1 The term *bilād al-Sūdān* ('the land of the blacks') was used by the early Arab geographers (who wrote between the ninth and fifteenth centuries) to describe the savanna lands that stretched from the Atlantic Ocean to the Red Sea, below the Sahara and above the rain forests. Modern scholars of Africa have continued this usage in their references to the Sudanic belt, which they divided into two or three main regions, eastern and western, or eastern, central and western. There is little unanimity about the precise boundaries between these regions, particularly because scholars have referred to these regions as culture areas rather than geographical divisions. (See for a good summary of the debate about definitions, Yūsuf Faḍl Ḥasan and Paul Doornbos, Introduction to *The Central Bilād al-Sūdān: Tradition and Adaptation; essays on the geography and economic and political history of the Sudanic belt*, Khartoum, 1984.) In the present study the term eastern Sudanic belt is used as a purely geographical term and denotes the area stretching from Wadai (the eastern part of modern Chad) across the modern Sudan to the Red Sea. However, the Nile valley and the historical Funj Sultanate are beyond the scope of this study.

2 A number of features of the eastern Sudanic states will be discussed in an article to be written by the present author and R. S. O'Fahey.

3 See Miers and Kopytoff, eds (1977) and Meillassoux, ed. (1975).

4 See Miers and Kopytoff (1977) and Klein (1978).

5 Cooper (1979), 104.

6 Meillassoux (1975) and (1978).

7 Cooper (1978) and (1979).

8 Klein and Lovejoy (1979), 199 and 207 (for quotation).

9 idem, 204.

10 Klein (1978), 601.
11 Klein and Lovejoy (1979), 208–9
12 Note that the emergence of a professional slave army had its parallels elsewhere in the Sudanic belt. See Smaldone (1972), 597.
13 The numerical increase of slaves as a result of warfare (*jihāds*) again had its parallels elsewhere in the Sudanic belt in this period. See Klein and Lovejoy (1979), 206 and Boutillier (1975), 273.
14 For a summary and critique, see Terray (1975), particularly 315–18.
15 idem, 335–6.
16 See Spaulding (unpublished 1981). The concept of administered trade is associated with the name of Karl Polanyi (Dalton, 1975; and Polanyi, 1975). Polanyi's theory, however, is so broad and non-specific about how trade was controlled, and is so interwoven with his (very controversial) general paradigm (which does not place enough emphasis on production), that it does not have the authority to support this case study. On the other hand, this case study could be used as supporting evidence for the purport of Polanyi's theory on foreign trade in archaic economies. See Kapteijns and Spaulding (1982).
17 For the concept of 'desert-side' economy', see Lovejoy and Baier (1975).
18 Amin (1976), 13–22; and (unpublished 1977). Compare Coquery-Vidrovitch (1976), 12. It is surprising that Amin and Coquery-Vidrovitch give the name of 'tributary mode of production' to societies in which the tribute paid by the subjects to the rulers often has only a symbolic and not a real, material value; that is to say, societies in which tribute is not the major way in which surplus is extracted.
19 Grele (1975), 127.
20 idem.
21 See for example the special issue of *Social Analysis*, 4 September 1980, 'Using Oral Sources: Vansina and Beyond'. The term 'converging lines of evidence' is taken from Renato Rosaldo's 'Doing Oral History'.
22 Miller, ed. (1980), 19–20.
23 Binsbergen (1980).
24 Miller, ed. (1980).
25 Grele (1975), 135.
26 idem, 133.
27 idem, 137.

Chapter 1 – The western Sudan before 1874

1 This and the following section are based on O'Fahey (thesis 1972),

48–90; O'Fahey (1980), 145–6; O'Fahey (forthcoming in *JAH*, 1982); and O'Fahey and Spaulding (1974), 108–116.

2 O'Fahey (1979) in Levtzion, 202.

3 Nachtigal (1971), 267, 356 comments upon the cannibalism of the Masālīt; Balfour-Paul (1955), 406 speaks of 'animism scarcely yet blanketed by Islam'. In Durham, Lewis (600/6/25), the Islam of the Masālīt is called only 'skindeep'.

4 For the concept of corporate Islam, see Spaulding (1980), 6–7. For the 'mixing stage' of Islam, see Fisher (1973), 31.

5 El-Tounsy (1851), 53 and 251; Nachtigal (1971), 237 and note. Note that there was a similar strip of uninhabited or unadministered frontier land between Dār Tāmā and Wadai in 1910 (Carbou, 1912, ii, 208); between Wadai and Bagirmi (El-Tounsy, 1851, 6); and between the sultanates of Dār Fūr and Dār Masālīt in 1918 (CRO Darfur 1/33/171). The term 'negative land' is taken from East (1965), 101. While El-Tounsy (1851), 52 described the frontier as a forest zone inhabited by wild animals, he feared human attackers as much as the beasts. Nachtigal (1971) mentioned two ranges of hills – the 'tirje' of Wadai (238) and that of Dār Fūr (239) on each side of the uninhabited zone – to which he referred as a 'boundary mountain' (149). These mountains were no real obstacles to communication and human movement between the sultanates.

6 El-Tounsy (1851), 251.

7 Nachtigal (1971), 71 and 231. In 1873–4 there were three routes linking al-Fāshir and Wārā (the capital of Wadai): a southern one, passing through Dār Silā, a northern one passing through Dār Tāmā, and a central one, the shortest, which formed almost a straight line between the capitals. Foreigners and traders could only use the latter route, which had frontier posts on either side of the border: Bīr Tawīl in Wadai and Tineat in Dār Fūr. The information collected by Burckhardt (1822), appendix 1, 437 indicates that there was a similar strip of uninhabited land with frontier posts on either side further to the south.

8 Nachtigal (1971), 239. For an analysis of the system of long-distance trade which confirms the lack of participation, see Chapter 4, 113–22 and Chapter 5, 155–61.

9 'CRO Int. 1/1/4, E. G. Sarsfield Hall; ʿAlī ʿAbd Allāh Abū Sinn (mimeograph 1968), 91–2; and Balfour-Paul (1956), 137.

10 CRO Civ.Sec. 1/19/59; CRO 2 Darfur, Dar Masālīt 51/1/1, R. B. Broadbent, 18 March 1931, 'Dar Gimr Administrative Organization'; and Durham, Lewis 600/3/30, Handing Over Notes 1952.

11 Nachtigal (1971), 214; El-Tounsy (1851), 187 ff. It is probably no coincidence that Sultan Sābūn of Wadai (1803–13), the conqueror of

the Tāmā, was also the initiator of Wadai's trade with Egypt *via* a northeastern route which passed close to the Zaghāwa of Dār Fūr and may therefore have passed through Dār Tāmā (idem, 218).

12 El-Tounsy (1851), 209 notes that the Tāmā Sultan, even after his defeat by Wadai, wrote to the Fūr Sultan: 'je me reconnais toujours ton tributaire.' According to El-Tounsy (1845), 121 and 137, Dār Tāmā was situated between the two larger sultanates and (476) paid tribute to both. Nachtigal (1971) commented upon the high degree of autonomy which the Tāmā Sultan enjoyed (157–8); placed Dār Tāmā on the map between Wadai and Dār Fūr, but noted that 'Dar Tama is now in fact a dependency of Wadai' (157).

13 The route Wadai–Egypt did not pass through Dār Qimr, in contrast to that between Wadai and al-Fashir.

14 For the Jabal, see Hasan and O'Fahey (1970), and Durham, Lewis 600/3/30–1, which gives a description of the similarities in the administrative organization of Dār Jabal and Dār Qimr. Ḥasan and O'Fahey (1970), 156 believe that Dār Jabal was part of Dār Fia. According to Nachtigal (1971), 355 it was part of Dār Madi. Yet he mentioned the Barkari – not a small border tribe related to the Sungor, as he said, but a subsection of the Jabal (Int. 23) – as one of the ethnic groups of Dār Fia. For the conquest by Dār Fūr, see Nachtigal (1971), 281.

15 Neither al-Tūnisī nor Nachtigal made mention of the Erenga, although the Awra (Oro), Asungor (Sungor), Marārīt, Girga, Dula and Shali do occur in the latter's account as separate (but related) ethnic groups, or as subsections of the Qimr (166, 168, 205, 240 and 355). Nachtigal called part of modern Dār Erenga, namely the east bank of the Wādī Kajja, 'Dar Shale'; the Shālī are today one of the subsections of the Erenga proper. It is possible that 'firsha Da'ud of Dar Sciara', who submitted to the Turkish governor of western Dār Fūr in 1879, was the chief of the Erenga-Shālī (Messedaglia, 1886, 29). The Italian travellers Massari and Matteucci mentioned Iringa only as a language widely spoken west of Dār Fūr and – with some variations – in Dār Tāmā (Massari, 1881, 821). The languages of the Erenga peoples all belong to the Tāmā group of the Nilo-Saharan language family (Doornbos, in Bender, forthcoming). Nachtigal (1971), 166 was of a different opinion. The interpretation of the identity of the Erenga offered here is based on oral data collected in Dār Erenga, in particular Int. 24 and 25. For the political events of 1889–90, see below, Chapter 4, 95–6.

16 Dār Sinyār's change of political allegiance from Dār Fūr to Dār Silā is attributed in the sources to four incidents, referred to separately or in combination. The first incident occurred in 1863, when the Dājū

Sultan, Muḥammad Būlād, passing through Dār Fūr on his return from Mecca, received Dār Sinyār, Dār Galfige, and Dār Fongoro as fiefs from the Fūr Sultan. The Sinyār refused to submit to the Dājū but were defeated in battle.

The second incident occurred in c. 1874, when the Sinyār Sultan turned to the Dājū Sultan for support against the Turco-Egyptian troops in his country. The Dājū fought a number of campaigns in Dār Sinyār and reinstituted the sultan.

The third incident occurred in 1879. The Sinyār refused to recognize Isḥāq Abū Rīsha's succession to the Dājū throne, but were defeated in battle and forced to submit.

The fourth incident is only mentioned by the oral sources. It involved a close male relative of Sultan Abū Rīsha, who lost his way during a slave raid and whom the Sinyār took to al-Fāshir rather than back to Dār Silā. For the Sinyār this incident led to war, defeat and incorporation into Dār Silā. The year was c. 1883. After one of these incidents, probably after the third, the Sinyār became divided into a pro-Dājū and a pro-Fūr section, which each had their ruler. Only the ruler of the pro-Dājū section had the title of sultan. (CHEAM, Berre, Mémoire 1804; Grossard, 1925, 325; B.I.F., Simonet, MS 6005; Int. 29; Int. 30.)

17 Nachtigal (1971) 231. See also the *laissez-passer* which Sultan Abū Rīsha issued to an important pilgrim in February 1892, and which specifically addressed Sultan Kussam of Dār Sinyār (1886–1904), in Durham, Arabic catalogue 101/13/12 (for the original) and CRO Cair. Int. 3/18/306 and Lavers (1968) 77 (for the translation). For the trade passing through Mogororo, see B.I.F., Simonet, MS 6005.

18 Nachtigal (1971), 81 and 347.

19 CHEAM, Berre, Mémoire 1804 and Mémoire 2005; Thelwall (1981); and Jungraithmayr (1978).

20 Nachtigal (1971) 81 and 347; El-Tounsy (1845) and (1851), maps.

Chapter 2 – Masālīt society during the Ancien Regime

1 The present study will not deal with two large and ancient groups of Masālīt in Central Chad (on the Wādī Batḥa) and in southern Dār Fūr (south of Nyala). See for the former, Carbou (1912), ii, 215–18; Le Rouvreur (1962), 125 ff.; Arkell Papers[2] 5/19, 6–8. For the former see, El-Tounsy (1845), 137; Nachtigal (1971), 325; and ANSOM Afrique VI, doss. 184.

2 According to Nachtigal (1971), 217, some Masālīt were subjects of Dār Silā. This was confirmed by Int. 1, xiii and Int. 15. The Gube and Fora

area originally belonged to Dār Silā, but became part of the Masālīt Sultanate in the 1890s. It was reconquered by the sultan of Dār Silā in 1896, but re-annexed by the Masālīt in about 1913, and formally incorporated into Dār Masālīt at the boundary delimitation of 1924. Part of the area reconquered by the Dājū in 1896 remained in Dār Silā. The western part of the area south of Habila still has a large Dājū population. Gube has two Dājū *maliks*.

As for the population of Dār Masālīt, estimates made in 1923 varied from 65,000 to 90,000 (CRO Darfur 1/34/175 and 1/35/177). The estimate made in 1936 was 120,000. According to the census of 1956, Dār Masālīt had 299,200 inhabitants. According to that of 1972, 385,956, compared to 2,076,733 for Dār Fūr as a whole (Census Office, Khartoum).

3 El-Tounsy (1851), 189.

4 ANSOM Afrique IV, doss. 183.

5 According to Nachtigal (1971), 170, Sultan Kharut (1655–78), Sultan Arus (1681–1707) and Joda (1747–95) had compelled the Masālīt to stay in Wadai.

6 Nachtigal (1971), 356. All the names by which he refers to the Masālīt – 'the Masalit el-Haush' (150), the Masālīt 'Ambūs' (267) and the 'el Tivje Masalit' (267) – are descriptive names or nicknames except for one, that of the Masālīt 'Zirban' (278), i.e. Surbang, which is the name of a Masālīt clan or *khashm bayt*. For the story of Sulaymān, see Nachtigal (1971), 278.

7 *Jadd al-Islām*, literally, 'the grandfather (or ancestor) of Islam'. It can be freely translated as 'the founding father of Islam' in the area.

8 The Kunjāra are now considered Masālīt, but their Fūr origins are well remembered. See Arkell Papers[2] 5/19, 40; and Int. 1, xviii. According to another version the Kunjāra descended from Fūr tax collectors who fled to Iffene after having been expelled by the Masālīt (personal information from Paul Doornbos). Compare for border guards Nachtigal (1971), 383 on the Ḥamar.

9 Int. 1, iii and xviii.

10 El-Tounsy (1851), 77; Nachtigal (1971), 149 and 238–9; Int. 1, xviii. The Borqū are the Boro Mabang speakers of Wadai.

11 Arkell Papers[2] 10/48, 55 and 5/19, 71.

12 The Anglo-French boundary negotiations (1898–1924), which were based on the principle that the Chado-Sudanese border would be drawn 'in such a manner as to separate in principle the Kingdom of Wadai from what constituted in 1882 the province of Dār Fūr' (CRO Int. 1/3/10) led to an intensive inquiry into the history of the border and the *tirja* by French and British officials. See CRO Int. 1/1/1, 1/1/3, 1/1/4, 1/1/5, 1/2/7 and 1/2/8; CRO Cair. Int. 10/22/55; ANSOM Afrique VI, doss. 184, 188 and 189; and ANSOM Tchad I, doss. 9. For a

detailed description of the *tirja*, see CRO Int. 1/1/3 and Int. 1, xviii. The *tirja* ran west of the present international boundary, leaving the area east of the Wādī Ḥamra in Dār Fūr.

13 El-Tounsy (1851), 55–61; Nachtigal (1971), 236, 241 and 244–7.

14 See Chapter 1, note 5.

15 W. G. Browne, who visited Dār Fūr in 1793–5, was virtually kept a prisoner throughout his stay. Both E. Vogel and M. von Beurmann lost their lives when attempting to visit Wadai in respectively 1856 and 1863. Boyd Alexander was killed in Dār Tāma in 1910. See also above, note 13.

16 Int. 29.

17 For details about the frontier zone, see El-Tounsy (1851), 51–7 and Nachtigal (1971), 237 and note.

18 For example, Jabal Fukkum of the Fukkunyang and Ḥajar Jabōk of the Mandara.

19 For 'Masalit et Tirge', see Nachtigal (1971), 149 and 267; for 'Ambus', see idem, 267 and Int. 29, i, 'Azza 'Alī, 16 May 1979.

20 Nachtigal (1971), 239.

21 Int. 1, iii and xviii. The Amm Būs allegedly had a language or dialect of their own (see also Arkell Papers[2] 5/19, 37) and were Muslims of doubtful quality, if at all. Their young men still had the traditional hair-style (long tiny plaits) and beads around their necks.

22 O'Fahey (1980), 70–1.

23 See CRO Darfur 6/17/19 for changes with regard to Dār Fia and Dār Kerne, and Arkell Papers[2] 10/48, 51–7.

24 The following section is based on MacMichael (1922), volume 1, 86; CRO Darfur 1/33/171 and 1/18/91; Nachtigal (1971), 244–5 and 324; Arkell Papers[2] 3/13, 34–49 and 10/48, 51–7.

25 For the exact border between Fia and Madi, see CRO 2 Darfur, Kuttum, 41/4/2. For *shartay* Ḥanafī, see Nachtigal (1971), 241, 245–6, 258 and 266; Int. 8, 15, 21 and 16. Ḥanafī's sister was the mother of *shartay* Muzammil Nūr of Kerne (see Arkell Papers[2] 10/48, 55).

26 Idem and Arkell Papers[2] 4/18, 23.

27 Dār Fia's southern border with Kerne followed (from east to west) the course of the Wādī Barei, the area north of the *wādī* being under Fia, that to the south under Kerne. Further west the boundary followed the line Kereinik–Dirjeil (Arkell Papers[2] 10/48, 55). For Dār Dīma, see O'Fahey (1980), 76 ff. and CRO Darfur 6/17/19.

28 See CRO 2 Darfur Dar Masalit, 6/1/1 and Darfur 6/7/19 for the different *shartaya*s (of Tebella, Zami Baya, Kulli and Zami Toya) during the Condominium period, when they no longer extended west of the Wādī Azūm. The *shartay*s of Dār Dīma were relatively modest figres (O'Fahey, 1980, 78). Oral testimonies were somewhat confusing

(Int. 8 and 15) with regard to the borders of Tebella, Kulli and Zami Baya.

29 O'Fahey (1980), 80 and Nachtigal (1971), 324–5.

30 Balfour-Paul (1957), 406.

31 Int. 1, viii.

32 According to R. Davies (CRO Int. 1/34/172) in 1921, the *midd* or *mudd* was eight *raṭl* (approximately four kilos). According to Int. 1, v the *midd al-madaq* (of the threshing floor) was fourteen *raṭl*, while the *midd al-fiṭra* was five and a half times two hands full of grain. In reality the *midd al-madaq* changed according to the circumstances. See below, 39–40 and glossary. For another definition of *midd*, see El-Tounsy (1845), 319; Klein and Lovejoy (1979), 191 (muude); and Nachtigal (1971), 431.

33 Int. 5 and compare O'Fahey (1980), 101.

34 Int. 1, ix and below, 29–30. Compare Haaland (1978), and Barth (1967), 154.

35 Int. 1, xv. *Būde* is Strigahermonthica.

36 See glossary. According to Int. 1, vii and x, *tukkiyya*s were usually ten cubits long, but varied in width. There were *tukkiyya*s with a width of 70 warpthreads (*abū sab'īn*), of 80 warpthreads (*abū tamanīn*), of 90 (*abū tis'*īn), up to 120 warpthreads. One *rubṭa* or spool of cotton thread had enough thread for ten warpthreads.

37 On raids into Wadai, see Int. 1, iii and x. For raids to the south, Int. 29 and 10. For the importance of raids to obtain bridewealth, see Int. 10 and compare the popular Fūr song quoted by O'Fahey (1980), 95. For their importance to prove one's virility, see Durham, Lewis 600/3/25 and 600/6/9.

38 Durham, Sandison 511/4/53–4 and Durham, Lewis 600/6/19–20.

39 The Masālīt gathered *nabaq* (*zizyphus spina christi*), the nuts of the *hijlīj* (*balanites aegyptica*) from which they made soap and oil, the fruit of the *gambīl* (*cordia abyssinica*), the fruit of the *aradayb* (*tamarindus indicus*), called the lemon of the western Sudan, *mukhayt* nuts (*boscia senegalensis*), honey, *jakhjakh* (*azanza garckeana*), *ḥimayd* nuts (*sclerocarya birrea*), rice, *difra* (*brachiaria spp.*), locusts and termites (which they ate fried). See Doornbos (unpublished 1979), 'Ecological Transformations in Darfur's Western District, Sudan'; and compare El-Tounsy (1851), 358 and (1845), 324–5 and Tubiana (1978).

40 For root doctors, see Arkell (1926); Durham, Lewis 600/6/33, who called them *kamarka*. For roots which could make someone invisible and for rainmaking charms, see Arkell Papers[2] 5/19, 34. The root doctors could put spells on people, make love potions, call up winds to restore the health of sick animals, cure sick people etc. A popular root among thieves was one which, when chewed and spit out on the tracks,

would immediately attract white ants and thus destroy the tracks. For the *dumbāri*, see Balfour-Paul (1957), 407; Arkell Papers[2] 5/19/30–34 (P. J. Sandison 'The Dumba:ri or Locust Charmer', Geneina, 18 November 1933); and le Rouvreur (1962), 142.

For the rainpriest, see Durham, Lewis 600/6/25–8; Durham, Sandison 511/4/36–6. Int. 1, ii gave an eyewitness account of the rainmaking ceremonies of the Masālīt Gernyeng, as they were held at the beginning of the twentieth century at Ḥajar Jerkone, not far from Dirjeil. Compare Tubiana (1964).

41 See Doornbos (unpublished 1981), 'The Haddad of Chad and Sudan; an African Pariah Caste'. *Maḥāya* are written *Qur'ān* texts dissolved in water, see glossary.

42 Int. 1, viii and x.

43 The leaders were the *warnang*, the leader of the young men (see below, note 85), and the *umm al-banāt* ('the mother of the girls'). Int. 1, xvi and 27, i.

44 Int. 1, ix and Doornbos (unpublished 1979), Interim rapport, 6.

45 Int. 1, ix. If one married a close relative, the price was much lower. Int. 10 and 15 give different versions. See also Durham, Lewis 600/6/31–34.

For *kumal*, see Int. 1, iii; Int. 27, i; and Int. 8.

46 Int. 1, vii and xvii was indignant at the suggestion that his father, a district governor in the 1890s, might have needed a *nafīr*, for he had plenty of slaves. Nevertheless he did hold *nafīr*s sometimes, at which he would regale the workers with game and bull's meat.

47 Sometimes these services would be exchanged for other services. If someone needed his farming tools to be repaired, the blacksmith might ask him to do some agricultural work for him. (Int. 1, vii), Int. 17, a man who combined the profession of *faqīh* with that of trader – not an unusual combination – made a small fortune by writing charms in Dār Zaghāwa. After a stay of three years he came back to Dār Masālīt with 75 goats, 28 sheep, two donkeys and clothing for his household.

48 For a fine characterization of the *jallāba* traders in Dār Fūr and Wadai, see Nachtigal (1971), 354.

49 Int. 1, x and compare the popular Fūr song quoted by O'Fahey (1980), 101.

50 Int. 1, vii; Int. 27, i (30 April); It is possible that this form of hired labour was also called *ngōre*.

51 Nachtigal (1971), 242 and Int. 1, xi and vii.

52 Int. 10 and personal information from Paul Doornbos.

53 Int. 1, x and xix; Int. 17, 20 and 23; CRO Darfur 1/33/171 for the salt trade between Dār Masālīt and Dār Fūr in 1922. See El-Tounsy

(1845), 317 and CRO Darfur 6/6/198 for how *falgo* salt was made.
54 Int. 1, xix. See Chapter 5, 156–7.
55 Int. 1, vii and ix, and see below, 54.
56 Int. 1, ix. Two Gernyeng bought a Dinka slave woman in Gereida. One of them married the woman, who bore him children. The other owner was compensated, when he demanded his share in the woman. See below, 54.
57 For the grooming of slaves for sale, see Int. 1, i and compare Walz (mimeograph 1977). See below 53–5 for slave trade from Dār Silā.
58 Int. 1, i, vii, viii and Int. 28. Compare O'Fahey (1980), 132.
59 El-Tounsy (1845), 319. Compare Nachtigal (1971), 125.
60 See for equivalencies Int. 1, x and CRO Darfur 1/34/172 for a list of customary fines recorded in Dār Erenga in the 1920s. One cow equalled 20 *tukkiyya*s and one bull 15. For the function of the currencies as measure of value, see Int. I, xix, and compare O'Fahey (1980), 110 (*toni*); El-Tounsy (1845), 319; and Felkin (1884/5), 250.
61 Int. 1, ix. *Nishkī* is *nashtakī*. *Iya* Amm Būsa was the mother of the Fūr Sultan Muḥammad al-Ḥusayn (1838–73) (according to the informant), or the mother of Sultan Muḥammad al-Faḍl (1803–38), according to O'Fahey (1980), 17 and Nachtigal (1971), 290 and 293.
62 El-Tounsy (1845), 316; Nachtigal (1971), 125, 203, 234, 241 and 247. Note that amber beads were almost worthless in Kobbei (253), probably because of Kobbei's proximity to Egypt.
63 Walz (1978), 46.
64 Nachtigal (1971), 125.
65 idem, 242.
66 Durham, Lewis 600/6/38: 'The Masalit have a bad name with neighbouring tribes for being cannibals (mingEEri)'; Int. 37; Nachtigal (1971), 267; Slatin (1896), 111; ANSOM Afrique VI, doss. 184; Alexander (1912), 272; CRO Cair. Int. 10/22/55, letter (translated from Arabic) from ʿUthmān Jānū to the Khalīfa, dated 27 Shaʿbān 1306 (28 April 1889); the Mahdist soldiers who campaigned in the frontier area of Dār Silā, Dār Sinyār and Dār Masālīt reported that they 'saw the Masalit El Aajem (the Masalit who speak a language foreign to the Arabs) who belong to Abu Risha (Sultan of Sula) and who eat the flesh of men, preferring it to any other. When a person falls sick his relatives lend the body to others for food. Evidence of this custom was found in every village by the Ansar. They saw human heads in clay pots on fires with the Belila (boiled grain).' According to Int. 2, i, it was one of the fighting tactics or ruses of the Masālīt to scare off the Mahdist pursuers by making them think they were cannibals.
67 O'Fahey (1980), 123; O'Fahey and Spaulding (1974), 112; Int. 13.
68 Int. 13.

69 According to Int. 1, vi, the Jabal, Tāmā and Erenga were all *massāsīn*. Examples were *shartay* Bukr of the Erenga (xiv) and the daughter of Sultan Dūd of the Marārīt (xi). El-Tounsy (1845), 355, reported that the Fūr believed that the Masālīt could change themselves into dogs, cats and hyaenas. For a similar belief of the Masālīt about the Fūr, see Int. 1, ii (below, note 106).
70 Int. 10 for first quotation; Int. 20 for the second.
71 Int. 10.
72 Int. 1, ix. For 'Abd Allāh Runga see below, 44–5.
73 See below, Chapter, 113–22 and Chapter 5, 155–61.
74 Int. 1, ix and above, note 49.
75 CRO Darfur 1/33/171 (30 June 1918).
76 CRO Darfur 1/33/186, P. J. Sandison, 'Notes on the Geography and Trade of the Emirate'. Compare CRO Darfur 1/1/2, where it is reported that control of country markets and regulation of the grain prices was one of the functions of the *shartay*.
77 CRO Darfur 1/37/188 for a reference to 1946 and CRO Darfur 3/1/5 for one to 1929. Compare CRO Darfur 1/34/172 for the discovery that *abbo* Badawī received a share of raided cows.
78 Int. 1, viii and below, 52.
79 For *dīwān* see Nachtigal (1971), 181–2 and 359. In Wadai the Masālīt paid gum arabic and lance shafts (182); see below, for what they paid in Dār Fūr. Compare Chapter 4, 111–12 for *dīwān* paid to Wadai in the 1890s.
80 For customary dues, see Chapter 5, 150–1.
81 Nachtigal (1971), 216 and his glossary for *salam*, *difa* etc.
82 All sources agree that the *warnang* (or *ornang*) was the leader of the young men of the village, responsible to an *ʿaqīd*, who was the head of the *warnang*s of a group of villages. The *warnang* saw to it that the young men were prepared for war, raiding parties, the pursuit of thieves or whatever, at any time. He summoned them to a *nafīr*, to repair the enclosure of the village herd etc. See El-Tounsy (1845), 147; Durham, Sandison 511/4/53–4; Durham, Lewis 600/6/20, 22–3; Haaland (1978); Int. 10. However, there is evidence that the *warnang* also had some responsibility for the public grainstores, and was the executive agent of the *malik* and village *shaykh*. According to Durham, Sandison 511/4/54 (referring to Broadbent's report on Dār Qimr), the *warnang* was responsible to the 'gebbei' (*jabbay* or collector of the graintax) for the grain payable by the commoners as *fiṭra* and *zakāh*. Int. 1, x described the *warnang* as *khalīfa* or *ghafīr* (deputy or 'tough guy') of the *malik*. When the Maghārba came to exchange salt for grain, the exchange took place between them and the *warnang*. See also note 83. In this context it is interesting to note that,

when the boys of a village or village group were circumcized, the first one to be operated was called 'dala gulfantami' (the chief or *malik* of the circumcised), the second one 'ornong gulfantami' (the captain or *warnang* of the circumcized), and the third 'kule gulfantami' (the blacksmith of the circumcized). See Durham, Lewis 600/6/19.

83 Int. 1, xvii.

84 CRO Darfur 6/7/19, Note by P. J. Sandison, 1931.

85 The Masālīt term *sutu* is equivalent to the Arabic *qabīla* and can denote both the ethnic group as a whole and the clan or section. The term variously given as *dusungu*, *jusungu*, *duchungu* or *tuchungu* (plur. *dusung*, *jusung* etc.) is the equivalent of the Arabic *khashm bayt* and can denote both the clan or section, or a section of the clan. (Int. 1, vii). According to the Masālīt, the number of clans was much smaller in the past. The historical process of fission and territorial expansion of the Masālīt clans requires further study.

86 The Masālīt term *dala* means drumchief, and can denote *malik*, *dimlij*, and *firsha*, three titles which are in common use throughout Dār Fūr. The use of the titles *malik*, *dimlij* and *firsha* in Dār Masālīt is both confused and confusing. The term *dimlij* is not used very often, but when it is, it refers to the head of a clan or subclan. The term *malik* is usually used in the same way, but sometimes denotes *firsha* or even village head. If one looks at functions rather than titles, there is less confusion. One can distinguish three levels of local authority from the bottom upwards. The village head will be referred to in this study as *shaykh*, which is his present title. The head of the clan or – if the clan had several *dinggar*s – the subclan, who was at the same time the head of several village *shaykh*s, will be referred to as *malik*, and as *dimlij* only when informants are quoted literally. This corresponds to a large extent to the use of the terms by the informants. The distinction between *malik* as head of the clan and *dimlij* as head of the subclan, proposed by R. Davies (CRO Darfur 1/34/172), was not confirmed by oral data collected by the present author. The same is true for the definition given by MacMichael in CRO Darfur 1/33/171. For *firsha* see below, 44. According to the Western Darfur District Handbook (CRO Darfur 6/7/19) the *dimlij* was the head of the tribal section, while the *malik* was the steward (or manager) of the 'fiefs' (*ḥākūras*) which the Fūr Sultans in the eighteenth and nineteenth centuries carved out of the territories of the *dimlij*s. When the British Condominium officials in the early 1920s revived the traditional *dimlijiyya*s, they appointed as *dimlij*s descendants of the *malik*s or stewards. This may have contributed to a confusion in terminology not only in Western Darfur District but also in the neighbouring Dār Masālīt. Compare Holý (1974), 95 for *sīd al-ḥākūra*, whose position

resembles that of the Masālīt *malik*. Among the Berti, the village *shaykh* was a more important figure than among the Masālīt, where the office of *shaykh* was not an institution in land tenure like that of the *malik*, but an administrative office.

87 For *fās* (or hoe) rights, see O'Fahey (1980), 65; Barth (1967), 152–3, and Holý (1974), 97. According to Int. 2, i, one owned a plot of land if the land belonged to one's clan and had either not been used for ten to fifteen years, or had been opened up by one's ancestors (*fās jaddak*, *fās abūk*; in Masālīt *kanya danya*). One could obtain permission to use land cleared and cultivated recently by someone else, but in that case that person would receive a small payment, possibly five *midd* of each *rayka* paid as *zakāh* (Int. 27, i). For other customary dues paid to the hereditary representative of the original clearer of the land, see CRO Darfur 1/35/177 ('salim ed darat' in Northern Darfur District), CRO Darfur 1/37/185 ('hagg el dar' and 'dugundi' in the Zalingei area), and Durham, Lewis 600/3/24 (for the *midd al-baraka* paid to the 'owner of the axe' for blessing the land which his ancestors had cleared.

88 Int. 2, iii.

89 Int. 1, i, ii, viii; Int. 28 and note 59.

90 CRO Darfur 1/34/172.

91 According to Int. 2, i, the *warnang* would administer corporal punishments to an offender sentenced by the *malik*, for if the *malik* were to dare to do so, he might be killed. See also Int. 1, i. Other titles used for persons who formed the *malik*'s 'strong arm' were that of *folqonāwī* (the man sent out to fetch an offender), that of *tanga* and *ghafīr*. Compare O'Fahey (1980), 150 (folgony), and Nachtigal (1971), glossary.

Ghafīr is probably a new (namely colonial) term used to denote an old function (personal information from Paul Doornbos).

92 For *ṣadaqa* or *karāma*, see Int. 5, 8, 9 and 28. Compare Arkell Papers[2] 4/18, 32–3 and 37–9. For the ceremony of 'biting the liver', see Int. 3,8,9, 15 and 28. For *diya* see Int. 8, 15, 28 and 29. Compare O'Fahey (1980), 103 (*dam kabīr* and *dam saghīr*). *Sadaqa* is much smaller than *diya*. It is a meal of reconciliation rather than payment of compensation.

93 Int. 1, i, ii, v and vii, and Int. 43.

94 Int. 1, vii; 'The *dala*s do not need *nafīr*s; they have slaves and in-laws', the informant said, probably referring to the *kumal* obligations of those young men who married the *dala*'s daughters.

95 Concrete information on early inter-clan disputes is limited, but see below, 46–7.

96 For greeting gifts, see Int. 13. For *ḥaqq al-naṣr*, see CRO Darfur 1/36/185 (1933); CRO Civ.Sec. 20/20/95 (1922); and Arkell Papers[2]

5/19, 40.

97 The sources do not agree about how the *zakāh* was divided among the *ḥukkām*. See glossary and see Chapter 5, 147–8.

98 Int. 1, ii; Int. 2, i; Int. 8; CRO Darfur 1/34/172: 'while perhaps it would hardly be true to say that the people elect their tribal leaders the Sultan certainly consults their wishes and removes oppressive and unpopular firash and dimalig.'

99 Int. 1, ii and vii; and Int. 9; Compare Doornbos (unpublished 1981), Interim Report, 6. For the hangers-on, see above note 62 (*tanga*, *gafīr*).

100 Int. 1, vii: 'The *firsha* is very different from the *miskīn*; perfume, scent, his clothes; Sulaymān had everything; red shoes on his feet, a red shawl, a rifle . . . ; and he had slaves, and his horse was tied up [nearby].'

101 For hospitality, see Int. 1, v and viii. How important it was for a *malik* to be hospitable is evident from the case of ʿAbd al-Jalīl, drumchief of the Nyerneng, who was rejected by his people and deposed on the grounds that he was a miser (Int. 15). The importance of having hangers-on and dependents in order to impress and command respect is visible even in the modern Sudan.

102 For *firsha* see O'Fahey (1980), 150; Nachtigal (1971), 407; CRO Darfur 1/33/171 (MacMichael); CRO Darfur 1/34/172 (Davies, 1921 and Arkell, 1926). The definition proposed here is based on Int. 5, 9, 10 and 12, and CRO Darfur 1/34/175 (Annual Reports for Dār Masālīt for 1936, 1937 and 1938); for the evolution of the titles and offices of *malik* and *firsha*, see Chapter 7.

103 For the four *firsha*s, see Int. 1, i; Int. 6, 8, 13 and 15. According to Int. 21 there were three *firsha*s, those of the Nyerneng, Fukkunyang and Surbang. According to Grossard (1925), 322 there were five. The break of the Mistereng and Minjiri with the Nyerneng was dated back to the reign of Sultan Muḥammad al-Faḍl (1803–38) (Int. 8), and the reign of Sultan Muḥammad al-Ḥusayn (1838–73) (Int. 13).

104 O'Fahey (1980), 90; Nachtigal (1971), 326; Ḥasan and O'Fahey (1972), 156; CRO Darfur 1/33/171 and 1/18/91 (MacMichael, 1918); and CRO Darfur 1/36/182.

105 Int. 43.

106 Int. 1, ii. One of the complaints of the Masālīt was that they had to pay a tax in *ḥimayd* nuts (see note 39), and that these nuts had to be cracked in such a way that the fruit inside would be in one piece. On the occasion of ʿAbd Allāh Runga's defeat and death, the Masālīt composed a song: "ʿAbdulla Runga was killed; where can we find his like? The cat turned into a fox; they [the Fūr] entered the holes [of animals] (Int. 1, ii). According to Durham, Sandison 511/4/42 ʿAbd

Allāh Runga was killed in a war with the Fezzān of Kobbei before the Mahdiyya.

107 Nachtigal (1971), 244 for Tineat, 241 for *urrundulung*. Compare O'Fahey (1980), 152 (*orrengdulung*) for the same title, but a different office. Int. 16 mentioned the *urrungdulung* as a tax collector at Amm Sibayḥa. See for ʿAbd al-Qaffā, Int. 1, i, iii and ix Int. 2, iii; and see Chapter 5. The *shaykhs* of the Tarjam, Ta'ālba and Maḥāmīd were at the end of the Ancien Regime respectively *shaykh* Ḥaqqār (near Ardeme), *shaykh* Angulu (at Kereinik), and *shaykh* Hārūn Adam Dallako (on the Wādī Barei). (Int. 1, i, xvii and xxiii, and Int. 2, iii).

108 For Ndelngongo, see Int. 1, v, vi and xv. Moku and Ḥajar Laban lie north and northeast of Dirjeil. For Andokoi, see Int. 1, v, ix, xv and xvi. Keira and Tineat lie east of Kereinik on the Wādī Barei.

109 See Chapter 5.

110 Int. 1, iv, v, vi and xi for *sambei*; Int. 1, v for *maqdūm* Bashīr of the Lere. Compare MacMichael (1922), volume 1, 86 and in CRO Darfur 1/33/171: 'In Fur days, they say in Dár Maṣálít, each *fersh* had also a *Sambei* as chief executive officer and representative attached to him, as was also the custom in the case of the Sultan of the *Dáju*; but since the chief fersh of the Maṣálít has become a "Sultan" this has been dropped.' According to Nachtigal (1971), 325, the *sambe* was an intermediate office between the *shartay* and the *dimlij* (dimilik), rather than between *firsha* and *dimlij*. Compare O'Fahey (1980), 70 and Arkell Papers[2] 3/13, 34. The songtext is not fully clear, but it is evident that the *sambei* was escorted to Dirjeil by the Fūr, and that the Gernyeng rejoiced that the days in which they went in fear of the Fūr were gone. The 'Arabs' of the area sang: '*niḥna surra, mā fī zōl barra*', which means literally, 'we are the navel, there is no one outside', i.e. we all belong together. (Int. 1, vi.)

111 Int. 5, 9, 10 and 12.

112 O'Fahey (1980), 93.

113 Int. 8. Compare Int. 13 and 15.

114 idem.

115 For tax collection see Int. 8, 15, 21 and 23. The reference to the Sinyār is from Int. 30. The term *dīwān* was used by Int. 8, 28, 30 and 31 and occurs in Durham, Lewis 600/3/6, who says that the Masālīt paid *dīwān* to the Fūr. Int. 29 said: '*al-ṣughayyar bidawwan al-kabīr wa al-kabīr bidawwan al-*ʿalī', i.e. 'the small ruler pays *dīwān* to the big one, and the big one to the one superior to him.' Compare above, 38 and note 79. See also below, Chapter 4, 111–12.

116 Int. 1, xxi; Int. 16, 9, 28 and 30.

117 For the story of the Fūr Sultan who marched against four Masālīt

villages whose inhabitants were reputed to be cannibals, see Int. 1, xiv. Paul Doornbos collected a tradition about a conflict between the Masālīt of the Kongo Haraza area and Fūr tax collectors (personal information). In B.I.F., Toureng M.S. 6013 it is recorded: 'En plein pays Fongoro . . . dans le cirque de Gallere, auraient habité assez longtemps de nombreux groupements Massalit qui s'y étaient enfui après avoir tué quelques collecteurs d'impôt foriens.'

118 Compare Nachtigal (1971), 383 and above, 19.

119 This section is based on Int. 1 (i–xxiii), Int. 16, 27, 32, 33 and 43. Much of the oral evidence used refers to the period after 1874, and is therefore used here anachronistically to throw light upon those aspects of the institution of slavery which were said or can be surmised to be continuations of the earlier situation, and can therefore be projected backwards into the past. Contemporary data would undoubtedly be preferable, but in their absence the cautious use of anachronistic data is allowable. Although slaves were numerous and omnipresent in western Dār Fūr until about sixty years ago, information about them is not easy to obtain. The travel accounts are silent about slaves owned by commoners, rather than sultans. Administrative reports by colonial officials venture surprisingly little information about slaves, either because the officials did not recognize many slaves as slaves, or because they did not want to elicit criticism of the policy of 'indirect rule', which let slavery be. Oral research on slavery is difficult as well. For the really old informants the past role and position of slaves are taken for granted, and so much regarded as insignificant and looked down upon, that they are an unpopular topic of discussion. Younger informants, more conscious of modern ideals of equality, are reluctant to bring to light, or to revive, inequalities which are still social realities today. Although a number of ex-slaves and their descendants are known to the author, so far she has not been able to create an atmosphere in which the discussion of matters related to slavery would be possible. This is a serious limitation in the present analysis. The latter has benefited from the introduction in Miers and Kopytoff (1979), whose limitations (see Cooper, 1979) it unfortunately shares. For many similarities, see Klein and Lovejoy (1979), those sections which deal with non-market-oriented societies.

120 Int. 10.

121 This definition resembles that of Miers and Kopytoff (1979), 11–12. Compare also Klein (unpublished 1977), 19; and Meillassoux (1975), 224.

122 See SHAT Tchad, carton 3, doss. 2 for reference to the slave trade by Fūr and Masālīt in Dār Silā in 1911. In 1912 the slave market of Goz

Beida had moved to the royal palace and traders came and went by night. After the Anglo-Egyptian occupation of Dār Masālīt in 1922, the Masālīt did the same to evade the new regulations which made the slave trade illegal (Int. 27, i). Slaves continued to be bought from Dār Silā after 1916. In 1914 Sultan Bakhīt of Dār Silā was still sending eunuchs to Mecca (CRO, Int. 2/31/258), while the slave trade with Dār Fūr remained brisk until the fall of ʿAlī Dīnār in 1916 (CRO Int. 2/2/11). Compare Warburg (mimeograph 1977).

123 See Chapter 4 for the wars of the Mahdiyya, and Chapter 5, 152.

124 *Ammo* Amm Tis was the daughter of Saʿīd Burūs, a Dinka *amīn* of Sultan Muḥammad al-Ḥusayn and his successors. ʿAsha al-Turkāwiyya (or ʿAsha Turkāya) was the daughter of ʿUmar wad Tirḥō, an important Turco-Egyptian official in al-Fāshir (Int. 1, i, ii and iv). *Bāsī* Aḥmad ʿUmar had two concubines who were ex-wives of Sultan Ibrāhīm (1873–4). (See Int. i and v). So was *dāda* Khayra, who was given as a concubine to *abbo* Sharaf al-Dīn, son of Ismāʿīl ʿAbd al-Nabī (Int. 1, iii). Just before the Mahdiyya the Masālīt captured a number of Maghārba women, who were on their way to the east to visit the Mahdī (Int. 1, i). See Chapter 5, 134–5. See also Carbou (1912), volume 2, 124.

125 For the political events of the 1890s, see Chapter 4.

126 The quotation is from Int. 1, iii; the reference to the slave wives from Int. 1, i and Int 2, i. For the story of the capture of the *jihādiyya*, see Chapter 5, 129–30.

127 Int. 1, iv and xix, and see Chapter 5, 156.

128 Int. 1, v and vii.

129 Int. 1, iii and Int. 43.

130 Int. 1, iv. At the conquest of al-Fāshir, Anjumma was taken to Wad Medani by one of the soldiers of the conquering army. It seems that the royal families of the eastern Sudanic belt pooled their resources in wives. Sultans not only married each other's sisters and daughters – which guaranteed them a safe refuge at neighbouring courts in times of need – but also incorporated into their family all the women they captured from neighbouring heads of state. Some of the wives and concubines seem to have circulated, giving birth to princes and princesses, wherever wars or raids forced them to go.

131 Int. 2, i; G. M. LaRue of Boston University (personal information) on the numbers of Masālīt captives; Int. 32.

132 See Chapter 6, 184.

133 Int. 1, viii. The man was called Aḥmad Donyokota, his wife Maryam Gendekkel.

134 The woman was called Amm Tajja. The reason why *abbo* Muḥammad Nimr did not succeed his father, Baḥr al-Dīn, was the fact

that his mother was not a free Masālīt woman (CRO 2 Darfur Dar Masalit 30/2/8). Another victim of drought who was lucky enough to become Sultan Baḥr al-Dīn's *maqdūm* for the northern part of Dār Masālīt, was Saʿīd Ab Dūdū. Saʿīd had been bought as a small boy by *ʿajūz* Toke, who bought him from hungry Arabs for some melon seeds and husks of grain. (Int. 1, viii). When Abbakr became sultan of the Masālīt in 1888, she gave the boy to him. Later Saʿīd was freed, and entered the service of Abbakr's son, Baḥr al-Dīn. See also CRO Darfur 1/33/171 and 1/34/172 for *maqdūm* Ab Dūdū. Khaffaltīnī probably comes from *ghaffaltīnī*, 'you proved me to be a fool', because the Masālīt sold their grain reserves in the first year of a drought, and then starved themselves in the second year.

135 Int. 1, ii and Int. 27, i (May 1979, Fāṭima ʿAlī).

136 SHAT Tchad carton 3, doss. 2, Simonet, 17 February 1914, reporting on the sultan's speech to his people.

137 Int. 5 and Int. 1, vi: The sister of *iya* Ḥumāra, Sultan Abbakr's wife, was kidnapped by Turco-Egyptian tax collectors in Dirjeil in the 1870s. Also G. M. LaRue, personal information.

138 For slaves paid as bridewealth by respectively Sultan Abbakr and Sultan Baḥr al-Dīn, see Int. 1, ix and CRO Darfur 1/18/96. For slaves paid as tribute, see El-Tounsy (1851), 206 (tribute paid by the Tāmā to Wadai); Chapter 4, 111. For slaves transferred in commercial transactions, see CRO Int. 2/31/258 (slaves exchanged for factory-made cloth etc. between Sultan Bakhīt of Dār Silā and Sultan ʿAlī Dīnār); Int. 1, vii and viii (slaves bought and sold by his father in Kobbei); Int. 1, ix (Fūr refugees in Dār Masālīt were, in the 1890s, taken to Abesher by the Masālīt and there sold as slaves, to cover travel expenses).

139 Int. 1, iii; of the slaves the informant brought from the Baḥr al-Ghazāl to the area of modern Gereida, he sold one male slave for three cows, and one female slave for one bull, two cows of four and three years and a calf.

140 Int. 1, i, iii, iv and vii; Int. 43 and 45 for the slave trade from Dār Silā; Int. 1, i and ix for that from Wadai.

141 Int. 1, i on ʿĀyisha, v on Bakhīta Bandiyya, iii on ʿAbd Allāh. The latter was bought in Mogornei. He was married to Bakhīta, when the latter did not bear *bāsī* Aḥmad any children. Eventually ʿAbd Allāh was freed and married a free Masālīt woman.

142 Int. 1, i, vii, viii, ix and x.

143 Int. 1, ii and vii. The Fartīt were hungry because the traders went south at the beginning of the rains, when the old crops had been eaten and the new crops were not yet ripe. In CRO Darfur 1/2/7 it was reported by W. M. Richards of the Baqqāra Markaz (Goz

Dango, 11 May 1922): 'the thing that impressed me most on this visit was the number of Habbania people one met on their way to Kafiakingi with bull loads of grain, which they state, fetches a much better price there than in Darfur.' The Ḥabbāniyya are the neighbours of the Masālīt of southern Dār Fūr. That slaves were transported in chains was confirmed by Int. 43.

144 Int. 27, i (28 April, 20 May and 5 June 1979).

145 Int. 43. Note the feminine ending of the verbs, which is a very common feature of Dār Fūr colloquial Arabic. The use of *ʿabīd* for *ʿabd* is also common. The fourth line of the song was not understood by either the author or those whom she consulted.

146 Int. 43.

147 Int. 1, vii.

148 idem.

149 According to Int. 1, iv the Dājū were notorious for selling slave children separately from the mothers, but he gave many stories about similar incidents among the Masālīt. ʿĀyisha, a Ninya girl from Birinjil, was bought by *iya* Ḥumāra, the wife of Sultan Abbakr, and her daughter *ammo* Zahra for two cows. After some years she was sold to *faqīh* Makkī of Murle, who wanted her as his concubine. The *faqīh* agreed to pay two cows for her, but paid only one. ʿĀyisha gave birth to a daughter, and at the *faqīh*'s death both mother and daughter were inherited by the *faqīh*'s son. *Iya* Ḥumāra, however, came to claim the second cow due to her and Zahra. The *faqīh*'s son, not knowing what to do with his father's concubine, instead returned ʿĀyisha to *iya* Ḥumāra. He kept the daughter, who later married a Maslātī and 'became free'. ʿĀyisha was married to a slave of Sultan Abbakr (remembered by name), and gave birth to six children. At least one of these six, Abbakr gave to his son, the future Sultan Baḥr al-Dīn. This son was eventually freed and married a daughter of another son of Abbakr. (Int. 1, i). See also SHAT Tchad carton 5, report on the massacre of the *faqīh*s.

150 Int. 1, vii and ix. Compare for this institution, Fisher and Fisher (1970), 49–50; and Klein (unpublished 1977), 24. The little boy who was kidnapped was *abbo* Mōmad Nyangarre, who is still alive but mute. *Bāsī* Aḥmad refused to accept the cow and gave the slave to Khadam Allāh as a present. If the parent of the child whose ears were cut refused to accept the slave, the slave's master had to pay compensation for the wound afflicted to the child. This the informant considered highly unlikely.

151 This is illustrated by a piquant story told by Int. 43 about Aḥmad Shaṭṭa, *maqdūm* of the south in the 1870s. Aḥmad had been kidnapped by nomads and was compelled to do all the (heavy)

women's work in the compound of his master, that is to say, to grind and pound grain, to make *ʿaṣīda*, to fetch wood etc. He resigned himself to this. However, when the son of his new master began to nag his father to be allowed to play with the captive's testicles, Aḥmad firmly declared that there was an end to the insults to his manhood he could accept. The story had a happy ending, for Aḥmad was freed by his sons.

152 Int. 1, vii; 'There is no one who does not farm with his own hands; everybody farms with his own hands, even the sultan.' The informant made an exception for the sultan's slave soldiers (see Chapter 5, 154) and for old people owning slaves (xiii).

153 Int. 1, i, iv, vii, x and xix. The slave could have as big a plot of land as he could cultivate. He could choose to have it where he wished, but it is likely that slave plots were, for example, further from the village than those of others. The slaves of *bāsī* Aḥmad also had a plot on a streambed to cultivate ocra, cotton and groundnuts.

154 Int. 1, vii and Int. 27, i.

155 Int. 1, iii and vii. The slaves received the *rūse*, the grain which had not been threshed well, and the *qār al-madaq*, the broken grain at the bottom of a pile. This often yielded four to five *rayka*s (Int. 1, vii).

156 An illustration (but not proof) of this is that the only people, apart from the *ḥukkām*, who ever tasted tea in Dār Masālīt in the 1890s, were the slaves of the *ḥukkām*. After the men had drunk the first two brews, and the free women the third, the slaves were allowed to suck the sweet tealeaves remaining in the pot (Int. 1, viii). Another illustration is the person of Somīt Abarranjāl, a freedman in the service of *bāsī* Aḥmad, who was very rich, had a horse, several wives, even slaves and hangers-on (Int. 1, vii). Finally, it is significant that the sultan's slaves tempted the slaves of the commoners or small *ḥukkām* into joining the sultan's household by showing off their nice clothes and by bragging about the good life they had (Int. 1, i).

157 Int. 1, vii.

158 Slaves were allowed to keep part of the booty they brought back from war (Int. 1, iv). If they worked hard in their leisure time, the fruits of this labour was theirs (Int. 1, 15). However, the informant mentioned a song composed by a slave woman who criticized her mistress for 'borrowing' food from her.

159 Int. 43: '*Al Allāh antū, ʿanduhum; al walā ʿanduhum, hum zāthum bakhdumū.*' Compare Int. 1, ix: 'If there are no slaves, life is hardship.' (*law ʿabīd mā fi*, *al-waṭaʿ taʿb*).

160 See above, note 134 and, for another example, Int. 1, iii.

161 Int. 1, ii.

162 Int. 1, i, iii, iv and vii. The quotation is from vii. What the father paid

as bridewealth to his wife depended on what she demanded from him as compensation for the disgraceful act of marrying her daughter to a slave. It was suggested that he paid very well. His daughter received a cow, a necklace called *tagāga*, and a garment.

163 See Int. 1, iv for *bāsī* Karam Allāh; idem, iii and ix for the daughter of *sambei* Nyanule. The latter, who had a Dinka slave mother, could not find a free husband, and was eventually married to a Masālīt-born slave.

164 Int. 1, iii and Int. 27, i. Int. 1, xiii mentioned another case in which a woman might marry a slave. If a man died, his wife, afraid to be married off and to be taken away from house and farm to another village, might take one of her slaves as her spouse, which is contrary to Islamic Law, since, 'the male slave [may marry] a free woman who is not his owner' (Schacht, 1964, 127).

165 Int. 1, vii.

166 Int. 1, ix: 'From the moment they read the *fātiḥa*, she became your wife. If she wants to marry someone else . . . , if she rejects you yourself, someone can come and marry her.'

167 Int. 43 and Int. 1, vii and x. Asked about the average number of the slaves owned by commoners, the informant said that this was hard to know: 'everyone who has cows has also slave women; there are also the slaves of his father and grandfather. Who has cows has also slave women with their children and childrens' children.' (Int. 1, x).

168 Int. 1, iii.

169 Int 1, i and ii.

170 For *diya* see Int. 1, i. For the freedman's marriage from among the relatives of his ex-master, see Int. 1, iii. Compare Schacht (1966), 129: 'The manumitted slave remains to his former master in the strictly personal relationship of clientship . . .; this has certain effects in the law of marriage and of inheritance.'

Chapter 3 – Prelude to the rise of the Masālīt Sultanate

1 See O'Fahey (1980), 12–13 and 98–100 (on the importance of fire-arms); Hill (1963), 136–8; Slatin (1896), 47–55. For the term *baḥḥāra* or *baḥrīna* (literally 'those of the river Nile'), see Nachtigal (1971), glossary, 405.

2 For districts and garrisons, see Jackson (1970), 76; Messedaglia (1886), 15; CRO Cair. Int. 10/22/55; Slatin (1896), 58–9; ANSOM Tchad 1, doss. 9 (Largeau). For the superior arms of the Turkish troops, see Messedaglia (1880), 78 and Fraccaroli (1880), 306.

3 A Banī Ḥusayn *shaykh* summarized the impact of the different

changes of regime upon his people as follows: 'When our grandfathers came they drove out the Mima who lived in the area around Jebel Khauran and Jebel Erliat north of Birket Saira. When the Fur Hukm arrived they took our land away and ruled us and we were scattered. When Zubayr came the tribe arose under Hamid Torjok and we received back our lands through his Mudir Nur Angara. Then came Jano and the Taasha and we became scattered again and with Sultan Ali the Fur were over us again. Now the Government has come *we are a tribe again* [my emphasis] and wish to cultivate our lands in peace.' (CRO 2 Darfur Kuttum 41/4/2)

4 For the impact of the fighting upon the local population, see Slatin (1896), 78–80; and Fraccaroli (1880), 205–6. For the impact upon trade, see Slatin (1896), 84; Messedaglia (1880), 77; Massari (1881), 822.

5 CRO Cair. Int. 10/22/55, information obtained from Sharīf Maḥmd Talāt by Naʿūm Shuqayr.

6 ʿAlī ʿAbd Allāh Abū Sinn (unpublished 1968), 86, for the Qimr sultan's participation in the war against al-Zubayr. For the decoration, see CRO Cair. Int. 10/22/55, letter dated 2 March 1878 written by the Governor General of the Sudan to the authorities in Cairo. For Sultan Idrīs' involvement in the final defeat of Hārūn, see Int. 40; Int. 1, xxiii; ANSOM Afrique VI, doss. 185 (Largeau interviewing Tāmā informants in 1913).

7 According to Int. 1, xxiii, and xi, Hajjām killed Hārūn with his own hands just before the Turco-Egyptian troops entered the palace of the Qimr Sultan, where Hajjām was hiding. Most other sources agree that it was al-Nūr ʿAnqara, who killed Hārūn, but Hajjām probably accompanied him. Ḥabbo Janna (Int. 43) said that she was born one day after Hārūn had been killed in Dār Qimr, on the day that Hajjām and his companions passed through her village (Konge) on their way back to Mogornei.

According to Int. 1, xxiii, Hajjām was appointed head of the Masālīt by Saʿīd Bey Jumʿa, commander of the troops of al-Fāshir (1878–1884). For the title bey, see Hill (1967), x.

8 Slatin (1896), 107; Fraccaroli (1880), 205; Massari (1881), 819. The Egyptian Government later allowed Slatin to reopen the road from Kobbei to Egypt, when the merchants complained that the route *via* Khartoum and down the Nile involved them in heavy transport expenses and long delays (Slatin).

9 The first Governor-General of Dār Fūr was Ḥasan Hilmī Pasha al-Juwaysar (1875–79). The prominent Kobbei merchant, Muḥammad Pasha al-Imām, was governor in 1879; on the latter and his brothers, see Hill (1967), 150–1.

Among those who were recommended for a decoration in 1875 was 'Shams el Din Mahmud, a merchant of Kobe' (CRO Cair. Int. 10/22/55). For al-Nūr ʿAnqara, see Hill (1967), 297; Slatin (1896), 11, and 101; and CRO Int. 5/3/7 (Messedaglia).

10 For details see ANSOM Tchad I, doss. 9 (Largeau); Fraccaroli (1880), 306; CRO Cair. Int. 3/9/172.

11 Messedaglia (1886), 29. He talked among others to *malik* Māḥī of Dār Jabal, *firsha* Dā'ūd of Dār Shāli ('Sciara'), and the son of the Tāmā Sultan Ibrāhīm. Compare Fraccaroli (1880), 306 for a different tax rate.

12 Slatin (1896), 90.

13 idem, 90–1.

14 Int. 1, v and vi for the labour migration. For the heavy taxes see below, 71; and see Chapter 5, 134–5.

15 Ensor (1881), 112–13. For *tōb* or *thawb*, see glossary, and Felkin (1884–5), 250, according to whom the *tōb* was a standard white imported cloth (two of which equalled a dollar), which were in use in the large towns.

16 CRO Cair. Int. 10/22/55 (information obtained from Sharīf Maḥmūd Talāt by Naʿūm Shuqayr).

17 For details see B.I.F., M.S. 6005, Simonet; idem, M.S. 6013, Toureng (who stresses the fact that the Sinyār were raided for taxes, not administered); SHAT Tchad Carton 9, Carnet de Poste de Sila; ANSOM Afrique VI, doss. 185; CHEAM Berre, Mémoire no. 1804; Grossard (1925), 325; Int. 28 and 29. The sources are all oral sources recorded by different people at different times. They differ in detail, but certain names of Turco-Egyptian representatives on the spot recur: Bābikr al-Ḥājj (compare Slatin, 1896, 270), 'Abd al-Rasūl Agha (compare Slatin, 1896, 169, 181 and 261), and al-Nūr ʿAnqara (compare Hill, 1967, 297).

18 The sources disagree about the extent to which Dār Tāmā was administered by the Turco-Egyptians. See CRO Darfur 1/33/170; CRO Int. 1/1/4; Cair. Int. 10/22/55 and Int. 1/1/4; Int. 1, i; ANSOM Afrique VI, doss. 185 and Tchad I, doss. 9; (which give evidence of a formal submission and the payment of 'presents' by the Tāmā to the Turco-Egyptians); Massari (1881), 819 and 822 for contradictory information, which seems to imply that eastern Tāmā was heavily taxed and that the foreign trade was seriously affected by the prohibition of the slave trade and the Turco-Egyptian monopoly on ivory. The Viceroy Muḥammad Saʿīd of Egypt was speaking the truth when he said: 'Nos frontières en Egypt son bien élastiques.' (ANSOM Tchad 1, doss. 9). For the garrison post at Abū Qurayn, see CRO Darfur 1/33/171; Massari (1881), 819 (who gives a description

and notes that it was inhabited solely by soldiers). I visited the old camp or *urdi* on 2 June 1978, but nothing but a mound remains of the fort. The big tree on the bank of the *wādī* was said to be the *mashnaqa*, the place where people were hanged. For the data on taxes, see Int. 22 and 23.

19 Int. 1, xvii and xxiii.

20 Int. 13.

21 Int. 13 and 15. Before Hajjām became *firsha*, he was probably *warnang* or *ʿaqīd* (head of *warnang*s).

22 Int. 9.

23 *Daftar* is here the cashbook of tax collectors. The quotation is from Int. 1, xxiii. See Int. 8 and 15 for Hajjām's consultation of, and confirmation by Isāgha Donkotch.

24 The story that the Fūr Sultan Ḥusayn appointed Hajjām as chief of the four Masālīt *firsha*s is from Int. 13. The story is suspect mainly because the informant, a close relative of Hajjām, and (in the past) a rival of the present *firsha* of the Mistereng, tended to exaggerate Hajjām's importance.

25 Int. 1, iii and xii.

26 CRO Int. 1/1/4 ('Sworn statement of Abd el Salam Agha Mohammed, sheikh of the section of the Gawazi tribe, formerly a Bimbashi in the old Egyptian Army of Darfur'). Compare CRO Cair. Int. 10/22/55 (notes 5 and 16 above); Maḥmūd Sharīf Talāt must have participated in the same expedition.

27 Int. 8. Other versions of Hajjām's 'Turkish' connection are: that Hajjām spent two years with the 'Turks' in al-Fāshir (where he had fled after an unsuccessful attempt to become *firsha*), and returned to Dār Masālīt in their company (Int. 15). The latter confirmed Hajjām's responsibility for collecting taxes for the 'Turks'. For Ismāʿīl, see below, Chapter 5.

28 Fraccaroli (1880), 306.

29 Int. 1, iii (for Kurra), xi (for the Amm Būs); Int. 15, 22 and 23 (for the Jabal and Erenga).

30 Int. 8 for the story of the rebellious youngsters; Int. 16 for the move from Wādī Nyala.

31 Int. 1, iii, xii and xviii and Int. 13.

32 Int 1, xvi. The Masālīt text is as follows:

Jaktūre tāre, korombo māte
Jaktūre tāre, dallunyimbo māte
Jaktūre tāre, nyōrimbo māte.

33 Int. 1, xv. The Masālīt text is as follows:

Toyayō, toyayō
Brahīm Bōsha wō toyayō
Fartāk Kunji mballa koto kaffel, toyayō.

Fartāk ('he who scatters or disperses'), was Hajjām's nickname. Kunji was not his father, but a close relative and one of his predecessors as *firsha* of the Mistereng.

34 Slatin (1896), 110–11.

35 Massari (1881), 823; The approach of two young Italian travellers in 1881 caused a real panic in Wadai (as it did in Dār Tāmā). It was thought, A. M. Massari reported, 'that there were a thousand of us, armed with no one knew how powerful cannons and wearing an iron casemate in which we were safe from the enemy's weapons' (translated from the Italian).

36 Int. 1, xv and vii.

37 Int. 1, xii (*qatal 'alā kayfuh*). Executing people on one's own authority was said to be the prerogative of independent rulers (Int. 1, iii). The other references are from Int. 6 and Int. 1, xii.

38 See for example Spaulding (1977), 411, who noted that someone who was found guilty in a lawcase presided over by the Funj Sultan was executed. The many stories about the arbitrariness and cruelty of Sultan 'Alī Dīnār of Dār Fūr are another example in case (Int. 47). Undoubtedly the mystique was fed by a rather bloody reality.

39 Int. 1, xii, xv and xvi. The Masālīt text is as follows:

Hajjām Bey wō kirei
Kebberre wō darja nggō ninda tunya
Torong ilā gāro nindāyong.

40 Int. 1, xiv and xxiii. The Manggere had given Hajjām hospitality when he held his honeymoon with Ḥumāra, the daughter of *sambei* Sulaymān Kijikinang.

41 Int. 1, xi.

42 Int. 1, xi and xxiii. The Masālīt text is as follows:

Hajjām Bey tarndiye
neirā ngatāngamboyong
agu kulang wāye
dāwinong kuri toyōrong.

43 The account of Hajjām's defeat and flight is based on Int. 1, xi; Int. 2, i; Int. 9, 13, 15, 16 and 21.

44 Int. 1, iii, ix, x, xviii and xii; Int. 13; and see note 27.

45 CRO Int. 1/1/4. Bikbāshi (Bimbāshi or Binbāshi) is a batallion commander (Hill, 1967, x).

46 Int. 13.
47 Int. 1, xviii and xxiii; Int. 2, i; Int. 20 and 22 (for quotation).
48 Int. 1, xi for song. The Masālīt text is as follows:

Hajjām Bey nggō kirei
Mogornei irijim kudei
'sallim' tirei
Isāgha lō darje tulong.

For accounts of the battles, see also Int. 21. During the Mahdiyya the *anṣār* tried to bring Hajjām back to power (see Chapter 4, 102). Hajjām died in Omdurman towards the end, or just after the Mahdiyya, when his house collapsed.
49 Int. 21 and Int. 1, xii; According to the latter Isāgha Choko gave the *ḥukm* to Ismāʿīl with the words: 'we are living on the mountain and cannot come here. I do not have the strong men [necessary] to become sultan and I have no one to give you. You, *faqīh*, rule justly. You know the Book, and the people . . . do not know what is right and what is wrong.' See also Chapter 5, 124.

Chapter 4 – The rise of the Masālīt Sultanate from a regional perspective

1 Holt (1970), 244–6.
2 Holt (1962).
3 Mūsā al-Mubārak [1970], 66 ff.
4 Mūsā al-Mubārak [1970], 63–4; Shuqayr (1903), 1027. CRO Mahdiyya 1/12, II doc. 121 (7 Shaʿbān 1305 = 19 April 1888), for a present of a skullcap, *jubba* (shirt) and banner sent by Zuqal to the sultan of Wadai.
5 CRO Cair. Int. 10/12/55; letter from Sultan Yūsuf of Wadai to Muḥammad Khālid Zuqal, translated by Naʿūm Shuqayr dated 8 Dhū'l-Qaʿda 1302 (18 August 1855). No original found.
6 Mūsā al-Mubārak [1970], 83–4; Holt (1970), 153; CRO Mahdiyya 1/10, doc. 5 (9 Jumādā I 1303 = 13 February 1886). The other two governors were Adam Kunjāra (Dāra) and Ḥasan Umm Kadōk (Umm Shanga).
7 Holt (1970), 155–7; Mūsā al-Mubārak [1970], 100–1.
8 CRO Mahdiyya 1/12, IV doc. 109 (2 Rajab 1305 = 15 March 1888) for the order concerning the sultans of the Qimr and Tāmā; doc. 123 (7 Shaʿbān 1305 = 19 April 1888) for the Qurʿān and Bidāyāt; doc. 129 (8 Shaʿbān 1305 = 20 April 1888) for the Zaghāwa. The death of Yūsuf, the 'shadow sultan', occurred on 14 Jumādā II 1305 (27

February 1888) and was reported on 4 Rajab 1305 (17 March 1888) in doc. 111.

9 For the Maslātī, see CRO Maydiyya, II doc. 166 (16 Ramaḍān 1305 = 27 May 1888); for the Qimrāwī, see idem doc. 169 (17 Ramaḍān 1305 = 28 May 1888); for the Silāwī, idem doc. 176 (17 Ramaḍān 1305 = 27 May 1888).

10 CRO Mahdiyya 1/12, III doc. 245 (8 Dhū'l-Ḥijja 1305 = 16 August 1888). See idem, doc. 267 (29 Dhū'l-Ḥijja 1305 = 6 September 1888) for Yūsuf's denial of having given refuge to enemies of the Mahdiyya. For the letters from the latter to Yūsuf, the Fūr 'shadow sultan', discovered by the *anṣār* see Mūsā al-Mubārak [1970], 141.

11 idem, doc. 245 (see note 10).

12 For the Zaghāwa, see Mūsā al-Mubārak [1970], 65–6 and 129; and CRO Mahdiyya 1/10, doc. 5 (9 Jumādā I 1303 = 13 February 1886). For the Qimrāwī and the expedition sent out to punish him in July 1888, see Mūsā al-Mubārak 1970, 145. For Ismā'īl, see CRO Mahdiyya 1/16, doc. 447 (7 Ramaḍān 1305 = 19 May 1888), Muḥammad Abūh Jūdā Fāt to the Khalīfa.

13 For the judicial system in the Mahdist state, see El-Fahal El-Tahir (1964); Holt (1970), 6–7 and Holt (1955), 6. That *qāḍī*s accompanied the armies is suggested by CRO Mahdiyya 1/12, IV doc. 309 (28 Muḥarram 1306 = 4 October 1888), and doc. 212 (29 Muḥarram 1306 = 5 October 1888). In 1896, when the Mahdist troops occupied Dār Tāmā, they put a puppet on the throne and subsequently withdrew to al-Fāshir. They left no garrison behind, but did leave a judicial representative (CRO Mahdiyya 1/14, III, doc. 718) (13 Jumādā I 1313 = 1 November 1895).

14 For the taxation system of the Mahdist state, see Holt (1970), 125–8. See also note 15.

15 For the reference to October 1891, see CRO Mahdiyya 1/13, II doc. 163 (22 Rabī' I 1309 = 26 October 1891). For the reference to January 1893, see CRO Mahdiyya 2/37, doc. 28 (22 Rajab 1310 = 22 January 1893), from Muḥammad 'Abd Allāh Abūh Jūda Fāt to Maḥmūd Aḥmad.

16 CRO Mahdiyya 1/12, III doc. 682 (2 Dhū'l-Qa'da 1307 = 20 June 1889); and CRO Mahdiyya 2/36, doc. 22 (20 Ṣafar 1313 = 8 August 1895), Salāḥ Abū to Maḥmūd Aḥmad.

17 For the maximum number of soldiers concentrated in al-Fāshir, see CRO Mahdiyya 1/12, IV doc. 387 (29 Rabī' II 1306 = 3 November 1888). For the garrison towns, see CRO Mahdiyya 1/13, II doc. 288 (6 Shawwāl 1309 = 4 May 1892). For the number of soldiers in November 1892, see CRO Mahdiyya 1/14, IV doc. 387 (29 Rabī' II 1310 = 20 November 1892). For the following of Maḥmūd's army,

see idem, III doc. 396 (28 Jumādā I 1310 = 26 November 1896).

18 CRO Mahdiyya 1/12, III doc 682 (2 Dhū'l-Qa'da 1307 = 20 June 1889).

19 CRO Mahdiyya 2/36, doc. 17 (13 Ṣafar 1313 = 5 August 1895), Muṣṭāfā Baḥr to Maḥmūd Aḥmad; the *anṣār* took 80 horses, 20 camels, 200 cows, 80 donkeys, 2,000 sheep and goats, and 20 slaves. Idem, doc. 22 (20 Ṣafar 1313 = 12 August 1895), Salāḥ Abū to Maḥmūd Aḥmad, conveys Zaghāwa complaints, while idem, doc. 16 (10 Ṣafar 1313 = 2 August 1895) gives the Mahdist side of the story.

20 CRO Mahdiyya 2/5, II doc. 127 (no date), Sultan Idrīs Abū Bakr to Maḥmūd Aḥmad.

21 For complaints by the governor, see CRO Mahdiyya 1/13, I doc. 80 (15 Dhū'l-Qa'da 1308 = 23 June 1891), and idem, doc. 79 (18 Shawwāl 1308 = 27 May 1891). For evidence of the dislike the western rulers had of the *hijra*, see CRO Mahdiyya 1/12, II doc. 144 (12 Sha'bān 1305 = 24 April 1888) and idem, doc. 94 (15 Jumādā II 1305 = 28 February 1888), both referring to Ismā'īl 'Abd al-Nabī's delay in performing the *hijra*.

22 For a discussion, see Holt (1970), 160 ff. and 'Uthmān Muḥammad 'Uthmān (1975).

23 See Holt (1970), 204–22 for the chapter on the Ta'āyishī Autocracy, 1892–96.

24 *'āmil* = agent (Holt, 1970, 121); *naqīb* = prefect. These terms replaced the older ones (*amīr* and *maqdūm*) in May 1884 by order of the Mahdī.

25 CRO Cair. Int. 10/12/55; translation by Na'ūm Shuqayr of the original Arabic which has not been found.

26 idem.

27 For Abū Rīsha, see CRO Mahdiyya 1/12, II doc. 121 (7 Sha'bān 1305 = 19 April 1888). For Ismā'īl's first excuse see idem, doc. 94 (15 Jumādā I 1305 = 28 February 1888); for his second excuse, see idem doc. 144 (12 Sha'bān 1305 = 24 April 1888). The quotation is from the latter document.

28 CRO Mahdiyya 1/12, II doc. 166 (16 Ramaḍān 1305 = 27 May 1888) for Ismā'īl's arrival in al-Fāshir; idem IV, doc. 277 (4 Muḥarram 1306 = 11 September 1888) for his deportation to Omdurman. Compare Mūsā al-Mubārak [1970], 145–6. In idem, III doc. 201 (27 Shawwāl 1305 = 8 July 1888) it is said that Ismā'īl was summoned to Omdurman, but was prevented by illness.

29 CRO Mahdiyya 1/12, IV doc. 279 (4 Muḥarram 1306 = 20 September 1888).

30 CRO Mahdiyya 2/5, I doc. 70 (no date, but probably January 1896), Abū Bakr Ismā'īl to Maḥmūd Aḥmad and appendix. Compare idem,

doc. 72 (no date), Abū Bakr Ismā'īl to 'Abd al-Qādir wad Dalīl: 'And I knew about the relationship between you and my father, that you were friends. I follow in the footsteps of my father and continue with you in everything [as he did]; but we were afraid because of what happened to our father, who went of his own free will and because of his desire to see his brothers, the companions of the Mahdī. So he went and never came back to us. That is the only reason why we have stayed calmly in our country for all that time.'

31 Int. 1, iii and xxiii; Int. 2, i and see Chapter 5, 129–30.

32 CRO Mahdiyya 2/5, II doc. 165 (no date).

33 For the events, see Holt (1970), 156–9; Shuqayr (1903), 1052–6; Mūsā al-Mubārak [1970], 147–60; ANSOM Afrique VI, doss. 184; CRO Cair. Int. 3/5/84; idem 3/10/192; idem 3/18/300. For the primary sources see CRO Mahdiyya 1/12, IV. For an example of Mūsā al-Mubārak's credulity see p. 160, where he reports that Bakhīt Abū Rīsha was killed in battle. Bakhīt, however, succeeded his father as sultan of Dār Silā towards the end of the Mahdiyya and ruled until 1916.

34 CRO Mahdiyya 1/12, IV doc. 288 (9 Muḥarram 1306 = 15 September 1888) and Mūsā al-Mubārak [1970], 158–9.

35 CRO Mahdiyya 1/12, IV doc. 275 (Ghurra Muḥarram 1306 = 7 September 1888); and idem doc. 312 (29 Muḥarram 1306 = 5 October 1888).

36 CRO Mahdiyya 1/12, IV doc. 325 (7 Ṣafar 1305 = 25 October 1888). Compare Mūsā al-Mubārak [1970], 151 who erroneously states that Abū Jummayza captured 21 boxes of ammunition.

37 idem, and compare Mūsā al-Mubārak [1970], 160.

38 CRO Mahdiyya 1/12, IV doc. 345 (10 Rabī' I 1306 = 14 November 1888) and doc. 348 (13 Rabī' I 1306 = 17 November 1888). The Qimr are not mentioned. Sultan Idrīs seems to deny his involvement in an undated letter to 'Uthmān Jānū, in which he stated that he had nothing to do with what the *faqīh*s of Dār Fūr did against the *anṣār* (CRO Mahdiyya 2/5, II doc. 167). According to Int. 25, the Qimr did take part. For the participation of the Banī Ḥalba, see CRO Mahdiyya 1/12, V doc. 420 (28 Jumādā I 1306 = 30 January 1889).

39 Mūsā al-Mubārak [1970], 151; CRO Mahdiyya 1/12, IV doc. 323 (7 Ṣafar 1306 = 13 October 1888) for first quotation and idem doc. 327 (same date), for the second. In idem doc. 352 (Rabī' I 1306 = 30 November 1888), 'Uthmān writes: 'May God destroy all who follow this deluded person and may the western regions become a pure mosque.'

40 For the number of soldiers, see CRO Mahdiyya 1/12, IV doc. 343 (5 Rabī' I 1306 = 9 November 1888); Holt (1970), 158; and Mūsā al-

Mubārak [1970], 154. For the route see idem, 154–5 and CRO Mahdiyya 1/12, IV doc. 343.

41 CRO Mahdiyya 1/12, IV doc. 347 (12 Rabīʿ I 1306 = 16 November 1888). The defeat was at Kānqa, i.e. Konge, not far from Kereinik. Compare Mūsā al-Mubārak [1970], 154–5.

42 CRO Mahdiyya 1/12, IV doc. 346 (12 Rabīʿ I 1306 = 16 November 1888); Holt (1970), 159; Mūsā al-Mubārak [1970], 159.

43 CRO Mahdiyya 1/12, IV doc. 352 (26 Rabīʿ I 1306 = 20 November 1888); Holt (1970), 159; Mūsā al-Mubārak [1970], 158.

44 CRO Mahdiyya 1/12, IV doc. 389 (29 Rabīʿ II 1306 = 2 January 1889).

45 CRO Mahdiyya 1/12, IV doc. 387 (29 Rabīʿ II 1306 = 2 January 1889) for numbers. Holt (1970), 159 and Mūsā al-Mubārak [1970], 157 for date of battle.

46 CRO Mahdiyya 1/12, IV doc. 325 (7 Ṣafar 1306 = 13 October 1888); doc. 363 (5 Rabīʿ II 1306 = 9 December 1888), and doc. 364 (same date). The assocation of the wearing of many rings with a locust charmer (*dumbāri*) is based on Arkell Papers[2] 5/19, 15–16; 'Note on a dumbaari': 'He wears a copper and a silver ring on one finger so that people know his trade', and again 'He wears 4 copper rings on one finger.'

47 CRO Mahdiyya 1/12, IV doc. 325 (7 Ṣafar 1306 = 13 October 1888); CRO Cair. Int. 3/5/84 and 3/18/300; Wingate (1968), 373 ff. Slatin (1896), 442–4; Hill (1967), 34. His real name is mentioned in doc. 363 (5 Rabīʿ II 1306 = 9 December 1888).

48 CRO Mahdiyya 1/12, IV doc. 310 (29 Muḥarram 1306 = 5 October 1888); Holt (1970), 157–8.

49 CRO Mahdiyya 1/12, IV doc. 310 (see note 148) and doc. 364 and 325 (see note 46) for reference to his claim to be the Sanūsī's son and the *khalīfa* of that son. See Shuqayr (1903), 1053, for the text of the Khalīfa's response and CRO Mahdiyya 1/12, IV doc. 364 (see note 46) for a summary of Abū Jummayza's letter. Compare Mūsā al-Mubārak [1970], 156.

50 CRO Cair. Int. 3/18/84 and 3/18/300. Wingate (1968), 374 and 376.

51 Int. 25. The informant's grandfather (Ibrāhīm) was a full brother of Muḥammad Zayn's father (Yaḥyā). Muḥammad Zayn was his mother's only child. His father begot another son by another wife, and the sons of this halfbrother of Muḥammad Zayn are allegedly still alive. Int. 1, xii confirmed that Muḥammad Zayn was born at Wāra.

52 Int. 2, i.

53 CRO Int. 1/3/10. The *faqīh* rose at Gokor (south of El Geneina); he was the son of a Wadaian (Borqū) father and a Fūr mother.

54 See Chapter 6, 203 ff. For the reference to 1892, see CRO Mahdiyya 1/13, II doc. 237 (23 Rajab 1309 = 22 February 1892). For that to 1922, see Chapter 7, 240.

55 CRO Cair. Int. 3/5/84; Wingate (1968), 377–8; Shuqayr (1903), 1053; Mūsā al-Mubārak [1970], 148. It was denied by Int. 1, ix.

56 CRO Mahdiyya 1/12, IV doc. 363 (5 Rabīʿ II 1306 = 9 December 1888): *ṣāḥib tadlīs wa maghshūshiyya . . . mustaʿīn ʿala ʿamalihi bi'l-iblīs w'l-istiʿdād fi'l-taʿyīn iblīs*'; and doc. 343 (5 Rabīʿ 1 1306 = 9 November 1888): '*sāḥir kadhdhāb wa shayṭān murtāb.*'

57 CRO Mahdiyya 1/12, IV doc. 290 (12 Muḥarram 1306 = 18 September 1888); compare idem doc. 343 (see note 56), and CRO Mahdiyya 2/36, doc. 7 (4 Shaʿbān 1313 = 20 January 1896), al-ʿAṭā Uṣūl to Maḥmūd Aḥmad; this compares the westerners to children who allow a swindler to ruin them.

58 Slatin (1896), 443 ff.

59 Int. 1, xxiii.

60 Int. 2, i and Int. 27, i (19 May 1979).

61 Int. 2, i.

62 Int. 1, iii (for song). For nickname 'Kubbū Kullu' see also Int. 43.

63 Int. 43.

64 For the term Taʿāyisha, see Int. 2, i; Int. 1, xxiii; and Int. 16. Int. 23 summed up Abū Jummayza's message as follows: 'we are *anṣār* and have to fight the "Turks".'

65 CRO Mahdiyya 1/12, IV doc. 325 (see note 47).

66 Int. 1, ix and xxiii.

67 Int. 37.

68 Int. 25.

69 For the prohibition of killing game, see CRO Mahdiyya 1/12, V doc. 453 (7 Rajab 1306 = 9 March 1889), and Int. 1, ix. For the taboos on food, chicken, rabbit, deer, camel, bull, goat, *wayka* (okra), hot pepper, *kawal* (a putrified, dried plant), see idem doc. 420 (28 Jumādā I 1306 = 30 January 1889).

70 Int. 1, xxiii.

71 That the *anṣār* believed in magic is evident from CRO Mahdiyya 1/12, IV doc. 101 (17 Jumādā II 1305 = 28 February 1888). For ʿUthmān's reassurances that the *anṣār* did not fear Abū Jummayza, see idem doc. 337 (18 Ṣafar 1306 = 24 October 1888), and doc. 348 (13 Rabīʿ I 1306 = 17 November 1888). For the Khalīfa's prohibition against calling Abū Jummayza a devil, see CRO Mahdiyya 1/12, V doc. 453 (7 Rajab 1306 = 9 March 1889).

72 Int. 1, xxiii, and CRO Mahdiyya 1/12, IV doc. 364 (see note 46).

73 Int. 1, xxiii.

74 CRO Mahdiyya 1/12, IV doc. 111 (4 Rajab 1305 = 17 January 1888)

for the references to the letters found. Compare Mūsā al-Mubārak [1970], 141. For the excuses which the Wadai Sultan presented to ʿUthmān Jānū for assisting Yūsuf Ibrāhīm, see idem doc. 109 (2 Rajab 1305 = 15 March 1888).

75 CRO Mahdiyya 1/12, IV doc. 235 (5 Dhū'l-Ḥijja 1305 = 5 May 1888). The quotation is from CRO Mahdiyya 2/5, II doc. 138 (no date), Sultan Isḥāq Abū Rīsha to Aḥmad ibn Isḥāq.

76 In his hostility towards Abū'l-Khayrāt, Abbakr probably continued his father's policy towards Abū'l Khayrāt's predecessor Yūsuf Ibrāhīm. On 20 November 1886 the Khalīfa had deemed it necessary to warn Yūsuf – then still governor of the Fāshir district – not to trouble Ismāʿīl when he passed through al-Fāshir on his way to Omdurman (Mūsā al-Mubārak [1970], 145). For Ismāʿīl's excuse that he could not come to Omdurman because of the hostility of Yūsuf see note 27.

77 Int. 1, xxiii. Int. 2, i, gave a similar account, but called the battle that of Abū Qurayn. That Abū Jummayza's people captured many firearms was confirmed by CRO Mahdiyya 1/12, IV doc. 363 (see note 46): 'of the weapons which were taken from the *anṣār*, many were destroyed, except those on which their eyes did not fall.' The story of the sword of the Tāmā Sultan gives the history of military success in this period in a nutshell. It was captured from the Tāmā Sultan by the Mahdist commander, Ḥāmid Majbūr, who was killed in the 'battle of Tāmā' and lost the sword to Abū Jummayza. The latter lost it to Sultan Abbakr of the Masālīt, who in turn lost it to ʿUthmān Jānū when the latter invaded Dār Masālīt. On ʿUthmān's death, the sword fell to the public treasury at al-Fāshir, from where it was sent to Maḥmūd Aḥmad, who presented it to the Khalīfa. (CRO Mahdiyya 1/12 VII, doc. 702 (15 Dhū'l-Ḥijja 1307 = 2 August 1890) and CRO Mahdiyya 1/13, I doc. 51 (6 Shaʿbān 1308 = 17 March 1891).

78 Int. 1, xxiii and Int. 2, i.

79 Int. 1, xxiii; Int. 37. CRO Mahdiyya 1/12, IV doc. 386 (21 Rabīʿ II 1306 = 25 December 1888) confirms that there was disunity within the ranks, but refers to the fact that the Masālīt refused to march against al-Fāshir because they were not willing to fight outside their *dār*. Compare Mūsā al-Mubārak [1970], 161. According to CRO Mahdiyya 1/12, V doc. 428 (15 Jumādā II 1306 = 16 February 1889), the leaders of the army were Abū'Khayrāt and Abū Jummayza's deputy.

80 Mūsā al-Mubārak [1970], 171.

81 For the letter of the sultan of Wadai see CRO Mahdiyya 2/5, II doc. 139 (1307 = August 1889–August 1890); and CRO Mahdiyya 1/12,

VII doc. 696 (15 Dhū'l-Ḥijja 1307 = 2 August 1890). The last letter refers to similar letters written to Abbakr by the sultans of Dār Silā, Dār Tāmā and Dār Qimr; all impressed upon Abbakr that he should not fight Abū'l-Khayrāt.

82 Mūsā al-Mubārak [1970], 171. I have not found the original, written in February/March 1890.

83 CRO Cair. Int. 10/22/55 (see note 5).

84 See below, 105–7. Even Ismā'īl had complained about his isolated position among the tribes and sultans of the west, and about their *ta*'aṣṣub ('fanaticism', or perhaps here 'tribalism'); see CRO Mahdiyya 1/12, II doc. 94 (see note 27).

85 Mūsā al-Mubārak [1970], 163.

86 CRO Mahdiyya 1/12, VII doc. 682 (2 Dhū'l-Qa'da 1307 = 20 June 1890); Mūsā al-Mubārak [1970], 175.

87 CRO Mahdiyya 1/12, VII *passim* and in particular doc. 682 (see note 86), doc. 700 (15 Dhū'l-Ḥijja 1307 = 2 August 1890), and doc. 709 (12 Muḥarram 1308 = 28 August 1890).

88 For the defeat of the Masālīt, see CRO Mahdiyya 1/12, VII doc. 692 (9 Dhū'l-Ḥijja 1307 = 27 July 1890); doc. 690 (idem) and 693 (15 Dhū'l-Ḥijja 1307 = 2 August 1890). The flight of the Masālīt was confirmed by Int. 1, xxiii, Int. 2, i and Int. 43.

89 For the first part of the quotation, see CRO 1/12, VII doc. 710 (12 Muḥarram 1308 = 28 August 1890) and compare Mūsā al-Mubārak [1970], 176. For the second part, idem doc. 709 (same date).

90 See Int. 2, i, for the story of the bull; idem and Int. 21, for the stories of the Wadaian *faqīh*s. Another version ascribes the catastrophe to a horsefly in a calebash which was smuggled into the Mahdist camp (personal information from Paul Doornbos).

91 Mūsā al-Mubārak [1970], 179. Int. 1, xxiii and 2, i confirmed that 'Uthmān died after he had left Dār Masālīt.

92 Mūsā al-Mubārak [1970], 181 and 185 (note 3).

93 CRO Mahdiyya 1/13, II doc. 197 (22 Rabī' I 1309 = 25 November 1891), quoted in translation; for original see idem doc. 196. See also idem doc. 163 (same date), for the economic recovery of the Kabkābiyya area and the western part of the country of the Banī Ḥalba.

94 idem doc. 229 (15 Rajab 1309 = 14 February 1892).

95 idem doc. 163 (22 Rabī' I 1309 = 26 October 1891). Compare idem doc. 264 (8 Ramaḍān 1309 = 6 April 1892); and CRO Mahdiyya 2/37, doc. 26 (Sha'bān 1309 = March 1892), Muḥammad Abūh Jūda Fāt to Maḥmūd Aḥmad.

96 Mūsā al-Mubārak [1970], 192.

97 CRO Mahdiyya 1/13, I doc. 27 (8 Jumādā II 1308 = 19 January 1891).

98 idem doc. 79 (18 Shawwāl 1308 = 27 May 1891); and again doc. 80 (16 Dhū'l-Qaʿda 1308 = 23 June 1891).

99 CRO Mahdiyya 1/13, II doc. 192 (22 Rabīʿ II 1309 = 25 November 1891).

100 idem doc. 128 (Ghurra Muḥarram 1309 = 7 August 1891); and Mūsā al-Mubārak [1970], 192.

101 Mūsā al-Mubārak [1970], 195 for the expansion of Wadai and Dār Silā; and see below, 109 ff.

102 CRO Mahdiyya 1/13, II doc. 60 (11 Shaʿbān 1308 = 22 March 1891) and 68 (Ramaḍān 1308 = April/May 1891), for the Wadai–Silā conflict. Idem doc. 275 (8 Ramaḍān 1309 = 10 April 1892), for the Masālīt–Qimr conflict. For the Qimr–Tāmā conflict, see CRO Mahdiyya 1/13, III doc. 452 (29 Ramaḍān 1310 = 16 April 1893). Idem doc. 342 (22 Rabīʿ I 1310 = 4 January 1893) for the Qimr–Zaghāwa conflict. CRO Mahdiyya 1/13, II doc. 275 (8 Ramaḍān 1309 = 10 April 1892), for the conflict between Abū Rīsha and Saʿīd Burūs.

103 CRO Mahdiyya 2/37, doc. 28 (4 Rajab 1310 = 22 June 1893), Muḥammad Abūh Jūda Fāt to Maḥmūd Aḥmad; and see above, 78.

104 CRO Mahdiyya 1/12, VII doc. 695 (15 Dhū'l-Ḥijja 1307 = 2 August 1890). For translation see CRO Cair. Int. 10/12/55. Compare Mūsā al-Mubārak [1970], 192. For Hajjām, see Chapter 3.

105 Mūsā al-Mubārak [1970], 195; and (but without date) Int. 1, iii and xv.

106 For the order to withdraw in 1895, see Mūsā al-Mubārak [1970], 195–8. For the events of 1896, idem, 200–1.

107 For the Masālīt, see CRO Mahdiyya 2/36, doc. 51 (5 Jumādā II 1313 = 23 November 1895). For the Silāwī, see idem doc. 30 (29 Shawwāl 1313 = 13 April 1896). The Qimrāwī (idem doc. 51) was secretly enquiring with Sinīn Ḥusayn of Kabkābiyya whether Maḥmūd Aḥmad was still in al-Fāshir.

108 For Abbakr's peace with Maḥmūd, see CRO Mahdiyya 1/13, I doc. 27 (8 Jumādā II 1309 = 19 January 1891); for Abbakr's attitude towards ʿAlī Dīnār, who surrendered to the *anṣār* on 13 November 1891, see Mūsā al-Mubārak [1970], 184; and CRO Mahdiyya 1/13, II doc. 128 (Ghurra Muḥarram 1308 = 7 August 1891) and idem doc. 155 (5 Rabīʿ I 1309 = 9 October 1891). In the last document, it was reported that Abbakr wrote to ʿAbd al-Qādir requesting him to eliminate ʿAlī Dīnār.

109 For Abbakr's acts of aggression, see CRO Mahdiyya 1/13, II doc. 275 (8 Ramaḍān 1309 = 6 April 1892) for a Qimr–Masālīt conflict; CRO Mahdiyya 2/5, II doc. 126 for a complaint by Aḥmad Bashar to Maḥmūd Aḥmad. CRO Mahdiyya 2/5, I doc. 13 and 145 and idem II

doc. 145 for a conflict between the Masālīt and the Banī Ḥusayn; For the use of Abbakr as a bogey, see CRO Mahdiyya 2/5, II doc. 142 (no date), Sultan Yūsuf to the *shaykh* of the Banī Ḥusayn; and CRO Mahdiyya 2/5, I doc. 62 (undated), Sultan Yūsuf to the sultan of Dār Tāmā, for the latter's fear of Abbakr.

110 Int. 1, xxiii; Int. 2, i; Int. 39 and Int. 40; CRO Mahdiyya 2/36, doc. 15 (18 Sha'bān 1313 = 3 February 1896), 'Abd al-Qādir wad Dalīl to Maḥmūd Aḥmad; idem doc. 13 (same date), al-Bishārī Rīda to Maḥmūd Aḥmad; idem doc. 10 (14 Sha'bān 1313 = 31 December 1895), Sinīn Ḥusayn to Maḥmūd Aḥmad; idem doc. 5 and 6 (20 Rajab 1313 = 6 January 1896), 'Abd al-Qādir to Maḥmūd Aḥmad, and doc. 7 (4 Ramaḍān 1313 = 8 February 1896), al-'Aṭā Uṣūl to Maḥmūd Aḥmad.

The quotation is from CRO Mahdiyya 2/5, II doc. 165 (no date), Sultan Idrīs Abū Bakr to Maḥmūd Aḥmad.

111 Mūsā al-Mubārak [1970], 198–9; Int. 1, xxiii.

112 Mūsā al-Mubārak [1970], 202; and note 110.

113 CRO Mahdiyya 2/5, I doc. 72 (no date), Abū Bakr Ismā'īl to Maḥmūd Aḥmad and appendix. Compare idem doc. 68 and 70, from the same to respectively al-Bishārī Rīda and Maḥmūd Aḥmad.

114 CRO Mahdiyya 2/5, I doc. 185 (no date). The *Sunna* is the Sunna of the Prophet, i.e. his sayings and actions, later established as legally binding precedents.

115 Int. 8. Compare Int. 1, xxiii; Int. 2, ii.

116 Int. 1, xxiii; *inta sulṭān wa anā sulṭān; kayf nadīk?*

117 Holt (1970), Chapter XI (204–22).

118 Holt (1970), 261; and Holt Papers 1/9, 1–5 ('tour of Sulaymān al-Hajjāz in Kordofan and Darfur, 1308/9') for the judicial centralization. Idem 2/4, no. 20 for a proclamation about cases involving bloodshed, dated 5 October 1885. For the divorce case, see Holt (1970), 261–2.

119 Holt Papers 3/4, no. 18 (15 March 1884).

120 For Maḥmūd's request, see CRO Mahdiyya 1/13, I doc. 46 (6 Sha'bān 1308 = 17 March 1891). For the battle of Shawai, see below, 66.

121 See above, 76 ff. For the peçuliar Remington, see CRO Mahdiyya 1/12, IV doc. 348 (13 Rabī' I 1306 = 17 November 1888). For Sultan Yūsuf's letter to Abū'l Khayrāt, see idem doc. 440 (25 Jumādā II 1306 = 26 February 1889). For the letters found in Abbakr's house, see CRO Mahdiyya 1/13, VII doc. 696 (15 Dhū'l-Ḥijja 1307 = 2 August 1890).

122 CRO Mahdiyya 1/14, doc. 802 (15 Shawwāl 1312 = 11 April 1895).

123 idem doc. 804 (11 Dhū'l-Qa'da 1312 = 15 June 1895), copy of a letter from Maḥmūd Aḥmad to Sultan Yūsuf of Wadai.

124 CRO Mahdiyya 1/14, III doc. 350 (20 Rabīʿ I 1310 = 11 November 1892). Initially 59 westerners were arrested at Kabkābiyya, 93 at Kutum and 7 at Dāra. Later numbers increased; see idem doc. 375 (23 Rabīʿ II 1310 = 14 November 1892) and doc. 398 (6 Jumādā I 1314 = 13 October 1896) for a breakdown indicating ethnic origin, profession and direction (east or west).

125 ANSOM Afrique VI, doss. 187, Rapport du Commandant Lucien au Lieut. Col. Commandant le Territoire Militaire du Tchad, Abéché, 5 Mars 1910. This includes the text of Lucien's interview with ʿAbd Allāh, *ʿaqīd al-Jaʿādnā*, the *ʿaqīd al-Salamāt* and Aḥmad, the *ʿaqīd al-Maḥāmīd*. For the tribute, see also SHAT Tchad Carton 8, doss. 2, Rapport du Col. Millot: Situation Wadai 1909.

126 For the tribute in horses and slaves, see Int. 1, ii, v, x and xviii (for Bagersa, the one-eyed horse). According to Int. 1, ix the *ʿaqīd al-Maḥāmīd* wrote the demands for a certain horse or slave, while Abū Aja, and later *faqīh* Wābī collected the tribute. This was confirmed by the correspondence preserved in CRO Mahdiyya 2/5, I and II. A number of letters were written by the *ʿaqīd*; Abū Aja figures in CRO Mahdiyya 2/5, II doc. 124 (no date), Sultan Yūsuf of Wadai to Sultan Sulaymān Ibrāhīm of Dār Tāmā, as Yūsuf's envoy to Dār Tāmā, and in idem, doc. 141 (no date) from same to Sultan Idrīs Abū Bakr of Dār Qimr. For *dīwān*, compare above, Chapter 2, note 115.

127 CRO Mahdiyya 2/5, I and II.

128 The ultimata are CRO Mahdiyya 2/5, I doc. 55; 2/5 II doc. 124 and 125 (referring to the same case) and doc. 123.

129 CRO Mahdiyya 2/5, II doc. 121: *jawād hazīl wa khāyib ḥatā mā yarkabahu ʿabdī*.

130 CRO Mahdiyya 2/5, II doc. 121: *anā talabṭahu minnak lā li-ajli ʿadamin bal bi'l -sharṭ al-khuwa*.

131 For *dīwān*, see Chapter 2, 38. For the Qimr incident, see above 103–4; for the Dājū invasion, see above, 104–5.

132 For Abbakr's war with Sinīn, see Int. 26, Int. 25, CRO Int. 2/3/13 (for Sinīn's version). According to Int. 1, x and xix and Int. 2, i, it was Sultan Yūsuf of Wadai who ordered Abbakr to go and fight Sinīn.

133 CRO Mahdiyya 1/14, III doc. 732 (7 Rajab 1313 = 3 January 1896).

134 For the first quotation, see CRO Mahdiyya 2/5, I doc. 46 (no date), Sultan Isḥāq Abū Rīsha to a number of *malik*s and *shartay*s mentioned by name and including the *shartay*s of Zami and Kulli. For the second quotation, see CRO Mahdiyya 2/5, II doc. 185 (no date), Sultan Isḥāq Abū Rīsha to *shartay* Riziq, Ḥāmid Shūk al-Balā and Aḥmad ʿAqīd.

135 CRO Mahdiyya 1/13, III doc. 275 (8 Ramaḍān 1309 = 6 April 1892).

136 CRO Mahdiyya 1/13, I doc. 60 (11 Shaʿbān 1308 = 17 August 1890).

137 This section is based on Cordell (1977), 21–36; see also Evans-Pritchard (1949) and Ziadeh (1958).

138 Cordell (1977), 32 for the products, and idem, 31 for the number of camels weekly passing through Kufra. Jālū was the headquarters of the Sanūsiyya from 1856 to 1895, Kufra from 1895 to 1899 and again after 1902. According to ANSOM Afrique VI, doss. 182 (Letter from M. Rais, 'Gérant du Consulat Général de France à Tripoli de Barbarie' to Delcasse, Minister of Foreign Affairs, 5 September 1899), half of the imports consisted of British cottons, while the French imported silks and sugar. Hides were exported to the USA, ostrich feathers to France, and ivory to the UK and Turkey.

139 For references to trade between the western front and al-Fāshir or Kabkābiyya, see the correspondence between Maḥmūd Aḥmad and the Khalīfa. In May 1897, for example, the vice-governor of al-Fāshir received a letter from the Maslātī requesting him to open the road for the traders. The traders were allowed to come as far as Kabkābiyya. (CRO Mahdiyya 1/14, III doc. 783, 28 Dhū'l-Qaʿda 1314 = 10 May 1897, Maḥmūd Aḥmad to the Khalīfa). Int. 1, x confirmed that trade continued on a limited scale.

140 See Chapter 2, 36.

141 Nachtigal (1971), 52.

142 Int. 1, viii; and Int. 46. For the escorts provided for the caravans, see, for example, El-Tounsy (1851), 49.

143 CRO Int. 2/5/125.

144 CRO Int. 2/3/14. In December 1900 and January 1901 ʿAlī Dīnār wrote two similar letters to the Director of the Intelligence Office, Khartoum, and to his trading agent Muḥammad Anīs, who was associated with the Egyptian firm of ʿAbd Allāh Kaḥḥāl. The text presented here is my translation of the original (Arabic) letter to Muḥammad Anīs, dated 6 Shawwāl 1318 (27 January 1901). The letter directed to the Intelligence Office, dated 6 Ramaḍān 1318 (28 December 1900), has been preserved only in a summary translation. For Muḥammad Anīs and ʿAbd Allāh Kaḥḥāl, see Walz (unpublished 1979), 9.

145 Bergen DF 23. 6/8: Sultan ʿAlī Dīnār to al-Dōma Muḥammad, 28 Ṣafar 1318 (27 June 1900).

146 Jennings Bramley (1940), 170 for an example of the evasion of import tax on ivory brought into Wadai from Dār Silā, and idem, 178 for the shrewdness of Yūnis' father.

147 idem. 170.

148 See El-Tounsy (1851), 55–62 and Browne (1806) for the elaborate immigration formalities on respectively Wadai's eastern border with Dār Fūr and Dār Fūr's northern border. See Nachtigal (1971), 230

for evidence that a caravan could not leave Abesher before the sultan's farewell presents had been received. See also Bergen DF 79. 10/4 ('Alī Dīnār to two traders mentioned by name, 17 April 1906), and DF 81. 10/16 ('Alī Dīnār to Muḥammad 'Uthmān Abū Takiyya), both trading licenses.

149 Nachtigal (1971), 70–1; Browne (1806), 249–50. Traditionally the trading season between the Zaghāwa Kobe and the Tāmā Sultanate was officially opened by the 'Takanyou', who made a ceremonial visit to Dār Tāmā to exchange presents (Tubiana, unpublished 1980, 6). For other examples of the closure of routes because of political reasons, see Chapter 6, 195.

150 For two *laissez-passers* issued by Wadai Sultans, see Bergen DF 86. 10/11 (issued by Aḥmad al-Ghazālī, 1901/2) and FF 84. 10/10 (issued by Dūd Murra, 21 April 1902). For a *laissez-passer* issued by Sultan Abū Rīsha of Dār Silā to a Kano pilgrim, see CRO Cair. Int. 3/18/306 and Lavers (1968), 77 (for translation), and Durham, Arabic Catalogue 101/13/12 (for Arabic original).

151 O'Fahey (1980), 144.

152 For the role of close relatives, see, for example, the correspondence of Bakhīt Abū Rīsha in CRO Int. 2/2/11 and Int. 2, i and Chapter 5, 143 ff. For *khabīr* see Nachtigal (1971), 56–7, and O'Fahey (1980), 141.

153 Nachtigal (1971), 51.

154 ANSOM Tchad I, doss. 7, Largeau to the Governor of Oubangi-Chari-Chad, and the attached declaration of Ibrāhīm al-Ḥājj, dated 5 December 1911. See Chapter 6, 195.

155 El-Tounsy (1851), 56–7 for the recording of imports on the border. For the duty to report to the sultan first, see Jennings Bramley (1940), 176 and Int. 1, v. Compare Chapter 5, 159.

156 For the greeting gifts (*salām* or *salāmāt*), see Nachtigal (1971), 130, and (in different context) Chapter 2, 42.

157 Jennings Bramley (1940), 176 for the royal monopoly of powder in Wadai in the 1890s. Rifles were a monopoly in Dār Fūr on the eve of colonial conquest (CRO Int. 2/2/11, and doc. III in Kapteijns and al-Hādī 'Abd al-Majīd (1981), dated 28 October 1916, 'Alī Dīnār to Bakhīt Abū Rīsha).

158 Int. 1, vi and viii; Chapter 5, 159.

159 See Chapter 5, 159; and Chapter 2, 43 (in a different context). Compare Nachtigal (1971), 248 for restrictions on the dress of nomads entering Abesher in the 1870s.

160 The question of coin currencies, analyzed for Sinnār by Spaulding (O'Fahey and Spaulding, 1974, 70–2), requires further study.

161 See Chapter 5, 150.

162 For the sultan's right to half of the ivory, see SHAT Tchad Carton IV,

Colonne de Sila, Col. Hilaire, and Int. 1, viii. See also Chapter 5, 160.

163 Nachtigal (1971), 203 and CHEAM, Berre, Mémoire 1804.

164 O'Fahey (1973), 29–43 and (1980), 135–8; El-Tounsy (1851), 467–95. For slave-raiding in Dār Masālīt, see Chapter 5, 161.

165 CRO Mahdiyya 2/36, doc. 29 (25 Jumādā I 1313 = 13 November 1895), Muḥammad Sa'īd Maḥmūd to Maḥmūd Aḥmad.

166 For a striking example see CRO Darfur 1/33/170 (February 1899), which refers to a present of a hundred camel loads of corn and a large number of camels sent to the Sanūsī by Sultan Ibrāhīm of Wadai. Ibrāhīm also intended to send ivory and ostrich feathers. In October 1900 he sent a present of fifty magazine rifles, three boxes of ammunition and two concubines to 'Alī Dīnār, sultan of Dār Fūr, who sent back clothing, coffee and a kettle (idem, April 1910). Compare my term 'diplomatic trade' with Polanyi's 'gift trade' (Polanyi, 1975, 151).

167 CRO Mahdiyya 2/5, I doc. 54 (no date), Sultan Yūsuf to Ibrāhīm Sulaymān of Dār Tāmā.

For *thawb* (*tōb*), see Nachtigal (1971), 416, where it is described as the standard men's garment in Borno; see also Cordell (unpublished 1977), 370 ff. The other names are all names of imported cloth. For *dubbalān*, see Nachtigal (1971), 406 (*dibelan*) and Cordell (unpublished 1977), 378–9. For 'alaj, see Walz (1978), 40 ('alaga). *Jukh* or *jokh* was another silk cloth. Int. I, viii mentioned most of these brand names, but *sūl* and *salam* were unknown to him. See also Chapter 5, 158–9.

168 For the presents to the Tāmāwī, see CRO Mahdiyya 2/2, II doc. 131 (no date), Sultan Yūsuf to Sulaymān Ibrāhīm; for that to 'Abd al-Raḥmān Firti of the Zaghāwa Kobbe, idem, doc. 103 (no date), Sultan Yūsuf to 'Abd al-Raḥmān Firti. For presents sent by Sultan Yūsuf of Wadai to Abbakr of the Masālīt, see Int. ix (nets with dates), and x (high quality cloth and gunpowder).

169 CRO Mahdiyya 1/14, doc. 819 (undated). The document is probably a fragment of a letter from Maḥmūd Aḥmad to the Khalīfa which summarized a number of letters Maḥmūd received from his *'āmils*. The quotation is from a letter received from Sinīn Ḥusayn of Kabkābiyya. The document is in a file with documents dating from 1312/3 (1894/6).

According to ANSOM Afrique VI, doss. 191, Report by the Chargé d'Affaires of France in Benghazi, 27 March 1911, there was a Sanūsī *zāwiya* (lodge) in Dār Masālīt in 1910. This was not confirmed by local oral sources.

170 Int. 1, ix and xix. Ḥarat is probably from the root *Khara'a*, to

defecate. Note the colloquial use of the feminine form in *ḥārat wa bālat*.

171 CRO Mahdiyya 2/5, II doc. 124 (no date), Sultan Yūsuf to Ibrāhīm Sulaymān.

172 See Chapter 6, 195 ff. Int. 1, explained the political dependence of the Zaghāwa Sultan on the sultan of Wadai in terms of the former's dependence on the Abesher market for grain.

Chapter 5 – The rise of the Masālīt Sultanate from within

1 CRO Mahdiyya 1/10, doc. 5 (9 Jumādā I 1303 = 13 February 1886).

2 CRO Cair. Int. 10/12/55; Proclamation in the Dervish Proclamation Register of 1302; only in translation.

3 See above, Chapter 4, 81.

4 CRO Mahdiyya 1/16, doc. 87 (7 Ramaḍān 1305 = 18 May 1888), Muḥammad Abūh Jūda Fāt to the Khalīfa.

5 ʿAlī Ḥasan (unpublished).

6 Int. 1, xi; Int. 2, i and Int. 15.

7 According to Int. 1, xxiii Ismāʿīl went all the way to Gedir. According to Int. 2, i and ʿAlī Ḥasan (unpublished) he visited the Mahdī in El Obeid.

8 Int. 1, xi and xxiii. I was told that this prayer is a usual part of the Friday sermon and that it is not a specifically Mahdist prayer. The text recorded here shows colloquialisms, e.g. *yā rabbanā al-ʿalamayn* (line 5) should be *yā rabb al-ʿalamayn*; *khāyibīn* (line 21) should be *khāʾibīn* (personal information from ʿAbd al-Ḥamīd M.U. ʿAbd al-Raḥīm).

9 Int. 1, xi.

10 Int. 15.

11 Int. 1, xxiii and Int. 43. *Tābā* was explained as 'tobacco'; compare Seetzen (1813), 149.

12 Int. 15. For Ismāʿīl's non-participation in the wars, see Int. 1, xi.

13 Int. 1, xi and xii; and above, Chapter 3, 72.

14 Int. 20.

15 See Int. 1, xi and xv for the war of Ṣarafāya and the deposition of the *firsha*. According to Int. 1, xv and xxiii, Int. 2, i, and Int. 23, Dār Jabal and Dār Erenga were conquered by Sultan Abbakr during the movement of Abū Jummayza. See also ʿAlī ʿAbd Allāh Abū Sinn (unpublished 1968), 47, and above, Chapter 4, 94 ff.

16 Int. 1, xxiii. According to Int. 2, i Ismāʿīl was cleared, but this is in contradiction with later developments, namely (i) that Ismāʿīl was imprisoned in Omdurman, and (ii) that Hajjām was allowed to go

back to the west to replace Abbakr when the opportunity occurred.

17 CRO Cair. Int. 10/22/55; letter from ʿUthmān Adam to the Khalīfa (15 Dhū'l-Ḥijja 1307 = 1 August 1890), translation by Naʿūm Shuqayr. For the original Arabic, see CRO Mahdiyya 1/12, VII doc. 695.

18 CRO Mahdiyya 1/12, II doc. 166 (16 Ramaḍān 1305 = 27 May 1888); Mūsā al-Mubārak [1970], 146; Int. 2, i; and ʿAlī Ḥasan (unpublished).

19 ʿAlī Ḥasan (unpublished). The Taʿāyisha, the ethnic group of the Khalīfa, belong to the cattle nomads called *baqqāra*.

20 Int. 16. According to Int. 1, xxiii; Int. 2, i and ʿAlī Ḥasan (unpublished), Ismāʿīl sent Abbakr back to Dār Masālīt in secret. The account of Int. 16 seems most trustworthy, because the presence of Abū'l-Khayrāt on the border was confirmed by written sources (Chapter 4, 94), and because Abbakr did not expel the Mahdist garrison immediately at his arrival in Dār Masālīt.

21 Int. 2, i.

22 Int. 1, iii and xxiii; confirmed by Int. 2, i.

23 Int. 1, xi.

24 Int. 1, vi, xii and xiv.

25 ʿAlī Ḥasan (unpublished).

26 Int. 16.

27 Int. 15. The Masālīt text was translated orally by Ibrāhīm Yaḥyā. This is the English translation of the Arabic.

28 Int. 1, iii.

29 Int. 27, i (28 April 1979).

30 Int. 1, ix. The song is in very colloquial and even broken Arabic. *Tijārnā* (line 3) should be *tijāratnā*.

31 Int. 1, ii and xiv. The Arabic terms used are *aṣnām* (idols), *ʿawā'id* (customs, customary ways) and *ʿadāt* (idem). Compare Tubiana (1964). The noise of the camels mentioned in the song refers to the noises made by the old woman and man who perform the ceremony.

32 Int. 1, ii; for the tree cut down in Beida, see Int. 27, i (22 May 1979).

33 For the reference to the teeth, Int. 1, vii and for the clean garment of *kalkaf* (fine cotton cloth either locally made or imported from the Jabal Marra), see Int. 1, xi.

34 Kapteijns and Ibrāhīm Yaḥyā (1980), 64–5 and 66–7; Bergen DF 367/58.1; and, see Appendix, Doc. I, 'From the Commander of the Faithful and Protector of the Oppressed, the Support of Islam in religion, Agent of the Mahdī, Lord Ismāʿīl ʿAbd al-Nabī.'

35 For *ʿāmil* and *amīr*, see Holt (1970), 121 and above, Chapter 4, 80 *ʿAmīl* was the traditional Islamic term for the collector of the *zakāh*, *amīr* that for army commander. For the titles used by Abbakr, see

CRO Mahdiyya 2/5, I doc. 70 (no date, probably January 1896), Abbakr Ismāʿīl to Maḥmūd Aḥmad: *Amīr Abbakr Isma*–ʿīl *ʿa–mil al-Mahdī ʿalayhi al-salām fī qism Masalāh.* See Appendix, Doc IV.

36 Int. 1, ix and above, Chapter 1, 00.

37 See Int. 1, i (for the grant of estates), iv (for *bāsī* Nyarmōl, son of the *sambei*), iv and vi (for the Gernyeng of Duwei), v and xi (for the Gernyeng Salāmī and *bāsī* ʿAbd al-Qādir). Ismāʿīl's daughter Arsho married *faqīh Ḥanāfī*, son of the Gernyeng *malik* Gōz (vi); Ismāʿīl's son Abbakr married the daughter of the son of the Gernyeng *malik* Gende (xii), and Ḥabība, daughter of the brother of *malik* Gōz (iv).

38 Int. 1, i and ix. Compare above, Chapter 3, 64 ff.

39 Int. 1, viii and ix. The nickname 'Abu Lafta' derives from a rifle of that name.

40 For *faqīh Abāy*, see Int. 1, i, iii and xii (for estate). He had been judge in Dirjeil Siminyang (with *maqdūm* ʿAbd al-Qaffā) and in the Kongyo area. For Ab Mondokōra, see Int. 1, vi; *iya* Amm Tas, daughter of the Fūr Sultan Ḥusayn, and ʿAsha al-Turkāwiyya, daughter of Saʿīd Burūs, *amīn* of a number of Fūr sultans, were married to Abbakr.

41 For those rulers who were left in place, see above, Chapter 2, 45; and Int. 1, v (for *maqdūm* Bashīr of the Lere), v and xvi (for *maqdūm* Andokoi), v (for *maqdūm* Marjān Ndelngongo); the latter was probably an agent of *maqdūm* ʿAbd al-Qaffā (x). For the defeat of ʿAbd al-Qaffā, see Int. 1, ix and xi.

42 Ismāʿīl's *faqīh*s were: Ḥamād Dorodoro of the Banī Ḥusayn with a *khalwa* at Affende; Muḥammad al-Maslātī of the Erenga; Muḥammad Hendeny of the Kunjāra, who was muezzin; Arbāb Barsham of the Jabal (Nyumuri); Makkī Maṭar of Murle; Zambūr of the Asumang; ʿId of the Jabal; *maqdūm* Bashīr of the Masālīt Lere (Int. 1, xii).

43 See Kapteijns and Ibrāhīm Yaḥyā (1980), 64–5 and 66–7; and Appendix, doc. i mentions 'the *faqīh*s, the people of *faqīh* Makkī'; doc. ii addresses the *faqīh*s 'who are in the hand of *faqīh* Makkī.'

44 Int. 16; *Ismāʿīl qawwāhum wa qarrabhum.*

45 Ismāʿīl's sister, Khadam Allāh, was married to *faqīh* Yūnis; his daughter ʿAsha married *faqīh* Muḥammad Tigil Abyaḍ, brother of Khalīfa Riziq (Int. 1, xi); Arsho married *faqīh* Ḥanafī, and Ḥawā' Dumbulla, *faqīh* ʿAlī al-Tamtam; the last two were also close relatives (vi). *Faqīh* ʿAlī was a pillar of Ismāʿīl's administration, and does hence not really belong to this group of *faqīh*s.

46 For estates of privilege, see below, 166 ff.

47 Kapteijns and Ibrāhīm Yaḥyā (1980), 67 and Appendix, Doc. II. That the *fiṭra* was not only their own but also that of the people they

led in prayer is not explicitly stated in the document.

48 idem and Int. 1, iii. During Abbakr's reign the local rulers and central government agents were explicitly so ordered: 'Do not interfere with him [*faqīh* Makkī] in his villages, unless with permission' (Kapteijns and Ibrāhīm Yaḥyā, 1980, 65–6 and 67–8, and Appendix, Doc. III.

49 See Int. 1, xi for the estate of *faqīh* Ḥanafī, and that of *faqīh* Abāy. Idem for *faqīh* ʿId.

50 Spaulding (1980), 6–7.

51 Int. 2, i. It is common among the Masālīt to call someone after his first child.

52 Int. 1, x and xv; Int. 2, i; Int. 16 and 20.

53 Int. 1, viii, xix (for *danga*); for *warra bāya* and *warra deiye*, see Int. 1, ix and O'Fahey (1980), 154, glossary (*orre baya* and *orre de*); for the doorkeepers, see Int. 1, vi and ix; and Int. 27, i (21 May 1979). The *ṭarbūsh* is the Turkish fez.

54 For syphilis (*bajl*), see Int. 1, xxiii and for its cure, xi. For eunuchs, see Int. 1, ii and Int. 16.

55 The *wazīr*, see Int. 1, xiv and xxiii; and compare O'Fahey (1980), 90; '*wazīr* appears to have been a honorific title more than an office.' For Kunji's treachery, see Davies (1924), 52; Int. 1, xii; Int. 2, i; Int. 6 and Int. 43. For the battle of Ab Saddara, see Int. 1, vii.

56 For *amīns*, see Int. 16 and Int. 1, xxiii and xiv ('they have no work but to sit with the sultan'). For the *korāyāt* and *ṭuwayrāt*, see Int. 16; Int. 1, xiv; and O'Fahey (1980), glossary 151 (kóriat). For the jester, see Int. 1, v and xv.

57 For the prayer leader and muezzin, see Int. 1, xii; for the judges, Int. 1, i, iii, viii and xv, and Int. 48 and 20. There was only one *qāḍī* in Dār Masālīt. *Qāḍī* Abāy, whom Ismāʿīl had inherited from the Turco-Egyptian Regime, was succeeded on his death by ʿAlī Aḥmar of the Borno of Konge. He was succeeded by his brother ʿAlī Azraq who married his late brother's wife and begot a son called ʿAbd al-Mālik. ʿAlī Azraq was killed by the Fūr in Shinggilba (the estate which he or his brother had received from Ismāʿīl). Since there was no one who was sufficiently proficient in Arabic to qualify for the office of judge, Sultan Abbakr sent *bāsī* Aḥmad ʿUmar and *bāsī* Arbāb Barsham to Dār Tāmā to recruit a judge from the entourage of the Tāmā Sultan. They brought *qāḍī* Ibrāhīm Sanūsī back with them. Ibrāhīm was the sultan's judicial adviser and secretary until ca. 1910, and was succeeded by ʿAbd al-Mālik (son of ʿAlī Azraq), who was still judge during the first decade of Condominium Rule. Informants confuse ʿAlī Aḥmar and ʿAlī Azraq. The *qāḍīs* intermarried with the royal family; ʿAbd al-Mālik's sister was married by Sultan Tāj al-Dīn (1905–10), and he himself married a daughter of Sultan Abbakr (Int.

27, i, 16 April 1979). The interview with *faqīh* Abū'l-Qāsim, son of *qāḍī* Ibrāhīm, was unsuccessful, since he wondered why I would want to write a book when the end of the world was at hand.

58 For *bāsī* see Int. 1, xvii ('The *bāsī* is called *bāsī* because he is Gernyengāwī'); Int. 16 ('a *bāsī* is every member of the clan of the Gernyeng'). Compare Nachtigal (1971), 450 ('an honorific title given to the brothers of the sultan and later applied to any male relative of his'); O'Fahey (1980), 33 and 150; and Kropàçek (1971), 45 (note 56).

59 Int. 1, xiv.

60 For *khalīfa* Riziq, see Int. 1, xiv and xvi (for quotation), and Int. 43. Riziq's son Yūsuf has become *firsha* and is regarded as a Gernyeng *firsha*. For Arbāb Barsham, see Int. 1, xiv.

61 Int. 1, iv.

62 Int. 1, vii, xvi and Int. 27, i (21 May 1979) for a reference to a eunuch called *bāsī* Nyurum.

63 Int. 1, xiv, and xvi (for 'the *bāsinga* of *faqīh* 'Alī al-Tamtam'; for '*bāsī Nduta zōl li 'Abd al-Qādir*'; and for the fact that *khalīfa* Riziq elected free and slave people whom he liked and made them *bāsinga*).

64 See above, Chapter 2, 45 and above, note 41.

65 See Int. 1, xvi (Ab Faḍḍāy), ix (Somīt), and xvi (Ab Daqdāq).

66 Int. 1, xiii. For example, *firsha* Māmā Barsham of the Surbang of Amm Dukhn and *shartay* Bukr of Dār Erenga.

67 Int. 1, iv and x for *khalīfa* Riziq and the *'aqīd al-Maḥāmīd*; see also above, note 57; Int. iv for *bāsī* 'Id Tokundāb who was Abbakr's envoy to Wadai together with Daldūm Abesher.

68 Estates of the types discussed here are called *ḥākūra* elsewhere in Dār Fūr. The Masālīt themselves do not use the term but use the word *dār* or *balad* (country). Only when referring to the estates granted to *faqīhs* by the Keira sultans of the Ancien Regime, do they use the word *ḥākūra*. Int. 1, iii and iv used the term and spontaneously distinguished between an administrative estate and an estate of privilege (*ḥākūrat al-jāh*), but only after the interviewer had shown that the term *ḥākūra* was familiar to her. No *ḥākūra* documents such as those collected by O'Fahey and G. M. La Rue have been found in Dār Masālīt. In land cases brought to court in El Geneina sworn statements of old men, rather than land documents are presented as evidence.

For a definition of *ḥākūra*, see Nachtigal (1971), glossary 408–9; O'Fahey (1980), 50–3 (a grant of administrative authority over the people of a certain area); and La Rue (unpublished 1980): 'A *ḥākūra* is a delimited area of land granted by the Fūr Sultan to individuals or ethnic lineage groups with the following aims: (i) to use it for productive activities; (ii) to benefit from its revenues; (iii) to rule it politically on behalf of the sultan.' This definition was presented as a provisional one.

69 Int. I, ii (for Adada Borqū), i and v (for Maymere). For the Borno estates, see Int. 1, i and ii; Int. 43 and 48, and Arkell Papers[2] 63–3: Note on conversation with Borno of Fata Borno, 15 February 1937.

70 Int. 1, xi and xii.

71 idem, iii, iv and xi.

72 idem, ii and iv.

73 idem, iii.

74 After the victory over the Erenga at Sarafāya (in 1888/9), Sultan Abbakr gave the village of Deleiba (northeast of El Geneina) to his maternal uncle Ndili who had distinguished himself in the war with the words: 'this village is yours, yours alone, and you will not have to give me *zakāh* or *fiṭra* from it' (Int. 1, xxiii). Ardeme, the village of *abbo* ʿAlī Ab Shanab, councillor of Sultan Baḥr al-Dīn (1910–51), is an example of a royal village of the type described here. The Tarjam *shaykh*, to whom the area of Ardeme belonged, moved to another part of his *dār*. Half of the *zakāh* collected in Ardeme was for the sultan. (Int. 1, iii and Int. 27, i, 28 April 1979.) For informal tax privileges, see Int. 1, vii and xi.

75 Int. 1, iii (for the estate at Kafānī); ii and iii (for the estate of Dār Jabal).

76 Int. 1, iii. For estates in other states of the Sudanic belt, see O'Fahey and Abū Salīm (1983), introduction.

77 Int. 1, iii, iv, vii and ix; for the local treasury, idem viii.

78 Int. 1, iv, v, vii, ix, x, xiv and xv.

79 Int. 1, v, xi and xii. See above, Chapter 2, 42.

80 Int. 1, xi.

81 CRO Darfur 1/34/172.

82 Int. 1, xv. Informants give different rates; Int. 1, xvii, ix and x; Int. 15 and 20.

83 Int. 1, xvii (on grain distributed in droughts); xvi (on the grain given to Dūd Murra).

84 For the term *kirsh al-fīl*, see Int. 1, xvi. For *kumal*, see idem, i, ii, v, xi and xvii.

85 CRO Darfur 3/3/20 for the labour service demanded from the people of Fofo (near Indirrabirro); Int. 1, iv (for the ditch dug for the ruler).

86 Int. 1, ix; compare Int. 1, i and v; El-Tounsy (1845), 175–6; Nachtigal (1971), 158–9, 181–2 and 233; CRO Darfur 5/3/39 for the taxes in Dār Fūr during the reign of ʿAlī Dīnār (1898–1916).

87 For *salām*, see above, Chapter 2, 42 and Chapter 4, 118, and Int. 1, ii, xiii, xvii and xxiii. For *ḍiyāfa*, see Int. 27, i (2 June 1979), Int. 1, x and

xxiii; Nachtigal (1971), glossary 406 (difa) and 179 (difa in Wadai).

88 For *hāmıl*, see above, Chapter 2, 42 (definition, but not the term); O'Fahey (1980), 103; According to Int. 1, ii, iii, iv and Int. 3 the *hāmil* was passed on to the sultan. For the sultan's right to ivory, see Int. 1, viii and xiii, and above, Chapter 4, 119. For the deposition of 'Id, see Int. 1, x.

89 Int. 1, iv, vii, viii and ix; Int. 2, i. For the importance of slave soldiers elsewhere in the Sudanic belt in this period, see Klein and Lovejoy (1979), 192; Fisher and Fisher (1971), 154–63; and Smaldone (1972) 596.

90 Int. 1, ix and Int. 16.

91 Int. 1, iii. Compare above, 143 and 147.

92 Int. 1, i, iii, iv and v. This confirms Smaldone (1972), although the development towards bureaucratization and centralization which he describes went further than in Dār Masālīt.

93 Int. 1, vii. See above, 141.

94 Int. 1, iv (for quotation), v, xii. 'The sultan became the sultan of the slaves'; 'the sultan rejected the Masālīt and sided with the slaves' (iv).

95 For Gernyeng resentment, see Int. 1, iv and xii; for the coup attempt of *faqīh* 'Alī, see Int. 1, xii. See below Chapter 6, 199.

96 Int. 1, iv, v, and xiii; 'the sultan did not want a strong man' (*al-sulṭān li'l-zōl al-qawī mā bidōr*), Int. 1, iv.

97 O'Fahey (1980), 39–40.

98 Nachtigal (1971), 247; confirmed by Int. 1, xvii and xviii.

99 See above, Chapter 4, 114 ff. According to Int. 48, the Dājū Sultan obtained (imported) cloth and other things from al-Fāshir or Dirjeil.

100 Nachtigal (1971), 233.

101 See above, Chapter 3, 69.

102 Int. 1, iv and ix, for the origin of Wiḥayda; Int. 1, ii for the fact that the *jallāba* obtained their goods from the Fezzān in Abesher. See above, Chapter 4, 114.

103 That the Fezzān supplied imports to the rulers on credit is evident from Int. 1, iii, vi and xviii; Int. 46; and Bruel (1935), 249.

104 Int. 1, i, xvii (for the fact that the Fezzān lived in one huge compound); see also Int. 46.

105 Int. 1, vi; this occurred during the reign of Baḥr al-Dīn (1910–51).

106 Int. 1, viii. *Nabaq* etc. are products collected from the bush; see above, Chapter 2, note 39.

107 See Int. 1, i, ii, v, vii, viii and xx. Compare above, Chapter 4, note 167. Compare Cordell (unpublished 1977), Appendix 3, 'Cloth in Dar al-Kuti region in the time of al-Sanusi', 367–80; idem Appendix 4, 'Beads in Dar al-Kuti in the time of al-Sanusi', 381–3. Compare also Walz (1978), 45–8 for beads, and 40–1 for cloth. For rifles see

CRO Int. 2/15/125. A number of local names of cloth are not known from other sources.

108 Int. 1, viii and xviii. The *kunjul* is an insect eating animal (lizard?) with a shiny multi-coloured neck. The tobe called after it was sold for one cow per *tāqa*, which was big enough for four women's garments (ca. 40 meters?). The Fezzān also brought pencils, ink, needles, scissors, mirrors, etc., and exported goat skins (Int. 1, xviii). Baier's hypothesis that the trans-Saharan trade had a much wider market than historians have believed does not take into account the existence of sumptuary laws (Baier, 1977).

109 See above, Chapter 4, 118 and Int. 1, ii. See note 103 (for credit).

110 Int. 1, ix (for the clothes given to Ismāʿīl's daughters); Int. 1, xvii and Int. 27, i (16 April 1979) for robes given to the *malik*s; for garments and rifles given to the slave soldiers, see Int. 1, xvii. Sultan Tāj al-Dīn gave to his cavaliers tobes 'which distinguish people' (Int. 1, xvi).

111 Note 110 and Int. 9; if a commoner dared to dress up in fine-quality (or even just clean) clothes, he would be stripped on the spot and receive a sound beating, 'for everybody must be *miskīn*.' Compare El-Tounsy (1851), 342, 371.

112 For the customary way of dealing with ivory, see Int. 1, ii, iii, viii and xix; Int. 27, i (1 May and 2 June 1979). Compare above, Chapter 4, 119 (note 162). For the ostrich feathers and rhinoceros horn, see Int. 1, viii, xvii and xviii.

113 For the hunting parties, see Int. 1, xvii; and Int. 27, i (for the reign of Baḥr al-Dīn); for tame ostriches, see Int. 1, xvii.

114 See above, 175 ff. for the sultan's slaves. For the slave raids, see Int. 1, i and vii. For the belief that the Fūr had become Fartīt, see Int. 1, xix. According to Int. 1, xvii even *faqīh*s were sometimes sold.

115 Int. 1, ix.

116 Int. 1, vii. The *malik*s put some pressure upon the owners of recalcitrant slaves to sell them to the visiting Fezzān. The Masālīt preferred selling to the Fezzān to selling to fellow Masālīt, because the former offered a better price. By allowing the Fezzān to travel through the *dār*, the sultan shifted the burden of acquiring slaves for export from the government to the people.

117 Int. 1, xvii. *Waṭa'* is colloquial for earth or ground. Compare the classical root *waṭi'a* (to tread under foot).

118 Int. 1, xiv; *bisawwū bāsī min fōq, min dārhum fōq, zayy rakūba*, 'they put a *bāsī* over them [the local rulers], over their district, as a straw roof.'

119 See below, Chapter 7, 220.

120 Int. 1, iii. Muḥammad Nyitirre, *firsha* of the Nyerneng of Konyose, was killed by Abbakr for submitting to Adam Rijāl, ʿAlī Dīnār's

governor of the Kongyo/Zalingei area after the restoration of the Fūr Sultanate in 1898. For the battle of Shawai, see below, 166.

121 Int. 1, v; *awīn al-sulṭān balbasū samḥ wa bāklū laḥm*, 'the sultan's wives dress nicely and eat meat.'

122 During the rains, when the new crop was standing in the fields but was not yet ripe, the governor of an estate opened his grain stores for those commoners who had run out of millet. Those who needed millet would come and borrow as much as they needed. After the harvest they returned exactly the same amount of millet as they had borrowed. This practice of borrowing grain was called *gurda*. On some occasions those who came to borrow millet were asked to participate in a communal labour party on the governor's fields. During this *nafīr*, they received beer and meat.

123 Int. 1, iii.

124 Int. 1, xvii and Int. 2, i.

125 See above, 161. For Masālīt expansion see CRO 2 Darfur Dar Masalit. This pride in being independent was not shared by the Jabal and Erenga. This is evident from the fact that they collaborated with the enemies of the Masālīt, whenever the opportunity arose; at first with the Fūr of ʿAlī Dīnār, and later with the French and British colonizers.

126 Int. 1, v and xii; Int. 8. Compare Abbakr's fate with that of ʿUmar Lel, sultan of Dār Fūr from ca. 1730–9, who was deserted in a war against Wadai (O'Fahey, 1980, 18). See also Davies (1924), 51 ff.

127 For heavy taxation, see Int. 1, iv; Int. 8; and above 154 ff. For greed, see Int. 1, xxiii and Int. 13. For the misbehaviour of the *jihādiyya*, see above 154–5.

128 For harsh justice, see Int. 1, xiii, xiv and xv, and Int. 6, 8 and 13. For the execution of the others, see Int. 1, iii, xiii and xvii.

129 Int. 9 and 13; and see above, 138.

130 Int. 13. The quotation is not literal. It is a free English translation of the oral Arabic translation of the original (Masālīt) text.

131 Int. 1, v.

132 See above, 146–7 (note 75).

133 Int. 1, ii and Int. 27, i (2 and 19 May 1979).

134 Int. 33. She was a Masālīt woman who had been captured by the Fūr in 1905 and had been brought up at the court of ʿAlī Dīnār. She was married off to one of the sultan's slaves.

135 Int. 1, iii for the story of the concubine. For the flight and capture of royal women, see above, Chapter 2, 51–2.

136 See above, 164–5 (note 122), and Int. 1, xvii.

137 Int. 1, ii and Int. 16, for eunuchs.

138 See above, 161, Cordell (1977), 34–5. Austen (1979) is of no help

at all.

139 A possible indication of this is the ease with which Abbakr sold his concubines to the Fezzān, and the ease with which Baḥr al-Dīn sold one of Badāwī's concubines to the merchants (see above, 157 and 169).

Chapter 6 – 'The sultan is like a buffalo in the fight'

1 Davies (1957), 153. The quotation is a line from a contemporary Masālīt song about the battle of Kirinding (see below, 183).

2 From a contemporary Masālīt song sung after the battle of Kejkeje (see below, 179).

3 Theobald (1965), 211 and 219.

4 O'Fahey (1980), 46.

5 CRO Int. 5/3/39.

6 See above, Chapter 4, 116 (note 144).

7 Theobald (1965), 58–9; CRO Int. 5/3/39. For the post in Dār Zaghāwa, see CRO Int. 2/3/14. For a survey of the relations between ʿAlī Dīnār and the Sanūsiyya, see ANSOM Afrique VI, doss. 190 (memorandum by Clayton), and CRO Int. 5/3/40; Int. 2/5/125; Int. 5/3/39; Arkell (1922); Darfur 1/4/17 and Darfur 1/33/170.

8 For Ibrāhīm's present, see CRO Darfur 1/33/170 and above, Chapter 4, 120 (note 166). For the *laizzez passers*, see above, Chapter 4, 117 (note 150).

9 For the exports from Wadai, see CRO Darfur 1/33/169; Darfur 1/33/170 (report April 1903); Darfur 1/33/171 (1918); in the *laissez passer* issued by al-Ghazālī the tradegoods are specified as 'animals and other things useful for the markets' (*ḥayawānāt wa mā yuṣliḥ ghayruhu al-aswāq*). In that issued by Dūd Murra, the exports are specified as 'what they possess of wealth and tradegoods consisting of camels, cows and other things' (see note 8). For the exports of Dār Fūr and Wadai ivory, see CRO Darfur 1/33/170 (report for November 1903). For the trade route, see idem, the *laissez passers* mentioned in note 8, and Int. 36.

10 CRO Int. 2/2/11, Muḥammad Bakhīt to ʿAlī Dīnār (3 Rabīʿ II 1333 = 18 February 1915).

11 ANSOM Afrique VI, doss. 189, Sultan Muḥammad Bakhīt to the French (8 Ramaḍān 1330 = 12 August 1912). The quotation is from the French translation. *Miskīn* means commoner rather than 'poor devil'.

12 CRO Darfur 1/33/70 (report for April 1903), and Int. 1, vii.

13 For the presents from Bakhīt, see CRO Int. 2/2/11, letters from

Muḥammad Bakhīt to ʿAlī Dīnār (6 February 1915) and Dhahab Muḥammad Bakhīt to ʿAlī Dīnār (same date). For ʿAlī Dīnār's presents, see idem, two undated lists of presents sent by him to Muḥammad Bakhīt, and CRO Darfur 1/4/18.

14 CRO Int. 2/2/10, for original letter and translation, dated 12 June 1901.

15 CRO Darfur 1/33/169, Monthly Intelligence Report, September 1905.

16 idem. Monthly Intelligence Report, July 1908 and April 1909.

17 CRO Darfur 1/33/170, Monthly Intelligence Report, December 1908.

18 CRO Int. 2/31/258, Arabic letters from Muḥammad Bakhīt to the District Commissioner of western Baḥr al-Ghazāl and to the Sirdar of the Sudan (15 February 1911 and 28 April 1912).

19 For the nickname, also in the variant of 'Ab Sarjan Barra', see Int. 2, i; CRO Darfur 1/133/169 (Monthly Intelligence Report, September 1910). For the marriage policy of Idrīs, see idem, Monthly Intelligence Report, March 1905, appendix I; Int. 2, i; Int. 1, vii; ANSOM Afrique VI, doss. 187 (interview with Idrīs himself, 9 March 1912); CRO Darfur 1/2/7. Compare Chapter 2, note 130).

20 Int. 1, v.

21 Int. 2, i.

22 Int. 1, iii. *Malik* Nyitirre of the Nyerneng was even executed.

23 For the battle of Shawai, see Int. 1, v and xxiii (for song); Int. 2, i; Int. 6; Int. 8; Int. 13; Int. 20; CRO Darfur 1/33/169; ANSOM Afrique VI, doss. 184 (Julien, Étude sur le Dar Masalit Ambouze, 15 June 1910). Informants disagree about the intentions of Kunji. All agree that Kunji's advice to divide the army was wrong and that he fled as a coward from the battlefield, but only a few (Int. 43 and 6) accused him of treachery.

24 Information from the wife of *amīr* Baḥr al-Dīn ʿAlī Dīnār, 8 June 1979, al-Fāshir.

25 CRO Int. 2/3/14 (for original); CRO Darfur 1/33/169, Monthly Intelligence Report, June 1905, for translation.

26 Int. 1, iii and xv; Int. 8, 13 and 20; CRO Darfur 1/33/169, Monthly Intelligence Report, August 1905: 'Forty-eight Emirs of the Masalat came and submitted to Ali Dinar at El Fasher and received the "aman" from him.' ʿAlī Dīnār forgave them and reinstated them in their offices and returned half of the camels and cattle they had brought. This is not confirmed by oral sources.

27 ANSOM Afrique VI, doss. 184.

28 According to Int. 2, i and ANSOM Afrique VI, doss. 187 (interview of Col. Julien with Wadaian *ʿaqīd*s in 1910), Dūd Murra did not assist the Masālīt in driving out the Fūr. According to CRO Darfur

1/33/169, Monthly Intelligence Report, September 1905 and December 1905, he did.

29 Int. 2, i (quotation). Accounts of Tāj al-Dīn's activities before the battle of Gilāni, see Int. 1, iii, viii and ix (who was himself with Tāj al-Dīn in this period); Int. 5, 6, 16 and 20.

30 Int. 1, iv. The song was composed by a man called Bugul, of the Shōtiyya, in the night that the Masālīt pursued the Fūr deep into Dār Fūr.

31 Int. 2, i (song: *Qamr al-Dīn, firka ḥarīriyya, Masālīt ḍarrū*). The best accounts of the battle were Int. 1, xvi and xxiii; Int. 16 and Int. 20 (who all participated). For the date see Int. 16 and CRO Darfur 1/33/169, Monthly Intelligence Report, December 1905.

32 Int. 16; *al-jurun, idhā kān bizakkī wa akhadhta gandūl mā binaqqis*, 'when the threshing floor (a heap of unthreshed millet) pays *zakāh* and you take one stalk, it does not become less.' See CRO Darfur 1/33/169, March 1906, for the execution of Abbakr.

33 Int. 1, vii (for the story of the banquet); xxiii; CRO Int. 5/5/39; and Davies (1924), 55 (for date). Andōka and Badawī were against peace with ʿAlī Dīnār (see note 102).

34 Int. 1, xvi (for song).

35 CRO Int. 1/33/169, Monthly Intelligence Report, January 1907 (for reference to *ra'īs*), and Int. 2/3/17, letter from ʿAlī Dīnār to Governor, Kordofan, 3 February 1910 (for idem and quotation).

36 Balfour-Paul (1957), 403.

37 Theobald (1965), 62; CRO Int. 5/3/39 (MacMichael); ANSOM Afrique VI, doss. 182 bis and doss. 183 bis.

38 ANSOM Afrique VI, doss. 187, 'Rapport du Commandant Lucien au Lieut. Col. Commandant le Territoire du Tchad à Fort Lamy, Abéché, 5 Mars 1910'. Only a fragment of the letter is given, in translation.

39 idem; and ANSOM Afrique VI, doss. 184, Col. Julien, 'Étude sur les Massalits Ambouzes'.

40 idem; the instructions were given in a letter dated 25 November 1909.

41 idem; this was reported by Delacommune from Nieri, the capital of Dār Tāma on 24 October 1909. *Kirdi* is a generic name given to all slaves coming from the southern marches of Wadai. Compare *Fartīt* for the slaves from the southern marches of Dār Fūr.

42 idem and ANSOM Afrique VI, doss. 185 (1910), for the tribute. Probably Idrīs paid only one half of this amount to the French, like the sultan of Dār Silā (see note 44).

43 ANSOM Afrique VI, doss. 187 (for original); doss. 185 (for a very rough French translation). The text here is my translation of the original. The letter is undated, but the date written on it in French is 9

November 1909.

44 ANSOM Afrique VI, doss. 187, Arabic letter from Muḥammad Bakhīt to the French (18 Rabīʿ I 1329 = 19 March 1911). Bakhīt protests against a tribute in money (coins), which he did not have and which had not been included in earlier (unwritten) agreements. It has been agreed that he would pay one half of one-thirtieth of the animal wealth (cows, sheep, donkeys) of his kingdom, Bakhīt said. He added rather indignantly that his kingdom only had the cows of the nomads and the sheep, donkeys and *tukkiya*s of the Dājū, and that he would only pay taxes from what was available.

45 ANSOM Afrique VI, doss. 184, Julien, 'Etude', letter no. 102.

46 'Un simple promenade militaire' was used by Delacommune in ANSOM Afrique VI, doss. 184. See also his last letters in Delacommune (1910), 233–48. The French text quoted here is not the literal translation of the Arabic translation. Apparently Julien did not have access to the original when writing his 'Etude'.

47 The French tried to cover up the fact that they had penetrated so far into Dār Fūr, and spoke consistently of 'the affair of Bir Tawil'. See ANSOM Afrique VI, doss. 184; and Delacommune (1910); Terrier (1910); Babin (1910); Gentil (1971), volume 2, 203–215; Davies (1924), 56–7.

48 Int. 15. The first three lines were reported in ANSOM Afrique VI, doss. 184. *Nammā* = *lammā*, meaning here 'until'.

49 See CRO Int. 2/4/17 for ʿAlī Dīnār's boastful letter (22 Muḥarram 1328 = 3 February 1910). For a translation of the original and evidence that the Intelligence Office realized that Tāj al-Dīn tried to impress ʿAlī Dīnār with a due sense of his capacity as a warrior, see CRO Darfur 1/33/169 (5 February 1910).

50 ANSOM Afrique VI, doss. 184 (Julien, 'Etude').

51 idem; CRO Int. 2/15/129; B.I.F. M.S. 6005, Largeau (1911–2); apparently the *ikhwān* accompanied Dūd Murra to Dār Masālīt, for Largeau reported that Andōka, when he met Col. Hilaire on 28 February 1912, admitted that Sī Ṣalīḥ Bū Krīmī had been present at Darōti with 70 *ikhwān*, but had not actually participated in the fighting.

52 ANSOM Afrique VI, doss. 184, Julien.

53 ANSOM Afrique VI, doss. 183 bis. From speech made by the President of the *Société de Géographie* on 15 December 1910.

54 ANSOM Afrique VI, doss. 184, Julien. The two letters are translations of originals which Julien must have had in front of him. Their dates are respectively 22 Dhū'l-Ḥijja and 28 Dhū'l-Ḥijja 1327, i.e. 4 and 11 January 1910. The text of Tāj al-Dīn's seal on both letters is: 'aides ô glorieux ton esclave l'Emir Tadj Eddine Ismail

1326'; (1326 H. = 4 February 1908 – 23 January 1909).

55 idem; the quotation has been translated from the French.

56 idem; the date and text of the seal are not given, but Julien had the original at his disposal when writing.

57 ANSOM Afrique VI, doss. 183 for original letter from: *'aqīd al-Baḥr* Ibrāhīm Bajūrī, *kamkolak* Burma walad Asad, *'aqīd Qarī* Absikkīn, *'aqīd 'Adrī* Jināyā, *kamkolak* Mursāl, *'aqīd al-Zabada, kursī* Qūnī and *shartaya* Aḥmad Abqayr, to *'aqīd al-Maḥāmīd* in Abesher, dated 22 Ṣafar 1328 (5 March 1910). Note that the authors had fled to Dār Fūr and had come back to the western frontier with the Fūr army.

58 ANSOM Afrique VI, doss. 183. The letters from the Fūr to Dūd Murra and his companions have not been preserved, but the two Arabic answers are in this file. CRO Int. 2/5/129 for confirmation that the *ikhwān* and northern desert tribes assisted Dūd Murra. See CRO Int. 7/5/10 for an original (Arabic) letter of Adam Rijāl, dated 2 Rabī' I 1328 (March 1910), in which he asked permission to punish the Tāmā and Qimr once more.

59 ANSOM Afrique VI, doss. 184, Julien.

60 Int. 1, ix.

61 According to ANSOM Afrique VI, doss. 184, Julien, Dūd Murra fled to Dār Masālīt on 23 April 1910, but on 3 May 1910 (22 Rabī' I 1328) he wrote to the various *shaykhs* and sections of the Maḥāmīd to come join him at Kapka in four days. (ANSOM Afrique VI, doss. 183 for original). Probably Dūd Murra fled soon after writing this letter.

62 CRO Int. 5/3/36; the British traveller was killed in Dār Tāmā just before the battle of Gereida (6 February 1910). For Dirjeil as a centre of refugees from the French and British, see Int. 1, v.

63 For details of Darōti, see ANSOM Afrique VI, doss. 183 bis, 'Attaque de la Colonne Moll'; SHAT Carton 1 (1909–11), doss. 4 (Reports by Lieut. Arnaud, who took the northern route, and by Col. Chauvelot of the column led by Col. Moll. For a Masālīt eyewitness account, see Int. 1, xxiii. Compare Caix (1910); Moll (1910) and (1912); Gouraud (1911); Payen (1910); Babin (1910a), (1911), (1911a) and (1911b); Gentil (1971), volume 2, 203–15; Davies (1924), 58–9.

64 According to Andōka (in his interview with Col. Hilaire at Todoronna in February 1912), the Masālīt lost 300 out of 1,000 horsemen, excluding the commoners. These 300 included 40 close relatives of Tāj al-Dīn. (B.I.F. M.S. 6005, Largeau, March/April 1911). The quotations are from Int. 1, iii and ix; idem in Int. 8.

65 For the first song, see Int. 1, ix; for the second, Davies (1957), 147. *Ab Tayra* was the name given to muskets and carabines no. 90–93 (B.I.F. M.S. 6005, Largeau, 1911). *Tūja* was a Masālīt traitor who

guided the French to Darōti. Compare Davies (1924), 58.

66 SHAT Carton II, doss. 1, Report of Col. Maillard on the 'Opérations au Massalit', from 17 January 1911 to 2 March 1911.

67 Int. 20. According to Int. 15 the Masālīt decided not to flee to ʿAlī Dīnār, because they realized that, if the troops he sent back with them crossed the Wādī Barei, that would mean the end of the Masālīt Sultanate.

68 For the Kodoi rebellion, see SHAT Carton I, doss. 4, Col. Hilaire, 'Pacification de Ouaddai' (from June to August 1911); and Largeau (27 October 1911). Int. 1, iv participated in Dūd Murra's raiding foray which ended in the skirmish with the French at Chokōyan. For the surrender of Dūd Murra, see Largeau (1938), 5–22, which includes translations of letters exchanged between Largeau and Dūd Murra, and Largeau and Andōka.

69 My translation of the original in ANSOM Afrique VI, doss. 187 (1329 = 1911). The seal reads: '*amīr* Muḥammad Andūka ibn Abbakr 1328'; (1328 = 1910).

70 ANSOM Afrique VI, doss. 187; my translation of the original (3 Dhū'l-Qaʿda 1329 = 26 October 1911), with the same seal as in the letter mentioned in note 69. Note that Andōka calls himself: *al-sulṭān Muḥammad Baḥr al-Dīn ibn al-marḥūm al-sulṭān Abbakr Ismā*ʿīl.

71 See ANSOM Afrique VI, doss. 184, for evidence that the French subdued the frontier *dār*s in the hope that this would affect the outcome of the border negotiations with the British in their favour. The Anglo-French negotiations are analyzed in Theobald (1965), Chapter 4 and appendix. For the French interpretation of the traditional border between Wadai and Dār Fūr, see ANSOM Afrique VI, doss. 184, Julien; ANSOM Tchad I, doss. 9, Largeau, 29 April 1913, 'Rapport ayant pour objet de faire ressortir les droits de la France sur le Tama et le Massalit'. See Chapter 7, note 11.

72 ANSOM Afrique VI, doss. 187. Two letters from ʿAlī Dīnār to Andōka, both dated 2 Ṣafar 1330 (22 January 1912). The file contains only the French translations of the originals. See also B.I.F. M.S. 6005, Largeau.

73 ANSOM Afrique VI, doss. 187. French translation of the original (22 January 1912), which is not included. The letter is from ʿAlī Dīnār to 'Cherefeddine Ismail, Ali Seman [Sennān] Ismail, Badaoui fils de l'Emir Ab Beker, Ahmed Abou Cjelouk [Shulūkh], Bassi Kerama, Bassi Kandasha, et l'Aguid Moudda'.

74 ANSOM Tchad I, doss. 7; my translation from the original Arabic, dated 7 Ṣafar 1330 (27 January 1912). The seal is not fully readable, but is probably the same as in the letter mentined in note 69.

75 ANSOM Tchad I, doss. 9, Largeau, 29 April 1913 (see note 71). He

adds 73 wounded and the costs of the troops guarding and policing the frontier with Dār Masālīt. For the *diya* idea among the Masālīt, see Int. 1, xxiii, and Int. 13; the French could not accept that their blood had been spent for nothing, and since the Masālīt had nothing to pay as *diya* they took in recompense the land west of the Wādī Asunga.

76 B.I.F. M.S. 6005, Col. Hilaire writing about 'une tournée en forces effectuée sur la frontière entre Ouadai et Massalit' (27 February–4 March 1912). On 13 August 1912 Andōka was still urging the French that they should send 'des soldats qui resteront auprès de nous' and should have with them 'un esprit (chef) extraordinaire', (ANSOM Afrique VI, doss. 188, letter dated 29 Shaʿbān 1331, in French translation only).

77 ANSOM Tchad I, doss. 7 (11 October 1911) for the first quotation; ANSOM Afrique VI, doss. 187 (6 March 1912), for the second quotation and for the statement that the Masālīt did not have to pay tribute.

78 ANSOM 6PA Julien, carton 1; B.I.F. 6004 (Largeau, 1913 and 1914); Int. 2, i; Int. 15; Int. 16; Int. 20.

79 Int. 1, ix. *Ammo* Zahra was the informant's wife. *Kinnaga* is Masālīt for members of the royal family, comparable (but less common) to *abbonga* and *bāsinga*; 'Ab Sōga' is a well near Dirjeil; *barḍū* probably comes from the Arabic root *raḍaʿa* = to suck or to nurse; *yidāriʿ* = from the Arabic root *daraʿa* = to armour or to provide with armour.

80 According to SHAT Tchad I, carton 19, doss. 1, B.I.F. M.S. 6004, Largeau (August 1914), and Int. 1, v and xvi, the capital was moved out of fear of ʿAlī Dīnār. For the lack of water, see ANSOM 6 PA Julien, Carton 1 (Decmber 1913); B.I.F. M.S. 6004, Largeau (1914). This is also the explanation usually given by the Masālīt. El Geneina (Ar. *al-junayna*) means 'the garden'; Sultan Abbakr had had his garden there since the 1890s (Int. 1, xv), and it had been the war capital of Tāj al-Dīn (Int. 1, xvi and SHAT Tchad I, carton 1).

81 B.I.F. M.S. Largeau (1914) and ANSOM 6 PA Julien, carton 1 (1913–14).

82 B.I.F. M.S. 6004 Largeau (February–April 1914).

83 idem, Largeau (September 1913–January 1914), for the obligation to pay taxes; idem, Largeau (June–August 1914), for reference to Julien.

84 Theobald (1965), 91–2. See CRO Civ. Sec. 112/2/7 for a worried letter from ʿAlī Dīnār to Slatin (1 Muḥarram 1330 = 22 December 1911). In this letter ʿAlī complained that the French had occupied Dār Masālīt; that he had believed that they only wanted Dūd Murra, but now realized that 'they want to satisfy their ambition by taking

possession of Darfur.'

85 ANSOM Afrique VI, doss. 183, 'Ouadai-Darfour. Pour-parlers au sujet de la délimitation. Actions sur le Sultan du Darfour. Année 1910.' (Letter dated 22 September 1909).

86 Theobald (1965), 92.

87 ʿAlī Dīnār tried to persuade Dūd Murra to take refuge in al-Fāshir. He sent three letters and presents to Dūd Murra in Dār Masālīt. The latter, however – advised against trusting ʿAlī Dīnar by the dignitaries who had fled to Dār Fūr in June 1909 and had managed to escape again – refused politely. He wrote to ʿAlī Dīnār that his subjects and the Masālīt had urged him to fight the holy war against the French. See CRO Int. 2/3/12 for the original of a letter to ʿAlī Dīnār (15 Shaʿbān 1329 = 11 August 1911); and ANSOM Tchad I, doss. 7.

88 ANSOM Tchad I, doss. 7, Largeau to Governor, Oubangi-Chari-Chad, and the attached declaration of Ibrāhīm al-Ḥājj, 5 December 1911.

89 SHAT Tchad, carton 8, reference to a letter from Asīl to al-Kaḥḥāl, dated 13 August 1911. Compare a letter from the latter to the former dated 21 May 1911, in which al-Kaḥḥāl complained that he could not do anything about the 'groupements senussistes' in Beskere and al-Dūr, and proposed to trade *via* the Kordofan–Kafiakingi route instead (ANSOM Afrique VI, doss. 183).

90 ANSOM Afrique VI, doss. 183 (letter from Grey to Cambon, 18 December 1912).

91 ANSOM 6PA Julien, Carton 1 (end 1912/beginning 1913 and January 1914) for the goods the caravans usually carried; compare CRO Int. 2/5/18 (for 1915). According to CRO Civ. Sec. 112/2/5 ʿAlī Dīnār opened the Abesher–Fāshir road in April 1912.

92 See for example ANSOM Tchad I, doss. 7: in 1912 traders and pilgrims were reported to travel *via* Goz Beida and Kafiakingi. See also ANSOM 6PA Julien, carton 1 (situation in 1912).

93 B.I.F., M.S. 6004, Largeau (1912). Letter is given only in translation. It was dated 28 Dhū'l-Qaʿda 1330 = 8 November 1912.

94 The Tāmā garrison was established to protect trade after Tāmā villagers had attacked a caravan travelling from Abesher to al-Fāshir (ANSOM 6PA Julien, carton 1, 1913). The Tumtuma route was open in April 1913 and probably stayed open until August (idem). Even Col. Largeau (B.I.F., M.S. 6004, 1915) pitied Sultan Idrīs of Dār Qimr, 'ce malheureux potentat noire', who was tormented by the double fear of displeasing the French and of being chastised by ʿAlī Dīnār, as happened to everybody who dealt with the French.

95 For French opinion on ʿAlī Dīnār's attitude, see B.I.F., M.S. 6004, Largeau (1913); for Andōka's complaint and the words of Julien, see

ANSOM 6PA Julien (August 1913).

96 Int. 46.

97 For fears of invasion in 1915, see CRO Darfur 1/4/18; CRO Int. 2/5/18 and Int. 2/5/19. For the declaration about the Silā route, see B.I.F., M.S. 6004, Largeau (1915).

98 Int. 1, xviii.

99 Int. 1, iii.

100 Int. 1, iv. Jimme (Jumʿa) was Jimme Tindil and Mursāl was Mursāl Jengge (the Dinka), both slaves of Tāj al-Dīn. Jimme commanded the frontier post at Amm Dukhn when Tāj al-Dīn had become sultan.

101 Int. 20 and Int. 1, xii; *al-shūqāy qāʿid fī rāsī hinā Allāh salla sut*, 'the thorn in my head God has pulled out like that'; *sut* = onomatopoeia indicating speed. ʿAlī al-Tamtam was the son of Ibrāhīm, the halfbrother of Ismāʿīl ʿAbd al-Nabī.

102 Int. 1, x and Int. 16. This occurred at Todoronna. Andōka was beaten up, tied up and imprisoned in Dirjeil, where he was guarded by Ab Sinnan Jīr. All his slaves, rifles and other possessions were confiscated. Compare Davies (1924), 55, who quotes a song which shows that Tāj al-Dīn's reconciliation with ʿAlī Dīnār was the cause of the conflict.

103 According to O'Fahey (1980), 33, the *bāsinga* in the Dār Fūr Sultanate usually played little part in the running of the state. For the opposite case in the frontier sultanates, see ANSOM Tchad I, doss. 9 (Largeau), and SHAT Carton 3 (Simonet, 19 July 1914).

104 Int. 1, x; Int. 2, i; and Int. 8. According to Int. 8 Tāj al-Dīn gave Andōka his ring and asked him to choose from among the axe, the sword and the hoe. Andōka chose the sword and was acclaimed by the bystanders '*wad Abbakr jāmūs*', 'the son of Abbakr is a buffalo.'

105 For the reference to ʿUthmān Jānū, see CRO Cair. Int. 10/22/55, letter dated 1 August 1890, and above, Chapter 4, 102. For the pretenders accompanying the Fūr armies in 1910, see ANSOM Afrique VI, doss. 184. For the flight of ʿAli Sennān in August 1914, see Int. 1, xxiii, Int. 16; CRO Civ. Sec. 112/2/5; B.I.F., M.S. 6004, Largeau (1914).

106 Int. 1, ix; in xxiii it was said that Idrīs Anggaroro had reproached Andōka. According to Int. 2, i, Dūd Murra invested Andōka with the turban while ʿAli Ab Shanab brought Tāj al-Dīn's ring.

107 ANSOM 6PA Julien, carton 1 (March/April 1915).

108 B.I.F., M.S. 6004, Largeau (1912); the letter (17 December 1912) is given only in translation.

109 idem, Largeau (1913), 8 April 1913.

110 For ʿAbd al-Sharīf, see ANSOM 6PA Julien, carton 1 (February 1914); he was said to be another son of *faqīh* ʿAlī al-Tamtam. For ʿAlī

Sennān, see note 105. The story and song of ʿAbd al-Karīm, are from Int. 1, xii. The song was sung by his sister-in-law.'The oil of your father you did not eat' means 'you refused to enjoy and be content with the high office and wealth bestowed upon your father.' Oil is often used as a metaphor for something good.

111 Int. 1, xiii; the *faqīh* was Abbakr's son-in-law and was called Adam Ngūje. For Shawai, see Chapter 5, 128 and above 177.

112 Int. 1, viii.

113 Int. 16.

114 Int. 15.

115 Int. 1, iii and xxiii. The first line means literally 'the one with the moustache, the lion'; *kinna* in *dūdkinna* is not clear; *shartay* Zayn was one of the leaders of the Fūr army.

116 CRO Darfur 1/34/175; in 1930 it was said that Andōka had sixty brothers and sisters, twenty 'uncles' and innumerable collaterals. See also Int. 16.

117 Int. 1, i, ix and xv.

118 CRO Darfur 1/34/172 (Davies, 9 April 1921) and Civ. Sec. 1/18/55 (Davies, 4 August 1920). Compare below, Chapter 7, 218.

119 Int. 15 and 16. The *abbonga* flogged and killed people, took cows, demanded hospitality for themselves, their followers and their horses (Int. 15). They took everything, even the spears one was carrying (Int. 8). They would take over a bridal hut (Int. 14). One could not complain about them, for one would lodge the complaint with the accused's brother (Int. 20). The *abbonga* came to a district to eat their fill and to clothe their followers from the fines they collected (Int. 20). When they visited a *firsha*, they administered justice and collected the fines over his head. They collected taxes and often took the *firsha*'s share. One could not complain to the sultan because the *amīn*s would not allow one into the palace (Int. 9). One *abbo* punished a man suspected of having stolen his bag by hanging him upside down from the branch of a tree and flogging the soles of his feet (idem). Compare CRO Darfur 1/34/172 (Redfern 17 September 1923), and below, Chapter 7, 218–19 for the trial of *amīn* Aḥmad Ab Shulūkh.

In ANSOM 6PA Julien, carton 1 (February 1914) it was reported: 'Les Massalits reprocheraient à leur sultan de se désinteresser par trop de l'expédition des affaires et notamment de celle de justice. Aucun écho officiel n'est parvenue à cet égard.'

120 Int. 1, x. This took place in the northeastern part of Dār Masālīt, in Ḥashāba (Timeit).

121 Holt (1970), 23.

122 For early *mahdī*s and prophets, see CRO Mahdiyya 1/13, III doc. 705

(14 Rabīʿ II 1313 = 4 October 1895); 1/14, III doc. 803 (25 Ramaḍān 1312 = 22 March 1895); idem doc. 825 (27 Rabīʿ I 1313 = 17 September 1895), for a Prophet Jesus, a prophet and a devil in Dār Tāmā. In CRO Mahdiyya 1/13, II doc. 237 (23 Rajab 1309 = 22 February 1892), it is reported that 'someone proclaimed himself (*daʿā lahu daʿwa*) and was killed by Abbakr.' For the prophet in al-Fāshir, see CRO Int. 2/3/17 (December 1905). For *faqīh* Abbo, see B.I.F., M.S. 6005 (and compare Int. 15). Idem, M.S. 6004, Largeau (1913), for the *faqīh*s and sorcerer of Ofoun. ANSOM 6PA Julien carton 1 (June 1913), for the *faqīh* of Gorane. For the 'war of the *faqīh*s', see below, 205 ff.

123 CRO Darfur 1/34/172, for the description of the meeting. Int. 1, viii and xxiii, for the belief in miracles.

124 Int. 1, xv and xxiii. According to Int. 20 the *faqīh* was a Marrāti (of the Marārīt), rose at Malam Gunji near Salāmi, where the informant himself lived, and was killed by *abbo* Sharaf al-Dīn. See also CRO Darfur 3/3/20 (Davies, 1924 and Arkell, 1926). For Abū Jummayza, see Chapter 4, 83 ff.

125 Accounts of the 'war of the *faqīh*s' were given by Int. 1, xix and xxiii; Int. 8, 10, 12, 13 and 15, and in CRO Darfur 3/3/20; Darfur 1/34/172 and ANSOM 6PA Julien, carton 1 (December 1913). Int. 8 and 15 are eyewitness accounts and give the story of the point of view of the rebels. Int. 1 gave the government's point of view. All accounts agree that the revolt was directed against the Gernyeng. The written sources emphasize the fact that Andōka joined the Tijāniyya and stopped being a Mahdist (*anṣāri*); the oral sources suggest that he did not do so until (just after) the arrival of the British in 1918 (Int. 15). See below, Chapter 7, note 131.

126 ANSOM 6PA Julien, carton 1 (December 1913).

127 Int. 8 and 15 (for the term *jizya*); *jizya* is in this context a head tax paid by free Muslims to a non-Muslim ruler. It is here undoubtedly used to emphasize the difference in religion between the Masālīt subjects and French rulers.

128 ANSOM 6PA Julien, carton 1 (December 1913).

129 Int. 15.

130 ANSOM 6PA Julien, carton 1 (December 1913), interview with *abbo* Badawī Abbakr, 26 December 1913.

131 All accounts agree on the aftermath of the revolt. The term *mubāḥ* was used by Int. 15; *kaseyeng* by Int. 8, 13, 3 and 5.

132 CRO Darfur 1/34/172.

133 B.I.F., M.S. 6004, Largeau (July 1913); for raids and punitive expeditions, see ANSOM 6PA Julien, carton 1 (1913–14, particularly March/April 1913).

134 Int. 3.

135 ANSOM 6PA Julien, carton 1 (March/April 1913, August 1913), for the raids held to make restitutions possible. For the sale of raided cattle in al-Fāshir, see CRO Int. 2/4/17; compare CRO Darfur 1/33/169 (August 1910).

136 ANSOM Tchad I, doss. 9, Annual Report by Largeau, 6 December 1911, mentions a raid by Ab Dūdū and tax collection by the *abbonga* Bashīr and Muḥammad in the area of Kudri. For the 'absolute lack of loyalism', see ANSOM 6PA Julien, carton 1 (March/April 1913).

137 SHAT Carton 3, Simonet, 24 November 1916.

138 ANSOM 6PA Julien, carton 1.

139 For Masālīt raids into Dār Fūr in 1915 and 1916, see ANSOM Afrique VI, doss. 190 (24 July 1916); CRO Int. 2/5/19 (17 October 1915); CRO Int. 2/6/23 (January 1916); In June 1916, just after the Anglo-Egyptian conquest of al-Fāshir and the fall of ʿAlī Dīnār, General Kelly heard from messengers of the *shartay* of Dār Kerne, that 'Andoka wrote to him June 2nd saying France has given him districts of Fea, Kerne, Madi, Tebella, Zami and Kunyir and that Niamaton = shartay should warn the respective headmen either to accept his authority or leave their country' (CRO Int. 2/5/20).

Chapter 7 – Some direct results of indirect rule

1 CRO Darfur 1/35/178, Lampen, October 1931.

2 CRO Darfur 1/4/21, H. A. MacMichael, 1916: 'At the present we are singularly ignorant of the country west of Fasher.' For the correspondence on ʿAlī Dīnār's *ḥarīm* retained in El Geneina, see CRO Darfur 1/18/96 (1917).

3 CRO Darfur 1/33/171, MacMichael, 'Report Dar Masalit', 1918; and CRO Darfur 1/33/172, Davies, 'The administration of Dar Masalit', 9 April 1921.

4 CRO Darfur 1/33/171, Letter of E. Gérard, Commandant la Circonscription du Ouadai, to R. V. Savile, Governor, Darfur, 18 October 1917. Both CRO Darfur 1/33/171 (MacMichael) and Darfur 1/33/172 (Davies) mentioned that Badawī made a coup attempt during one of Andōka's visits to the French in Tumtuma or Abesher, possibly in October 1916. Oral sources confirm the incident, but add that the people of Dirjeil believed that Andōka had been imprisoned by the French, and that there were no hostilities when Andōka came back (Int. 13).

5 For the Qimr Sultan, see CRO Int. 1/1/3 (for Col. Hilaire's letter to Idrīs dated 14 June 1916); and CRO Civ. Sec. 1/19/59 (for Idrīs's

reception in al-Fāshir). For Andōka's letter, see CRO Darfur 1/33/171.

6 CRO Darfur 1/33/171, letter from R. V. Savile to Andōka dated 9 February 1918.

7 idem; instructions given by R. V. Savile to J. H. Hardy on 14 February 1918.

8 idem.

9 idem.

10 idem; the original letter is enclosed in this file; it is dated 4 Muḥarram 1327 (10 October 1918). The Governor of Dār Fūr wrote to Hardy on 4 November 1918: 'As Dar Erenga is under Dar Masalit, I fear we cannot at present interfere with Endoka's appointment or dismissal or imprisonment of Shartais in that Dar.' The Sudan Government was also approached by Ḥusayn Muḥammad Attok Ḥasab Allāh, who defended the claim to the sultanate of his father, a decrepit old gentleman living in Sinnār Province, who was a brother of Hajjām (CRO Int. 2/13/105, letter dated 1 April 1919).

11 CRO Civ. Sec. 1/18/55, and Darfur 1/33/171 (for the scare about an attack on the Kereinik post on 4 May 1918). Even Andōka clamoured for a real occupation. For the dates and details of the settlement of the Anglo-French boundary dispute, see Theobald (1965), appendix (220 ff.); and SHAT Tchad, carton 19, doss. 1, Darfour: Capt. Canavaggio, 'Representations sur le Dar Massalit', 8 March 1955, 1–53. See above, Chapter 6, note 71.

12 CRO Civ. Sec. 1/18/55, Civil Secretary to Governor Dār Fūr, 27 December 1919, and *vice versa*, 17 January 1920.

13 For the Nyala rising, see CRO Civ. Sec. 122/1/1; Darfur 1/2/7; and Daly (1980), 79–88. The sources emphasize excessive taxes, the release of slaves and hatred of the 'infidel' government as major causes of the revolt. For the unrest in Dār Masālīt, see CRO Darfur 1/33/172 (R. Davies, 15 December 1921), 'Report on the recent unrest in Dar Masalit'; and CRO Darfur 1/35/76, Mr Laidlaw, 1939, 'Note on Kereinik'. The quotations are from R. Davies in Darfur 1/33/172. For the function of the Resident, see below, 215.

14 CRO Darfur 1/33/172, R. Davies, 'Note on the objects of the Patrol in Dar Masalit, attitude of its population, and the events leading up to the patrol', 19 January 1922.

15 Int. 15; CRO Darfur 1/33/172, R. Davies, 'Report on the occupation of Dar Maṣalit', 19 March 1922. The occupying force consisted of two camel companies, two M.I. companies, one infantry company, three cars of the M.M.G. Battery.

16 CRO Darfur 1/33/172, R. Davies, 'Report on the recent unrest in Dar Masalit'.

17 CRO Darfur 1/34/172, R. Davies, 9 April 1921.
18 Sanderson (1980), 46–7. Sanderson's introduction is a lucid analysis of the Sudan Civil Service's 'official mind' and administrative policy. See also Daly (1980), 168–83 ('The beginnings of Indirect Rule') and 177–8 ('the Dar Masalit "experiment" '). Daly mentions that Davies left for Dār Masālīt with the major works on indirect rule in his luggage. He missed the point that the influence of the Resident and his staff was pervasive.
19 CRO Darfur 1/34/172, Sir Lee Stack to Andōka, 24 March 1924; idem to the sultan of Dār Qimr, Idrīs Abū Bakr.
20 CRO Darfur 1/35/177, R. Davies to Governor, Dār Fūr, 'The Finances of Dar Masalit', 1 January 1924.
21 CRO Darfur 1/34/175, A. J. Arkell, 'The Dar Masalit Native Administration', 4 December 1926, Am Shokaba.
22 CRO Darfur 1/33/172, Governor, Dār Fūr to Civil Secretary, 29 July 1925.
23 Sanderson (1980), 47, for quotation.
24 CRO Darfur 1/34/172, R. Davies, 9 April 1921, 'The administration of Dar Masalit', 1921.
25 See above, Chapter 6, 199 ff.
26 See above, Chapter 5, 146–7.
27 For *abbonga*, see above, Chapter 6, 198–9. See CRO Civ. Sec. 1/18/55, R. Davies; Int. 1, ii and Int. 2, i.
28 CRO Civ. Sec. 20/21/96, E. Campbell, Resident, Dār Masālīt, 26 September 1928.
29 CRO Civ. Sec. 20/21/96, E. D. M. Batty, Assistant Resident, Dār Masālīt, 28 September 1928.
30 Int. 2, i. See above, Chapter 6, 202–3.
31 CRO Civ. Sec. 1/18/55, R. Davies, 'Sultan Endoka and his brothers', 4 August 1920; and CRO Darfur 1/33/172, R. Davies, 'The administration of Dar Masalit'.
32 Andōka's most important slave official was *maqdūm* Saʿīd Ab Dūdū, who had been given to Abbakr as a small boy (see Chapter 2, note 134). Ziyāda and Kafōti were slave governors of the area of Beida and Arara probably in the 1930s. They succeeded and were succeeded by *abbonga* (Int. 9). CRO Darfur 1/34/172, R. Davies, 'The administration of Dar Masalit', 1921, for the quotation.
33 The quotation from 1918 is from CRO Darfur 1/33/171, unsigned, probably MacMichael. For the murder of the pilgrim, see CRO Civ. Sec. 1/18/55, R. Davies, 4 August 1920, 'Murder of Hausa Pilgrim Abukr by Endoka's brother Khalil Abukr'. The reference to 'Endoka's harpies' is from idem, Civil Secretary to Governor, Dār Fūr, 17 December 1919. The quotation about the abolition of the

dārs is from CRO Darfur 1/34/172, R. Davies, 1921.

34 CRO Darfur 1/34/172, R. Davies, 1921; and Darfur 1/34/175, W. M. H. Pollen, Resident, Dār Masālīt, report on 1924.

35 CRO Darfur 1/34/172, R. Davies, 19 March 1922; and S. Redfern, 17 September 1923, 'Trial of El Amin Ahmed Ijeiber Vizier of Dar Masalit'.

36 See note 29. For Badawī's deposition, see CRO Darfur 1/35/175, report for 1928, and Int. 27, i.

37 CRO Darfur 1/34/172. P. B. Broadbent, Resident, to Governor, Dār Fūr, 'Intimidation of El Hag Endeili by the Sultan's Brothers', 21 February 1931.

38 CRO Darfur 3/3/21, Governor of Dār Fūr (Dupuis) to Civil Secretary, 17 April 1930: 'Brought up in a court atmosphere they neither expected to work for a living nor learnt to do so. Some of them were allotted areas ("Hakouras") upon the inhabitants of which they were allowed to batten, others simply roamed the country at will, taking almost without protest, whatever served their need or took their fancy. These people have quite failed to adapt themselves to the changed conditions. Very few of them are employable under the Native Administration.' For the sultan's sons, see CRO Darfur 1/34/175, annual report 1928.

39 CRO Civ. Sec. 1/18/56, R. Davies to H. A. MacMichael, 10 October 1922.

40 CRO Civ. Sec. 56/2/18, A. J. Arkell, 1926, 'Notes on Mahdism in the Western Sudan'.

41 CRO Darfur 1/34/172, P. B. Broadbent, annual report 1931, speaking about the period 1927–30.

42 For the judicial powers of the local rulers, see CRO Civ. Sec. 1/18/58, report for 1928; and Darfur 1/34/172, R. Davies, 1921. For the tax assessment boards, see CRO Darfur 1/34/172, R. Davies, 1921; and Int. 2/51/430, R. Davies, 22 October 1922, 'Report of the first Zeka Assessment in Dar Masalit'. For the 'tax payers strike', see below, 236–7.

43 CRO Darfur 1/34/172, R. Davies, 1921.

44 CRO Darfur 1/34/175, A. J. Arkell, annual report 1925–6. Compare Int. 13 for an account of how the informant refused to assist in the assessment and collection of taxes from his people if Andōka recognized a rival as *firsha*.

45 CRO Darfur 1/34/175, E. A. V. de Candole, annual report for 1938; for details on how the 25 Masālīt *firsha*s were reduced to 17, see CRO Darfur 1/34/173, 'Administrative changes in Dar Masalit made in the course of 1937 by the Sultan', possibly by P. Ingleson.

46 Int. 2, i; the suggestions were made among others by the sultan and

the *qāḍī* (Darfur 1/34/172, A. J. Arkell, 4 December 1926).

47 CRO Darfur 1/34/172, R. Davies, 1921.

48 CRO Darfur 1/33/177, R. Davies to Governor, Dār Fūr, 'The Finances of Dar Masalit', 1 January 1924.

49 CRO Darfur 1/34/172, R. Davies to Governor, Dār Fūr, 24 March 1922.

50 See note 48.

51 CRO Darfur 1/33/171, MacMichael, 1918.

52 See note 48. Compare e.g. Dorward (1976).

53 CRO Darfur 3/3/21, annual report for 1932.

54 CRO Darfur 1/35/177, R. Davies, 1923.

55 See note 48.

56 For the sultan's salary, see CRO Darfur 1/35/177, R. Davies, 'The Finances of Dar Masalit', 1 January 1924 (idem in Darfur 3/3/24); Darfur 1/35/177, Governor, Dār Fūr (Dupuis), 16 April 1931, 'Notes on Development of Dar Masalit Native Administration Finance'; Civ. Sec. 20/20/95 (budgets 1925/6); Civ. Sec. 20/21/96; in 1927 his salary was reduced from LE 975 to LE 750. For the salaries of the others, see CRO Darfur 1/34/172, Arkell, annual report 1925/6. For the sultan's relatives, see Darfur 1/34/175, Dupuis, 17 April 1930. For the sultan's horses, see Darfur 1/35/177, R. Davies, 'The Finances of Dar Masalit', 1 January 1924.

57 CRO Darfur 1/34/173 and Darfur 1/34/175, annual reports.

58 CRO Darfur 1/34/172, R. Davies to H. A. MacMichael, 6 January 1924; reply, 4 March 1924.

59 CRO Darfur 1/34/175, annual report for 1933.

60 CRO Darfur 1/34/175, Arkell, 1926.

61 CRO Darfur 1/34/175, P. B. Broadbent, annual report for 1932.

62 CRO Darfur 1/34/175, annual reports for 1925, 1929 and 1933.

63 CRO Darfur 3/3/20, Resident, Dār Masālīt, 29 September 1928.

64 For shrouds, see Int. 1, xvii; for the incident with the money, Int. 1, v and vi.

65 CRO Darfur 1/34/175, P. Sandison, annual report for 1934.

66 idem.

67 CRO Darfur 1/34/173; Darfur 1/34/175; and Darfur 3/1/2, 'Report on Dar Masalit Khalwas', 20 March 1927, by *shaykh* Muḥammad Faḍl. According to Int. 15 the British tried to convince the sultan that their education was not 'infidel' education. 'Don't say that this is the education of the "Turks", for you will study the *Qur'ān* and [Islamic] science, and will show your fathers and mothers the right way. In your country there is no education and the jallāba have taken possession of your *dār*. Tell your people that they should be educated and take over their own *dār*.'

68 CRO Darfur 1/34/173, P. Ingleson, 25 May 1939, 'Note on Dar Masalit Sultanate'.

69 SHAT Tchad, carton 19, doss. 1 (see note 11); and CRO Darfur 1/37/188, for the Government's plans for after the sultan's death, formulated in 1946.

70 CRO Darfur 1/34/172, R. Davies, 1921.

71 CRO Civ. Sec. 20/20/95, R. Davies, 22 October 1922, 'Zeka Assessment 1921–1922'.

72 See note 70.

73 See note 71 for the amounts of taxes assessed and collected in 1922 and for the census.

74 CRO Darfur 1/34/175, W. M. H. Pollen, annual report 1924. Apparently R. Davies had proposed lower tax rates (CRO Civ. Sec. 20/20/95).

75 CRO Darfur 1/34/175, W. M. H. Pollen, annual report 1924; and Civ. Sec. 20/20/95, MacMichael to Financial Secretary, 2 October 1924.

76 Quoted from CRO Darfur 1/34/175, Arkell, annual report for 1925; see also Darfur 1/34/172, Arkell, 4 December 1926. Out of a total of LE 2,904 (LE 1,099 herd tax and LE 1,805 hoe tax) only LE 102 was not collected.

77 CRO Darfur 1/34/175 and Darfur 1/34/173, annual reports.

78 CRO Civ. Sec. 20/20/95, Davies, 1922; and CRO Darfur 1/35/177, 'Notes on Development of Dar Masalit Native Administration Finance System'.

79 CRO Darfur 3/3/24, Resident to Governor, Dār Fūr, 30 June 1929.

80 CRO Civ. Sec. 20/20/95, Davies, 1922.

81 Int. 27, i

82 For the old system, see above, Chapter 4, 147–8 ff. For the innovations, CRO Civ. Sec. 20/20/95, Davies, 1922. For the disasters, see the annual reports for the respective years in CRO Darfur 1/34/173, Darfur 1/34/175, Civ. Sec. 20/20/95 (1924) and Civ. Sec. 20/21/96 (1925–7) and Hartwig (1978).

83 ANSOM Afrique VI, doss. 187, Muḥammad Bakhīt Abū Rīsha to the French (18 Rabīʿ I 1329 = 19 March 1911); and Int. 15. According to Int. 8, the Masālīt refused to pay taxes before the occupation, because it was more than they were used to. 'After the taxlists had come out', he said, 'we paid by the nipple; two piaster for a goat, since it has two nipples, and four for a cow, since it has four.'

84 CRO Civ. Sec. 20/21/96, Resident (Grigg) to Governor, Dār Fūr, 20 January 1927. The oral reference is from Int. 15. For *ardabb*, see glossary.

85 Int. 5.

86 CRO Darfur 1/34/172, Davies, 1921 (first quotation); Darfur

1/25/177, Davies, 1924 (second quotation).

87 CRO Darfur 1/35/177, Davies, 1924.

88 Civ. Sec. 1/19/59, 'Report on Dar Gimr', 1931, possibly by P. Broadbent.

89 CRO 2 Darfur Dar Masalit 51/1/1, Broadbent, 18 March 1931.

90 CRO Darfur 6/7/19.

91 SHAT Tchad carton 8, doss. 2, Col. Millot, 'Situation Ouadai 1909'.

92 SHAT Tchad carton 3, doss. 2, Rémond, 25 February 1929.

93 CRO Darfur 1/33/171, MacMichael, 1918.

94 CRO Darfur 1/34/172, Arkell, 4 December 1926. Dār Fūr (including Dār Masālīt) was a closed district after 15 October 1922. However, according to Darfur 3/3/2 the Government put restrictions on *jallāba* who were not genuine traders, rather than on traders. 'It has been brought to my notice that a considerable number of small gallaba traders roam about in the closed areas. The class of persons to whom I refer is not a genuine trader and has no capital or stock in trade .... He always poses as the educated Easterner well-versed in the ways of the Government and invariably pushes himself forward when the District Commissioner-Muauins etc. happen to pass by. This type of person is not to be encouraged' (Governor, Dār Fūr Province, 30 May 1925).

95 CRO Darfur 3/3/24, P. Sandison, 1935.

96 CRO Darfur 6/7/19.

97 CRO Darfur 1/34/175, P. B. Broadbent, annual report 1932.

98 CRO Darfur 5/3/11, Northern Darfur District (1931).

99 See note 97.

100 CRO Darfur 5/3/11, Northern Darfur District (1932).

101 CRO Darfur 1/34/175, E. Campbell, annual report 1933.

102 CRO Darfur 5/3/11, Northern Darfur District (1935).

103 CRO Darfur 1/34/175, P. J. Sandison, annual report 1934.

104 CRO Darfur 3/3/20, P. J. Sandison to Governor, Dār Fūr, 18 September 1934.

105 In Masālīt this was called *gonja* (Int. 5 and 12).

106 CRO Darfur 1/34/175, E. Campbell, annual report, 1934; He reported that the traveller was impressed by 'the efforts recently made, at the instigation of the Sultan, to cultivate a money crop in the form of cotton, chillies and onions.'

107 CHEAM, Berre, Mémoire 1804.

108 CRO Civ. Sec. 1/19/59, P. B. Broadbent, 'Report on Dar Gimr', 1931.

109 CRO Darfur 3/1/5, S. Redfern, 16 September 1923; 'The people were absorbed in existing villages', 'but number would be equivalent to about 30 villages.' See also 'The Political Situation in Wadai' (27

August 1928) in this same file.

110 The quotation is from CRO Darfur 1/34/175, P. Broadbent, annual report 1931. The reference to 'système dé' is from Darfur 1/34/172, R. Davies, 'Note on a visit to Abeshsha', 17 February 1921.

111 CRO Darfur 3/1/5, *passim*.

112 CRO Darfur 1/34/175, annual report 1928.

113 CRO Civ. Sec. 20/21/96, Grigg to Civil Secretary, 20 January 1927; and Int. 1/34/175, Sandison, annual report 1934.

114 CRO Darfur 1/34/172, Arkell, 4 December 1926; and Birks (1978), *passim* and 48–52.

115 For the flight of slaves at the beginning of colonial rule and the arrival of wage labour opportunities and colonial courts in French Africa, see Roberts and Klein (1980); and Warburg (unpublished, 1977). Int. 1, x, stressed that the slaves took the initiative in detaching themselves from their old masters if they had not been treated well. Those who had been treated properly continued to cooperate with their old masters in house-building, watering animals etc. Many slaves stayed 'but did not cooperate with ex-masters.' Many of the descendants of slaves figuring in his accounts now live in southern Dār Fūr. More research is certainly required on this topic.

116 For the definition of *ahl warrai*, see CRO Darfur 1/34/172, Arkell, 4 December 1926; and Int. 27, i. For the sultan's reluctance to pay taxes for his slaves, see CRO Civ. Sec. 1/18/58, Governor Dār Fūr (Bembroke) to Civil Secretary, 2 January 1927: 'Of the L.E. 500 outstanding December 1st, 1926, no less than L. 300 are due from villages lying within a 15 mile radius of Geneina, the inhabitants of which are all connected in one way or another with the Sultan himself.' For the figure 41%, see CRO Int. 1/21/120, 'List of Villages in Dar Masalit whose male cultivators show a marked decrease on 1925 list', under *amīn* Barra, who was responsible for the *ahl warrai* (according to CRO Civ. Sec. 57/7/28, September 1928).

117 See e.g. CRO Civ. Sec. 57/7/28 (June 1938); 'There is a normal exodus to the Gezira for "hishing" [cultivating]. The District Commissioner, Western Darfur District reports that the women are inciting their menfolk to go, in order that they may return laden with fancy silks etc.' Compare Civ. Sec. 1/19/59, 'Report on Dar Gimr', 1931, for references to the enormous number of deserted villages, among other things as a result of 'the migration of young men to find work'. Compare also CRO Darfur 1/21/120, for a list of villages which lost almost 50% of the male cultivators in 1925/6. According to Int. 5, people went east to earn the bridewealth.

118 For studies of neomahdism and the Sudan Government's relations with Sayyid 'Abd al-Raḥmān, see Daly (1980), 51–89; and Ḥasan

Aḥmad Ibrāhīm (1979 and 1980). This section is to a large extent based on CRO Darfur 1/21/120; Darfur 1/24/134; Darfur 3/3/20; Int. 9/2/28; Civ. Sec. 56/2/18, which includes A. J. Arkell's 'Note on Mahdism in Western Sudan'.

119 CRO Int. 9/2/28, and Darfur 3/3/20, which includes both the Arabic text and English translation of the Sayyid's answer, dated 19 September 1921.

120 CRO Int. 2/51/431, for English text of the translation.

121 CRO Darfur 3/3/20, 'Reported Rising in Zalingei District'; and a report by the Resident (Grigg), 8 February 1927.

122 CRO Civ. Sec. 56/2/18, Arkell, 1926.

123 CRO Darfur 1/24/134, Arkell, 22 September 1926.

124 idem.

125 CRO Darfur 3/3/20, Assistant Resident to Governor, Dār Fūr, 7 August 1936.

126 For the listing mania, see CRO Darfur 1/24/134, Arkell, 'Mahdism and Sultan Masalit', 22 September 1926; and Int. 1/21/120 (list of villages). 'They shall measure the land' etc. is a prophecy of the 17th century holy man Faraḥ wad Taktūk (Hillelson, 1935), 158. For the *faqīh*s who had been active in the risings of 1913–14, see CRO Darfur 1/21/20, Arkell, 21 August 1925.

127 CRO Darfur 1/3/20, Arkell, 4 August 1925.

128 CRO Darfur 1/24/134, Arkell, 22 September 1926, 'Mahdism and Sultan Masalit'; and CRO 1/21/120, Arkell to Governor Dār Fūr, 13 September 1925.

129 CRO Civ. Sec. 56/2/18, Arkell.

130 Int. 8.

131 Int. 15. According to Davies (CRO Darfur 1/34/172, 9 April 1921), Andōka became a Tijānī before the British came on the scene, namely on his succession. See Chapter 6, note 125. *Bushka* = *bukhsa* or pumpkin, often used as an ablution vessel by poor *faqīh*s; *andarāb* = *cordia rotii. Hijlīj* = *balanites aegyptica*; *tamtarūn* explained by the informant as the *rātib* of the Mahdī.

132 CRO Darfur 1/24/124, Intelligence Department, 27 October 1926, 'Report on Dar Masalit'.

133 Idem. The hymn was not unique to the Masālīt.

Appendix

Document I

بسم الله الرحمن الرحيم الحمد لله الوالى الكريم والصلاة على سيدنا محمد وآله مع التسليم وبعد فمن حضرة امير المومنين وناصر المظلومين وراحة الاسلام فى الدين عامل[1] المهدى السيد اسماعيل عبد النبى اطال الله ايامه وادام عزه ونصره آمين الى احبابنا فى الله الفقراء اهالى الفقيه مك كافة منا اليكم جزيل السلام ومزيدة التحياة والاكرام اما بعد فقد يكون معلومكم فها هو واصل لكم جوابنا بصحبة الفقيه مك هو المومة [2] من طرفنا فى امر الدين لاجل امار [3] بلدنا ونزول الرحمة فينا والبركة فى جميع افعالنا والنصر على اعدائنا والسكون مواطننا [4] فاجتمعوا عنده فى كل جمعة لاجل ختمة كتاب الله واشتغلوا بذلك فلو غاب

١٤ احد منكم او تخلف ٥ منه فيلزمه الاب ٦ فى ذلك

هذا ما عرفناكم به والسلام الف

١٣٠٣
سنة

جماد الثانى ٢١

Translation

In the name of God, the Compassionate, the Merciful. Praise be to God, the Ruler, the Noble, and blessing and peace upon our Lord Muḥammad and his family.

And thereafter: from the Commander of the Faithful and Protector of the Oppressed, and Support of Islam in religion, Agent[1] of the *Mahdī*, Lord Ismāʿīl ʿAbd al-Nabī, may God grant him a long life and make his fame and victory last, Amen.

To our beloved in God, the *faqīh*s, the people of *faqīh* Makki, from us to you many greetings, best wishes and respect.

And thereafter: Let be known to you this, what is reaching you through my son, *faqīh* Makki, sent by me[2] as representative in religious affairs, so as to make our country prosperous,[3] and so as to let God's mercy descend upon us, his blessings upon all our acts, victory over our enemies, and order in our home-country.[4] So gather around him on every Friday to recite the entire Book of God. Occupy yourselves with this. If any of you absents himself, or disobeys[5] him, then the Father[6] must compel him [to do] this.

This is what I informed you of. Thousand greetings.

21 Jumād II 1303, [i.e. 27 March 1886].

Notes

1 *ʿāmil*: title of Mahdist agent; it was substituted for the title of *'amīr* in May 1884. (See Holt 1970: 121)

2 *al-mūma*, for *al-muwajjah*, 'one who is sent'.

3 *amār* for *iʿmār*.

4 Correctly, *sukūn mawāṭininā*.

5 *takhalafa*: the final *fā'* is written with the dot below and short tail characteristic of the West African form of the Maghribī script.

6 *al-'Ab*: lit. the father; meant is here probably *al-faqīh* Makkī, but possibly the Sultan.

Document II

بسم الله الرحمن الرحيم الحمد لله الوالى الكريم
والصلاة على سيدنا محمد وءاله مع التسليم
ومن عبد ربه اسماعيل ابن عبد النبى الى اخوانى
الفقراء حملة فى يد سيدنا مك بن سيدنا الصمد
المرحوم مطر منى لكم السلام عليكم ورحمة
الله وبركاته فالذى نعلمكم به كان سابقا
انا امرت له لسيدنا المك فى افطار الفقراء
واعطوه ولا تخالفوه ابدا هل يكيل ولا
تتعارض له احد من الملوك ولا غيره
هذا ما عرفناكم به ١٣٠٣
سنة

الختم ١

Translation

In the name of God, the Compassionate, the Merciful. Praise be to God, the Ruler, the Noble, and blessing and peace be upon Our Lord Muḥammad and his family.

From the Servant of his Lord Ismāʿīl, son of ʿAbd al-Nabī, to my brothers the *faqīh*s, all those who are in the hand of our Lord Makkī, son of our Lord the late Lord Maṭar. Greetings from us to you, may the mercy and blessings of God be upon you.

What I inform you of [is this]:
Formerly I ordered *faqīh* Makki to collect *fiṭra* from the *faqīh*s; so give it to him and don't ever disobey him; let him measure out [the measure of grain due as *fiṭra*]. Let no one of the *malik*s or others oppose him.

This is what I have informed you of.

1303 [i.e. the year from October 1885 to October 1886].[1]

Note

1 The seal is illegible.

Document III

بسم الله الرحمن الرحيم الحمد لله الوالى الكريم وصلاة والسلام
على سيدنا محمد وآله مع التسليم وبعد [1] فمن [2] عبد ربه الفقيه مك
ابن الفقيه مك [3] الى حضرة من ايده الله الودود وخصه بالكرم
وجمله ظلا ظليلا وبحرا موردا محل الشفاعة [4] من الاباء
والجدود اعنى واخص بذلك صاحب المقام [5] العليه والقلب
امر نعيم واليد السخيه نسيل الله الكريم ان يحفظه
وينجيه من كل شر وبليه فداك امير المومنين سلالة
الطاهرين السلطان ابكر ابن سيد المرحوم اسماعيل عبد النبى
فسلام عليك ورحمة الله لديك فالذى نعرفكم به من جيهة
الحلال للفقيه مك ولا تتعرض فيهم من البوا . . . [6] والملوك [7]
والخلفاء [8] والنياب [9] والوزرا [10] والنجباء [11] و ملة الخداديم
لا تتعرضوا فى [12] حلاله الا باذن ولو فى حبلهم العرم الحظر
ثم الحظر بر خزى [13] وبلا فوة الراس ولكن المتعد لا
لا يلوم الا نفسه والسلام الف [14] ست فى شهر
الحجة

١٣٢٠

الختم : وفق يا
خليل ابكر
اسماعيل

Translation

In the name of God, the Compassionate, the Merciful. Praise be to God, the Ruler, the Noble, and blessing and peace upon Our Lord Muḥammad and his family.

And thereafter:[1] from[2] the Servant of his Lord, *faqīh* Makki, son of *faqīh* Makki.[3]

To him – may the loving God support him and bestow special kindness upon him, and make him an umbrageous shelter and a fresh lake, a place [to ask] for intercession[4] from the forefathers and ancestors – I mean, and I specifically refer thereby to him who has a high rank[5] and a contented heart, and a generous hand – we ask God, the Generous to preserve him and to protect him from all evil and calamity – him, the Commander of the Faithful, Offspring of the Blameless, Sultan Abbakr, son of the late Lord Ismāʿīl ʿAbd al-Nabī.

Greetings to you and may God's mercy be upon you. We inform you of [something] concerning the villages of *faqīh* Makki: Let no one of the [. . . . .][6] and *maliks*[7] and *khalīfas*[8] and deputies[9] and ministers[10] and prefects[11] interfere with them. Do not interfere with him in[12] his villages unless with permission, not even if [it concerns] a rope which has been thrown away.[13]

Beware, yes beware of violation[14] and stubbornness. Indeed the trespasser has no one to blame but himself.

Thousand greetings.[15]

The sixth [day] of the month of *al-Ḥijja* 1321 [i.e. 23 February 1904].

Exalted One
Give success
to
Abbakr Ismāʿīl

Notes

1 This letter is peculiar because it is in form a letter from *al-faqīh* Makki to Sultan Abbakr, while it is in content a decree from Sultan Abbakr to a number of local authorities and central government officials on behalf of, or in favour of *al-faqīh* Makki.
2 *fa min*: the fā has the dot below the letter.
3 *ibn al-faqīh Makki*: should be *ibn al-faqīh Maṭar*; see document II; this is also confirmed by oral tradition.
4 *al-shifāʿa*: the fā has the dot below the letter.
5 *al-maqām*: the qāf is written with only one instead of two dots; probably this is another 'Maghribism' or western influence.
6 *al-bawā* . . . : *lacuna* because of a hole in the paper.
7 *al-mulūk*: singular of *al-malik*, a local or 'tribal' authority, head of a section or subtribe of the Masālīt and title-holder to its land. (Compare the Masālīt title *dala*.)
8 *al-khulafāʾ*: plural of *al-khalīfa*, the traditional title of a village head in Dār Masālīt, now called *shaykh al-hilla*.

9 *al-niyāb*: plural of *al-nāyib*, deputy or representative; so far I have found no evidence of an official bearing this title in the Masālīt Sultanate, but meant is possibly a deputy of the Mahdist government.
10 *al-wuzarā'*: plural of *al-wazīr*, vizier or prime minister. Each Masālīt Sultan had only one *wazīr* at the time, namely: *Wazīr* Kunji during the reign of Sultan Abbakr (1888–1903), *Amīn* Dāʿūd Bōbale during that of Sultan Tāj al-Dīn (1905–1910), and Aḥmad Abū Shulūkh during the reign of Sultan Baḥr al-Dīn (1911–51).
11 *al-nujabā'*: plural of *al-najīb*, prefect, Mahdist title substituted for the title of *maqdūm* in May 1884. (See Holt 1970: 121.)
12 *fī*: the fā has the dot below the letter.
13 *ḥablihim al-marmi* (their thrown away rope) or *ḥablihim al-mubram* (their twined rope). In the first case one would have expected a yā at the end of the word, where there is none; in the second case one must read a dot under the bā where there is none. I prefer to read *al-ḥabl al-marmi* since the same expression is found in one of the documents of the Fūnj. (See Muḥammad Ibrāhīm Abū Salīm 1967:78.) Either way the expression means 'the smallest and most unimportant thing'.
14 *Khilāf*: the fā has the dot below the letter.
15 *'alf*: the fā has the dot below the letter.

Document IV (CRO Maydiyya, 2/5 I, doc. 72)

بسم الله الرحمن الرحيم الحمد لله الولى الكريم و
الصلاة على سيدنا محمد وءاله مع التسليم من بعد فمن
عبد ربه امير ابكر اسماعيل عبد النبى كان الله فى عونه
ونصر حزبه ءامين الى عند والدنا العامل عبد القادر
دليل دام الله قدره ءامين السلام عليك ورحمة الله و
بركاته قد حضر عندنا عزيز جوابك المبارك مع رسلكم
وفهمنا بما فى ضميره بارك الله فيك حبيناه ورضيناه
وانا نعرف الذى بينك وبين والدنا ان انتم اصحاب خير
ونحن كذلك على اثر والدنا ونحن متواصلين معكم
فى كل امر الا خفنا من امر الذى بقى فى والدنا هو مشا

بمراده وشوقه على اخوانه اصحاب المهدى و مشا ولم رجع عندنا الا ذلك نحن صبرنا فى بلدنا الى هذه الوقت وفى هذه السنة قصدونا البرقاو و السلاو والقمراو كلهم امرهم واحد ومكروا بى ويقولوا ان تدخل فى ديننا وتدرك [1] دين المهدى وانا قلت لا نحن امرنا وجدنا بامر المهدى وانتم سلاطين اهل العادات ولم نتبع كلامكم ولا دينكم والبرقاو اجتمع [2] حروبه مع ابو ريشة على ثلاث مواضع ودخلوا بمودعا واحد ونحن حروبنا قسمنا خمسة مكانات ها هو الخرب لنا دارنا ونحن سابقا قبل جوابك كتبنا

للمكرم محمود لاجل نحن كنا غرب وانتم اهلنا و مفزعنا وسنين كتب لنا وتعلم من هذا السنة [3] نحن امرنا معكم وفزعنا معكم ان كان تدخلوا بداجوا نحن معكم وان كان بدار برقو معكم وصول مكتوبى عندك ان البرقاو ارسل اقيد [4] المحاميد بالغش يتوجع ابو ريش وانا ما ندخل فى كلامهم والسلام الخ

الختم : وفق يا
خليل ابكر
اسماعيل

ان رفعوه انا نعرف كلامى وامرنا معكم سواء وان ما رفعوه انا نرسل لكم جواب باسرع
وانتم تفيضونا [5] بما يكون وانا وجملة اهلى كنت عند

جيهتكم

وها هو واصل لك ثلاث بغرات لاجل الدين هدية لك

وتعلم نحن مشغولين كنا فى الخلا ما عندنا شى فى يدنا

حتى نقصروا ونرجبوا ونعدوا لك شى طيب حتى ترضاه وتشكرنا

به والسلام الف

الختم : وفق يا

خليل ابكر

اسماعيل

Translation

In the name of God, the Merciful, the Compassionate. Praise be to God, the Noble Protector, and prayers and salutations be upon our Lord Muḥammad and his relatives.

Thereafter. From the servant of his Lord, *amīr* Abbakr Ismāʿīl ʿAbd al-Nabī – may God help him and make his party victorious, Amen.

To our father, *ʿamīl* ʿAbd al-Qādir Dalīl[6] – may God make his power last, Amen.

Peace be with you and God's mercy and blessings be upon you. Your noble and blessed letter reached us with your messengers. We have understood its contents – may God bless you. We loved it and were pleased with it. I know about [the relationship] between you and my father, that you were friends. We, in the same way, follow in the footsteps of our father, and we continue with you in everything [as he did]. But we were afraid [because] of what happened to our father. He left voluntarily and [because of] his desire [to see] his brothers, the companions of the Mahdī. He went away and did not come back to us. Therefore we patiently remained in our country until now. In this year the Borqāwi, Silāwi and Qimrāwi came to me sharing the same cause. They [tried to] deceive me saying, 'you must enter our religion and you must abandon the religion of the Mahdī.' I said, 'no, we earnestly adhere to the cause of the Mahdī, and you are sultans who adhere to traditional religion.[7] We will follow neither your words nor your religion.' The Borqāwi concentrated his troops, together with [those of] Abū Rīsha, on three spots, and they invaded [my country] on one spot. We have divided our troops into five parts. This caused the ruin of our country.[8] Earlier on, before the letter to you, we wrote to the Honourable Maḥmūd, because we are outsiders.[9]

You are our kinsmen and our refuge, and Sinīn[10] wrote to us. Know that from this year onwards, we will be on your side and you will be our refuge.[11] If you invade the Dājū, we will be on your side; if [you invade] Dār Borqū, we will be on your side. [After] the arrival of my letter, if the Borqāwi sends the *'aqīd al-Maḥamīd* with the deceit[ful message] that Abū Rīsha will return [to his own country], I will not heed their words. Thousand greetings.

[Seal:] Oh Exalted One, give success to Abbakr Ismā'īl. If they remove him [Abū Rīsha, from our country], we know that we are on your side both in word and deed. If they do not remove him, I will send you a letter as soon as possible. You must write to us about what will happen, and I and all my people are on your side.

Reaching you [from us] are three cows for the sake of the religion, a present to you. Know that we are busy and are residing in the bush. [Therefore] we have nothing with us [to give to you], so that we are falling short and are apologetic.[12] We will prepare something pıoper for you, so that you will be pleased with it and thank us for it. Thousand greetings.

[Seal:] Oh Exalted One, give success to Abbakr Ismā'īl.

Notes

1 Reading *tatruk* for *tadruk*; what appears to be a *dāl* is probably a discrete *tā'*.

2 Note the colloquial use of *ijtama'a*, which in standard (classical) Arabic cannot take an object.

3 One would expect here the feminine form of the demonstrative pronoun.

4 The usual spelling is *'aqīd*, meaning war captain. See glossary.

5 Reading *tufīdūnā* for *tufīḍūnā*.

6 'Abd al-Qādir Dalīl was one of the important army commanders of the *anṣār* in Western Sudan. He had been vice-governor of al-Fāshir during one of Maḥmud Aḥmad's absences. At the time of this letter he was in the country of the Banī Ḥalba.

7 An alternative translation is 'You are sultans of people of traditional religion.'

8 The expression *al-kharaba* is colloquial for *alladhī kharaba*.

9 *Gharab*: the translation is tentative. Compare below, document V, note 10.

10 Sinīn is Sinīn Ḥusayn, the Mahdist governor of Kabkābiyya.

11 Translating 'refuge', as if the text read *mafza'* rather than *faza'* ('fright').

12 The literal translation of *narjabū* is 'we are awed.' Note the colloquial verb endings. Colloquially *narjab* would mean 'I am in awe'; *narjabū* 'we are in awe.'

Document V (CRO Mahdiyya 2/5 I, doc. 70; no date, but probably written early in 1897)

بسم الله الرحمن الرحيم الحمد لله الولى الكريم والصلاة على سيدنا محمد وءاله مع التسليم من بعد فمن عبد ربه امير ابكر اسماعيل عبد النبى عامل المهدى عليه السلام بقسم مسلاة كان الله فى عونه ونصر حزبه ءامين الى عند سيد محمود احمد عموم دار فور [١] كان الله له معين ءامين السلام عليك ورحمة الله تعالى وبركاته سبب خطابى الباعث عليك تعلم ان امر المهدى جاء به كما جاء به رسول الله صلى الله عليه وسم [٢] كان سابقا والدى مشا عند السيد المهدى عليه السلام واعطاه المناشير وجع [٣] عند اهلنا مسلاة وطبعوا [٤] امر المهدى وطابعين [٤] حتى اتى الينا بدار فور سيد عثمان وفرحنا به وقلنا هذا المقصود نحن كنا غرباء ليس لناطبيق لعمالة المهدى وابى اسماعيل قام بمراده ولا غصبوه ولا جبروه الا لاعانه الدين وقدم بغاشر ولا رجع عندنا لهذا اليوم الاجل ذلك نحن خفنا ومن انت حضرت بدار فور ولا نظرنا فسالتك الا خايفين من امر الذى كان بوالدنا وتعلم ان انا طابع [٥] امر المهدى وانتم كذلك نحن ليس لنا اهل ءاخرين الا انتم اهلنا تعلم من هذا اليوم انا واهلى كلهم امرنا كنا معكم ان سابقا نحن نعاملوا مع البرقاو والداجاو وهم كانوا لى اعداء وعادونى

لا جل هم مخالفين امر المهدى وانا طابع[٥]

المهدى واخذة منهم نحاسات ادريس و

هم عادونى بالحروب ان شاء الله نجاهد معهم

دين الله منصور وانت اعانة لنا ونحن اعانه لك

وان كان حصل لنا امر فاسد نساونا واو

لادنا على طرفكم وشىء الذى نعطى لبرقوا

او لداجوا نعطوك انت تاكله افضل لنا والسلام الف

الختم : وفق يا

خليل ابكر

اسماعيل

Translation

In the name of God, the Merciful, the Compassionate. Praise be to God, the Noble Protector, and prayers and salutations be upon our Lord Muḥammad and his relatives.

Thereafter. From the servant of his Lord, *amīr* Abbakr Ismāʿīl ʿAbd al-Nabī, *ʿāmil* of the Mahdī – peace be upon him – in the district of Masalāh – may God support him and make his party victorious, Amen.

To Lord Maḥmūd Aḥmad, [Commander] General of Dār Fūr – may God help him, Amen.

Peace be with you and the mercy of God – Elevated is He – and his blessings be upon you. The reason of my letter, which I send to you, is [as follows]: Know that the Mahdī brought forward his cause as the Prophet of God – God bless him and grant him salvation – did. In the past my father went to his Lord, the Mahdī – peace be upon him. He was given the proclamations and returned to our people of Masalāh. They followed the Mahdist cause and continued to do so until Lord ʿUthmān came to us in Dār Fūr. We were glad about this, and we said, 'this is what we wanted.' We were outsiders and were not yet subject to the *ʿimāla* of the Mahdī.[6] My father Ismāʿīl left voluntarily, without being forced or compelled, and only to[7] support the religion. He went to al-Fāshir and has not come back to us until this day. Therefore we took fright, and from the time you arrived in Dār Fūr we did not look up or ask you,[8] but we were only afraid [because] of what happened to our father. Know that, from this day, I and all my people are on your side. In the past we cooperated with the Borqāwi and the Dājāwi. [However] they became enemies to me and treated me hostilely because they do not adhere to the Mahdist cause, while I follow the Mahdī. I took from them the kettle-drums of Idrīs [of Dār Qimr] and they sent troops against me. If God wills, we will fight the holy war with them, and God's religion will be victorious. You are a support for us as we are a support for you. If a grim fate befalls us, let our wives and children be on your side. What we used to give to Borqū or Dājū, we will give to you, for you to consume; for that is preferable to us. Thousand greetings.

[Seal:] Oh Exalted One, give success to Abbakr Ismāʿīl.

Notes

1 *ʿumūm Dār Fūr* should probably be *amīr ʿumūm Dār Fūr*, i.e. Commander-General of Dār Fūr. Compare Holt (1971), 76. Sultan Abbakr used the old titles which, by a decree of May 1884, had been changed.
2 The *lām* of *sallam* is missing.
3 I read *wa rajaʿa* for *wajaʿa*, but the *rā'* is missing.
4 Reading *tabaʿū* for *ṭabaʿū*, and *tābiʿīn* for *ṭābiʿīn*. The alternative reading, *ṭayaʿū*, and *ṭayiʿīn*, is excluded in the case of *ṭaba'ū*, in which the second consonant is clearly a *bā'*.
5 Reading *tābiʿ* for *ṭābiʿ*.
6 The translation of this sentence is tentative. As it has been interpreted here, Abbakr claims that the Masālīt had been independent from the governor (*ʿāmil*) before the arrival of ʿUthmān Jānū. The word *ghurabā*, the plural of *gharīb*, has the same root as *gharb*, meaning 'west', and may denote westerners here, although this would be impossible in standard (classical) Arabic. Compare document IV (CRO Mahdiyya 2/5 I, doc. 72), above note 11. For *ʿimāla*, see Holt (1971), 121, note 1.
7 This is a very colloquial use of *illā*.
8 The translation of *walā naẓarnā fa-sa'altak* is tentative. The construction is so colloquial that it is hard to understand.

Sources and bibliography

1 The oral sources

The oral sources used in this study have been collected in Dār Masālīt, during three field trips totalling seven months in 1978, 1979 and 1980; in al-Fāshir, during a shorter visit in 1979, in Dār Qimr, during a short visit in April 1980; and in Khartoum, in a series of interviews held from October 1980 to May 1981.

Although it may seem strange to emphasize gender in a discussion of oral data collected in western Dār Fūr, gender affected both the way in which oral sources were collected and what kind of data were collected from whom. As a foreign non-Muslim woman, the author could speak with male informants, but usually not in the same informal way as was possible with the women. Most of the oral information obtained from men, therefore, was collected through formal interviews and usually tape-recorded. The women – with some of whom the author spent several months in the same hut and compound – answered questions while cooking, pounding grain and watering the donkeys, shared spontaneous reminiscences of past times, but claimed ignorance in any situation distantly resembling that of a formal interview. Their oral testimonies have therefore often not been tape-recorded. In western Dār Fūr the social position and role of the men has always – even before a more thorough Islamization during the 1880s – been very different from that of the women. Politics and war, administrative matters such as taxation and justice, everything related to the public sphere, were traditionally, and still are, in the male domain. Most oral information about the political and administrative history of the sultanate was therefore collected from male informants. The women, whose responsibilities lay and lie mainly within the family, often knew little of past politics, but much about the facts of past daily life. Their testimonies are valuable for the social history of the Masālīt.

The author has held formal interviews with male informants of advanced age and of various social backgrounds all over Dār Masālīt (including Dār Sinyār, Dār Jabal and Dār Erenga). Most research among women was done in the district capital of El Geneina, where many old ladies remembered their royal past fondly and talked about it with pleasure. A small number of informants was selected for more intensive interviewing, partly because they were particularly knowledgeable, and partly because their openness and place of residence made them easily accessible. In El Geneina these were ʿAzza, ʿIda and Faṭima ʿAlī Ab Shanab, whose father had been a councillor of Sultan Baḥr al-Dīn (Int. 27); *ḥabbūba* Janna Ayyūb (Int. 43), whose father was a *faqīh* highly respected by Hajjām Ḥasab Allāh, and whose late husband was *khalīfa* Riziq, one of Sultan Abbakr's *bāsinga*; and al-*ḥājj* Dafaʿ Allāh ʿAjab Ibrāhīm (Int. 2), who has been a tax clerk and accountant in Dār Masālīt from 1927 until today. In Khartoum a long series of interviews was held with al-*ḥājj* Muḥammad Aḥmad ʿUmar Abū Lafta, who is about 103 years old and proved to be the most knowledgeable informant of all (Int. 1). Abū Lafta left Dār Masālīt in 1916 and joined the Sudan Defence Force. His father, *bāsī* Aḥmad ʿUmar, was one of Sultan Abbakr's *bāsinga* and district governors. He himself participated in all the sultanate's wars from 1905 onwards and married Sultan Baḥr al-Dīn's sister Zahra.

The oral sources used in this study are of four types:

1. eyewitness accounts;
2. topical songs composed (usually by women) to express grief, pride, praise or criticism on memorable occasions such as wars (these songs form an important control on the veracity of types 1 and 3);
3. hearsay accounts, oral testimonies transmitted to the informant by an eyewitness of his own or the previous generation;
4. public accounts, i.e. oral accounts of famous or generally known events, the sources of which are hard to trace. (Public accounts can be of great value not so much as evidence of facts, but as evidence of values; 'Once none of an audience can remember details of an event, or have their own perceptions and opinions about it, what is needed is a simplified, stylised account which concentrates on the meaning of the story' (Thompson, 1978, 111)).

Since slavery is in Dār Masālīt much more a taboo subject than e.g. in al-Fāshir, it has so far been impossible to interview (ex-)slaves, some of whom are still alive and known to the author. When reading the analysis of the social position and role of slaves in Dār Masālīt, the reader should keep this serious limitation in mind.

Wherever possible the author has referred to more than one source when annotating arguments presented in the text. The evaluation of a source or informant becomes even more crucial if that source is the only source for particular historical facts and phenomena, as was the case with some of the information obtained from al-*ḥājj* Muḥammad Aḥmad Abū Lafta. Abū Lafta was interviewed weekly for about four hours over a period of more than six months. The internal consistency of his accounts, which was checked by bringing up the same (and similar) topics more than once with an interval of a few weeks, proved very high, although the informant was weak on numbers and on dates before 1890. Abū Lafta's accounts often ended with a topical song or with a detailed account of the descendants of the persons who had figured in the anecdotes, including persons known to the author. Much of Abū Lafta's information was moreover confirmed by other oral sources, by the Arabic documents of the Mahdist Archives, or other archival material. For example, Abū Aja and *faqīh* Wābī, whom Abū Lafta (spontaneously) presented as the Wadai Sultan's envoys to Dār Masālīt in the 1880s and 1890s (Int. 1, vi), also figure in the Mahdist documents (CRO Mahdiyya 2/5, II doc. 141) and in Works (1976, 56/7). *Faqīh* Ḍalma, mentioned by Abū Lafta as a Dājū envoy to Dār Tāmā and the subject of a vulgar little song (Int. 1, ix, xix), figures in the correspondence of Sultan Bakhīt Abū Rīsha of Dār Silā (CRO Int. 2/2/11, 18 February 1915). Abū Lafta's stories about the battle of Chokōyan (Wadai 1912), in which he fought the French under the banner of Sultan Dūd Murra (Int. 1, iv), are confirmed by military reports in the French Archives (SHAT Tchad, Carton 1, doss. 4). Because examples of this kind are innumerable, information obtained from this informant has been used as the basis for a provisional analysis of some elements of the Masālīt past otherwise unknown.

List of informants

Int. 1 : al-*ḥājj* Muḥammad Aḥmad Abū Lafta, Khartoum, about 103 years old, in Arabic.

(i) 26 November 1980
(ii) 1 December 1980
(iii) 8 December 1980
(iv) 15 December 1980
(v) 21 December 1980
(vi) 24 December 1980
(vii) 27 December 1980
(viii) 31 December 1980
(ix) 6 January 1981
(x) 11 January 1981
(xi) 19 January 1981
(xii) 26 January 1981

(xiii) 28 January 1981
(xiv) 9 February 1981
(xv) 16 February 1981
(xvi) 23 February 1981
(xvii) 2 March 1981
(xviii) 9 March 1981
(xix) 16 March 1981
(xx) 23 March 1981
(xxi) 30 March 1981
(xxii) 6 April 1981
(xxiii) 13, 14 April 1978, in Masālīt and Arabic.

Int. 2 : al-*ḥājj* Dafa' Allāh 'Ajab Ibrāhīm, El Geneina, about 70 years old, in Arabic.
(1) 20–21 April 1978
(ii) 20–21 May 1978
(iii) 21 April–5 June 1978 (not taped).

Int. 3 : *shāyib* Kidik, Foro Buranga, 26 April 1978, over 60 years old, ex-*malik*, in Masālīt.

Int. 4 : Isḥaq Nahīd Haqqār and his brother Muḥammad, Foro Buranga, 30 April 1978, under 60 years old, *firsha* of the Sinyār, in Arabic.

Int. 5 : Adam Ḥasan Aḥmad, Kajenggessa, 2 May 1978, over 60 years old, cultivator, in Masālīt.

Int. 6 : Adam Ḥasan Zambūr and Bilāl Tūtū, Habila, 3 March 1978, over 60 years old, in Masālīt.

Int. 7 : *Shaykh* Ḥasan Muḥammad and others, Kujunung, 5 May 1978, under 60 years old, village head, in Masālīt.

Int. 8 : *Sayyidnā* Mā̧ Muḥammad 'Umar Ḥasan), Kaboska, 6 May 1978, over 60 years old, *faqīh* and leader of a *khalwa*, in Masālīt and Arabic.

Int. 9 : Mūsā Karāma Adinggi, 'Alī Arbāb Nūr Adinggi, Yaḥyā Karāma Addinggi, and others, Arara, 8 May 1978, varying ages, *firsha* of Arara and relatives, in Masālīt and Arabic.

Int. 10 : Muḥammad Ḥasan Adam (*shāyib* Tillo) and his wife, Beida, 10 May 1978, 92 years old, cultivator, in Masālīt and Arabic.

Int. 11 : *Abbo* Abū Bakr Badawī, Beida, 11 May 1978, under 60 years old, son of Badawī Abbakr, brother of Sultan Baḥr al-Dīn (1910–51), in Arabic.

Int. 12 : *Malik* Ibrāhīm 'Umar, Beida, 12 May 1978, under 60 years old, *malik* of the Manggare, in Arabic and Masālīt.

Int. 13 : *Shāyib* Maḥmūd Jambe and al-*ḥājj* 'Abd Allāh Ḥasan, Misterei, 13 May 1978, over 60 years old, son of a late *firsha* of the Mistereng and his relative or friend, in Masālīt and Arabic.

Int. 14 : *Shāyib* Bishāra ʿUmar Ijeibir, Misterei, 15 May 1978, over 60 years old, relative of the *wazīr* of Sultan Baḥr al-Dīn, *amīn* Aḥmad Ijeibir ʿAb Shulūkh', in Masālīt.
Int. 15 : *Shāyib* ʿAbd al-Banāt, Abū Sōga, 15 May 1978, over 60 years old, cultivator, in Masālīt.
Int. 16 : *Shāyib* ʿUmar Jihādiyya, El Geneina, 17 May 1978, over 60 years old, member of the royal clan, in Arabic.
Int. 17 : *Shāyib* ʿAbdullāhi Dingeis, El Geneina, 20 May 1978, *faqīh*/trader, in Masālīt.
Int. 18 : Jār al-Nabī Sayyāf Digeis, Kereinik, 23 May 1978, under 60 years old, ex-*amīn* of Sultan Baḥr al-Dīn, in Arabic.
Int. 19 : *Firsha* ʿAbdullāhi Abū Bakr Zubayr, Kereinik, 23 May 1978, about forty years old, *firsha*, in Arabic.
Int. 20 : *Shāyib* Dunggi, Salāmī, 24 May 1978, over 60 years old, cultivator, in Masālīt.
Int. 21 : *Shāyib* Bilāl, Mogornei, 28 May 1978, over 60 years old, cultivator, in Masālīt.
Int. 22 : *Firsha* Dā'ūd Idrīs, Sirba, 2 June 1978, under 60 years old, *firsha* of the Erenga, in Arabic.
Int. 23 : *Bāsī* Abbakr Muḥammad, Silaya, 3 June 1978, over 60 years old, in Arabic.
Int. 24 : Muḥammadayn Muḥammad Adam, Abū Surūj, 4 June 1978, cultivator, in Arabic.
Int. 25 : *Shāyib* al-Dūm Adam Ibrāhīm, Sirba, 5 June 1978, óver 60 years old, cultivator, in Arabic.
Int. 26 : Maḥāsin and Khadīja Yaʿqūb Abū Bakr, Kabkābiyya, 15 June 1978, under 40 years old, in Arabic (not taped).
Int. 27 : ʿAzza, ʿIda, Faṭima and Zamzam ʿAlī ab Shanab, El Geneina.
(i) 21 April–5 June 1979 (not taped)
(ii) April 1980 (untaped)
Int. 28 : Ibrāhīm Haqqār Ḥanafī, Foro Buranga, 7 May 1979, 62 years old, janitor, relative of a former *firsha* of the Sinyār, in Arabic.
Int. 29 : Al-*ḥājj* Sulaymān ʿAbd Allāh Muḥammad Bannata, Tamar, 9 May 1979, 71 years old, cultivator, in Arabic.
Int. 30 : Al-*ḥājj* Daldūm Khalīfa Daldūm, Foro Buranga, over 60 years old, in Arabic, interviewed by Ibrāhīm Yaḥyā in 1977.
Int. 31 : *Shaykh* Khamīs and others, Marissa, varying ages, in Arabic, interviewed by Ibrāhīm Yaḥyā in 1977.
Int. 32 : *Ammo* Ḥalīma Abbakr, al-Fāshir, 8 June 1979, over 60 years old, daughter of Sultan Abbakr (1888–1905), in Arabic (untaped).
Int. 33 : *ʿAjūz* Ashta, al-Fāshir, 8 June 1979, over 60 years old, in Arabic (not taped).

Int. 34 : Ṣadīq Abū Yamanī, al-Fāshir, 9 June 1979, under 60 years old, trader, in Arabic (not taped).

Int. 35 : Manṣūr and Ismāʿīl Abū Safīta, al-Fāshir, 9 and 11 June 1979, under 60 years old, traders, in Arabic (not taped).

Int. 36 : ʿAlī al-*hājj* Badawī Zayn al-ʿAbdīn, al-Fāshir, 10 June 1979, over 60 years old, trader, in Arabic (not taped).

Int. 37 : *Amīr* Sulaymān ʿAlī Dīnār, al-Fāshir, 11 and 12 June 1979, over 60 years old, son of Sultan ʿAlī Dīnār (1898–1916), in Arabic (not taped).

Int. 38 : *Abbo* ʿAlī Idrīs Abū Bakr and Muḥammad Bāliḥ Sarjayn, Kulbus, 12 April 1980, over 60 years old, of the Qimr royal family, in Arabic (untaped).

Int. 39 : A daughter of Sultan Idrīs Abū Bakr of Dār Qimr, Kulbus, 12 April 1980, about 60 years old, in Arabic (partly taped).

Int. 40 : Sultan ʿUthmān Hāshim of Dār Qimr, Kulbus, 12–13 April 1980, in Arabic (partly taped).

Int. 41 : *Shāyib* Umbaḍḍī Aḥmad Abbakr, Kulbus, 13 April 1980, over 60 years old, trader, in Arabic.

Int. 42 : *ʿAjūz* Ḥalīma, El Geneina, 16 April 1981, over 60 years old, wife of the late Sultan Tāj al-Dīn (1905–10), in Arabic (untaped).

Int. 43 : *Ḥabbūba* Janna Ayyūb, El Geneina, 17, 19, 21 April 1980, about 100 years old, wife of the late *khalīfa* Riziq, right hand of the first sultans of the Masālīt, in Arabic.

Int. 44 : *Faqīh* Ismāʿīl ʿUmar, El Geneina, 19 April 1980, over 60 years old, *faqīh*, in Arabic.

Int. 45 : *ʿAjūz* Atiyya Aḥmad Abū Lafta, El Geneina, 22 April 1980, over 60 years old, sister of informant 1, in Arabic.

Int. 46 : Sanūsī al-Naffār, El Geneina, 6 June 1979, under 60 years old, trader, in Arabic.

Int. 47 : Adam ʿAbd al-Raḥmān Nurayn and Muḥammad Adam Nurayn, El Geneina, 5 June 1979, under 60 years old, *firsha* of the Nyerneng and his close relative, in Arabic (not taped).

Int. 48 : *Faqīh* Abū'l-Qāṣim Ibrāhīm Sanūsī, El Geneina, 3 June 1979, over 60 years old, son of a former judge (*qāḍī*) of Dār Masālīt, in Arabic (not taped).

Int. 49 : Sultan ʿAbd al-Raḥmān Baḥr al-Dīn, El Geneina, 2 June 1979, under 60 years old, in Arabic.

Informants 3–25 were interviewed by myself and Ibrāhīm Yaḥyā together.

2 The archival sources

(i) Khartoum, Central Records Office (CRO)

(a) The Mahdist Archives

Mahdiyya, *Daftar qabad al-awāmir al-ṣādira min al-Mahdī li umarā' al-jabhāt*, 1–23 (19 December 1884 to 27 May 1885).

Mahdiyya 1/10, *Muḥammad Khālid Zuqal to the Khalīfa*, volume I, 21 April 1885 to 5 June 1890. The earlier correspondence of Muḥammad Khālid could not be located in the storerooms.

Mahdiyya 1/12,	*'Uthmān Adam to the Khalīfa*,
volume II,	28 February to 30 May 1888
volume III,	9 June to 5 November 1888
volume IV,	6 September 1889 to December 1889
volume V,	4 January 1889 to 26 August 1889
volume VI,	28 April 1889 to 26 August 1889
volume VII,	14 September 1889 to 17 September 1890

Mahdiyya 1/13,	*The Khalīfa to 'Uthmān Adam*,
volume V,	10 September 1889 to May/June 1891.

Mahdiyya 1/13,	*Maḥmūd Aḥmad to the Khalīfa*,
volume I,	17 August 1890 to 7 August 1891 (1308 H.)
volume II,	7 August 1891 to 26 July 1892 (1309 H.)
volume III,	26 July 1892 to 15 July 1983 (1310 H.)

Mahdiyya 1/14,	*Maḥmūd Aḥmad to the Khalīfa*,
volume III,	4 October 1895 to 10 May 1897.

Several files of correspondence of Maḥmūd Aḥmad could not be located in the storerooms.

Mahdiyya 1/16,	Miscellaneous

Mahdiyya 2/5,	Miscellaneous correspondence
volume I	
volume II	

Mahdiyya 2/36,	Miscellaneous correspondence

Mahdiyya 2/37,	Miscellaneous correspondence

(b) The Condominium Archives

Darfur

1/1/1 : Darfur Province Native Administration.
1/1/3 : Darfur Nyala Rising, 1921, Patrol 99.
1/1/4 : Nyala Rising outlaws, general correspondence.
1/1/5 : Darfur Nyala Rising outlaws, individual cases.
1/2/7 : Rumoured Uprising in Northern Darfur.
1/4/17 : Occupation of Darfur, Senussi activities and western frontier posts 1916.
1/4/18 : Army, Occupation of Darfur, Int. reports from H. A. MacMichael, 1915–16.
1/4/19 : Army Occupation of Darfur, Correspondence with 'Ali Dinar, 1915–16.
1/4/21 : Memorandum concerning future status of Darfur, 1916.
1/18/19 : MacMichael's Reports, 1918, on Darfur Masalit.
1/18/95 : MacMichael's Darfur Who is Who
1/18/96 : The Fur Royal Family.
1/19/102: Nyala Rising, 1921.
1/21/120: Religion, Mahadism, Pilgrimage to Aba.
1/23/126: Religion, Mahadism, Mahadist Agents, Fiki Muhagir at Guggu, January 1927.
1/23/128: Religion and Mahadism, Nebi Isa Cult.
1/24/134: Mahadism in Darfur, October 1923–March 1936.
1/31/163: Zaghawa, Dar Gilla, Dar Artag, Dar Tour.
1/31/164: Undesirables 1923.
1.31.165: Undesirables 1929, individual cases.
1/33/169: Events in Darfur 1898–1912.
1/33/170: Events on Western Frontier, 1899–1910.
1/33/171: Dar Masalit Administrative Affairs General 1918.
1/34/172: Idem, 1921–6.
1/34/173: Idem, 1927–44.
1/34/174: Dar Masalit Administrative Affairs, Judicial System.
1/34/175: Dar Masalit Confidential Annual Reports, 1924–39.
1/35/176: Dar Masalit Reports 1939.
1/35/177: Dar Masalit Finance General.
1/35/178: Local Government Policy, General Correspondence.
1/34/173: Dar Masalit Administrative Affairs General, 1927–44.
1/36/182: Local Government, Local Administration, Northern District 1925–32.
1/36/183: Idem, Western District, Zalingei.
1/37/185: Local Government, Native Administration, Zalingei, 1929–32.
1/37/188: Darfur Province, Local Government Reports, Notes on Darfur Administration, 1928.

3/1/1 : Dar Masalit, Agriculture.
3/1/2 : Dar Masalit, Education.
3/1/5 : Dar Masalit, Immigration and Emigration.
3/3/17 : Dar Masalit Legal, Criminal Cases
3/3/20 : Mahadism, Special Cases in Dar Masalit.
3/3/21 : Dar Masalit, Annual Reports, 1924–32.
3/3/22 : Dar Masalit, Slavery.
3/3/23 : Trading in Closed Districts.
3/3/24 : Finance Dar Masalit.
4/1/5 : Religion.
4/1/6 : Slavery.
5/2/9 : Northern Darfur District, Annual Reports, 1935–37.
5/3/11 : Idem, 1931–1934.
6/2/5 : Dar Fur Province, Annual Reports 1939–44, Zalingei.
6/6/14 : Western District Reports.
6/7/19 : Handbook of Western Darfur by Mr Beaton; introduction by J. E. H. Boustead.
64/6/42 : Control of Markets Darfur.

2 Darfur Kutum

41/4/2 : Dar Fia – Fur boundaries 1922–70.
41/4/13 : Gimr 1931–41.
41/4/14 : Beni Hussein subfiles, 1948–70.

2 Darfur Dar Masalit

6/1/1 : District Boundary Western Darfur/Dar Masalit, 1920–40.
30/2/8 : Death of Bahr al Din.
41/2/7 : Weights and Measures General.
48/1/1 : Dar Gimr, Administrative Organization, 1931–58.
50/1/1 : Local Administration, 1928–57.
51/1/1 : P. B. Broadbent, Dar Gimr Administrative Organization, 18 March 1931.

Intelligence

1/1/1–
1/3/10 : Ten files with Wadai/Darfur Boundary Correspondence, 1909–25.
1/3/11 : Darfur/Wadai Boundary Incidents, 1926–8.
1/19/98 : Darfur, Report on Dar Masalit by H. A. MacMichael, 1918.
2/1/3 : Ali Dinar, Darfur/Wadai Frontier Affairs, 1911.
2/2/10–
2/5/20 : Ali Dinar Historical, 1901–16 (11 files).

2/5/21 : Ali Dinar, Sharif Mahmud Talaat, 1911–23.
2/6/25 and
2/5/26 : Darfur Miscellaneous.
2/6/27 : Darfur Administration, 1916.
2/2/102 : Darfur, Report on Tour of Inspection by H. A. MacMichael, 1916–17.
2/12/103: Darfur Historical.
2/13/105: Darfur, Hussein Mohd. Hasaballa of Masalit, 1919.
2/15/125: Western Sudan, Senussi, Wadai, 1901–7.
2/15/126: Western Sudan, Borgu.
2/15/127: Wadai, Historical and Descriptive, Senussi, Wadai, Western Sudan etc.
2/31/258: Letters and Messengers from Mohammed Bakhit, Sultan of Dar Sula, 1911–15.
2/51/429: Darfur, Unrest in Dar Masalit, Report by Resident Kereinik.
2/51/430: Darfur, Unrest in Dar Masalit 1922; Zeka Assessment Dar Masalit, 1921–2.
2/51/431: Darfur, Dar Masalit 1922.
5/3/17 : Translation of Extracts from Diaries of Messedaglia, 1878–81.
5/3/20 : Proclamation by Sultan of Dar Sula.
5/3/27 : Memorandum on Western Sudan.
5/3/36 : Journey and Death of Boyd Alexander, 1909–10.
5/3/37 : Precis of the History of Darfur since 1874, H. A. MacMichael, 1915.
5/3/38 : Notes on the Tribes of Darfur, H. A. MacMichael.
5/3/39 : Notes on Darfur, Wadai, Dar Tama, H. A. MacMichael, 1916.
5/8/88 : Mr R. Davies, Confidential Reports.
7/4/10 : Ali Dinar, Translations of Letters, 1914–16, Syme's Private file.
7/5/1–
7/5/14 : Ali Dinar Miscellaneous Letters, 1901–13.
8/1/1 : Darfur.
9/1/8 : Nyala Rising.
9/1/12 : Who's Who (Darfur Province).
9/2/26 : Nebi Isa.
9/2/28 : Writings and Circulars 1916–20, Miscellaneous.
11/3/12 : Sudan Intelligence Reports, 1903–4.

Civ. Sec.

1/18/55 : Occupation and Administration of Dar Masalit.
1/18/56 : The Administration of Dar Masalit.
1/18/58 : Dar Masalit Administrative Headquarters, 1926–8.
1/19/59 : Dar Masalit Administration.

20/20/95: The Finances of Dar Masalit.
20/21/96: Darfur Province, Dar Masalit Native Administration Budget.
56/2/18 : Mahdism General.
57/7/28 : Province Monthly Diaries 1938, Darfur Province.
66/6/19 : Visit of Mr R. Davies, Resident of Dar Masalit, to Nigeria.
66/8/51 : Sultanate of Dar Kabja.
66/10/96: Powers of Nomad Sheikhs, Darfur.
112/2/5–
112/2/7 : Ali Dinar Historical.
112/3/9 : Notes on the Tribes of Darfur by H. A. MacMichael.
112/9/64: Anthropological and Historical Records, Tribal: Masalit, Gimr, Erenga, Mun, Tama.
122/1/1 : Southern and Western Darfur, Patrol 99.
122/1/3 : Darfur, Narrative of Events, 1916–17.
122/1/4 : Darfur Miscellaneous.

Cair. Int.

3/5/84 : Early Events in Darfur; Statement of Bim. Abdalla, Cairo 2.7.1890.
3/9/172 : Notes au sujet de la liquidation des provinces soudaniennes envahies, 1884, Vaillant.
3/10/192: Memorandum on the Sudan, Wingate, Cairo, 12 May 1889.
3/11/200: Wingate, General Report on the Egyptian Sudan.
3/18/300: Memorandum on the Western Sudan and Proclamation of Sultan of Dar Sula, Wingate 1891–3.
10/22/55: Darfur Boundaries, 1913.

(ii) Dār Fūr Province

(a) al-Fāshir

The Dār Fūr Province Archives in al-Fāshir no longer exist in the form in which they were consulted by R. S. O'Fahey. Some of the files have been sent to the CRO, Khartoum, while the rest have been dumped in a far from perfect storeroom. The author was kindly permitted to dig out a number of old files, but a systematic and thorough study of the archives was impossible.

(b) El Geneina

The storeroom in El Geneina, which the author together with Ibrāhīm Yaḥyā, has thoroughly searched, contains only a few early files from the 1920s and 1930s. Dar Masalit District 95.A, Dar Gimr administrative Policy 1931–61, was one of these files; it contained many original letters from Sultan Idrīs Abū Bakr. More recent files (1940s and 1950s) were in a very poor state.

(iii) Paris

(a) Archives Nationales Section Outre Mer (ANSOM)

Afrique VI

dossier 177:	Affaires diplomatiques: 1901–5.
dossier 182:	Affaires diplomatiques: 1899–1902: (a) Centre Africain et Soudan Oriental (b) Situation au Baguirmi et au Kanem
dossier 182 bis:	Affaires diplomatiques: Ouadai–Darfour: 1906–1907.
dossier 183:	Affaires diplomatiques: 1910 (a) Renseignements sur la situation du Ouadai et l'affaire du Massalit: Délimitation Ouadai–Darfour et rapports avec le sultan du Darfour (b) Attaque de la colonne Moll au Ouadai: Opérations de police anglaises au Kordofan
dossier 184:	Affaires diplomatiques: Ouadai–Darfour: 1910–11 (a) Rapport Julien sur le Dar Massalit Ambouze et sur les opérations des troupes du Ouadai au Tama et contre le Massalit. (b) Attaque massalit des colonnes Fiegenschuh et Moll à Bir Taouil et Dridjéle. (c) Opération contre les Massalit et Doudmourah, le soulèvement des Kodoi et le projet d'occupation de Borkou.
dossier 185:	Affaires diplomatiques: Ouadai: 1910–1913 (a) Politique saharienne et droit de suite dans les régions inorganisées: Darfour et Fezzan (b) Relations extérieures: Tripolitaine, Senoussia, Massalit; Délimitation avec le Darfour.
dossier 186:	Affaires diplomatiques: Ouadai–Darfour: 1911–1913, Délimitation.
dossier 187:	Affaires diplomatiques: Ouadai–Darfour: 1910–13; Agissements du sultan du Darfour Ali Dinar; Demande anglaise de délimitation et question du Massalit et du Tama, considerés comme parties du Darfour par les autorités du Soudan anglo-egyptien.
dossier 188:	Affaires diplomatiques: 1913; Délimitation Ouadai–Darfour; Mémoire du colonel Largeau sur les droits de la France sur le Tama et le Massalit.

dossier 189: Affaires diplomatiques: 1912–1914; Délimitation Ouadai–Darfour.

dossier 190: Affaires diplomatiques: 1915–1916: Ouadai–Darfour
(a) Opérations anglaises contre Ali Dinar, sultan du Darfour;
(b) Agissements d'Ali Dinar et opérations anglaises au Darfour
(c) Opérations dans le centre africain et capture du sultan Sila, appuyant les opérations anglaises au Darfour.

Tchad I

dossier 6: Correspondance générale: 1911–12, Ouadai, Borkou, Tibesti.

dossier 7: Correspondance générale: 1910–12, situation au Tibesti, au Borkou, au Ouadai–Darfour.

dossier 8: Correspondance générale: 1912–14, Rapports sur les événements de mars–avril, mai–juin 1914, du colonel Largeau.

dossier 9: Correspondance militaire: 1913, Mémoire ayant pour objet de faire ressortir 'les droits de la France sur le Tama et le Massalit', par le colonel Largeau.

Papiers d'agents

6PA Papiers Julien, carton 1, including Extraits des Bulletins de Renseignments de 1912 à 1914, and Détail de Correspondance, 1910.

(b) Service Historique de l'Armée de Terre (SHAT)

carton 1 : including Opérations environs d'Abéché, 1909–11.

carton 2 : Tchad 1911, Tchad 1912–14.

carton 3 : Chad 1909; Correspondance, Notes, Ordres de Mouvements, Circonscription du Ouaddai, 1909–18; Correspondance du Territoire militaire du Tchad du 2 février 1910–29 mai 1914; Régistre de Correspondance de la subdivision de Goz Beida, 1913–14.

carton 4 : Capt. Mounier, Reconnaissance au Djebel Zaghawa et Ennedi, 18 juillet–16 septembre 1915; Col. Hilaire, Colonne du Sila.

carton 5 : including notes on the massacre of the *faqīh*s, 1918; and Col. Largeau's 'Colonne au Dar Sila, mai/juin 1916'.

carton 8 : Tchad: Ouadai, Archives 1904–22; Correspondance du départ, Abéché, 8 mai 1911–20 juin 1914; Régistre du correspondance du Bataillon du Ouaddai, 12 avril 1916–8 mars 1918.

carton 9 : includes Carnet de Poste Sila, 1912–1937.
carton 12: includes Étude Géographique du District d'Adre, 1956; Capt. Nalgas, Monographie du District de Biltine, 1948; Ouaddai, 1908–20; Historique des operations militaires au Ouaddai, 1955; Monographie Abéché, 1961.
carton 19: Documentation sur le Soudan; Capt. Canavaggio, Documentation sur le Dar Massalit, 8 mars 1955, 1–53; Col. Grossard, Délimitation de frontières Ouadai–Darfour, 1921; Darfour.
carton 20: Tchad, Région du Tchad, Département du Ouadai, 1962.

(c) Centre des Hautes Etudes Administratives sur l'Afrique et l'Asie Modernes (CHEAM)

Berre, H.: El Hadj Mustapha Ould Bakhit, Mémoire 1804, 10 novembre 1951, 1–124.
Berre, H.: Les Sultanats du Tchad, Mémoire 2005, 10 octobre 1951.
Cazenave, A. J.: Les Minorités Musulmanes au Nord Est Tchadien; Sultanats des Dâr Zaghawa et Dâr Tama.

(d) Bibliothèque de l'Institut de France (B.I.F.)

MS 6004: Papiers Colonel Largeau, 1911–1912.
MS 6005: Papiers Colonel Largeau, 1914; Col. Simonet, Rapport de Reconnaissance sur les confins du Sila, Goz Beida, le 28 juillet, 1914.
MS 6006: Rapport de la reconnaissance Goz Beida – Djale – Kafiakingi, 15 avril–14 juillet 1913; Rapport du Capt. Gillet, Toumtouma, 13 août 1913; Aperçu géographique de la région du Dar Tama parcouru en juillet 1913.
MS 6013: Capt. Toureng, Soudan anglo-égyptien, reconnaissance de février et mars 1913 et de mai, juin, juillet 1913 dans le Sud-Est de la Circonscription du Selamat et la région frontière de l'Oubangui-Chari-Chad et du Soudan Anglo-Egyptien; Col. Grossard, Soudan égyptien, 1924; Mission d'Albert Bonnet de Mezières en Égypte, 1911.

(iv) London

(a) School of Oriental and African Studies, University of London (SOAS)

The Papers of Dr A. J. Arkell, who served in Dār Fūr in 1921–6 and again in 1932–7, and was Assistant-Resident of Dār Masālīt from December 1921–October 1926. The papers were deposited in two batches. The

material used in this study is all from the second batch. Prof. P. M. Holt has made a checklist of the papers. Dr R. S. O'Fahey has described them in SNR, 1974, 172–4.
The Papers of Prof. P. M. Holt, which have been deposited only recently, contain notes and copies of documents from the Mahdist Archives.

(b) Public Records Office (PRO)

The Foreign Office Series (Boundaries, Soudan, Wadai, Darfur, Tripoli, and Massalit) contains much valuable information for the present subject. Part of these files has been consulted.

(v) Durham

School of Oriental Studies, University of Durham, Sudan Collection

The Arabic Archive contains a number of letters of the western sultans during the Mahdiyya.
Of the papers deposited by ex-members of the Sudan Civil Service, those of P. J. Sandison and B. A. Lewis proved most useful for this study.

(vi) Bergen

Photographic collection of Arabic documents photographed by R. S. O'Fahey in Dār Fūr between 1970 and 1976.

3 Travel literature

Browne, W. G. (1806), *Travels in Egypt, Syria and Africa*, London, 2nd edition.
Burckhardt, J. L. (1822), *Travels in Nubia*, London, 2nd edition.
Cuny, C. (1854), 'Notice sur le Darfour', *BSG*, 4e série, viii, 81–120.
Ensor, F. S. (1881), *Incidents on a Journey through Nubia to Darfoor*, London.
Felkin, R. W. (1884–5), 'Notes on the For Tribe of Central Africa', *Proceedings of the Royal Society of Edinburgh*, xiii, 205–265.
Fraccaroli, A. (1880), 'Gita commerciale nel Cordofan e Darfur', *L'Esploratore*, v, 161–6, 205–7.
Massari, A. M. (1880), 'Spedizione Principe Borghese', *L'Esploratore*, v. 34–7.
Massari, A. M. (1881), 'La Spedizione Borghese, Conferenza di A. M. Massari tenuta alla Societa Geografica il giorno 18 dicembre 1881', *Bolletino della Societa Geografica Italiana*, 812–37.

Matteucci, P. and A. M. Massari (1880), 'La Spedizione Borghese', *Bolletino della Societa Geografica Italiana*, 598–600, 708 ff.

Messedaglia, G. B. (1879), 'Via Commerciale del Sudan, Dongola-Cordofan-Darfur-Uadai', *L'Esploratore*, iv, 84–89.

Messedaglia, G. B. (1880), 'Via Commerciale nel Darfur', *L'Esploratore*, v, 70–79.

Messedaglia, G. B. (1886), *Diario Storico Militare delle Revolte al Sudan di 1878 in poi*, Alexandria.

Nachtigal, G. (1871), 'Beschreibung von Wara, der Hauptstadt von Wadai', *Zeitschrift der Gesellschaft für Erdkunde zu Berlin*, vi, 526–41.

Nachtigal, G. (1875), 'Originalkarte der Länder im Süden von Wadai und Dar-For Nach seiner Reisen und Erkundigungen zusammengestellt von Dr. —, *Zeitschrift der Gesellschaft für Erdkunde zu Berlin*, x, Tafel II (Maasstab 1:3,000,000).

Nachtigal, G. (1876–7), 'Handel im Afrika', *Mitteilungen Geographische Gesellschaft, Hamburg*, 305–326.

Nachtigal, G. (1971), *Sahara und Sudan*, vol. iv: Wadai and Darfur, transl. A. G. B. and H. J. Fisher, London.

Parravicina, E. (1881), 'Societa d'Esplorazione commerciale i Africa. Commemorazione Pellegrino Matteucci', *L'Esploratore*, 321–8.

Seetzen, U. J. von (1813), 'Nouveaux Renseignements sur l'intérieur de l'Afrique, III, notions sur le Dar-Four, du pays de Four, recueillies de la bouche d'un indigène', *Annales des Voyages de la Geographie et de l'Histoire*, xxi, 145–179.

Stone, le Général (1881), 'Le Général, E. S. Purdy Pacha, Notice Nécrologique', *BSKG*, 2e série, i, novembre, 57–64.

El-Tounsy, le Cheikh Mohammed Ebn-Omar (1845), *Voyage au Darfour*, transl. N. Perron, Paris.

El-Tounsy (1851), *Voyage au Ouadây*, transl. N. Perron, Paris.

Al-Tūnisī, Muḥammad ibn 'Umar, see El-Tounsy, le Cheikh Mohammed Ebn-Omar.

Vecchi, H. de (1885), 'Pellegrino Matteucci', *BSKG*, série 2, vi, February, 295–312.

Vedova, G. Dalla (1885), 'Pellegrino Matteucci ed il suo Diario inedito', *Bolletino della Societa Geografica Italiana*, 641–73.

4 Theses, forthcoming papers and articles and mimeographs

'Alī 'Abd Allāh Abū sinn (1968), 'Mudhakira 'an mudīriyya Dār Fūr', CRO, Khartoum.

'Alī Ḥasan Tāj al-Dīn (no date), 'Tārīkh Dār Masālīt', Cairo.

Amin, S. (1977), 'The Debate on Precapitalist Societies. Is It Useful?',

United Nations, African Institute for Economic Development and Planning, Dakar.

Cordell, D. (1977), 'Dar al-Kuti: A History of the Slave Trade and State Formation on the Islamic Frontier in Northern Equatorial Africa', PhD thesis, University of Wisconsin, Madison.

Davies, R. (no date), 'The Masalit Language', M.S. University of Khartoum.

Doornbos, P. A. (1979), 'Arabisation, Ethnic Identity and Social Change in Western Darfur', Interim Report.

Doornbos, P. A. (1979), 'Ecological Transformation in Darfur's Western District, Sudan'.

Doornbos, P. A. (1980), 'Arabisation, Ethnic Identity and Social Change in Western Darfur', Interim Report.

Doornbos, P. A. (1981), 'The Haddad of Chad and Sudan; an African Pariah Caste'.

Doornbos, P. A. (1982), 'The Languages of the Chad–Sudan Border (Wadai and Darfur)', in M. L. Bender, ed., *Eastern Sudanic Studies*, vol. ii, Linguistics.

Hill, P. (1977), 'Comparative West African Farm-Slavery (south of the Sahel) with Special Reference to the Muslim Kano Emirate (N.Nigeria)', presented to the Conference on Islamic Africa, Slavery and Related Institutions, Princeton University, June 12–19.

Ibrāhīm Yaḥyā 'Abd al-Raḥmān (1980), 'Contribution on some Aspects in the Description of the Masalit Language', B.A. Honours Thesis, University of Khartoum, Department of Linguistics.

Kapteijns, Lidwien (1980), 'The Emergence of the Masālīt Sultanate; the contribution of written and oral sources to the history of western Sudan', paper presented to the International Oral History Conference, Amsterdam, 24–6 October.

Kapteijns, Lidwien (1981), 'The Organization of Trade in Precolonial Western Sudan', paper presented to the Workshop 'Staat en Maatschappij in Afrika', Leiden, 15–16 December.

Klein, M. A. (1977), 'Domestic Slavery in the Muslim Societies of Western Sudan', Princeton Papers on Slavery.

La Rue, G. M. (1978), 'A Preliminary Paper on Bagirmi: Issues and Questions for Future Research', Boston University.

La Rue, G. M. (1980), 'Ḥākūras in the Area between al-Fāshir, Kobbei and Kutum', paper presented to the Postgraduate Seminar, History Department, University of Khartoum, 16 December.

O'Fahey, R. S. (1972), 'The Growth and Development of the Keira Sultanate of Dār Fūr, PhD Thesis, University of London.

O'Fahey, R. S. (1977), 'Slavery and Society in Dār Fūr', Princeton Papers on Slavery.

O'Fahey, R. S. (1980), 'Fūr and Fartīt: A Sudanic Frontier', in J. Mack and P. Robert Shaw, eds, *Culture History in the Southern Sudan*, Nairobi, 1982.

O'Fahey, R. S. (forthcoming 1984), 'The Tunjur: a Central Sudanic Mystery', forthcoming in *JAH*.

Spaulding, J. L. (unpublished 1981), 'The Heroic Age in Sinnār: The Management of Exchange', paper presented to the African Studies Association Meeting, 21 October 1981, Bloomington, Indiana.

Tubiana, M. J. (1980), 'Nouveaux Aperçus sur le structure du pouvoir au Dar For', Colloque: L'Esprit de Découverte, Valbonne, Décembre.

Varga, J. S. (1980), 'History and Theory: Long-Distance Trade between Dār Fūr and Egypt, 1750–1850', BA Honors Thesis, University of California, San Diego.

Voll. J. O. (1981), 'Abū Jummayzah; The Mahdī's Musaylimah', presented to the Mahdiyya Conference, Khartoum, November.

Walz, T. (1977), 'Black Slavery in Egypt during the Nineteenth Century as reflected in the Maḥkama Archives of Cairo', Princeton Papers on Slavery.

Walz, T. (1979), ''Abd Allāh al-Kaḥḥāl and the Northeast Africa Trade of Egypt, 1880–1920'.

Warburg, G. (1977), 'Slavery and Labour in the Anglo-Egyptian Sudan', Princeton Papers on Slavery.

5 Secondary sources

'Abd al-Ghaffār Muḥammad Aḥmad (1974), *Shaykhs and Followers: Political Struggle in the Rufa'a al-Hoi Nazirate, Sudan*, Khartoum.

Abū Salīm, M. I. (1967), *al-Funj wa'l-arḍ: wathā'iq tamlīk*, Khartoum.

'L'Affaire de Bir Taouil', *L'Afrique Française*, xx, juin, 194–6.

Alexander, H. (1912), *Boyd Alexander's Last Journey*, London.

Amin, S. (1976), *Unequal Development: An Essay on the Social Formations of Peripheral Capitalism*, transl. by B. Pearce, Hassocks, Sussex.

Arkell, A. J. (1922), 'The Southern Route to Kufra From El Fasher to the Senussi and Back with Ali Dinar's Caravan, 1915–1916, Told by Bidi Awdi, The Guide', *SNR*, v, 130–6.

Arkell, A. J. (1926), 'Magic and Medicine in Dar Masalit', *SNR*, ix, 89–94.

Atlas Practique du Tchad (1972), Institut Nationale Tchadien pour les Sciences Humaines, Fort Lamy.

Austen, R. A. (1979), 'The Trans-Saharan Slave Trade: A Tentative Census', in Gemery, H. A. and J. S. Hogendorn, eds, *The Uncommon Market: Essays in the Economic History of the Atlantic Slave Trade*, New York, San Franciso, London, 23–68.

Babin, G. (1910), 'Les événements du Ouadai', *L'Illustration*, 24 décembre, 481–2.

Babin, G. (1910a), 'Le Guet-apens de Bir Taouil', *L'Illustration*, 20 février, 196–8; 1 juin, 509–10.

Babin, G. (1910b), 'Un combat sanglant du Ouadai', *L'Illustration*, 10 décembre, 438.

Babin, G. (1911), 'Le Ouadai depuis Drijele', *L'Illustration*, 25 février, 131–4.

Babin, G. (1911a), 'Au pays massalit – les opérations des colonnes Moll et Arnaud', *L'Illustration*, 25 mars, 221–3.

Babin, G. (1911b), 'Moll et ses camarades vengés', *L'Illustration*, 15 avril, 288.

Babin, G. (1911c), 'La Rude Conquête du Ouadai', *L'Illustration*, 2 octobre 307–9.

Baer, G. (1967), 'Slavery in Nineteenth Century Egypt', *JAH*, viii, 3, 417–41.

Baier, S. (1977), 'Trans-Saharan Trade and the Sahel: Damergu, 1870–1930', *JAH*, xviii, 1, 37–60.

Balfour-Paul, H. G. (1955), *History and Antiquities of Darfur*, Khartoum.

Balfour-Paul, H. G. (1956), 'Cave-paintings and Camels', *Blackwood's Magazine*, 280, July–December, 132–47.

Balfour-Paul, H. G. (1957), 'The very rich hours of the Sultan of Geneina', *Blackwood's Magazine*, 281, January–June 405–20.

Barth, F. (1967), 'Economic Spheres in Darfur', in R. Firth, ed., *Themes in Economic Anthropology*, London, New York etc., 149–74.

Binsbergen, Wim, M. J. van (1980), 'Interpreting the Myth of Sidi Mhâmmad: Oral History in the Highlands of North-western Tunisia', *Social Analysis*, 4 September, 51–73.

Birks, J. S. (1975), 'Overland pilgrimage in the savanna lands of Africa', in L. S. Kosinski and R. M. Prothero, eds, *People on the Move. Studies on internal migration*, London, 297–303.

Birks, J. S. (1978), *Across the Savannas to Mecca: the Overland Pilgrimage Route from West Africa*, London.

Björkelo, A. and G. E. Wickens (1981), *A Bibliography of the Dār Fūr/Wadai Region*, Historisk Institutt, Universitetet Bergen, Occasional Papers, 5, Bergen.

Boutillier, J. -L. (1975), 'Les trois esclaves de Bouna', in C. Meillassoux, ed., *L'Esclavage en Afrique précoloniale*, Paris, 253–80.

Brown, K. and M. Roberts (1980), 'Introduction', *Social Analysis*, 4, Special Issue, Using Oral Sources, Vansina and Beyond, 3–12.

Buchta, R. (1888), *Der Sudan unter ägyptischen Herrschaft. Rückblicke auf die letzten sechzig Jahre*, Leipzig.

Caix, R. de (1910), 'Les Événements du Ouadai et la mort du Colonel

Moll', *L'Afrique Française*, décembre, 357–64.

Carbou, H. (1912), *La Région du Tchad et du Ouaddai*, Paris, 2 vols.

Claessen, H. J. M. and P. Skalnik (1978), 'The Early State: Theories and Hypotheses', in Claessen, H. J. M. and P. Skalnik, eds, *The Early State*, The Hague.

Cooper, F. (1978), review of S. Miers and I. Kopytoff, eds (1977), *African Economic History*, 5, Spring, 41ff.

Cooper, F. (1979), 'The Problem of Slavery', *JAH*, xx, 1, 103–25.

Coquery-Vidrovitch, C. (1976), 'La mise en dépendence de l'Afrique noire: essai de périodisation, 1800–1970', *Cahiers d'Etudes Africaines*, xvi, 1–2, 7–58.

Cordell, D. (1977), 'Eastern Libya, Wadai and the Sanūsīya: a Tarīqa and a Trade Route', *JAH*, xviii, 1, 22–36.

Dalton, G. ed., (1971), *Primitive, Archaic and Modern Economies: Essays of Karl Polanyi*, Boston.

Dalton, G. (1975), 'Karl Polanyi's Analysis of Long-Distance Trade and His Wider Paradigm', in J. A. Sabloff and C. C. Lamberg-Karlovsky, eds, *Ancient Civilizations and Trade*, Albuquerque, 63–132.

Dalton, G. (1978), 'Comment: What Kinds of Trade and Markets?', *African Economic History*, 6, Fall, 134–38.

Daly, M. W. (1980), *British Administration and the Northern Sudan, 1917–1924. The Governor-Generalship of Sir Lee Stack in the Sudan*, Nederlands Historisch-Archaeologisch Instituut te Istanbul.

Davies, R. (1924), 'The Masalit Sultanate', *SNR*, vii, 49–62.

Davies, R. (1957), *The Camel's Back: Service in the Rural Sudan*, London.

Delacommune, Lieut. (1910), 'Lettres du Lieutenant Delacommune', *Afrique Française*, août, 233–48.

Delavignette, R. (1939), *Les vrais chefs de l'empire*, Paris.

Doornbos, P. A. (1982), 'A Sinyar Tale of Friendship', *Sudan Texts Bulletin*, iv, 36–46.

Dorward, D. C. (1976), 'Precolonial Tiv Trade and Cloth Currency', *IJAHS*, ix, 4, 576–91.

East, W. G. (1965), *The Geography Behind History*, London and Edinburgh.

Evans-Pritchard, (1949), *The Sanusi of Cyrenaica*, Oxford.

El-Fahal El-Tahir Omer (1964), 'The Administration of Justice during the Mahdiyya', *The Sudan Law Journal and Reports*, 167–70.

Ferrandi, Lieut.-Col. J. (1930), *Le Centre-Africain Français: Tchad, Borkou, Ennedi*, Paris.

Fisher, H. J. (1973), 'Conversion reconsidered: some historical aspects of religious conversion in black Africa', *Africa*, vol. XLIII, 27–40.

Fisher, A. G. D. and H. J. (1970), *Slavery and Muslim Society in Africa.*

The Institution in Saharan and Sudanic Africa and the Trans-Saharan Trade, London.
Gentil, P. (1971), *La Conquête du Tchad (1894–1916)*, Paris, 2 vols.
Goody, J. (1971), *Technology, Tradition and the State in Africa*, London.
Gouraud, Col. (1911), 'Le Lieutenant-Colonel Moll', *La Géographie*, xxiii, 1–4.
Grele, R. J., ed., (1975), 'Movement without Aim: Methodological and Theoretical Problems in Oral History', in R. J. Grele, ed., *Envelopes of Sound*, Chicago, 126–54.
Grossard, Lt.Col. (1925), *Mission de Délimitation de l'Afrique Equatoriale Française et du Soudan Anglo-Egyptien*, Paris.
Haaland, G. (1978), 'Ethnic Groups and Language in Darfur', in R. Thelwall, ed., *Aspects of Language in the Sudan*, Occasional Papers in Linguistics and Language Learning, 5, The New University of Ulster, 181–99.
Hartwig, G. W. (1978), 'Louse-Borne Relapsing Fever in Sudan, 1908–1951', in G. W. Hartwig, ed., *Disease in African History: An Introductory Survey and Case Studies*, Durham, N. C.
Ḥasan Aḥmad Ibrāhīm (1979), 'The Mahdist Rising Against the Condominium Government, 1900–1927', *IJAHS*, 12, 3, 445–71.
Ḥasan Aḥmad Ibrāhīm (1980), 'Imperialism and Neo-Mahdism in the Sudan. A Study of British Policy towards Neo-Mahdism, 1924–1927', *IJAHS*, 2, 3, 214–39.
Ḥasan Imām Ḥasan and R. S. O'Fahey (1970), 'The Mileri of Jebel Mun', *SNR*, 51, 152–61.
Hilaire, Col. (1917), 'L'Occupation du Dar-Sila', *L'Afrique Française*, mai–juin, 105–18.
Hill, R. (1959), *Egypt in the Sudan, 1820–1881*, London.
Hill, R. (1967), *A Bibliographical Dictionary of the Sudan*, London, 2nd edition.
Hillelson, S. (1935), *Sudanese Arabic Texts*, London.
Holt, P. M. (1955), 'The Archives of the Mahdiyya', *SNR*, xxxvi, 71–78.
Holt, P. M. (1962), 'The Mahdist Archives and Related Documents', *Archives*, v, 28, Michaelmas, 193–200.
Holt, P. M. (1970), *The Mahdist State in the Sudan, 1881–1898: A study of its origins, development and overthrow*, Oxford, 2nd edition.
Holý, L. (1974), *Neighbours and Kinsmen: A Study of the Berti People of Darfur*, London.
Jackson, H. C. (1970), *Black Ivory or The Story of El Zubeir Pasha, Slaver and Sultan, as told by himself*, translated and put on record by—, New York.
Jennings Bramley, W. E. (1940), 'Tales of the Wadai Slave Trade in the Nineties, Told by Yunes Bedis of the Majabra to—', *SNR*, xxiii, 169–83.

Jungraithmayr, H. (1978), 'A Lexical Comparison of Darfur and Wadai Daju', in R. Thelwall, ed., *Aspects of Language in the Sudan*, Occasional Papers in Linguistics and Language Learning, 5, The New University of Ulster, 141–54.

Kapteijns, Lidwien and al-Hādī 'Abd al-Jalīl (1981), 'The Chado-Sudanese frontier on the Eve of Colonial Conquest: Five Letters from the Correspondence of Sultan 'Alī Dīnār of Dār Fūr and Sultan Muḥammad Bakhīt Abū Rīsha', *Sudan Texts Bulletin*, 3, 56–74.

Kapteijns, Lidwien and Ibrāhīm Yaḥyā 'Abd al-Raḥmān (1980), 'Three Administrative Documents from the Sultans of Dār Masālīt', *Sudan Texts Bulletin*, 2, November, 62–72.

Kapteijns, Lidwien and J. Spaulding (1982), 'Precolonial Trade between States in the Eastern Sudan, ca. 1700–c. 1900, *African Economic History*, 11, 29–62.

Kaye, A. S. (1976), *Chadian and Sudanese Arabic in the Light of Comparative Arabic Dialectology*, The Hague, Paris.

Klein, M. A. (1977), 'Servitude among the Wolof and Sereer of Senegambia', in S. Miers and I. Kopytoff, eds, *Slavery in Africa: Historical and Anthropological Perspectives*, Madison, 335–63.

Klein, M. (1978), 'The Study of Slavery in Africa', review article, *JAH*, xix, 4, 599–609.

Klein, M. and P. E. Lovejoy (1979), 'Slavery in West Africa', in H. A. Gemery and J. S. Hogendorn, eds, *The Uncommon Market: Essays in the Economic History of the Atlantic Slave Trade*, New York, San Francisco, London, 181–210.

Kropàçek, L. (1970), 'The confrontation of Darfur with the Turco-Egyptians', *African and Asian Studies* (Bratislava), vi, 73–86.

Kropàçek, L. (1971), 'Title-Deeds in the Fief System of the Sultanate of Darfur', *Acta Universitatis Carolinae Philologica*, (Prague), iv, 33–50.

Largeau, Col. (1913), *La Situation de Territoire Militaire du Tchad au début de 1912*, Paris

Largeau, Col. (1938), 'Reddition du Doudmourra', *Revue Militaire de l'AEF*, iv, 11, 1 janvier, 5–20.

Lavers, J. E. (1968), 'The Adventures of a Kano Pilgrim, 1892–1893', *Kano Studies* I, 4, 69–78.

Lebeuf, A. M. D. (1959), *Les Populations du Tchad (Nord du 10e Parallèle)*, Paris.

Lebon, J. (1965), *Land Use in Sudan*, Budge, Cornwall.

Longhena, M. (1965), *Scritti di Pellegrino Matteucci raccolti et annotati*, Ravenna.

Lovejoy, P. E. (1978), 'Plantations in the Economy of the Sokoto Calphate', *JAH*, xix, 3, 341–68.

Lovejoy, P. E. and S. Baier (1975), 'The desert-side economy of the central Sudan', *IJAHS*, viii, 4, 551–81.

McEvedy, C. (1980), *The Penguin Atlas of African History*, Harmondsworth.

MacMichael, H. A. (1922), *A History of the Arabs in the Sudan*, Cambridge, 2 vols.

Malval, J. (1974), *Essai de chronologie tchadienne (1701–1940)*, Paris.

Meillassoux, C. (1975), 'État et Condition des Esclaves à Gumbu (Mali) aux xixe siècle', *JAH*, xiv, 3, 419–52.

Meillassoux, C. (1978), review of Miers and Kopytoff (1977), *African Economic History*, 5, Spring, 37–40.

Miers, S. and I. Kopytoff (1979), ' "African Slavery" as an Institution of Marginality', in S. Miers and I. Kopytoff, eds, *Slavery in Africa: Historical and Anthropological Perspectives*, Madison, 3–81.

Miller, J. C., ed. (1980), *The African Past Speaks: Essays on Oral Tradition and History*, Folkestone, Kent.

Miller, J. C. (1980), 'Listening for the African Past', in J. C. Miller, ed., *The African Past Speaks: Essays on Oral Tradition and History*, Folkestone, Kent. 1–59.

Moll, Lieut.-Col. (1910), 'Les Dernières Lettres du Lieutenant-Colonel Moll', *L'Afrique Française*, décembre, 364–69.

Moll, Lieut.-Col. (1912), *Une Ame de Colonial: Lettres du Lieutenant-Colonel Moll*, Paris.

Mūsā al-Mubārak al-Ḥasan (1970), *Tārīkh Dār Fūr al-siyāsī, 1882–1895*, Khartoum.

Mynon, T. H. B. (1949), 'The adventures of a Darfur slave', *SNR*, xxx, 273–75.

O'Fahey, R. S. (1970), *States and State Formation in the Eastern Sudan*, African Studies Seminar Paper no. 9, Sudan Research Unit, University of Khartoum.

O'Fahey, R. S. (1973), 'Slavery and the Slave Trade in Dār Fūr', *JAH*, xiv, 1, 29–43.

O'Fahey, R. S. (1979), 'Islam, state and society in Dār Fūr, in N. Levtzion, ed., *Conversion to Islam*, New York, 189–206.

O'Fahey, R. S. (1980), *State and Society in Dār Fūr*, London.

O'Fahey, R. S. and M. I. Abu Salim (1983), *Land in Dār Fūr: Charters and Related Documents from the Dār Fūr Sultanate*, Cambridge.

O'Fahey, R. S. and J. L. Spaulding (1974), *Kingdoms of the Sudan*, London.

Payen, E. (1910), 'Le mort du Colonel Moll: Le combat de Dridjéle', *Questions Diplomatiques et Coloniales*, xxx, juillet–décembre, 753–57.

Polanyi, K. (1975), 'Traders and Trade', in J. A. Sabloff and C. C. Lamberg-Karlovsky, eds, *Ancient Civilizations and Trade*, Albuquerque, 133–54.

Polanyi, K., C. M. Arensberg and H. W. Pearson, eds (1957), *Trade and Market in the Early Empires: Economies in History and Theory*, New York.

Roberts, R. and M. A. Klein (1980), 'The Banamba Slave Exodus of 1905 and the Decline of Slavery in the Western Sudan', *JAH*, xxi, 3, 375–94.

Rosaldo, R. (1980), 'Doing Oral History', *Social Analysis*, 4, Special Issue, Using Oral Sources: Vansina and Beyond, 89–99.

Roth-Laly, A. (1969), *Lexique des Parlers Arabes Tchado-Soudanais*, Paris.

Rouvreur, A. le (1962), *Sahariens et Sahéliens du Tchad*, Paris.

Sanderson, G. N. (1980), 'Introduction', in Y. Bedri and P. Hogg, eds, *The Memoirs of Babikr Bedri, vol. 2*, translated from the Arabic and edited by—, London.

Schacht, J. (1964), *An Introduction to Islamic Law*, London.

Shuqayr, Naʿūm (1903), *Tārīkh al-Sūdān al-qadīm wa'l-hadīth wa jughrāfiyyatuhu*, Cairo, 3 vols.

Slatin, R. C. (1896), *Fire and Sword in the Sudan. A personal narrative of fighting and serving the dervishes, 1879–1895*, translated by F. R. Wingate, London.

Smaldone, J. P. (1972), 'Firearms in the Central Sudan: A Revaluation', *JAH*, xiii, 4, 591–607.

Spaulding, J. L. (1977), 'The Evolution of the Islamic Judiciary in Sinnār', *IJAHS*, x, 3, 408–26.

Spaulding, J. L. (1980), 'Towards a Demystification of the Funj: Some Perspectives on Society in Southern Sinnār, 1685–1900', *Northeast African Studies*, ii, 1, 1–18.

Terray, E. (1974), 'Long-distance exchange and the formation of the state: the case of the Abron Kingdom of Gyaman', *Economy and Society*, 3, 3, 315–46.

Terray, E. (1975), 'Technologie, État et tradition en Afrique', *Annales, Economies, Sociétés, Civilisations*, xxviii, 5, sept.–oct., 1331–38.

Terray, E. (1975a), 'La captivité dans le royaume abron de Gyaman', in C. Meillassoux, ed., *L'Esclavage en Afrique précoloniale*, Paris, 389–454.

Terrier, A. (1910), 'Le Drame de Bir Taouil', *L'Afrique Française*, xx, mai, 181–3.

Thelwall, R. (1981), 'Lexicostatistical Subgrouping and Lexical Reconstruction of the Daju Group', in Th. C. Schadeberg and M. L. Bender, eds, *Nilo-Saharan*, Dordrecht-Cinnaminson, 167–85.

Theobald, A. B. (1965), *ʿAlī Dīnār: Last Sultan of Darfur, 1898–1916*, London.

Thompson, P. (1978), *The Voice of the Past: Oral History*, Oxford.

Tothill, J. D. (1948), *Agriculture in the Sudan*, London.

Trenga, G. (1947), *Le Bura-Mabang du Ouadai: notes pour servir à l'étude de la langue maba*, Paris.

Tubiana, M. J. (1960), 'Un document inédit sur les sultans du Wadday', *Cahiers d'Etudes Africaines*, 2, 49–112.

Tubiana, M. J. (1964), *Survivances Préislamiques en Pays Zaghawa*, Paris.

Tubiana, M. J. and J. (1978), *The Zaghawa from an Ecological Perspective*, Rotterdam.

Tubiana, M. J., J. Khayar, P. Delville (1978), *Abd El-Karim, propagateur de l'islam et fondateur du royaume du Ouaddai*, Paris.

Tully, D. (1980), 'Dar Masalit Today: Dynamics of Ecology, Society and Politics', in M. L. Bender, ed., *Eastern Sudanic Studies, vol. 1*, Lansing, Michigan.

ʿUthmān Muḥammad ʿUthmān (1975), 'Siyāsat al-tahjīr fī ʿahd al-khalīfa ʿAbd Allāh', *Majallat al-dirāsāt al-sūdāniyya*, v, 1, August, 135–74.

Walz, T. (1978), *Trade between Egypt and Bilād al-Sūdān, 1700-1820*, Cairo.

Watson, J. L., ed. (1980), *Asian and African Systems of Slavery*, Berkeley and Los Angeles.

Wingate, F. R. (1968), *Mahdiism and the Egyptian Sudan*, London, 2nd edition.

Works, J. A., Jr. (1976), *Pilgrims in a Strange Land*, New York.

Ziadeh, N. A. (1958), *Sanusiya. A Study of a Revivalist Movement in Islam*, Leiden.

Index

Ab Daqdāq, 143
Ab Julla, 152
Ab Maṭar, 50
Ab Mondokōra, 135
Ab Runga, 111, 152
Ab Sinān Jīr, 138
Ab Tarbūsh, 138
Abāy, 50, 135–6, 145
Abba Maṭar, 50, 138
Abbakr b. Ismā'īl, Sultan of Dār Masālīt (1888–1905), 128–31, 135, 137–70, 244–5; consolidation and centralization, 137–61; and French, 176–7, 179, 198–202; kingship, 138–9; and Mahdist state, 82, 85, 88, 92–112 *passim*, 118–21; ruling elite and estate system, 139–52, 216; slave army, creation of, 152–5; trade, control of, 155–61
abbo/abbonga, 244; under Abbakr, 141, 157, 167; under 'Ali Dīnār, 198–9, 203, 207; under Ancien Regime, 52, 54; under Condominium, 216–20, 224, 230; under Mahdist state, 111
Abbo Jiddo Sa'd, 128
'abd/abīd, 48; *see also* slaves
'Abd al-Khayr Ab Faḍḍay, 143
'Abd Allah al-Kaḥḥal, 151, 173, 195
'Abd Allāh Abū Ḥaraka, 53
'Abd Allāh al-Suḥaynī, 212
'Abd Allāh Runga, 37, 44
'Abd al-Qādir (*bāsī*), 154, 176
'Abd al-Qādir wad Dalīl, 84, 94, 100, 105, 129, 142
'Abd al-Qaffā, 45, 135, 154
'Abd al-Raḥmān b. Baḥr al-Dīn, *abbo*, 219
'Abd al-Raḥmān al-Mahdī (the Sayyid), 239–43
'Abd al-Raḥmān of the Konjorong, 205
'Abd al-Salām, 71
'Abd al-Sharīf, 200
Abū Aja (*faqīh*), 111
Abū Jummayza, 50, 77–8, 82, 130; movement, 83–99
Abū Rīsha, Sultan of Dār Silā, 76–7, 80–1, 94–7, 103–7, 112–13, 117
Abū Rō, 141
Abū Takiyya, 173
Abū'l-Khayrāt b. Ibrāhīm Qaraḍ, Shadow Sultan of Dār Fūr (1888–91), 53, 76–7, 85, 88, 92–7, 109, 129, 143
Abūlonggo, 166
Adam 'Alī, 177
Adam Asīl b. 'Abd al-Maḥmūd b. Muḥammad Sharīf, Sultan of Wadai (1909–12), 180–5, 188–9, 195
Adam Bosh, 80
Adam Kebberre, 69, 142
Adam Mīr Ya'qūb, 113
Adam Rijāl, 52, 176
ahl warrai, 239
Aḥmad Ab Shulūkh, 205, 218, 221
Aḥmad Abū Lafta, *see* Aḥmad 'Umar Abū Lafta
Aḥmad al-Ghazālī b. 'Ali b. Muḥammad Sharīf, Sultan of Wadai (1901–2), 110, 173
Aḥmad Bayḍa, 184
Aḥmad Duway, 198

Index

Aḥmad Shaṭṭa, 44
Aḥmad 'Umar Abū Lafta, 51, 53, 56, 134, 142–3, 149–50, 332
ajāwīd, 41, 42, 75, 244
al-'Aṭā Uṣūl, 81, 84, 94
al-bay' *wa' l-shīra'*, 120
al-Bishārī Rīda, 81, 124
al-Dūm (*shāyib*), 87
al-Khatīm Mūsā, 84
al-Nūr Bey 'Anqara, 64, 67
al-Tūnisī, Muḥammad b. 'Umar, 14–15, 17, 34
al-Zubayr Raḥma, 50, 62–3, 75
'alaj, 120–1, 158
alcohol, prohibited, 127, 131, 136, 212
Alexander, B., 187
'Alī Ab Shanab, 54, 200, 218, 332
'Alī al-Tamtam, 136, 141–3, 154, 199, 200
'Alī b. Muḥammad Sharīf, Sultan of Wadai (1858–74), 114, 119
'Alī Dīnār b. Zakāriyya b. Muḥammad al-Faḍl, Shadow Sultan of Dār Fūr (1898–1916), 50–2, 80, 101, 113, 116, 249; and French, 181–4, 191–7, 200, 207; versus Masālīt, 171–81
'Alī Dunyuru, 71
'Alī Ḥasan Tāj al-Dīn, 124–5
'Alī Sennān, 199–200, 206
'Alī Taher Keru, 80
'Alī Umm Belōlo, 218
'āmil, 81–2, 85, 133, 244
amīn, 244; under Abbakr, 139, 141, 143, 167; under 'Alī Dīnār, 198, 201; under Condominium, 218–21, 230
amīr, 82, 133, 174–6, 188–90, 244
Amm Būs, 68–9
Amm Nabūd, 111, 152
amm dallu, 130
Amm Ḍīfān, 198
Amm Gazza, 198
Amm Raqīq, 175
ammo/*ammonga*, 136, 192, 244; *see also abbo*
Amunong people, 68
Ancien Regime (before 1874), 2, 5, 18–61; commoners and means of subsistence, 24–40; nobility, local, and Fūr overlords, 40–8; slaves and masters, 48–61; Turkiyya, beginning of, 62–5
Andōka, *see* Baḥr al-Dīn
Andokoi (*maqdūm*), 45
Anglo-Egyptian Sudan, *see* Condoinium
Anjumma bint H'alīma, 51–2
anṣār, 50, 53, 73, 76–109 *passim*, 115, 124, 129–30, 135, 138, 168, 201, 241–2
'aqīd, 110–12, 134, 144, 244, 262; under Ancien Regime, 27, 42, 47–8; under French, 186, 188, 197
'Arafa (*mayram*), 177
Arbāb Barsham, 134, 140
archival sources, 337–45
ardabb, 228–9, 231, 244
Arkell, A.J., 215, 220–1, 240, 242
army, *see jihādiyya*; military activity
Arsho *bint*, Ismā'īl, 129
'Asha Shaddo, 136
Asīl, *see* Adam Asīl
Asongor people, 85
Awra people, 45, 69, 178, 211
'Āyisha, 53
Ayyūb Dā'ūd al-Sanūsī, 70, 145
'Azza *bint*, Idrīs, princess of the Qimr, 176

Badawī b. Abbakr, 110, 157; under Condominium, 209, 218, 221, 223; under French, 186, 199–200, 205–6
baḥḥāra, 62–4, 96, 174, 245
Baḥr al-Dīn (Andōka) b. Abbakr b. Ismā'īl, Sultan of Dār Masālīt (1910–51), 132, 242, 244; and Condominium, 209–26 *passim*, 237, 240–1; and French, 178, 188–92, 197–207, 211
Bakhīt Kurjūk, 134
Bakhīt b. Abū Rīsha, Sultan of Dār Silā (1900–16), 175–6, 181–2, 184, 231
Bakhīta Bandiyya, 53
balance of power, new, in western Dār Fūr, 94–7
Banī Ḥalba people, 72, 78, 85, 97–8, 101, 105
Banī Ḥusayn people, 23, 32, 62, 77, 80, 84–5, 100–1, 103, 145
Baqqāra people, 75, 129, 208
Barre (*malik*), 149–50
barter, *see* trade
Bashīr (*maqdūm*), 142
bāsī/*bāsinga*, 59, 216, 245; under Abbakr, 51, 56, 140–6, 149, 153–4, 157–60, 166, 168; under French, 176, 198, 202; under Ismā'īl, 53, 134

battles, *see* military activity
beads, 34–5, 157–8
Bidāyāt people, 16, 76, 85, 186
bikbāshī, 71
Borno people, 45, 70, 139, 144–5
Borqāwī/Borqū people, *see* Wadai
Boutillier, J.-L., 5
brideprice, 24; reduced, 131–2, 136
British colonialism, 2, 87–8, 181, 189, 191, 194, 204; Condominium (1898–1956), 3, 172–3, 208–43
Bukhārī (*bāsī*), 134, 142, 157–8, 166
Bukr (*shartay*), 143

cannibalism myth, 22, 36, 48, 260
circumcision of women, 44
colonialism, *see* British; Condominium; French
commoners: in Ancien Regime, 24–40; and brideprice, 132; and colonial rule, 228–43; and import goods, 159; rise of sultanate, impact of, 164–7; *see also* taxation
communal labour, 29–31, 149–50
Condominium period (1898–1956), 3, 172–3, 208–43
consolidation and centralization, *see* Abbakr
Cooper, F., 4
Coquery-Vidrovitch, C., 6
Cordell, D., 170
crafts, 28–30, 259
crime, *see* judicial; raiding; robbers
currency: coin/cash, 34, 172, 222–3, 228–37; goods as, 32–5, 38–9; introduction of, 63, 222–3; *see also* taxation

dabbalān, 120–1
Dājū people, *see* Dār Silā
dala/dalajei, 40, 245, 262
dallu, 130
danga, 138, 167
dār, 245; under Abbakr, 141–4; under Ancien Regime, 40, 41, 42, 47, 55, 58; under Condominium, 212–13, 218, 225, 233; under French, 177, 181, 189, 202, 203; under Mahdists, 78–9, 88, 98, 109
Dār Dīma, 24, 44
Dār Erenga; under Abbakr, 143; under Ancien Regime, 16–17, 18–19, 32, 36, 45; under Condominium, 211, 216, 218, 221, 223, 227, 229, 234; under French, 178, 188, 191, 199; under Hajjām, 65, 69; under Ismā'īl, 125, 128; under Mahdists, 84, 88, 90, 93, 94–5
Dār Fartīt, *see* Fartīt people
Dār Fia, 23–4, 38, 44–5, 155, 178
Dār Fongoro, 17, 77, 193
Dār Fūr, 1; under Abbakr, 154–6, 161, 164, 166, 170; under Ancien Regime, 13–17, 27, 36, 38; and balance of power, new, 94–7; under Condominium, 208–12, 215, 222–4, 229, 233–9 *passim*; under French, 171–204 *passim*; under Hajjām, 62; under Ismā'īl, 124; under Mahdists, 73–81, 85, 94–6, 99–106, 112, 117, 121; and Wadai, 107–22; western, 73–7, 94–103, 107–22
Dār Jabal: under Abbakr, 146–7; under Ancien Regime, 16, 18–19, 45; under Condominium, 211, 216, 221, 229; under French, 178, 188, 191, 199; under Hajjām, 65, 68–9; under Ismā'īl, 125, 128; under Mahdists, 85, 101, 104
Dār Kerne, 20, 23–4, 38, 44–5, 68, 177–8, 211
Dār Kibet, 119
Dār Kūtī, 119
Dār Masālīt, *see* Masālīt
Dār Qimr, 1; under Abbakr, 166, 168; under Ancien Regime, 16, 37; under Condominium, 209, 211, 232, 237; and French, 174, 176, 181–91 *passim*, 196, 198; under Hajjām, 63; under Mahdists, 76–8, 83–4, 88, 96, 100–7, 110–12, 120
Dār Runga, 17
Dār Silā, 1; under Abbakr, 142, 144, 161, 170; under Ancien Regime, 17, 24, 27, 33, 51–5; and Condominium, 231–2; and French, 174–84, 191, 193, 197, 199, 206–7; under Hajjām, 65, 71; under Ismā'īl, 125; under Mahdists, 69, 76–81, 85, 94–6, 101–3, 105–6, 112, 116–17, 121
Dār Sinyār, 17, 19, 22, 24, 47, 65, 71, 77, 112
Dār Tāmā, 1, 16, 19, 21, 63, 65, 129, 144, 211; and French, 174, 181–8 *passim*, 191, 193, 203; and

Dār Tāmā (*cont.*)
Mahdists, 76–7, 80–9 *passim*, 100–7, 111–12, 120–2
Dār Zaghāwa, 16, 23, 32, 39, 52, 149; and French, 173–4, 181; and Mahdists, 76–80, 85, 88, 101–8, 111, 121
'Dardama', *see* Muḥammad Jūda Fāt
Darok people, 124, 127–8, 143
Dā'ūd Bōbale, 201
Davies, R., 213–15, 217, 221–5
depression, world, 234–5
daym, 78, 184
Dervish Proclamation Register, 80
dimlij, 40, 220, 245, 262
dinggar, 40, 131, 134, 206, 245
Dinka people, 44
Dīseng people, 70, 135, 146
dīwān, 38, 47, 67, 111–12, 245
diya, 41, 60, 191, 245
ḍiyāfa, 143, 163–4, 230, 245
doctors, 258
documents, 319–30
drought and famine, 28, 52, 192–9, 203
drums, 40, 112, 130–1, 134, 206
Dūd Murra, Sultan of Wadai (1902–9), 115, 149; and French, 172–4, 178–80, 184–6, 188, 194–5, 200, 206
Dudbanga, *see* 'Abd Allāh Dudbanga
Dūdū Somītkilō, 142, 153
Dugdug, 204, 241
dumbāri, 28, 31, 86, 245

'ear-cutting ceremony, 56, 59
economic: boycott, 195–6; dimension of political domination, 113–22
education, 125, 135, 227
Egypt, trade with, 15–16, 33, 64, 119, 172–3; *see also* Condominium
El Tounsy, *see* al-Tūnisī
Ensor, F.S., 65
Erenga people, *see* Dār Erenga
estate system, creation of and ruling elite, 139–52; *see also dār*
eunuchs, 138, 169
exchange relationships in Ancien Regime, 29–40; *see also* trade
export goods: under Abbakr, 7, 8, 160–3, 170; under 'Ali Dīnār, 174; under Condominium, 233; under Mahdists, 108, 114, 119–22; *see also* trade

factionalism, 3, 197–203
Faḍl Allāh al-Daghūr, 103
falgo, 32–3, 36, 39, 245–6
famine, *see* drought
faqīh, 28–9, 246; under Abbakr, 140–1, 144–8, 153, 157–61, 165, 167; under 'Ali Dīnār, 179–80, 199–205; under Ancien Regime, 50, 53, 58, 59, 60; under Condominium, 212–13, 216–17, 219, 228, 239–40; under Hajjām, 67, 70, 72; under Ismā'īl, 124–5, 128–37 *passim*; under Mahdists, 75, 86–8, 92–5, 99, 111, 115, 121
farming, 8, 25–31, 42, 169, 237
Fartīt, 49, 53, 161, 246
fās, 40, 263
fātiḥa, 29, 59, 60, 169, 246
Felkin, R.W., 249
Fezzān traders, 55; under Abbakr, 156–61 *passim*, 166, 169–70; and French, 173, 185–6, 196; and Mahdists, 114, 118, 120–1
Fiegenschuh, Colonel, 181–3
fines, *see* judicial system; taxation
firearms, 8, 158–9, 173–4, 184, 212
firka, 158–9, 179, 246
firsha, 246; under Abbakr, 95, 146–51, 157, 161, 166, 264; under 'Ali Dīnār, 162, 178; under Ancien Regime, 44–8; under Condominium, 217–21, 227–30, 235, 240; under Hajjām, 66–8, 71; under Ismā'īl, 128, 130, 137; *see also furūshiyya*
fiṭra, 136, 201, 246; under Abbakr, 145–6, 148–50, 153, 162; under Condominium, 224, 228–30; under Mahdists, 77, 96
Fongoro, *see* Dār Fongoro
foreign trade, *see* export; import
Fraccolari, A., 67
freedom, slaves', 59–60
French colonialism, 2, 171–5, 180–97, 200–4, 209–11
frontier areas, 15–17, 107–13, 209
Fukkunyang people, 44, 45–6, 66–8, 70, 72, 124, 127, 146
Fūr, *see* Dār Fūr
fursān/*fāris*, 197, 201, 246
furūshiyyas, 44, 45–7, 140, 144, 147, 220, 246; *see also firsha*

game, *see* hunting
gathering, 27–8

Gernyeng people, 46, 69–71; under Abbakr, 140–2, 149, 151, 154, 165, 216; and French, 171, 187, 199, 201–2, 205; under Ismā'īl, 124, 128–36
ghanīma, 78, 229
Girga people, 101
Gonykokong people, 70
government, central, 36, 39–40, 46–8
Grele, R.J., 11

Habbo Janna, 57
Ḥabība, mother of Abbakr, 146–7
ḥajar, 246
Ḥajar wad Baḥr, 80
Hajjām Ḥasab Allāh, ruler of the Masālīt (1880–83), 2, 36, 66–72, 102–3, 105, 137, 145, 156, 166, 199; overthrown, 123–4, 127–9; and unification of Masālīt, 62–72
ḥākim/ḥukkām, 44, 58, 246
ḥākūra, 45, 144, 246; *see also dār*
Ḥāmid Majbūr, 81, 84
ḥāmil, 41, 151, 160, 246
Ḥanafī of Dar Fia, 23, 45
Ḥanafī, *faqīh*, 136
Hardy, J.H., 210
ḥarīm, 52, 135, 169, 246
Hārūn b. Sayf al-Dīn b. Muḥammad al-Faḍl, Shadow Sultan of Dār Fūr (1874–79), 63, 68
Ḥasan Ya'qūb, Sultan of the Tāmā (1909–10), 181, 185–6
Ḥasan Kunji, 129, 134, 139, 169
Ḥasan Umm Kadōk, 128
Hāshim b. Idrīs, 176
Ḥawā' Dumballa, 136
Hayati, Sheikh, 80
hereditary nobles, 43
hijra, 79–83, 101, 105, 124, 246–7
Hilaire, Colonel, 191
Holt, P.M., 244
ḥubb al-riyāsa, 77, 124
ḥukkām/ḥākim/ḥukm, 40, 47–9, 68, 115, 128–31, 135, 147, 169–70, 180
Ḥumāra, 52
hunting, 25, 27, 41, 42, 92
Ḥusayn, Sultan of Dār Fūr, *see* Muḥammad al-Ḥusayn

Ibrāhīm al-Ḥājj Muḥammad al-Maghribī, 195
Ibrāhīm b. Yūsuf b. Muḥammad Sharīf, Sultan of Wadai (1898- 1901), 110, 173
Ibrāhīm Bōsha, 45, 68
Ibrāhīm Burām, 125, 142
Ibrāhīm Qaraḍ b. Muḥammad al-Ḥusayn, Sultan of Dār Fūr (1873–4), 50, 51, 63, 68, 75, 138
Ibrāhīm b. Sulaymān, Sultan of Dār Tāmā, 80
Ibrāhīm Yaḥyā, 335–6
'Id (*faqīh*), 137
Idrīs Abū Bakr, Sultan of Dār Qimr, 77, 79, 82–3, 94, 103–4, 176, 181–2, 209, 232
ikhwān, 184, 186, 247
imām, 92, 131, 139, 195, 247
impact of rise of sultanate (1888–1905), 161–70; on commoners, 164–7; on new masters and slaves, 168–70; on nobility, local, 162–4
import goods: under Abbakr, 156–9; under 'Alī Dīnār, 173–5; under Ancien Regime, 7–8, 33–4, 37; under Condominium, 233; under Mahdists, 114–15, 118–22; *see also* trade
independence, struggle for (1898–1916), 173–207; 'Alī Dīnār versus Masālīt, 171–81; factionalism and popular revolt, 197–207; French, slaughter of, 180–97
indirect rule, direct results of (1920s and 1930s), 3, 208–43
insecurity problem, and foreign trade, 115–18
Isāgha Choko, 72, 128
Isāgha Daldūm, 205
Isāgha Donkotch, 66–7
Isḥāq Abū Rīsha, *see* Abū Rīsha
Islam, 13–15, 125–32; *see also* Mahdist faith
Ismā'īl b. 'Abd al-Nabī, Sultan of Dār Masālīt (1883–88), 67, 72, 75–7, 80–2, 85, 97, 123, 168, 205, 245; consolidation and centralization by, 137–61; founding state, 133–7; kingship and leadership qualities, 130–3, 138–9
Ismā'īl al-Wālī, 125
Ismā'īliyya brotherhood, 125
īya, 52, 247

Jabal people, *see* Dār Jabal
jabbāy, 157, 247
jalāla, 127, 131
jallāba, 247; under Abbakr, 51, 155–7; under Ancien Regime, 31, 33, 55; under colonialism, 173, 226; under Hajjām, 63–4; under Mahdists, 108, 114, 117
jallābiyya, 133, 135, 247
Jesus, prophet, 203–4, 239–40; *see also nabī 'Isā*
jibba/jubba, 175, 179, 201, 247
jihād, 88, 247
jihādiyya, 62, 247; under Abbakr, 50–1, 141, 147, 150–5, 159, 163–4, 169–70; under Ismā'īl, 135; under Mahdists, 91, 98, 111; *see also* military activity
Jimme Tindil, 143
jubbāy, 133, 247
judicial system: under Abbakr, 139, 147, 165; under Ancien Regime, 41–2, 44–6; under Condominium, 212, 220, 224, 227; under Mahdists, 77
Julien, Colonel, 192–3, 196, 205–6, 207
jummayza tree, 86, 89

Kajjām Zubayr, 157, 218
kalamshiyya, 138
Karam Allāh (bāsi), 57
Karyeng people, 142
Keira sultanate, 1–2, 137, 163; *see also* Dār Fūr
khabīr, 117
Khadam Allāh Ismā'īl, 56, 136, 145–6
khādim/khadīm, 48
khalīfa, 40, 67, 87, 108, 140–1, 144, 247
Khalīlo, 157
khalwa, 124–5, 137, 145, 247
khashm al-bayt, 40
khawāja, 180, 242
khidmat al-māl, 148
khidmāt/khadāmāt, 150, 247
Khuzāmī people, 205
kidnapping, 52–3
kingship, grandeur of, 138–9
kinsmen, artificial, slaves as, 56, 58–9
Kirdī people, 49, 182, 247
kirsh al-fīl, 149–50
Klein, M., 4
Kobbei, 33–4, 53, 64
Komore people, 70
Kondojo, 203
Konjorong people, 205
Kopytoff, 4–5
korāyāt, 139
Kropàçek, L., 245
kumal, 146, 149–50, 247
Kusubei people, 66, 71
Kuttūk, 32–3, 157

La Rue, G.M., 246
labour: communal, 29–31, 149–50; migration, 65; service, 149–50; slave, 56–8, 146, 169
land allocation, 144–52; *see also* estate; *dār*
Largeau, Colonel, 185–6
law and order, *see* judicial
Lereng people, 70
livestock, 20–1
local resistance to Mahdists, 77–83
Lovejoy, P.E., 4–5
lubūs, 78, 102

Ma'āliya people, 175
Mābā, 14
MacMichael, H.A., 210–11, 213, 222, 225
Maghārba people, 32, 58, 195
Maḥādī people, 142
maḥāya, 29, 125, 247,
Maḥāmīd people, 32, 35, 45, 65, 76, 80, 144, 186
Mahdist faith, 2–3, 106, 123, 237; *see also* prophets; Mahdist state; neo-mahdism
Mahdist state and Mahdism, 2, 6, 47–8, 73–122 *passim*; and Dār Fūr, 73–7, 99–103; neomahdism, 239–43; prophets, 203–4, 239–43; re-activated, 171; resistance to, 77–83; and Wadai, 107–13; warfare, 50–1; *see also* Islam
maḥmal, 248
Maḥmūd, Aḥmad, 78, 82, 99–105, 109–13
Maḥmūd 'Ali al-Dādingāwī, 177
Mahriyya people, 86, 93
Maillard, Colonel, 188
Majābra, *see* Fezzān
maji/majir, 48; *see also* slaves
Makki, 53, 136
malik, 248; under Abbakr, 148–51,

160–1, 162; under Ancien Regime, 40–7, 58, 262; under 'Ali Dīnār, 176–8; under Condominium, 216–21, 227, 230, 240; under Hajjām, 68–70; under Ismā'īl, 130–1, 134, 137; under Mahdists, 112
Manggere people, 70
manumission of slaves, 60
maqdūm, 248; under Abbakr, 142–3, 146–53 *passim*, 161, 168; under Ancien Regime, 41, 44–6, 47; under Condominium, 211–12, 218, 221
Marārīt people, 45, 65, 80, 143, 211
marissa, 131, 136, 141, 224
marriage, 30–1, 131–2, 136; of slaves, 55–6, 58–9, 169, 271
masīk, 29, 131
martu, 27
masjid, 248
mayram, 153, 177, 248
Mecca, 17, 183
Meillassoux, C., 4
Messedaglia, G.B., 64
midd, 246, 248–9; under Abbakr, 148, 162, 164, 166; under Ancien Regime, 26, 34, 39–40; under Condominium, 228, 230; under Hajjām, 64
Miers, S., 4–5
migration, 65; and Mahdist faith, 237–43
military activity: under Abbakr, 152–5, 162, 169–70; under Ancien Regime, 14–15, 36, 48, 49–52, 255; under Condominium, 212; under French, 173–97 *passim*, 201–2; under Hajjām, 62; under Ismā'īl, 128–30, 135; under Mahdists, 68–70, 91, 98, 111
Miller, J.C., 10
Millot, Lieut. Colonel, 194, 232
Minjiri people, 43, 45–7, 67
miracles, 92–3
miskīn/masākin, 40, 248
Mistereng people, 142, 227; under Ancien Regime, 44–7; under French, 199, 201; under Mahdists, 63, 66–7, 71, 102
mōgāy, 139
Mokony, 146
Moll, Colonel, 187
Mōmad Nyiterre, 166
mondokōra, 135, 138
money, *see* currency
morota, 30
Mudda (*'aqīd*), 111, 134, 197
Muhājir, 130–1, 240
muhājirīn, 240, 242
Muḥammad Aḥmad 'Umar Abū Lafta, 51, 332–3
Muḥammad al-Faḍl, Sultan of Dār Fūr (1803–38), 145, 174
Muḥammad al-Ḥusayn b. Muḥammad al-Faḍl, Sultan of Dār Fūr (1838–73), 44, 54, 62, 144, 177
Muḥammad al-Mahdi, 173
Muḥammad Bishāra, 88, 111
Muḥammad Jūda Fāt, 50, 104
Muḥammad Khālid Zuqal, 73–5, 80, 108, 124, 134
Muḥammad Nimr Baḥr al-Dīn, 52, 219
Muḥammad Sāja, 124
Muḥammad Ṣāliḥ Dūd Murra b. Yūsuf b. Muḥammad Sharīf, Sultan of Wadai (1902–9), *see* Dūd Murra
Muḥammad Sharīf, Sultan of Wadai (1834–58), 114, 117, 145, 180
Muḥammad Tigil Abyad, 136
Muḥammad Zayn, *see* Abū Jummayza
mulūkiyya, 140, 144, 147, 220, 248; *see also malik*
Mūsā al-Mubārak al-Ḥasan, 3, 84
muwalladīn, 168
Muzammil nūr, 45

nabī 'Isā, 203–4, 212, 239–40, 248; *see also* Prophet Jesus
Nachtigal, G., 14, 17, 34–5, 115, 155–6, 245–6, 249–50
nafīr, 29–31, 42, 248
naḥāsāt, 130, 138
nā'ib shar'ī, 107
Ndelngongo, 45
Ndili, 218–19
neomahdism, 239–43; *see also* Mahdist faith
ngōre, 30
nobility, local, *see* rulers
nomads, 32
Nūr wad Bakr, 80
Nyarmōl, 142, 154
Nyerneng people, 44, 45–7, 66–7, 131, 142, 166, 201

occupation, British, 209–14

O'Fahey, R.S., 3, 8, 14, 46, 154, 172, 244–6, 249–50
Omdurman, 74–5, 79–80, 82–3, 108, 124, 128
opposition party under Abbakr, 154
oral history, 9–12, 331–6
overlords, Fūr, and Ancien Regime, 40–8

pagans, 17, 49, 106, 132
poet, 139
political domination, economic dimension of, 113–22
prices, 38–40; of slaves, 53
prophets, Mahdist, 203–4, 239–43

qāḍī, 50, 135–6, 139, 144, 221, 224, 248
Qamr al-Dīn 'Abd al-Jabbār, 179
Qimr, *see* Dār Qimr
Qur'ān, 29, 125, 128, 135, 195
Qur'ān (Tubu) people, 186
qūz/*qōz*, 26, 169, 248

Rafa, 132
raiding, 119, 155, 161, 206–7, 258; under Ancien Regime, 27, 32, 36, 42
rainfall, 25–6, 28
rainmaking, 132, 259
Ramla (*faqīh*), 156
rātib, 86, 201–2, 248
raṭl, 26, 249
rayka, 26, 32, 53, 228, 230, 249
reciprocity, 29–31
regional perspective on rise of Masālīt Sultanate (1883–98), 73–122; Abbakr's dilemma, 103–7; Abū Jummayza movement, 83–99; Mahdist administration as cause of local resistance, 77–83; western Dār Fūr and Mahdist state, 73–7, 99–103; western Dār Fūr and Wadai, 107–22
religious message, text of, 125–7
revolt of Abū Jummayza, 83–99; aftermath of, 97–9; balance of power, new, in western Dār Fūr, 94–7; causes of, 88–94; events of, 84–6
revolt, popular (1905–16), and factionalism, 3, 197–207
Rijāl, Adam, 52, 176–7
riyāl, 182, 249
Riziq Batanjān (*maqdūm*), 142, 166
Riziq Qāsī (*bāsī*), 140–2, 144
robbers, 32, 36, 206; *see also* raiders
rubṭa/*rabṭa*, 34, 58, 151, 249
rulers/nobility: under Abbakr, 139–52, 158–64; under Ancien Regime, 6–8, 40–61; under Condominium, 219–21; and estate system, creation of, 139–52; under French, 202; import goods and, 158–61; and indirect rule, 219–21; under Ismā'īl, 134, 136; new, 6, 134, 136, 158–61; and rise of sultanate, 162–4; and slaves, 6, 48–61; and trade, 6–8

ṣadaqa, 41
Sa'īd Ab Dūdū, 211, 218
Sa'īd Burūs, 50, 102
salām, 38, 42, 120, 151, 249
Ṣaleḥ/Ṣāliḥ, *'āmil* of the Zaghāwā, 80
Ṣaliḥ (faqīh), 130–1
sambei, 46, 71, 130–1, 249
Sammaniyya, 125
Sanderson, G.N., 214
Sandison, Assistant Resident, 227, 236
Sandukka (īya), 146
Sanūsi al-Naffār, 197
Sanūsiyya (Sanūsi), 75, 86–7, 108, 114, 172–4, 181, 184, 195–6
shahāda, 127, 131
Sharaf al-Dīn Ismā'īl, 146, 204
Sharī'a, 106
shartay, 249; under Abbakr, 143, 155; under 'Ali Dīnār, 178, 202; under Ancien Regime, 44–5, 47; under Condominium, 211, 218; under Hajjām, 68; under Ismā'īl, 135; under Mahdists, 101, 112
shaykh, 249; under Abbakr, 148, 157; under Ancien Regime, 40, 42, 44–6; under Condominium, 218, 221, 227, 229; under Hajjām, 67; under Mahdists, 74–5, 87, 97, 102
shīt, 121, 158
Shūsha, 185
Sī Ṣaliḥ Abū Krīmī, 195
Silāwī, *see* Dār Silā
Sinīn Ḥusayn, 103, 112, 145, 175–6, 204
Sinyār, *see* Dār Sinyār
Slatin, R.C. von, 64, 69, 73, 89–90, 134
slaves: under Abbakr, 138–9, 152–5, 160–1, 168–70; under Ancien Regime, 48–61, 266–71; under

Ismā'īl, 135; as kinsmen, artificial, 56, 58–9; labour, 56–8, 146, 169; under Mahdists, 117, 119; manumission of, 59–60; marriage of, 55–6, 59, 169, 271; prices of, 53; runaway, 41, 151, 160, 246; theories about, 3–7; trade, 17, 33, 49, 53–5, 57, 63, 160–1, 170, 182, 238–9; war captives, 49–52, 153; women, 48–52, 55–7, 138–9, 168–9, 202; *see also jihādiyya* (slave army)
Somīt Abarranjal, 57, 143, 150
songs: about Abbakr, 177; about 'Abd al-Karīm, 200–1; about tobacco and alcohol prohibition, 127; about 'Ali Dīnār, 180; of battle, 68, 177–9, 187, 192, 197, 202; about brideprice, 132; about Condominium, 208; about *falgo* trade, 33; about Hajjām Ḥasab Allāh, 69–70, 72, 275–6; about Mahdists, 90–1; about Mudda, 197; rainmaking, 132; about slave trade, 54–5; about Tāj al-Dīn, 198
state formation before 1874, 13–15
subsistence, means of, 24–40
Sudan Government, *see* Condominium; western Sudan
Sudanic tradition, 2, 3, 123, 137, 196
Sulaymān Ibrāhīm, Sultan of Tāmā, 111
Sulaymān Kijikinang, 130
Sulaymān Nīdim, 43
Sunna, 106
syphilis, 138–9

Ta'ālba people, 45, 65
Ta'āyisha people, 74, 76, 80, 91, 95, 107
tahjīr, 79–80, 83, 249
Tāj al-Dīn b. Ismā'īl, Sultan of Dar Masālīt (1905–10), 103, 146, 148–50, 154; and French, 177–89, 198–200, 201–2, 203
Tāmā, *see* Dār Tāmā
ṭarīqa brotherhood, 242
Tarjam people, 35, 45, 65, 85
taxation: under Abbakr, 145, 147–51, 153–4, 162–4; under 'Ali Dīnār, 172, 207; under Ancien Regime, 7–9, 16, 26, 35, 38–42, 47, 265; in coin or cash, 172, 224, 228–37; under Condominium, 207, 212, 220–25, 228–37; under French, 182, 193, 203; under Hajjām, 64–5; under Mahdists, 77, 119
Terray, E., 5, 7–8
tōb/thawb, 27, 120, 249
tobacco, prohibited, 127, 131, 136
Torong people, 69
trade: under Abbakr, 156–61, 163, 170; under 'Ali Dīnār, 172–6, 196; under Ancien Regime, 8, 15–17, 29–40, 253–4; boycott, 195–6; under Condominium, 233; under Hajjām, 62–3; local, 29–31; long-distance, 3, 6–8, 33–4, 37–40, 108, 114–22, 156–63, 170–5, 233; under Mahdists, 100, 108–10, 114–22; regional, 31–7; *see also* export; import; slaves
travel literature, 345–6
tukkiyyas, 220, 223, 249; under Abbakr, 147, 150–1; under Ancien Regime, 27–8, 34, 38–9, 47, 52, 53; under French, 180; under Hajjām, 68, 71; under Ismā'īl, 132
Turco-Egyptians, 45, 48, 50, 62–5, 73, 91, 110, 128, 133–5, 137, 140, 169
Turjūk, *shaykh* of Banī Ḥusayn people, Ḥāmidwad, 80, 100–1, 125–6
Turkiyya, *see* Turco-Egyptians
Turūj people, 136–7, 145, 169
ṭuwayrāt, 139

'Umar (*aqīd*), 54
'Umar Ismā'īl, 142
'Umar Wad Tirhō, 128, 134
Umbadda al-Raḍḍī, 103
unification of Masālīt, 62–72
'Uthmān Adam or Jānū, 50, 76–8, 81, 85–9, 93–9 *passim*, 105, 108–10, 124, 156, 199
'Uthmān ibn 'Affān, 87
'Uthmān Baṣal, 99
'Uthmān Adam, Sultan of Dā Tāmā (1896–1909), 181, 203

Van Binsbergen, 10
Vansina, 9–10

Wābī (*faqīh*), 95, 111, 333
Wadai: and Abbakr's regime, 137, 144–5, 155–7, 170; and Ancien Regime, 13–17, 27, 36, 38, 51, 52–3; and Condominium, 209, 211, 231, 237–8; under Hajjām, 69;

Wadai (*cont.*)
under Ismā'īl, 125; and Mahdists, 75–119 *passim*; and western Dār Fūr, 107–22
wādī, 32, 58, 87, 145, 169, 189, 213, 249
wakīl, 103, 249
Walz, T., 8
war, *see jihadiyya*; military activities
waraq, 86
warnang, 39, 41, 42, 150, 163, 249, 261–2, 263
warra bāya and *deiye*, 138
water supply, 25–6, 28
wayba, 250
wazīr, 134, 139, 221, 250
weapons, *see* firearms
western Dār Fūr: balance of power, new, 94–7; and Mahdist state, 73–7, 99–103; and Wadai, 107–22; *see also* Dār Fūr
western Sudan before 1874, political and geographical context, 13–17
Wingate, General, 87
women: and beads, 34–5; circumcision of, 44–5; as farmers, 26; as gatherers, 27; informants, 331–2; as landholders, 144–7; and *rites de passage*, 29–30; slaves, 48–52, 55–7, 138–9, 168–9, 202

Ya'qūb (faqīh), 205
Yūnis Bādis, 117
Yūnis Kirdī, 136
Yūsūf b. Ibrāhīm Qaraḍ, Shadow Sultan of Dār Fūr (1884–88), 75–6, 80–1, 89, 94
Yūsūf b. Muḥammad Sharīf, Sultan of Wadai (1874–98), 75, 80, 103–4, 108–13, 120–2, 171

Zaghāwa people, *see* Dār Zaghāwa
Zahra *bint* Abbakr, 192, 332
zakāh/*zakāt*, 26, 77, 100, 136, 146–54 *passim*, 228, 249
zāwiya, 172–3, 195, 249
Zokko (*'aqīd*), 54
Zuqal, *see* Muḥammad Khālid Zuqal
Zuwayya people, *see* Fezzān